What American Women Did,
1789–1920

WHAT AMERICAN WOMEN DID, 1789–1920

A Year-by-Year Reference

by

Linda Miles Coppens

McFarland & Company, Inc., Publishers

Jefferson, North Carolina, and London

Library of Congress Cataloguing-in-Publication Data

Coppens, Linda Miles, 1944–
What American women did, 1789–1920 : a year-by-year reference
/ by Linda Miles Coppens.
p.   cm.
Includes bibliographical references and index.
ISBN 0-7864-0899-5 (illustrated case binding : 50# alkaline paper) ∞
1. Women — United States — History.
2. Women — United States — Social conditions.
I. Title.
HQ1154.C665   2001
305.4'0973 — dc21
00-64010

British Library cataloguing data are available

Front cover image ©2000 Index Stock

Manufactured in the United States of America

*McFarland & Company, Inc., Publishers
Box 611, Jefferson, North Carolina 28640
www.mcfarlandpub.com*

To Alan

Acknowledgments

It is a pleasure to thank the many people who helped make this book possible. At Warren Wilson College, I would like to thank Willis M. Hubbard, director of the Shelley Mueller Pew Learning Center and Martha Ellison Library, for his support and interest and for allowing me a flexible schedule while completing this work. I am indebted to librarian Mary O. Brown and her interlibrary loan crew for their good work getting the needed books and journal articles. I am grateful to Barbara Hampe Hempleman, former college archivist, for her expertise and interest and for many good discussions on American women.

For help with photographs, I acknowledge with much appreciation: John Lovett, librarian at the Western History Collections at the University of Oklahoma; archivist Thomas Featherstone at the Archives of Labor and Urban Affairs at the Walter P. Reuther Library at Wayne State University; Marguerite Miller, director of the Allegan County Historical Society; the librarians for the North Carolina Collections at the Pack Memorial Library in Asheville, North Carolina; and the staffs at the Library of Congress and the National Archives.

For help of various kinds, I am grateful to Jan Bower, Otto and Grete Heinz, Laura Livrone, Nancy Springer-Ochs, Cynthia Sutton, Florence Wallin, and Vickie White.

Special thanks goes to my wonderful family. My sister Margaret M. Miles strongly encouraged me to write this book years ago when I first had the idea. She helped me with its organization and format and has been a wonderful source of inspiration and encouragement. My sister Karen E. Voigts took time from her busy schedule to find and reproduce some excellent photographs of women in Allegan, Michigan, and she also directed me to sources on craftswomen. My daughter Lynne Miles-Morillo helped me with research on African-American women, despite her busy schedule and an active toddler. Dione Miles, my mother, has always believed in me and was my best editor from grade school through graduate school. She gave me several excellent books on women from her personal library and called my attention to Agnes Inglis and Voltairine deCleyre. My father, Richard D. Miles, carefully read the entire manuscript, and his excellent editing, good ideas, and thoughtful suggestions have made the book much better than it otherwise would have been.

Alan B. Coppens, my husband, read the whole text, and his sound and wise comments and suggestions have improved the book immensely. He has been very supportive, and his wit and cheer helped me during the entire process.

Table of Contents

Women are the majority of humankind
and have been essential to the making of history.

— *Gerda Lerner, "Placing Women in History:
A 1975 Perspective"*

Introduction

Since the mid–1970s, both scholars and the general public have shown enormous interest in women's history. This demand for information has generated considerable scholarship, resulting in hundreds of general and specialized histories, narratives, and biographical studies. There is still much more to do, discovering and interpreting new sources, as well as synthesizing published works to better understand patterns and trends within the complexity of women's history.

This book, built on the past two decades of scholarship, chronicles what American women did from the emergence of the Republic through the end of World War I and the passage of the Nineteenth Amendment. I have selected this era because it was transitional for many women. The possibilities of new rights and opportunities for females emerged from the period's immense political, social, technological, and ideological changes. Some American women organized and established collective political voices, crusading for civil rights, better labor conditions, more education, and suffrage. Others preferred the status quo and actively resisted change. And still others, in harsher economic circumstances, saw little variation in their daily lives.

This book provides a broad picture of what these women did and thought, portraying their many activities and accomplishments and the events, trends, movements, and forces affecting them. I have chosen a chronology format because it illuminates the flow of history and shows how events are interconnected.

The goal of this book is to provide a picture of the accomplishments of American women from 1790 through 1920. Women's activities are examined within a framework of seven categories: *domesticity, work, education and scholarship, religion, arts, joining forces*, and *law and politics*.[1]

The first category, *domesticity*, examines attitudes about women's roles through published writings and speeches. Should women speak in public, work outside the home, occupy themselves with only marriage and childhood, be granted the vote? A range of opinions and attitudes are incorporated.

Work portrays activities of females in paid and unpaid jobs. This category includes statistics showing general employment trends.

Education and scholarship includes women who founded schools or departments, pioneered as teachers or students, and crusaded for better educational opportunities. As Gerda Lerner has pointed out, the struggle to learn, to teach, and to define is a major part of the history of American women.[2]

The fourth category, *religion*, depicts visionaries, ministers, missionaries, volunteer church workers, and founders of religious sects.

Arts includes writers, poets, painters, architects, musicians, and arts patrons.

Joining forces traces organized efforts to achieve reform, including associations dedicated to moral, social, and political improvement. Recent scholarship has emphasized the importance of these women's groups. Anne Firor Scott wrote that they "lay at the very heart of American political and social development."[3]

Law and politics encompasses general political activity, legislation, and court decisions that affected women.

Some men are included, particularly in *domesticity* and *law and politics*. Examples of males include those who were supportive of or opposed to women's reform, those who figured in judicial and legislative develop-ments, and those whose work affected women's lives in significant ways.

Statistical data are included for certain years. For example, in a particular year, census data illustrate percentages of female wage earners, college graduates, or workers in various occupations. In addition, the results from some consecutive censuses are occasionally brought together to reveal changes through time in certain activities (e.g., percentages of women in selected occupations).

Sources include published histories, journal articles, biographical works, writings by contemporary authors, published diaries and letters, and various statistics. The proliferation of scholarship and publications made it difficult to decide whom to include or exclude; the selections of women represent the author's subjective decisions. I have attempted to show a representative sample of American women and to offer a balance of race, class, ethnicity, prominence, and geographical distribution as source availability permitted.

What American Women Did, 1789–1920

— 1789 —

DOMESTICITY

Newlywed **Elizabeth Foote Washington**, who lives in Virginia, vows in her diary to be an ideal wife: pious, obedient, and submissive. "The Lordly sex," she writes, "can never be wrong in their own opinion." Troubled marriages are the wives' fault, she believes, since "it is their business to give up to their husbands." Her views reflect typical eighteenth-century attitudes. When Elizabeth was growing up, female behavior was a common discussion topic. She learned that because women inherited Eve's legacy of sin, they are inferior and should be ruled by men. Most women she knows consider themselves "naturally" patient, pure, cheerful, and modest, and often deprecate themselves as "just women."[1]

WORK

Grace Mulligan has completed midwifery studies with Philadelphia physician William Shippen, and opens a practice in Wilmington, Delaware. Females have traditionally delivered babies, a skill they learned from female relatives or community healers. Mulligan's training with Shippen will help her establish a practice; but eventually male doctors will replace midwives in cities. Medicine is becoming specialized, and more male physicians study in Europe's new medical schools where they learn anatomy, forceps use, and other new birthing techniques. Women, viewed as too delicate to learn medicine, are barred from medical schools. Eventually urban middle- and upper-class women will prefer to be attended by the professionally trained and more prestigious male doctors; and midwives will practice primarily in rural or isolated areas, or in urban ghettos.

EDUCATION AND SCHOLARSHIP

Students and parents attend the third annual commencement at the Philadelphia Young Ladies' Academy, a school founded by educator Benjamin Rush. A commencement guest cites a verse he has written on women's education. He speaks of expanding the mind and exploring sciences, and then concludes, "To form the maiden for th' accomplish'd wife, and fix the basis of a happy life!"[2] Indeed, preparation for marriage and family is one goal of the academy's founder. Rush is helping define a new role for the American

Painting, Martha Washington, Our First War Time Knitter, *c. 1776. (Library of Congress.) Washington and her guests are garbed in typical dress of upper class women. Wealthy colonial Americans imported elegant fabrics from which their tailors made garments, copying the latest European fashions. Dresses had tight bodices and full, floor-length skirts, which were often covered with elaborate overskirts of rich fabrics. Sleeves generally reached below the elbow and were edged with ruffles. For indoor warmth, women wore small shawls (fichus) and mobcaps, as Martha wears.*

When George Washington became president in 1789, Martha kept her political views private and assumed a limited official role. She hosted dinners, entertained female visitors, and made public appearances. Her primarily domestic role set the precedent for future First Ladies.

woman. She will be called a republican woman, and her civic job will be to ensure virtue in the home. She will set a virtuous example for her husband, and teach her sons liberty and justice. This will guard against national corruption and safeguard the nation's existence. To become proper mothers and wives, American girls need to be moral, literate, competent, and educated. Rush and other reformers endorse separate female schools, and his is among the earliest girls' private school. Students learn reading, writing, spelling, grammar, bookkeeping, math, history, geography, natural philosophy, and religion.

Massachusetts legislators pass a law mandating that public schools admit girls as well as boys. As more girls attend school and learn to read, the literacy gap between the genders in New England will close.

RELIGION

Secretary of War Henry Knox wants more territory for American settlers who are moving west. Much good land is under tribal ownership, and although some tribes have sold or traded land, they now resist further ceding. Rather than declare war and win lands through conquest, Knox proposes the Indians be "civilized," by converting them to Christianity and persuading them to become Americans, living in nuclear families on individual homesteads.

Missionaries are eager to convert Indians, and the Quakers send workers to a western New York Seneca village. They urge the women to give up farming for domestic work, and the men to give up hunting for farming, but the response is unenthusiastic. Senecas have little interest in lifestyle changes, and they cling to the familiar, having suffered much recent devastation. The tribe sided with the British during the war, and as a punishment American troops burned their crops and orchards; and outbreaks of smallpox and other diseases have killed nearly 8,000 Senecas.[3] Seneca women especially resist change. They have farmed for centuries; they own the lands and handle food distribution. Nor do the men want to forgo hunting and fishing for agriculture, which they consider "women's work." The Quakers' program is unsuccessful. Seneca females agree to learn spinning, weaving, and soapmaking, but they also continue to farm.

Arts

Since the mid–1700s, American publishers have founded magazines that were often imitations of British publications featuring news from Europe. Most were short-lived, through lack of subscribers and the low literacy level of the American public. Now patriotic sentiment is high and there is a demand for publications about the United States, with stories, poems, and articles by Americans. A new publication, *The Christian's, Scholar's, and Farmer's Magazine*, is founded. The editors, noting the "dignity, importance, and merit" of women, announce they will publish stories, articles, and essays for them, and their magazine will be a forum for discussion on women's role in the United States.[4]

— 1790 —

Work

Fewer than 10 percent of all women work outside the home.[5] Most of these wage earners are free black women, impoverished native-born white single and married women, immigrants, and white widowed and divorced females. There are few places where women can learn job skills; apprenticeships in crafts and trades are reserved for males, and the common perception that women are mentally inferior to men limits most other opportunities. Most women have scant education, and have been trained for housework or farm chores. The jobs wage earners hold are usually an extension of domestic work. Urban women often manage boardinghouses, work in small businesses, sell dry goods, food, or liquor, or teach children to read and write. Others are milliners, dress or cloak makers, seamstresses, healers, midwives, or household servants. Rural women often run taverns or shops, or keep house for the wealthy. Black women, facing prejudice, work in the low-paying jobs as laundresses, domestic servants, or child care workers.

Most married women's work is centered in the household. Here they spin, weave, sew the family's clothing and bedding, quilt, brew beer, make soap, candles, butter, and cheese, grow and produce fruits and vegetables, cure and salt meat, raise poultry and other animals, and help run family businesses. Many also help manage family farms, since the economy is primarily agricultural. Those who need additional income sell household products, take in boarders, sewing, or laundry, or do piece work for businesses as spinners and weavers, shoe binders, and hatmakers.

Nearly 700,000 slaves live in the United States. Female slaves on President George Washington's plantation spin, weave, sew, clean house, iron, clean stables, heap dung, thin swamp trees, carry fence rails, make fences, kill hogs, thresh wheat and rye, break and chop flax, strip tobacco, plow, level ditches, plant, and harvest corn. Young slave girls bake bread, help care for babies and children, make fences, plow, shell corn, work on roads, help clean stables, and help with harvests. The dictum that women are too fragile for heavy outdoor work does not apply to slave women.[6]

EDUCATION AND SCHOLARSHIP

A London firm publishes *Letters on Education; With Observations on Religious and Metaphysical Subjects*, written by British historian **Catharine Macaulay**. She maintains that women are not inferior; it is their environment and lack of schooling that limits them. She calls for better education for women, equal to men's. Macaulay and her husband, who supported the Revolution, have frequently visited America, often staying with President George Washington, and she has many friends here. Her pamphlet is circulated in the United States. Many applaud her critique, including Abigail Adams, wife of the vice president. Adams and other upper- and middle-class literate women are fascinated with revolutionary rhetoric and how it applies to their lives.

Lexicographer Noah Webster publishes a volume of essays in Boston. In "On the Education of Youth in America," he describes the ideal republican woman who will instill morality and virtue in the household. He emphasizes that females have a powerful influence "in controlling the manners of the nation" and that they need to study "what is *useful*."[7] Arithmetic and writing will help them run efficient households, and studying history, geography, and moral philosophy will help them become virtuous. While Webster insists that today's woman needs practical skills, many Americans ridicule the idea that women need education. The topic will be debated in the press for decades.

ARTS

Current writings on citizenship emphasize men. Patriots, who viewed politics as men's sphere, wrote tracts and essays that focused on male rights and obligations. Later, the founding fathers drew upon Enlightenment writings in developing America's political framework, but these writings were silent about female patriots and citizens. Yet American women participated actively in the cause, are citizens, and their obligations and responsibilities need addressing. Many writers are trying to define a female patriot and citizen, and some ideas are expressed in fiction.

Writer **Mercy Otis Warren** publishes *The Ladies of Castile*, a poetic drama set in revolutionary Spain. Maria, the heroine, is patriotic and brave, and after her husband's death, she leads his troops to victory. In contrast, Louisa, a passive romantic, eventually kills herself. Warren shows how women should act in a national crisis, indicating that the courageous and self-reliant will survive, while the weaker may not.

Warren, an outspoken and well-read woman, grew up in a wealthy and politically prominent Massachusetts family. She was bright and eager to learn. She had no formal education, but her father allowed her to observe her brother's tutoring sessions, and she spent hours reading in her uncle's library. Warren is now married to a legislator and former revolutionary, and her home is a gathering place for political leaders and thinkers. She maintains that although domesticity is women's main role, they need more education, and that a well-organized wife can find time for intellectual pursuits.

JOINING FORCES

Writer **Judith Sargent Murray**'s essay "On the Equality of the Sexes" is published in *Massachusetts Magazine*. She maintains that women are as smart as men, but because they are confined and limited they never reach their potential. She pleads for better education, arguing that women should be allowed to think about more than "the mechanism of a pudding or the sewing of the seams of a garment."[8] Murray, like her contemporaries, had little formal education, but she read widely and when a local minister tutored her brother for Harvard, their father allowed her to join the sessions. She later studied her brother's college texts. Murray has a wide readership and is one of few American women who publish.

LAW AND POLITICS

Martha Jefferson Randolph is newly married, and her father, Secretary of State Thomas Jefferson, counsels her always to please her husband, for her own happiness depends on it. Parents often give this advice to daughters. It is not only social custom for wives to defer to husbands, but at marriage a woman loses all legal rights. Under British common law, recognized in America, an unmarried women is a *feme sole*, under her father's legal protection, but lawfully able to own property, transact business, and make a will. At marriage, she becomes a *feme covert*, with her rights legally subsumed under her husband's. This system is based on the traditional Western viewpoint that all women are "politically and legally irresponsible."[9]

New Jersey legislators enact a law making election procedures consistent. The revised code offers suffrage to free inhabitants who are properly qualified and refers to voters as "he or she." This new law implies that married women can vote. Single New Jersey women have been voting since 1776. Framers of the American Constitution gave no specific political rights to women, leaving local lawmakers to address this issue in their state constitutions. Some states prohibited female enfranchisement; others were silent on the issue. New Jersey lawmakers, however, gave suffrage to all who met age, residency, and property qualifications, thus including qualified single women. They were continuing a colonial tradition, when single women participated in public affairs, often spoke at town meetings, and were sometimes involved in litigation; and lawmakers also drew on their Quaker heritage with its liberal attitudes toward women.

Sarah Woodward petitions Connecticut legislators for permission to sell land she owned before marriage. She needs the money because her husband, now insane, is unable to support the family. The lawmakers grant her petition but caution her to reapply for further business transactions. Although married women lack individual legal rights, they can appeal to equity courts or petition their state legislature for temporary *feme sole* status if their husbands are absent or incapacitated.

— 1791 —

WORK

Treasury Secretary Alexander Hamilton presents a report on manufacturing to the U.S. House of Representatives. Hamilton, envisioning a self-sufficient nation, independent of British and European imports, praises the nation's young textile and shoe industries and encourages greater capitalization for continued industrial growth. He then addresses the question of factory employees, stating, "It is worthy of particular remark that ... women and children are rendered more useful by manufacturing establishments than they would otherwise be." He later adds that without factory work, women might be "idle" and a "burden" on the community.[10] Although Congress does not accept all of his recommendations, Hamilton's comments help set national policy. His endorsement of a female factory labor force sets a precedent for hiring women. His comment about idle females reflects a growing disparagement of women's household labor as a contribution to society.

Allegory of the restoration of peace and prosperity to America after the Revolutionary War, engraving, 1781. (Library of Congress.) Artists traditionally used the female form to show symbols or ideals, and this picture is a good example. The left side shows the anguish of the Revolutionary War. America, wearing furs, feathers and jewels, is an Indian queen. She kneels by a monument honoring her destroyed cities; she has flung her sword on the ground, and several war victims lie nearby. In the background cities burn and storm clouds threaten overhead. America looks up at Peace, who appears above, offering an olive branch. On the right, more figures approach America. Hercules, representing heroic virtue (and thought by some to represent George Washington), leads Liberty, Industry, Concord, and Plenty, all in female form.

In colonial days the household was a unit of production. Most families lived on farms and were self-sufficient. They grew crops and raised livestock, and produced household goods and equipment which they bartered or sold for additional goods and services. The economy is still primarily agricultural, but with growing commerce and industry, cash is becoming more important. Many men whose grandfathers farmed now earn wages, and the workplace is viewed as the crux of the economy. Married women's household labor, though it clothes, feeds, and maintains the family, is often regarded as unproductive since women earn no wages.

English immigrant Samuel Slater builds a cotton thread manufacturing mill in Pawtucket, Rhode Island, the nation's first factory with water-powered spinning machinery. His employees are primarily female: young unmarried girls spin the thread, and married women weave cloth at home. The mill does well and begins a factory boom in New England.

In colonial days many young girls left home to work, often apprenticing as servants in other households where they did domestic chores. Now in some towns a new class of young women workers is established as factory workers whose wages supplement the family income. Females, traditionally spinners and weavers, are seen as "natural" employees for the new mills.

Hiring women saves factory owners money. That women should earn less than men has been proposed by political economists, such as the influential Adam Smith. In *The Wealth of Nations*, he envisioned a gender-divided labor force and proposed that men should earn enough to support a family, while women need only enough to support themselves, since child rearing takes most of their time and they are already supported by husbands. It became common to view all women as dependents regardless of age, race, economic class, or marital status. This theory became practice, and it is now traditional to pay women lower wages.[11]

President George Washington, touring the South, stops in Charleston to visit **Eliza Lucas Pinckney**, widow of a wealthy plantation owner. They are friends from revolutionary days, when her late husband loaned money to South Carolina for the war effort. Now nearly seventy, she is well known for her contributions to agriculture. As a young women she managed her father's extensive rice plantation. Enjoying the work and finding it challenging, she later experimented with crops and adapted the indigo plant to South Carolina's soil and climate, becoming the first person to grow it successfully. Local planters prospered using her methods, and indigo had become the colony's major export. Washington admires Pinckney, and at her death two years later he will be a pallbearer.

RELIGION

Reverend Freeborn Garretson is traveling on the East Coast, preaching and converting thousands to Methodism. His wife, **Catherine Garretson**, writes to him, effusing, "They that turn many to righteousness shall shine like stars, forever and ever," and suggests that he preach with "strong words, soft and persuasive."[12] Garretson, daughter

of a wealthy New York family, is steeped in religion. She keeps a journal and corresponds with friends about her religious beliefs, pastors she admires, sermons she has heard, and the importance of her faith. Although piety is viewed as a "natural" female trait, most denominations forbid female ordination and preaching. For women like Garretson, marrying a minister is a good decision. Their home in the Hudson Valley is a gathering place for traveling ministers. Catherine leads prayer meetings and offers Bible study in the community, and is a role model of the good Christian woman.

ARTS

Writer **Susanna Rowson**, who is living in London, publishes her novel *Charlotte, A Tale of Truth*. A morality tale, it concerns a young woman who is seduced, gets pregnant, is abandoned, becomes impoverished, and dies in childbirth. It becomes a best-seller in England and America. Philadelphia bookseller Mathew Carey pirates a book and reprints a thousand copies, which sell so quickly that he prints two more editions. Everyone loves the tragic heroine. Young girls resolve to behave themselves, fearing the consequences. Parents like it because it shows what happened when Charlotte ignored her parents' advice. Even men see it as warning against selfishness. Because women's virtue is a popular theme, some even view the novel as a metaphor for what might happen if American society became corrupted. The book will eventually have more than 200 editions and be popular through the early 1900s. Someone will erect a tombstone for Charlotte Temple in New York's Trinity Cemetery, which thousands will visit, leaving flowers, locks of hair, and letters to the fictional heroine.

LAW AND POLITICS

Nancy Shippen Livingston's husband sues for divorce in a Pennsylvania court. His suit is granted, which is a relief to Nancy, who has already left him. Her father had chosen her bridegroom, a much older man who has become indifferent and cruel. Many other women have similar plights in unhappy wedlock. Parents usually choose husbands for young women, and marriage is considered permanent. Divorce, difficult to obtain and unavailable in some states, is frowned upon as a threat to the Republic's morality. It generally requires a private bill passed by the legislature, although Pennsylvania lawmakers now allow some courts to grant divorces. Few women initiate divorce, since as *feme coverts* they cannot act legally for themselves. Nancy's only option would have been to petition a judge's wife to request a hearing with her husband.

— 1792 —

DOMESTICITY

Philadelphia bookseller and publisher Matthew Carey reprints *The Ladies Pocket Library*, an advice book for girls by **Hannah More**, a British writer. More believes that female education should be pragmatic. Girls should not study needlework, music, or French, as these skills will not help them "perform the *duties* of life,"[13] which are being a thoughtful wife, running a proper household, and educating children. More's attitude toward women reflects a common conservative viewpoint: girls should become educated, but not aspire to scholarship or to activity outside the domestic sphere.

WORK

Deborah Sampson Gannett, a wounded Revolutionary War soldier, petitions the state of Massachusetts for a pension. As a young woman, Gannett read Enlightenment and revolutionary tracts and wanted to join the war. She dressed as a man, and under the name of her dead brother, Robert Shirtliffe, she enlisted and went into battle. A doctor tending her discovered her gender but kept quiet. Long after the war, married and with children, she decided to reveal her service. She travels, talking about being a soldier. She will eventually receive a soldier's pension from the United States government.

Gannett is not the only woman who fought in battles, although most women participated in the Revolution in other ways. Many donated or raised funds to support the military, and stayed home running family businesses and farms. Nearly 20,000 women followed their husbands' military units, often with their children in tow; and they cooked, cleaned, nursed, and fired weapons for sick or exhausted husbands. Others spied, collecting and delivering secret information; joined anti–British demonstrations; wove homespun, or threw tea off English ships. Many others joined mobs who tarred and feathered traitors and looted Tory-owned businesses.

EDUCATION AND SCHOLARSHIP

Sarah Pierce opens a girls' school in her house in Litchfield, Connecticut. Pierce views females as intelligent and rational and agrees that future republican wives and mothers need to be educated and self-reliant. She teaches her students to think, reason, and cultivate imagination. Her curriculum includes composition, spelling, math, history, literature, philosophy, and religion. Wanting her students to be physically sound, she encourages evening walks. Most of Pierce's students are upper- and middle-class white girls. Their parents pay for this schooling as a patriotic duty, and they hope their accomplished young daughters might marry into a higher social class. Pierce's academy will receive substantial bequests, expand, and gain national fame. Many other New England women will found similar institutions. These new academies are permanent. They are housed in large buildings, have trained staff,

Triumph of Liberty. Dedicated to Its Defenders in America, *engraving by Peter C. Verger, based on a draw-ing by John F. Renault, 1796. (Library of Congress.) This allegory portrays the flourishing of liberty and the de-cline of monarchy. The obelisk honors America's fallen cities and heroes. Minerva, the goddess of war, holds a shield representing the United States; she feeds the flames of liberty burning on a sacred altar. To her right sev-eral female figures celebrate America's victory. Plenty burns crowns, scepters, and nobility titles. Peace holds an olive branch; Justice holds scales and a sword. Behind them Liberty stands on a column. She holds a wreath aloft, and points to copies of the Declaration of Independence and the Constitution, near the pillar's base. At the right, several monarchs turn from the scene in horror, and one stabs himself. In the left foreground, a priest watches the Hydra of Despotism writhe and die.*

Artists frequently drew females as virtues or ideals rather than as actual women. Men were considered the makers of American history. In murals, illustrators drew men fighting wars, traveling west, and building cities, while female figures, goddesses or representations of treasured national values, hovered above.

and receive community support. Many grad-uates will become the next century's writers and reformers.

Young American females today have a different upbringing from their mothers' and grandmothers.' In colonial days most females were not expected to become educated, and most women were illiterate. Schooling was considered a waste since their adult life would be spent in domestic duties. Some girls in wealthier families were tutored in reading and writing, and some learned French, danc-ing, drawing, and to play the harpsichord. Others attended dame schools where they learned to read, spell, and do arithmetic and

needlework in the homes of their teachers, often widows or single women with limited education.

JOINING FORCES

Two years ago, English writer **Mary Wollstonecraft** published *A Vindication of the Rights of Men*, on equality and civil and religious rights. Her new book, *A Vindication of the Rights of Woman, with Strictures on Po-litical and Moral Subjects*, is published this year in London, Boston, and Philadelphia. She dedicates it to French leader Talleyrand, who declared it "natural" to deny women political rights in the new French republic. Wollstonecraft analyzes women's oppressed place in society and urges radical reform. Women are equal to men, she insists. They deserve the same educational and vocational opportunities and should have full civil and political rights. She attacks the marriage structure, women's confinement in the home, and the sexual double standard.

Her book is widely read on both sides of the Atlantic and is discussed at parties and salons and in newspapers and magazines. Britons and Americans are shocked; they believe that gender roles are part of the "natural" order and sanctioned by the Bible. They denounce her personally for living with a man and giving birth out of wedlock. Many critics even refused to read the book. Reaction in the press is vitriolic, and she is branded immoral, labeled an "amazon" with wicked proposals and a "hyena in petticoats."[14]

While some American readers privately agree with some of her ideas, they do not want radical change. They want better education and legal rights for married women, but believe females should be wives and mothers, not doctors, ministers, or political leaders. Others think these issues are private and inappropriate for public discussion. Most American women do not care about reform; they are still recovering from war hardships, glad to be alive, and their household labors leave little time for reflection on gender roles. Although Wollstonecraft's work inspires no reform movement, it brings many women's issues to public attention and is one of the earliest women's rights tracts. Her book will be rediscovered and lauded by women in the early twentieth century and again in the 1970s.

A woman writes to the *Lady's Magazine, and Repository of Entertaining Knowledge,* questioning the word "obey" in wedding vows and calling for marriage reform. This woman has more confidence in herself, like many others who survived the Revolution. While their husbands fought, they headed the household; they managed family farms and businesses and made economic decisions. This independence has led some women to question the traditional patriarchal structure. More parents now allow their daughters a choice in husbands, and the social status of wives is higher than in prewar days. Even marriage has changed for some, becoming a social as well as economic relationship.

Judith Sargent Murray begins an essay series, "The Gleaner," in *Massachusetts Magazine.* She addresses how upper- and middle-class young women are raised, and comments on education, manners, politics, and religion. Influenced by Wollstonecraft's ideas, Murray believes in the importance of education for women. She realizes most will marry and have children, and insists that schooling will uphold the dignity of motherhood. For those who remain single, she writes, an education will qualify them for employment. Murray, having survived the war, is aware of the danger of dependence on a father or husband and argues that any woman might someday need to be self-sufficient. Murray has a wide readership and this series is popular, though many reject her ideas as too radical. Murray, who writes to support her sick husband and child, is an important figure in defining the role of the new American woman. Her series will run for two years, and then be published in three volumes.

— 1793 —

DOMESTICITY

New Hampshire minister John Ogden publishes *The Female Guide, or Thoughts on the Education of Sex, Accomodated* [sic] *to the State of Society, Manners in the United States.* He is concerned about the recent questioning of traditional values. He reminds readers that ideal women are pious and submissive, worship God, and serve, obey, and love their husbands. He compares marriage to a master/servant relationship, explaining that marriage is an economic contract and that husbands will always take care of loving and respectful wives. He warns against idleness and asks women to stay busy with spinning, sewing, or supervising servants. Preachers have long used the pulpit for guidance in moral living. Now that more Americans are moving to the West, where few churches are founded, some preachers are publishing their views in order to reach a wider audience.

WORK

Martha Ballard, age fifty-eight, writes in her journal that she has delivered fifty-three babies this year. Ballard, who lives in rural Maine with her family, is a skilled midwife and healer. She provides medical care to nearby communities, often traveling by horseback, in a canoe, or on snowshoes. Her husband works as a surveyor and sawmill operator, and their joint wages buy coffee, prepared foods, brooms, cloth, sewing supplies, and farming tools. Assisted by her daughters, Ballard also makes candles and soap, knits socks, sews her family's clothing, preserves food, brews beer, grows vegetables and fruits, and raises poultry. Her diverse work is typical of many American married women. Although current writings emphasize women's role as mothers, women in rural areas still produce most household goods. While child rearing is important, it does not consume most of their time.

Hannah Wilkinson Slater registers a patent for cotton sewing thread. Thread has been traditionally made of flax, which is weak and breaks easily. Her invention makes sewing easier and more efficient and contributes to the prosperity of mills owned by her husband, Samuel Slater.

Eli Whitney has designed and built the first cotton gin. He has spent six months working on it in **Catherine Littlefield Greene**'s Georgia plantation home. They had met while traveling, and Greene liked the intelligent young man and suggested he visit. During his stay he made her a new embroidery frame. She admired his skills and suggested he invent a machine to discard seeds from short-staple cotton. She offered some design ideas, for which he will later pay her royalties.[15] His new machine will separate seeds ten times faster than doing it manually. Its use will revolutionize the cotton industry. Short-staple cotton grows rapidly in the nation's interior. With Whitney's machine, cotton can be more quickly prepared for market and planters can increase production. It is in great demand by English manufacturers, and there will be a greater domestic need for it as more American cotton mills are built. His machine will also increase the need for slaves, which will be required for harvesting the increased cotton crops.

EDUCATION AND SCHOLARSHIP

Quaker women who are members of the Pennsylvania Abolition Society buy land and build a school for black children. Philadelphia has a large free black population, but the children have no access to education. There is no public school system, and private schools are not only costly but usually prohibit blacks. The Quakers hire a local black teacher, **Eleanor Harris**, and thirty students enroll. Other Friends pay Harris's salary, donate firewood, and buy texts.

Valedictorian **Eliza Laskey** speaks at the Philadelphia female academy commencement, emphasizing modesty as an important female accomplishment. Laskey has learned to balance her pride in learning with adherence to traditional values. There is a controversy about women's education. Many conservative Americans believe that educating women will make them unfeminine. Some parents fear it will make their daughters unmarriageable. Others point out that women, "whose brains are smaller than men's," have less capacity for learning, so why spend money to educate them?

RELIGION

New Yorker **Catherine Ferguson**, a former slave, starts an integrated Sunday school in her house. She enrolls forty-eight young students and teaches them to read the Bible and care for themselves. She works as a caterer and house cleaner to support her school. Later, a local minister, impressed by her work, asks her to move her classes to his church, and the early Sunday school continues to flourish.

ARTS

Ann Eliza Bleeker, who lived in upstate New York during the Revolution, endured Indian raids, British invasions, the deaths of her mother, sister, and young baby, and the kidnapping of her husband by Tories. After the war she expressed her grief by writing letters, poetry, and stories about the hardships. After Bleeker's death, her daughter **Margaretta Faugeres** collects her mother's writings and publishes *The Posthumous Works of Ann Eliza Bleeker in Prose and Verse.* The book is well received. Americans want publications about their history, and they praise the work for its realistic description of western American wilderness and the vivid account of wartime chaos.

JOINING FORCES

Priscilla Mason addresses the commencement audience at the Young Ladies' Academy in Philadelphia. She expresses frustration at the lack of opportunities for women. She complains that colleges are closed to them, as are the church, the bar, and the senate. Why, she wonders, are women not allowed a broader role?

— 1794 —

WORK

Fifty-two-year-old **Coincoin** is an exslave in Louisiana whose lover purchased her

freedom, gave her land, and provided her with a lifetime annuity. An industrious worker with an astute business sense, she grows tobacco and raises cattle and turkeys in Louisiana's Red River Valley. She is qualified to apply for a Spanish land grant and receives 600 additional acres. With the extended holdings she will plant corn, raise cattle, and find and buy her ten enslaved children. In a decade, with Louisiana's annexation to the United States, Coincoin will be among the most wealthy American citizens, owning nearly 1,000 acres of land and sixteen slaves. Her offspring will later extend her agricultural empire to nearly 20,000 acres, worked by 500 slaves, and they will establish their own school and Catholic church.[16]

Tench Coxe publishes his recent speech, "Address to the Society for the Employment of Manufactures and the Useful Arts." Encouraging industrial growth, he echoes Alexander Hamilton in suggesting that women (when not doing other work) are ideal factory employees. Coxe, like many other leaders, does not consider work in the household as labor, since it is unpaid.

RELIGION

Since mainstream religions offer women no authority, some organize their own sects, often establishing separate religious communities. **Jemima Wilkinson,** who calls herself a "Publick Universal Friend," founds Jerusalem Township, a religious settlement in western New York. Wilkinson was raised as a Quaker but was later banished for attending a Baptist revival. Her new sect is based on her visions and dreams and incorporates the Golden Rule, plain dress, universal salvation, peace, and abolition. She wants her people dissociated from mainstream society, which she regards as sinful. A dynamic and persuasive leader, she attracts the poor and rich, and some even free their slaves and give up their homes to join her community. The sect will flourish until Wilkinson's death when lack of leadership will dissolve the group.

— 1795 —

JOINING FORCES

Quakers allow women an active public role; they can be lay preachers and have a voice in community affairs. But because they are barred from leadership in philanthropic work, some women organize their own groups. Philadelphian **Ann Parrish**, a young Quaker, organizes the Friendly Circle to help the poor. Starting as an informal gathering with friends, they will attract new members, raise funds, and aid hundreds of the city's poor women and children. They will build a "house of industry" where needy women can earn money spinning flax and wool or minding the workers' small children. This early group foreshadows hundreds of other benevolent societies that church women will found.

— 1796 —

DOMESTICITY

Vice President John Adams reminds his married daughter **Nabby Smith** of the importance of her role as republican mother. He writes, "You, my dear daughter, will be responsible for a great share of the duty and opportunity of educating a rising family, from whom much will be expected."[17] Like Adams, many upper- and middle-class parents approve of the new role for their daughters. Smith, like other wealthy wives with servants or slaves, has the leisure to devote time to instructing her sons about liberty and government. But the republican motherhood rhetoric has little reality for most American mothers, who spend lengthy days in arduous household labor, wage work, or both. Nor

does it apply to slave mothers, whose children are often sold.

Engaged in the debate on women's role, **Abigail Adams**, wife of the vice president, writes to a friend, "Government of States and Kingdoms, tho' God knows badly enough managed, I am willing should be solely administered by the lords of creation," and adds, "I should only contend for Domestic government, and think that best administered by the female."[18] Adams, like most Americans, believes that separate spheres for men and women are "natural" and that both roles give important. Caring for her family gives her pleasure and also allows her husband to be in public service. Adams is outspoken about her strong political opinions. She argues for improving women's status, although her changes would be within society's structure. She wants more education for females, legal rights, and a sense of a partnership for married women. Although she maintains that women are men's intellectual equals, she does not envision gender equality. Because women's domestic work is so time consuming, she cannot imagine a society with women in business or politics.

RELIGION

Elizabeth, an ex-slave, begins an itinerant ministry in Maryland and Virginia. When white officials request her preaching credentials, she replies that man did not ordain her, but if God did she needs nothing better. The bemused officials allow her to continue her work. A persuasive orator, she will gain a large multiracial following and the Quakers will later publish her autobiography. Like many other slaves, Elizabeth found comfort and strength in the salvation message, and it was often the slave women who preached or led prayers, following the West African tradition of female religious leaders.

Shakers have lived in America since 1776, when **Ann Lee**, an English immigrant, established the first New York settlement.

Portrait of Abigail Adams by Gilbert Stuart, c. 1801. (Library of Congress.) This picture shows Adams in her late fifties, shortly after her husband John Adams lost the election for a second presidential term. Abigail's hairstyle of tight curls accommodates a soft cap decorated with ribbons and lace. Her ruffled collar, called a Betsie (after Queen Elizabeth's ruff), was in vogue in England and the United States. The high waistline of her dress reflects the popular empire style. She abhorred the more revealing fashionable European styles, and hoped to set a precedent for more modest dress.

Adams' interests, however, went far beyond fashion, as reflected in her serious demeanor. A well-read woman with an inquiring mind and strong opinions, she enjoyed discussing politics and current affairs. She vehemently opposed slavery and was appalled by the violence of the French Revolution. She believed women deserved more education and should be less submissive in marriage. Her husband respected her intelligence and often consulted with her on national affairs during his presidency. This angered his political foes, who deplored Abigail's outspokenness. Critics often contrasted her unfavorably with Martha Washington, her more domestic predecessor.

Lucy Wright and Joseph Meacham were appointed Lee's successors, and Meacham's death this year leaves Wright as leader. She will expand membership, sending missionaries west, who will found seven more settlements in Ohio, Kentucky, and Indiana. Wright establishes uniformity in rituals and adds singing and dancing to the worship. She also founds a school for the community's children.

The Shakers worship a male and female god, offer members racial and sexual equality, and stress simplicity in work and lifestyle. They live in self-supporting communities, each working at a craft or trade. Although work is divided by gender, with women indoors and men outdoors, celibacy is enforced, giving some women freedom from marriage, child care, and running a household.

JOINING FORCES

Many northern free black families are impoverished, since racism bars them from education and keeps them in poorly paid jobs. They are usually ineligible for charity from white benevolent groups, so they establish their own organizations. A group of free black women in Philadelphia organize the Benevolent Daughters for self-help and community support. Their dues fund members' medical or burial expenses and aid local churches and needy families.

— 1797 —

ARTS

Boston writer **Hannah Foster** publishes *The Coquette*, a seduction novel whose heroine is betrayed and dies. This cautionary tale of the importance of virtue for women also exposes the sexual double standard, and criticizes women's limited options in society. It is a popular novel and will be reprinted in more than thirteen editions.

The Revolutionary War inspired many women to express patriotism in diaries, letters, essays, stories, and poems. Boston poet **Sarah Apthorp Morton** publishes "Beacon Hill, A Local Poem, Historic and Descriptive," a paean to war soldiers. A spirited patriot, she supported the Revolution despite her aristocratic family's Loyalist sentiments. Proud of her new country, she encourages writers to write and publish material on the nation's history, geography, and people. She is a beloved writer whose fans have dubbed her "America's Sappho."

JOINING FORCES

In urban areas, the gap between rich and poor is widening and little public relief is available other than crowded almshouses. More women who want to do useful work are getting involved in charitable work. New Yorker **Isabella Graham**, a widowed schoolteacher, establishes the Society for Relief of Poor Widows with Children. The founders apply for a state charter, elect officers, and run the group efficiently, holding regular meetings and keeping careful financial records. Applicants are carefully screened, keeping out the "immoral." Their goal is to train clients to become self-supporting. They will buy a large building where they hold classes in sewing, spinning, and other trades and where the children can attend schools. The group will later extend services, setting up food kitchens in the city. Membership and funding will grow, and hundreds will be helped.

LAW AND POLITICS

In New Jersey, Republican congressman John Condict is almost defeated by the last-minute votes of seventy-five Federalist women. Condict and other irate Republicans write to local publications complaining about female voters. A pro–Republican newspaper publishes lyrics of a song hailing the downfall of male "tyrants" and welcoming a "government in petticoats."[19] This uproar, rousing public opinion against female suffrage, will continue, and lawmakers will later disfranchise New Jersey women.

— 1798 —

WORK

Betsey Metcalf develops an efficient technique to braid straw for leghorn hats and teaches it to her Providence, Rhode Island, neighbors. Word of the new process spreads, and braiding straw becomes a fad; hundreds of women and children braid straw and make leghorn hats and bonnets at home. This stimulates the straw bonnet industry, a boom that brings local prosperity and offers women wage work. The straw-braiding, weaving, and bonnet-making industry will later be valued at half a million dollars in Massachusetts, and many New England towns will be dubbed "straw towns."

Metcalf could have patented her invention. Congress passed the Patent Act in 1790 to promote scientific and artistic progress and allow inventors initial freedom from competition. It allows male and female candidates, but Metcalf declines to apply. She claims satisfaction with her income and is unwilling to be named on official records and before Congress, reflecting traditional attitudes that respectable women stay out of the public eye.

ARTS

Quaker writer Charles Brockden Brown publishes a novel, *Alcuin: A Dialogue on the Rights of Women*. Alcuin, a young man, talks with Mrs. Carter, an astute older women who runs a salon. They discuss society's injustices to women, and she outlines the issues. On political neglect, she illustrates, "Even the government of our country, which is said to be the freest in the world passes over women as if they were not.... Lawmakers thought as little of comprehending us in their code of liberty, as if we were pigs, or sheep."[20] Later Alcuin envisions an imaginary world with gender equality. In writing this, Brown encourages young women to find a new role, and this popular work helps later reformers envision change.

— 1799 —

WORK

New York City's Lying-in Hospital, offering maternity care for the poor, publishes a handbook that lists duties of the resident matron: buy the hospital's wood and provisions; maintain and administer goods, including wine, spirits, sugar, molasses, linens, blankets, and furniture; visit the sick twice a day; supervise nurses; inspect the building for cleanliness; and attend all deliveries. The hospital is a teaching facility where male doctors can learn skills by treating patients unable to afford medical care. The hospital employs a few female nurses, but the resident matron is one of few female staff positions.

EDUCATION AND SCHOLARSHIP

Quaker **Rebecca Jones** helps found Pennsylvania's Westtown School, modeled after English Friends' schools she has visited. The school's goal is to train teachers, and it admits Quaker girls and boys, both poor and wealthy. The sexes are segregated physically but have similar curricula, including grammar, penmanship, arithmetic, botany, ornithology, scientific experiments, religion, and needlework for the girls. One of several boarding schools the Friends founded, it is intended to simulate a Quaker family. Few visits home are allowed, and discipline is strictly enforced. Although Quakers advocate gender equality, they follow tradition by paying female teachers less than males.

The Catholic Church founds the Visitation convent school in Washington, D.C., with instruction from nuns. It is open to girls of all faiths, and many socially prominent Protestant parents enroll their daughters. They approve of the curriculum, which includes excellent French classes and training in social etiquette as well as solid academic work. The school will gain an excellent reputation for scholarship, and John Adams and James Madison will be among those who speak at commencements. The school's good name will help balance the growing anti–Catholicism movement.

Historian **Hannah Adams** publishes *A Summary History of New England.* Among the earliest American women to support herself through writing, she has already published on the history of religion. Reviewers consider her work competent and industrious, and her community patronage includes liberal Boston ministers. Like most contemporary female scholars, she had little formal schooling. She educated herself reading history, geography, and logic in her father's library, and learned Greek and Latin from some family boarders. Her writings add to the growing body of literature on America.

LAW AND POLITICS

Although slavery is still legal in some parts of the United States, some northern states have been enacting laws for gradual emancipation. This year the New York legislature mandates that daughters of slave mothers will remain indentured to their mothers' owners until age twenty-five, and sons until age twenty-eight. This puts the burden on slave mothers, who may die before their offspring are freed. Many slaves had looked forward to emancipation after the war; they hoped the rhetoric on freedom and liberty would apply to them. Although there is increasing anti-slavery sentiment in the North, it will be another decade before Congress prohibits foreign slave trade.

Free black communities are growing in the North. After the Revolutionary War some northern slaves successfully petitioned for freedom, and many southern slaves escaped north. In the last nine years the number of free blacks has increased nearly 80 percent, and next year almost 108,000 African Americans will be free.[21]

— 1800 —

RELIGION

Mary Webb and fourteen other women form an interdenominational group, the Boston Female Society for Missionary Purposes. At weekly meetings they pray for the unsaved, collect dues, plan fund-raising events, and hear reports of evangelical work. Webb's group anticipates many more groups supporting missionary work. Although most churches prohibit women from being missionaries, in these groups they learn organizational skills that they will later use to build larger groups and obtain more control over evangelical work.

JOINING FORCES

Eliza Southgate, from a prosperous Maine family, writes to her cousin, "I do not esteem marriage absolutely essential to happiness.... I congratulate myself that I am at liberty to refuse those [potential husbands] I don't like and that I have firmness enough to brave the sneers of the world and live an old maid, if I never find one I can love."[22] More young women are questioning women's limited role in marriage, and more are choosing to remain single, especially in parts of New England where women outnumber men.

Elizabeth Peck Perkins establishes the Boston Female Asylum, a home for the mentally ill. She will run it and support it. A successful businesswoman, Peck was widowed before the war and left with eight children. She opened a china, glassware, wine, and imports shop, which she expanded into a prosperous enterprise, and supported her family through the war. Her prosperity allowed her to donate one thousand dollars to the war effort. Now, with children grown, she is prominent in civic and benevolent causes and is among the earliest Boston women to found a major charitable institute.

— 1801 —

DOMESTICITY

Like most Americans, **Alice Izard** believes God created men and women for different roles and that this is part of the "natural" order. She has just read Wollstonecraft's *A Vindication of the Rights of Woman*, finds it appalling, and tells her reaction to her daughter. She defends women's traditional role, insisting, "The rank of a good Woman in society leaves her little to complain of. She frequently guides where she does not govern, & acts like a guardian angel by preventing the effects of evil desires & strong passions & leading them [men] to worthy pursuits." Her husband also condemns the book and denounces Wollstonecraft as a "vulgar, impudent hussy." The Izards' reaction is typical of most Americans, though it is not just her ideas they deplore. Their disapproval of her blunt and "unladylike" style and their shock at her unorthodox personal life intensify their rejection of Wollstonecraft's work.[23]

RELIGION

Boston Congregational women found the Female Society for Propagating the Diffusion of Christian Knowledge to support missionary work. Many Protestants are eager to proselytize. They link the Bible to progress and believe that Christian America is the pinnacle of "civilization." Evangelical work will become a national movement, and by the century's end women in Protestant churches will support missionary programs.

The revival movement is growing, and leaders have targeted the frontier. Thousands of settlers are moving west; in the past decade the populations of Tennessee and Kentucky alone have nearly tripled.[24] Christianity has not kept pace with this expansion; many communities have no churches, and the Sabbath is often ignored. Church leaders want to bring piety and morality to the West.

Revivalists hold a camp meeting in Cane Ridge, Kentucky. Nearly 20,000 people have traveled by horseback, wagon, and foot to hear the words of Baptist, Methodist, and Presbyterian ministers and exhorters. The preachers' offer of universal salvation means that everyone can convert and avoid eternal damnation. Unlike the predestination doctrine of older and more conservative eastern churches, this more democratic concept of universal salvation means that people can control their destiny. The gathering is emotional; would-be converts offer impassioned and expressive personal testimonies, and the newly saved shout prayers of joy, cry, laugh, sing, and dance. Revivalists urge women — who are considered "naturally" pious and moral — to convert. It is, after all, a duty of the new republican woman to instill piety and morality in the home. Because women are encouraged to be religious, the majority of revival participants and church members are female.[25]

The Cane Ridge revival is part of a national movement. Ministers are displeased that church membership and support have declined. The new republic is a secular society with no official ties to the church and no state taxes to support them. During the Revolution, writings by Deists were esteemed. This weakened religion's influence, and commercial and industrial development, rather than the Bible, have become society's focus. The revival movement will be successful. In the next forty years, Americans will found new sects and denominations, build thousands of churches, and establish Sunday schools. The term "God" will be evoked in public policy, and ministers will be influential in education, speaking at school dedications and commencements and being selected as college trustees. It will be women who will be the major church supporters; they will raise thousands of dollars to support the institutions.

ARTS

New Hampshire writer **Tabitha Tenney** publishes *Female Quixotism: Exhibited in the Romantic Opinions and Extravagant Adventures of Dorcasina Sheldon*, a two-volume work printed in Boston. About a gullible and shallow-minded woman who is duped by a rogue, it satirizes a society that keeps women pure and innocent and shows the consequences when reason is sacrificed to passion and romance. The novel is widely read and will have a fifth reprinting in 1841. Although the work shows some personal bigotry, it is nationalistic and is appreciated by Americans who want literature about their new nation.

Current American thought frowns upon females reading novels, believing that it causes excessive romanticism and flights of fancy and, moreover, takes time from domestic duties. Tenney's book is, in part, a response to this sentiment, offering entertainment and instruction. Novels have been popular in America since the mid-eighteenth century, and recently more female writers are turning to fiction, which offers both a paid occupation and a public voice. Tenney's work ushers in a new era of novels written by and about women, and read by women.

JOINING FORCES

Rebecca Gratz, at age twenty, helps found Philadelphia's Female Association for the Relief of Women and Children in Reduced Circumstances and serves as its secre-

tary. Gratz grew up in a prosperous and leading Jewish Philadelphia family. The family home was a gathering place for young writers and thinkers; continuing the tradition, she will host an ongoing salon of prominent Philadelphians and visitors. Gratz will devote her life to charitable work, founding and supporting many secular and religious groups, and will later offer religious instruction for young Jewish children in her home. An active and independent woman, she chooses to remain single; later she raises her nine nieces and nephews after the death of her sister.

— 1802 —

WORK

Mary Orne Tucker, who lives with her husband in Haverhill, Massachusetts, writes in her diary, "I have been so entirely engrossed today by domestic avocations, that I have hardly time for reflection."[26] Like Tucker, the lives of most white upper- and middle-class wives are centered in the home. Although their income allows purchase of ready-made goods and services, alleviating some household production, the duties of child care, cooking, cleaning, and sewing seem endless.

The ease of a married woman's life depends, of course, on class, race, and residence. Some wealthy urban women with servants have much leisure time, although mistresses of large southern plantations have full-time jobs supervising slave labor. Lower-income wives and those in rural or isolated areas still need to produce most household goods. Some supplement their husband's income by taking in boarders, by doing sewing, laundry, or wage work outside the house, and by doing domestic chores.

Thirty-eight-year-old **Jane Aitken** takes over the family's Philadelphia printing and bookbinding business. Her father has died and willed her the business. Aitken learned printing while growing up, and she is a skilled printer and bookbinder. She will run the business successfully and publish many works under her own imprint, including a new Bible translation. Like the Aitkens, many colonial families owned printing presses and children learned the business, as did wives, who often took over after being widowed. Recently, printing is being viewed as a male occupation and fewer women learn it.

ARTS

Susannah Rowson, head of a Medford, Massachusetts, female academy, organizes an exhibition of her students' work for parents and townspeople. She displays a selection of the girls' needlework, ink sketches, mourning pictures, paintings, and drawings. Some pupils recite or read their poems, essays, and stories. Local newspapers give the event a rave review, and Rowson decides to do it annually.

Rowson, a writer and former actor, opened her academy five years ago, believing girls have a right to a good education. Her school offers a serious curriculum, including math and sciences. She writes texts as needed, and recently she printed a geography text depicting women in other countries. Her school is best known for its excellent art curriculum and its skilled instructors, in contrast to most recent female academies, which have eliminated most fine arts. A music lover and former song composer, she buys a piano for the school and offers lessons in piano, guitar, dance, drawing, and painting. Many graduates will become artists.

— 1 8 0 3 —

EDUCATION AND SCHOLARSHIP

The Moravian female academy in Salem, North Carolina, which opened in the late 1700s, now accepts students of all faiths. The academy has a good reputation and is one of few southern schools for girls. Academic courses include physics, optics, and geometry, and the school is noted for its excellent training in the arts. Females can take classes in music, drawing, engraving, printmaking, and sewing. Some spend seven hours a week learning ornamental stitching, and they create elaborate samplers, pictures, and needlework globes.

LAW AND POLITICS

Thomas Jefferson completes negotiations for the Louisiana Territory. This purchase doubles America's size, gives the nation more fertile land for cotton and sugar plantations, and adds to the nation's slave territory. Cotton is booming since the widespread use of the cotton gin, and the crop is in demand by British cotton mills. Plantation owners want to expand their holdings, and to do this they need more slave labor. This causes additional great hardship for slave women, who are caught between owners' need for workers and for a self-replenishing labor force. Women are forced to bear many children while still laboring in the fields. This burden raises the infant mortality rate for blacks and destroys slave women's physical and mental health.

— 1 8 0 4 —

WORK

Meriwether Lewis and William Clark, hired by the government to explore and map the Louisiana Territory, need a guide. They hire a French Canadian fur trader, Toussaint Charbonneau, and his family accompany him. **Sacagawea**, his wife, whom he purchased from her former owners, is an unpaid but invaluable member of the party. She translates and interprets as the explorers encounter other tribes. She also fishes, gathers edible plants, cooks, cleans, and will rescue valuable equipment and records when a storm overturns their boat. The addition of a baby gives the group a friendly appearance, which is helpful when they meet other tribes who might otherwise have considered them belligerent.

ARTS

Mary Green, a schoolgirl in Worcester, Massachusetts, writes to her father about her needlework picture she has designed and sewn. It is about liberty, symbolized as a woman, who offers a golden goblet to an eagle, representing the United States, and a flag with fourteen stars waves in the background. Americans feel pride in their country, and young women often express their patriotism in the arts.

Although needlework is being phased out in the newer academies, it has a long tradition as a skill for young women. Needlework pictures teach discipline and creativity. Samplers are another popular needlework form. Girls create designs and embroider poems or sayings expressing selflessness, cheerfulness, humility, or piety. They are proud of their samplers. They display them on parlor walls, and often they will these heirlooms to a daughter or favorite niece. As needlework is dropped from school curricula, this expertise will die out and become a leisure-time hobby.

Nancy Dunham, who lives in Colchester, Connecticut, completes a mourning picture honoring her mother. Using needlework and paint, she depicts her mother's tombstone surrounded by the grieving family. Mourning pictures have become more fashionable since George Washington's death, when hundreds of women created tributes to the first president. Women sew them for family members or close friends, and some even make them for their own future death. The works are often embroidered on silk or velvet or are painted on glass.

Sometimes they include a piece of the deceased's clothing. Classical motifs such as funeral urns and weeping willows are used, reflecting the current art and architecture style; backgrounds may portray New England villages, with churches, angels, birds, flowers, and pine trees.

These works reflect a new sentimentality about death. In earlier days, death rates were high, especially for infants; and it was impractical to dwell on death. As mortality rates dropped in the late 1700s, people have felt freer to express emotions about death. Women will create these pictures for the next several decades, but their popularity declines as fewer girls learn needlework. Later, these sentiments will be reflected in photographs of the deceased.

— 1805 —

EDUCATION AND SCHOLARSHIP

Twenty Boston women organize a Gleaning Circle to discuss books they have read, including history and geography as well as essays and poems. In keeping with the current disapproval of novel reading, fiction is considered frivolous and is not part of their program. Many women in urban areas are forming such groups for continued self-improvement. Reading is an acceptable activity and a way women can learn morality and self-discipline. These groups give women a chance to socialize with a serious purpose.

Writer **Mercy Otis Warren** publishes her three-volume *History of the Rise, Progress, and Termination of the American Revolution* in Boston. She was inspired by Catharine Macaulay's history of England, and she began research during the 1770s. She collected tracts, books, essays, magazines, and newspaper clippings. She also interviewed many leaders of the Revolution, whom she knew growing up, and later she requested their diaries and private writings. She asserts America's special moral destiny, and like other contemporary histories, her work is moralistic as well as nationalistic. She calls for an end to poverty and for better treatment of the Indians. In the introduction she affirms that waging war and writing history are men's province, and she apologizes for writing it. It is sold by subscription, and reviewers judge it as scholarly. Warren's history is about men, and her exclusion of females is common. Although there are some published biographical sketches of American females, it will be another thirty years before a writer will publish a history of American women.

RELIGION

Women in Jericho Center, Vermont, found the Female Religious and Cent Society. At meetings they pray, discuss the Bible, and organize fund-raising events to support church and missionary activities. As more women attend revivals and are reawakened, they form these groups as a practical way to affirm their faith. They often call their clubs "cent" or "mite" societies to denote their small (but faithful) weekly dues.

LAW AND POLITICS

Loyalists Anna and William Martin fled to England during the Revolution and have since died. Their son and heir William sails to America to claim the Massachusetts family property, which the state impounded in 1781. Although William's father held a lifetime interest in the land, it was his mother's before marriage. Martin's lawyers argue that as a married woman who vowed to obey, it was natural and correct for Anna to accept her husband's allegiance to the king, and she had no choice in becoming a Loyalist. Only those who actively betrayed the cause had property confiscated, therefore seizure of her land was unlawful. In *Martin v. Commonwealth of Massachusetts*, a state judge upholds Martin's case and rules that as a *feme covert*, Anna had "no *political* relation to the *state*, any more than an alien." The ruling will be cited in other decisions, reinforcing married women's legal invisibility.[27]

— 1806 —

JOINING FORCES

Quaker **Alice Jackson Lewis** speaks at the Philadelphia annual women's meeting, imploring Friends to boycott sugar, cotton, and all slave products. Purchasing power is one political voice women have, and Lewis will be followed by many other women who call for boycotts.

— 1807 —

ARTS

Pennsylvanian **Susanna Heebner** completes a hand-lettered calligraphy picture. Entitled "A Song of Summer," the text is entwined and bordered by an ink and watercolor design. This is a folk art form that German settlers in Pennsylvania brought to America. Under German law, births, deaths, and marriages must be recorded on official documents, which are then often reproduced in hand-lettered and -designed certificates. Called *frakturs*, these illustrated documents become popular with Americans, and artists create them for school awards, marriage certificates, house blessings, and commemoration gifts. Later they will be replaced by lithographs, which are cheaper to produce.

LAW AND POLITICS

New Jersey voters go to the polls to decide the location of a new courthouse, but corruption is discovered and the election voided. The fraud is blamed on female, black, and immigrant voters. Republican men have long demanded female disfranchisement, and Federalist males are still angry about a high Republican female turnout in 1800 that helped Thomas Jefferson become president. The arguments against women's voting have ranged from claims that "female reserve and delicacy are incompatible with the duties of a free elector" to allegations that they are ignorant about politics and vote as their husbands or fathers do. Congressman John Condict, who started the crusade against women's voting a decade ago, submits a bill to the state legislature prohibiting suffrage from everyone except free white men. The law is enacted.[28]

— 1808 —

DOMESTICITY

The second edition of Samuel Jennings's book *The Married Lady's Companion, or Poor Man's Friend* is published in New York. He advises married women on health, happiness, and marriage. "It is in your interest to adapt yourself to your husband, whatever his peculiarities," Jennings admonishes. He emphasizes that men's "natural" rights are explained in the Bible and "It is well to remember that when you became his wife, he became your head, and your supposed superiority was buried in that voluntary act." His didactic style is typical of contemporary works on how women should behave. Not all females accept these proscriptive writings, and there is continued debate on marriage reform.[29]

RELIGION

Nineteen-year-old **Nancy Thompson**, a Connecticut resident, attends a religious revival and is so moved that she vows to devote her life to religion. Like Thompson, most revival converts are women, and in New England two out of three who accept salvation are females.[30] Religion provides meaning for young New England women. Their lives are less stable than those of their mothers and grandmothers, who often lived in the same community from birth to death. Now there are more choices for young women; some move west to Ohio or Indiana, and others work in mills or teach. Yet women's options are still limited. Marriage and motherhood are praised more than ever, but married women have few rights. Choosing a religion is one decision a woman can make, and church work is approved by society. Church membership offers young women a supportive community with people of shared values and ideals, a lifetime of work for the church, and comfort in an uncertain world.

LAW AND POLITICS

Congress passes an act prohibiting all foreign slave trade. This act puts a heavy burden on slave women, who are forced to reproduce as often as possible, ruining the health of many.

— 1809 —

WORK

Mary Kies of Killington, Connecticut, invents a method to weave straw with silk or thread, for more efficient hatmaking, and patents the process. Her method spurs New England hat manufacturing. Because of the Napoleonic Wars there is an embargo on imported goods, and national leaders encourage manufacturing and industrial growth. First Lady Dolley Madison writes to Kies, complementing her on the invention and thanking her for contributing to the American economy.

EDUCATION AND SCHOLARSHIP

Jacob Mordecai founds a female academy in Warrenton, North Carolina, modeled after the northern schools, with an academic

Portrait of Dolley Madison by Gilbert Stuart, 1804. (Library of Congress.) Dolley was married to James Madison, President Thomas Jefferson's secretary of state. She wears a fashionable empire style dress, inspired by the French Revolution as a revolt against the excessively decorative and aristocratic court dress. These new dresses had lighter fabrics and colors and a more natural shape, offering more physical freedom. Skirts were long and narrow, waistlines high, and necklines low-cut. Dolley's oblong scarf and decorative folding fan were popular accessories.

The Madisons and President Thomas Jefferson were neighbors in Virginia, and good friends. Because mixed dinner parties at the White House required a hostess, the widowed Jefferson asked for Dolley's assistance. She loved parties and became known for her skillful blending of social affairs and politics. Five years later, as First Lady, she hosted more brilliant White House gatherings.

curricula. His daughter **Rachel Mordecai** helps him run the school, and she also teaches. The academy is one of few new schools in the South, and it is convenient for southern families who prefer that their daughters be educated locally.

The South lags behind the North in education, and building schools is a low priority. The southern countryside was ravaged in the war, and many buildings are in ruin; agricultural equipment has been damaged, and thousands of slaves fled the South. Plantation owners and farmers need to plant new crops and buy more equipment and slaves.

RELIGION

Elizabeth Bayley Seaton, a widow and recent convert to Catholicism, founds the Sisters of Charity of St. Joseph in Emmitsburg, Maryland. This early Catholic American community's mission is to educate girls and help the poor. The sisters wear a simple uniform and live in a two-story log house. They teach at a Catholic school for wealthy girls and later found a free school for poor girls and an orphanage. The order will grow and inspire other Catholic women to build similar communities in Philadelphia and New York. Seaton will later be beatified for her pioneering work in religious education and charity.

Philadelphian **Jarena Lee**, a member of the African Methodist Episcopal Church, has a vision in which God tells her to spread the gospel. After being refused permission to preach in her church, she begins an itinerant ministry. She travels throughout the Northeast preaching to people of all races. A powerful and persuasive speaker, she will travel more than 2,000 miles and convert thousands. Lee's work inspires a later generation of women to preach, and much later her church will create official positions for women.

JOINING FORCES

Newport, Rhode Island, formerly a leading slave port, has a large black community. Last year some black men founded a benevolent group; while women can join, they are barred from voting or holding office. A group of Newport women decide then to form their own organization, and this year they establish the African Female Benevolent Society. They help each other as well as needy widows and orphans, and they support the local school by raising money for teachers, books, and supplies.

— 1810 —

WORK

The cotton industry is booming in the United States, due in part to the Embargo and Non-Intervention Acts passed two years ago to prohibit British imports. As more mills are built, women are the majority of employees. This year, Secretary of the Treasury Albert Gallatin investigates conditions at eighty-seven cotton mills and reports that 500 men and 3,500 women and children work there.[31]

RELIGION

Seventeenth-century ministers commonly preached on female wickedness, emphasizing their inheritance of Eve's sins. This viewpoint has been shifting, and in the last few decades sermons more often emphasized good women in the Bible, upholding them as models of female behavior. Many ministers now address women as a special class of citizens with important duties in the home and community. Boston minister Joseph Buckminster speaks to members of a local charitable organization. He praises their work and encourages them to bring religion into their homes, reminding them, "We look to you ladies to raise the standard of character of our own sex."[32]

— 1811 —

DOMESTICITY

Mary Lee, a young New England wife despondent over her child's death, writes to her sister, "It seems as if all my occupation is gone."[33] Her comment reflects changing ideas on parenthood. In colonial times both parents reared the children. Men worked on farms or in nearby businesses or craft shops where they had daily contact with their offspring, whom they would help to guide, discipline, and educate. Men's work patterns have now changed. Many have left farming or life in small communities for urban occupations, farther from their households.

While fathers have a lesser parenting role, American mothers are now being told that child rearing is their highest priority. Few can meet this standard. While wealthy women like Mary Lee have servants and leisure time, most mothers are occupied with strenuous domestic chores and others earn wages in factories.

WORK

Traditionally, shoes have been produced in two steps: women sewed the leather uppers, and then men did the heavier work of hand-stitching the uppers to the soles. The invention of the wooden shoe peg simplifies production. Lightweight shoes can be assembled by women and children. They first bind the upper parts, then attach them to light soles with the pegs. Although some people still prefer the older and heavier shoes, the light ones are cheaper and gain popularity. The demand creates more employment for women, whom factory owners prefer to hire since they can be paid less.

ARTS

Artist **Susan Sedgwick** paints a commemorative watercolor of **Elizabeth Freeman**, her housekeeper. Freeman, a former slave, illiterate but smart, challenged her bondage in 1781. She based her case on the Massachusetts Constitution, which proclaims all men are born free and equal, and she won with the help of Sedgwick's father, a pro-abolition lawyer. She is one of the earliest slaves to sue for freedom using a state constitution for her defense. There is affection and respect between Freeman and her employer, and she will be buried in a Sedgwick family plot.

— 1812 —

WORK

Elleanor Eldridge starts a weaving, soap making, and nursing business in Warwick, Rhode Island. At age ten, working as a domestic servant, she learned to weave, and by fourteen she was a skillful carpet maker. Her business will serve many Warwick citizens, earning her the community's respect. Eldridge is one of few free northern black women with their own businesses. Most blacks have little education and work as domestic servants or laundresses.

Martha Laurens Ramsay's memoirs are published by her husband, David, who is grieving over her death. Ramsay's friends in Charleston considered her a model southern upper-class woman. She was obedient to her husband and acknowledged his superiority. Her life was steeped in religion. She read the Bible and prayed with her family daily, wrote prayers, attended church faithfully, and instructed her slaves in Christianity. She took her role as mother of eleven seriously, tutoring her sons for college and educating her daughters. As a good wife, she helped her husband with his medical research. She experimented with growing olives and devised a preserving and debittering process for them. Behind this paragon was a brilliant woman who had learned to read at age three, later learned Greek and Latin, and became well read in history and philosophy. Yet her father insisted that learning domestic skills should be her priority. Her memoirs, based on her diaries, will be reprinted ten times, portraying the contemporary ideal American woman.

JOINING FORCES

Eleven women form the Boston Fragment Society to help families who lost husbands and fathers in the current war with the British. The members are from Boston's leading families, who have time and money for charitable work. They sew newborns' layettes, collect children's clothing to loan to clients, and help widows find jobs. Applicants for assistance are carefully selected so that most have British ancestry. The group serves three purposes: they are doing God's work for the needy, learning business skills, and socializing. They will maintain their activities long after the war and well into the twentieth century.

New York women form a Ladies' Stocking Society. They meet to knit socks, and they hold fund-raisers to buy uniforms for soldiers fighting the British. Like the Boston group, these women want to feel needed and useful and they seek fellowship. These groups are typical of many that women establish after the Revolution. Although initially responding to wartime hardships, many continue their work, using the organizational skills they have learned for other causes.

— 1813 —

WORK

The Boston Manufacturing Company incorporates with $400,000 in capital, the largest amount ever financing the American textile industry. These entrepreneurs, led by Francis Cabot Lowell, build mills in Waltham, Massachusetts. Putting all stages of cloth manufacturing in one location will give them better coordination and lower shipping costs. They will hire female labor to save costs, since women can be paid less and weaving and spinning are traditional women's work.

American leaders are encouraging industrial development. Because of the war with the British, imported goods are restricted and there is a demand for American-made ones. Entrepreneurs like Lowell are eager to invest in American manufacturing. There are now more than one hundred cotton and woolen mills in New England.

RELIGION

Ann Hasseltine Judson travels to Burma with her missionary husband. She is one of the earliest American women to accompany a missionary husband abroad. In Rangoon she runs the household, teaches native women hygiene and Christianity, and helps translate the Bible into Burmese. Though the public views her travels abroad as wild and romantic, and church officials are dubious about wives in the field, her many accomplishments force officials to see the value of a wife's work. Eventually husband-and-wife missionary teams will be accepted and sanctioned. Judson's writings will inspire a later generation of single women to be missionaries.

ARTS

Folk artist **Eunice Griswold Pinney**, who lives in Windsor, Connecticut, completes a watercolor mourning picture for herself, leaving a space for her death date. Pinney, age forty-three, recently taught herself to paint, and she has more leisure now that her eight children are grown. She paints memorials, landscapes, genre scenes, portraits, and interiors using literary and religious themes. She will complete some fifty works and gain local fame for her fresh colors, good composition, and skillful drafting.

JOINING FORCES

Seventeen wealthy New Jersey women found a charitable society. They donate personal funds and ask local businessmen for additional support. They run the operation efficiently, dividing the community into districts, each administered by an individual member. This group is unusual in that they help blacks and immigrants as well as native-born whites. They will continue their work for nearly sixty years.

LAW AND POLITICS

A divorcing couple both want custody of their children. In *Commonwealth v. Addicks*, a Pennsylvania judge awards the wife temporary custody because the children are so young, though he affirms the father's rights of ownership and gives him unlimited visitation. The judge upholds traditional common law, which gives fathers all legal rights to their children, but he also establishes a "tender years" doctrine according to which mothers are viewed as the best custodians of the very young. The courts will not view women as appropriate legal guardians for another seventy years.[34]

Dower rights are a widow's inheritance of one-third of her husband's real property. This long-standing legal tradition ensures against a widow's becoming destitute and a burden on society. Many men also will property to their wives, and unless specified that it is in lieu of dower, widows have customarily kept both. Now dower rights are being legally challenged. There is more competition for land in a nation experiencing commercial and industrial growth. In *Herbert v. Wren*, Supreme Court justice John Marshall rules that a widow has no legal claim to both a property bequest from her husband and land from her dower rights; she must choose between them.[35]

— 1814 —

WORK

The introduction of power machinery in factories allows large-scale cloth production, which will make it cheaper to buy than make at home. Many young women who traditionally spun and wove at home now often take jobs outside the house. Some work in the mills, hire out as domestic servants, or enter the growing profession of teaching. Daughters in wealthier families who can purchase cloth now have more leisure time for writing, reading and socializing. Women living in isolated or rural areas, especially in the South and West, will continue to weave and spin at home for many decades, since the cloth from factories is not available everywhere.

Mill employee **Deborah Skinner** operates one of the nation's first power looms at the Waltham cotton mill. She is among hundreds of young single female employees recruited from the region's farms. Factory owner Lowell will develop a paternalistic system for housing employees, to keep them on schedule and encourage *esprit de corps*. He will build company housing that will provide family-style meals, planned social activities, and church services. These young women who work and live together will establish close friendships.

Philadelphian **Mary Clarke Carr** founds a new magazine, *Intellectual Female, or Ladies Tea Tray*, with fiction, morality tales, theater reviews, death notices, and fashion and beauty advice. Like many other contemporary magazines, it is short-lived due to lack of subscribers. Her publication does anticipate later women's magazines whose editors will imitate Carr's personal style. Philadelphia is a magazine publishing center, as are New York and Boston. These cities have growing audiences of literate women with leisure to read and money to subscribe.

EDUCATION AND SCHOLARSHIP

Catherine Fiske opens a girls' high school in New Hampshire and hires six teachers. Her curriculum emphasizes moral instruction, considered important for future wives and mothers. Her facility will operate for more than two decades and have nearly 2,500 alumnae. Many women are founding similar schools in New England, the country's center of education. While Americans still debate the wisdom of educating girls, supporters point out that they need practical training for their future domestic life.

RELIGION

Women are active in churches. They are the majority of members, and their efforts and the money they raise are needed to sustain the institutions. Though church officials appreciate this supportive work, they fear that women may covet a greater voice in church affairs. New Hampshire Congregationalist minister Walter Harris reminds women of their place. "God has made known," he states, "that females should not be public teachers of religion, nor take an active part in governing his church on earth."[36]

LAW AND POLITICS

The British, still at war with America, are concentrating on their land campaign. They enter Washington, D.C., bombard buildings, then burn them. First Lady **Dolley Todd Madison**, who is in the presidential house, rescues valuable items. She wrests Gilbert Stuart's cherished portrait of George Washington from its embedded frame, then collects state papers and documents and flees in her carriage to the Madison home in Virginia.

— 1815 —

DOMESTICITY

Writers are publishing books, pamphlets, articles, and essays on the value of motherhood, and young single upper- and middle-class females are reading them. Many are enchanted with their future roles. Eighteen-year-old **Mehitable May Dawes** reads **Hannah More**'s *Strictures on the Modern System of Education*. Impressed with More's depiction of motherhood, Dawes writes in her journal that raising children is an honorable job, and adds, "What an important sphere a woman fills!"[37]

— 1816 —

WORK

Massachusetts women establish the Dorchester Maternal Association. As Christian mothers they take their responsibilities seriously, gathering to discuss child rearing, offer mutual help and advice, and pray together. This is a grassroots response to the current elevation of motherhood and the imperative to raise a moral generation of children. Hundreds of middle-class mothers in the Northeast and Midwest are forming similar groups.

A congressional committee studies the status of industrial workers. It reports that 100,000 people are employed in cotton mills, and two-thirds of these are women and children. The committee concludes that the growth of the cotton industry has created a new class of textile workers: young, white, and female.[38]

RELIGION

Joanne Graham Bethune, who grew up in Scotland, observed the active Scottish Sunday school movement and was inspired by it. Now a prominent and wealthy New Yorker who works for charity, she organizes the Female Union Society for the Promotion of Sabbath Schools. The group sponsors interdenominational Sunday classes in Christianity, reading, and writing, and thousands of children are converted and educated. Her group will later merge with the American Sunday-School Union, and Bethune will be considered the mother of American Sunday schools.

Many African Americans have attended religious revivals that are still sweeping the country. Though they converted eagerly, they need a church. In Philadelphia many blacks are tired of the hostile reception at white churches. This year a group of African Americans found the African Methodist Episcopal Church. Most new members are women, and their work ensures its success. They raise money for the building and programs, recruit new members, lead prayer meetings in their homes, and help clothe and feed the minister and needy parishioners.

ARTS

Methodist **Peggy Dow** has traveled throughout the nation attending religious revivals with her husband, who is a minister. She has been awed by the jubilant spirit pervading the gatherings and has carefully transcribed the songs for posterity. This year she publishes a music book of camp meeting hymns.

— 1 8 1 7 —

WORK

Amanda Elliot, a young Connecticut woman, accepts a teaching position. Although wages are low, it is a respectable position and, with more schools established, teachers are needed. This is not the only work Elliot does this year. She also splits and braids straw for hats, binds shoes, and helps her mother care for boarders living with the family. Her work is typical of many young New England women, who hold many different jobs. Earlier generations of white young single females also worked away from home. Many did domestic chores in other households, hired out to farms, or worked in small businesses or shops. Now, with growing industry and commerce and the proliferation of female schools, Elliot and her contemporaries have more vocational choices than their mothers and grandmothers did.

JOINING FORCES

American agents are negotiating with Cherokee leaders for tribal land in the Southeast. They have already bought or taken Cherokee territory, but they want more for westward expansion and settlement. This purchase would require the remaining tribe members to emigrate west of the Mississippi. Cherokee women have a voice in tribal government, and during the proceedings a petition signed by **Nancy Ward**, an esteemed elder, and twelve other Cherokee women is presented to the male Cherokee council. The petitioners note that their home is land their foremothers farmed for centuries. "We do not wish to go to an unknown country," they plead. "Your mothers and sisters ask and beg of you not to part with any more of our lands." The tribal men consider the petition; although they cede some parcels to the Americans, they refuse to sell all of it. They will all be evicted from their home nearly two decades later.[39]

— 1 8 1 8 —

EDUCATION AND SCHOLARSHIP

Rose Philippine Duchesne, a French nun, establishes a girls' boarding school on the Missouri frontier and welcomes black and Indian as well as white students. Thousands of Americans are moving west; in the Missouri Territory alone the population has tripled in the past eight years.[40] Schools are needed for children of the pioneers, and

Catholic nuns are among those founding them. American parochial schools have a good reputation, and Protestant as well as Catholic students enroll.

ARTS

Few women become professional artists, since this is considered men's work. It is difficult for women to get training, and apprenticeships are closed to them. Even if they could acquire skills they would find it difficult to attract patrons, and social restrictions would discourages public exhibits. However, there are some successful female artists; these are usually the daughters, nieces, or wives of well-known male painters.

Anna Claypoole Peale travels to Washington this year with her uncle, artist Charles Willson Peale. He introduces her to potential patrons and shares his studio with her. Peale is a miniaturist who trained with her artist father, and she specializes in portraits on ivory. She has developed a distinctive style using dark backgrounds, and her pictures are noted for their warmth. She has already exhibited and will later be elected academician of the Pennsylvania Academy of Fine Arts. On this trip she paints President James Monroe, Andrew Jackson, and Henry Clay.

JOINING FORCES

Forty black women organize the Colored Female Religious and Moral Society in Salem, Massachusetts, for mutual help. Many African-American women are establishing such groups, which are often crucial for their survival. Because prejudice against blacks is so common in the United States, most white benevolent groups are unwilling to help even destitute black families.

Hannah Mather Crocker publishes *Observations on the Real Rights of Women with Their Appropriate Duties, Agreeable to Scripture, Reason, and Common Sense.* She describes women's accomplishments and pleads for more education for them. She advocates egalitarian marriages based on mutual affection and trust and argues that women deserve legal rights. She defends some of Mary Wollstonecraft's ideas — one of few Americans to do so publicly. Hoping to avoid criticism by focusing on women, she includes an appendix of men's accomplishments. Subscribers purchase it, but the work has no major impact on current thinking.

LAW AND POLITICS

In *Connor v. Shephard*, the Massachusetts Supreme Court rules that a widow cannot claim her dower on unimproved lands because uncultivated property is not subject to dower rights. The judgment extends the restrictions of *Herbert v. Wren*, and sets a second precedent for the erosion of dower rights. These court rulings reflect Americans' desire for land for commercial and industrial expansion.[41]

— 1819 —

DOMESTICITY

Boston writer **Nancy Sproat** publishes *Family Lectures*. She contrasts the peaceful setting in an ideal home with the poisonous atmosphere of the workplace. Home should be a retreat, she argues, and a sanctuary for men after a day's labor. Sproat and other writers of this genre help strengthen the idea that home and work are separate. They describe the home as women's sphere, linked to love, while work is men's sphere, tied to greed and exploitation. Although these writers disparage the effects of industrialization, their solution is to ensure ideal homes rather than to reform industry.

WORK

A Savannah publisher starts the *Ladies Magazine*, one of the earliest publications for southern women. Like northern publications, it provides jobs for female writers and offers readers the latest fiction and fashion.

A duty has just been slapped on imported ready-made clothing, and there is demand for American-made apparel, especially military uniforms and garments for slaves. Master tailors in New York City who need more assistance at low cost are hiring seamstresses. This angers journeymen who worry that the seamstresses will replace them, and they strike.

The garment industry is changing as more clothing is being mass-produced. Mill workers weave the cloth; then it is cut and delivered to seamstresses who complete the garments at home. These seamstresses underbid each other. Tailors, who measure, cut, and sew in the customer's house, are being underpriced by the growing clothing industry.

Cherokee **Nancy Ward** is forced to leave her hometown of Chota, in the southern Appalachians, because her tribe ceded it to the United States. She moves south and works as an innkeeper. Ward, known as "War Woman" for her courage in battle, is an honored leader. She heads the women's council and has a voice in the tribe's general council. She helps negotiate treaties and has a prominent role in ceremonies. She is among one of the few remaining Cherokee women with power. Within the next decade the tribe will restructure their government, denying women voting or council privileges.

EDUCATION AND SCHOLARSHIP

Julian Froumountaine, a Santo Domingo immigrant, opens a free high school for blacks in Savannah, Georgia. This is needed because black parents want learning for their children. Most white schools prohibit enrollment of blacks, and southern African-American youth have scant educational opportunities. Slaves, of course, are already prohibited from receiving any instruction.

More free blacks live in the United States now, with territorial additions from the Louisiana Purchase and the Adams-Onís treaty. Southern lawmakers, threatened by this increase and fearful of uprisings, pass more restrictive laws. When education for free blacks is prohibited, Froumountaine will operate the school secretly, one of a few brave southern women who run underground schools.

Emma Willard presents a plan, *An Address to the Public; Particularly to Members of the Legislature of New York, Proposing a Plan for Improving Female Education*, to the New York State legislature. It is a request for state-supported female colleges. She believes that women can learn college-level subjects, and has proved this. Some years ago, preparing to open a girls' school in Vermont, she studied her nephew's college math and philosophy texts, and learned other subjects as well. She then designed courses for her students, who did well. She appeals to the legislators' patriotism, noting that college-educated mothers could raise exemplary American sons. Her plan, well thought out, includes a history of female education, justification, and a description of an ideal female seminary. President James Madison endorses it, as do distinguished statesmen John Adams and Thomas Jefferson. The legislature, unwilling to commit funds, does not approve it, though they grant her a charter for a female school.

RELIGION

The New York Missionary Society wants to send workers to the Buffalo Creek Seneca village in New York. Missionaries, encouraged and subsidized by the national government, are eager to transform Indians into Christian Americans. For decades they have urged Senecas to adapt to white society and offered help. Finally, this year, the tribal council agrees to let them build a church and a school. Here the girls are trained in sewing, spinning, and other domestic work, and the boys learn to farm.

Already the Senecas have experienced change; white settlers are encroaching, and government agents have pressured them to give up communal living and farming. While some males are willing to accommodate, appreciating men's higher status in white society, many older women resist. They have always farmed and distributed food, and are unwilling to abandon traditional ways. Earlier, some who fought change were accused of witchcraft and executed.

The remaining Senecas accept the mission's presence and will learn to live like Americans. The school becomes an important community center, as many convert to Christianity and older women learn domestic skills.

LAW AND POLITICS

In a Supreme Court decision upholding the legality of a college's charter, *Dartmouth College v. Woodward*, the brief includes comments about men's rights in marriage. Justice Joseph Story rules that Dartmouth College's charter is a legal contract, protecting the school from state interference. He compares the college's legal rights to men's rights in the civil contract of marriage, affirming, "A man has just as good a right to his wife, as to *the property* acquired under a marriage contract [and] ... he has a legal right to her society and her fortune." To divest him of these "would be as flagrant a violation of the principles of justice as the confiscation of his own estate." This opinion reflects current legal thinking on matrimony and married women's rights.[42]

— 1820 —

WORK

More than 8,000 immigrants arrive in the United States, 92 percent from Europe.[43] Many are tired of high taxes, the rigid social structure, and harsh winters and want to start a new life. American land is available, plentiful, and inexpensive, and soils on the western frontier are fertile. Others, living in poverty, hope to find jobs in the new country.

This year 43 percent of all immigrants are from Ireland.[44] In Ireland, an ongoing agricultural depression has caused loss of farms and destitution for thousands. Many young unmarried men who would have farmed now have no land, and they immigrate to America hoping to find jobs. Young unmarried Irish women would also face a bleak future at home, and they too immigrate to the United States. Most have few skills and must compete with native-born women for jobs at mills and in domestic work. The majority become household maids, and in some cities they will comprise more than half of all domestic servants.

The New York *Emigrant's Directory* is published to help newcomers find jobs and housing. This year's edition cautions tailors of the severe competition for sewing jobs, warning them they are unlikely to get fair wages. Thousands of women and children work as seamstresses, earning one-half or three-fourths of tailors' standard wages, thus "damaging" the trade.

Of the 870,800 black female Americans, 86 percent are slaves. In the large southern plantations they grow cotton, now in greater demand for the northern mills. On other plantations and farms they cultivate tobacco, wheat, corn, and grain. They are bought primarily as laborers but are expected to reproduce, giving them extra value. Thomas Jefferson attests, "I consider a women who brings a child every two years as more profitable than the best man of the farm."[45]

EDUCATION AND SCHOLARSHIP

Anne Marie Becroft opens a school in Georgetown for black girls, who are barred from most local academies. She is an excellent teacher and will run the school successfully for eight years. Later, converting to Catholicism, she will open a larger school under the church's aegis, at the local priest's request. Becroft had been unable to complete her own education. Racial animosity forced her out of one northern institution, and community hostility compelled closure of the next one. Educating blacks is often unsafe even in the North, but Becroft wants to offer them the training she missed.

Zilpa Grant enrolls in a coeducational academy in Byfield, Massachusetts, run by Joseph Emerson. She receives not only an excellent education but inspiration and encouragement from Emerson, who respects his female students and treats them as equals of male pupils. He offers higher-level work to students who want it and predicts that there will be women's colleges one day. Grant is one of many females Emerson influences. Next year **Mary Lyon** will enroll, the two will become good friends, and both will pursue educational careers. Lyon will found Mt. Holyoke, and Grant will establish an academy for women.

ARTS

The Boston Handel and Haydn Society hires **Sophia Hewitt Ostinelli** as their organist, a position she will keep for ten years. Her musician husband collects her pay, since a married woman's wages legally belong to her husband. Ostinelli, daughter of a composer, was a prodigy at age seven and studied piano, organ, and harp. Her parents supported her talent and allowed her to perform in public.

Young girls often learn harpsichord or piano, since musical knowledge is an expected social grace for daughters in well-off families. Music is part of courtship and family life in upper- and middle-class families. Amateur playing is desirable, but women are discouraged from continuing beyond that, and few become professional musicians.

Miniaturist **Sarah Goodridge** opens an art studio in Boston, where she will paint and exhibit for twenty years. Unlike the few females who are professional artists, Goodridge comes from a family that is neither wealthy nor artistic. As a child she drew pictures on the sand kitchen floor, and with a pin on bark. Her parents could not afford lessons, so she trained herself and later sold paintings and taught school to support formal art instruction. She will become well known for her skillfully colored miniatures. She is acquainted with Gilbert Stuart, and he later asks to sit for her. Her portrait of him will have "fire and energy," and he will declare it his only true portrait.[46]

— 1821 —

WORK

Priests at the San Gabriel Mission, north of Pueblo de la Reina de Los Angeles, appoint **Eulalia Perez** the llavera, or key keeper. The mission houses priests, nuns, and Indian laborers and hosts traveling missionaries, cowboys, Spanish and Mexican officers, visiting dignitaries, and upper-class travelers. Running the establishment requires considerable work. Her duties include maintaining stores of food and supplies, making candles and soap, distributing sheepskins and hides for saddles, sewing clothing for the men, and doing laundry and cooking. She also makes chocolate and lemonade and operates the olive press. She works with Indian assistants and will keep her post for fourteen years. Other Hispanic women hold similar jobs in missions along the Pacific coast. This sparsely populated region has few women, and those with domestic skills can find work. Perez is among thousands of Hispanics who will become Americans when California is annexed.

EDUCATION AND SCHOLARSHIP

Emma Willard moves to Troy, New York, to open a female seminary. She has a state charter, and local merchants donated land for the buildings. Willard believes women are capable and intelligent and deserve a good education. The school even offers some college-level instruction. The curriculum includes history, geography, geology, botany, chemistry, physics, physiology, algebra, Greek, Italian, Spanish, fine arts, dance, and rhetoric. She has a scholarship program and also gives personal loans, believing education should not limited to the wealthy. The school flourishes, and it will gain fame for its rigorous standards, strong academic curriculum, and establishment of regular testing and exams. Nearly 12,000 will graduate, and many will teach or found schools based on the Troy model.

JOINING FORCES

Black women in Philadelphia establish the Daughters of Africa Society for mutual help, and nearly 200 working-class women join. They lend each other money for rent, medical, and burial expenses. Most American black women earn little, and they rarely receive assistance from the government or local charitable groups.

— 1822 —

DOMESTICITY

On her wedding day, **Eunice Wait Cobb** writes in her diary, "in everything I must consult the interest, the happiness, and the welfare of my *Husband*."[47] Cobb has been taught that if she makes him happy her marriage will be successful, and she wants to be the ideal American wife.

WORK

Pennsylvania legislators award **Mary Hays McCauley** a pension for her service in the Revolutionary War. When her husband,

a gunner, joined the troops, she followed him to camps and battle sites, washed his clothing, cooked meals, and helped nurse the militia. She frequently brought water to thirsty soldiers, who dubbed her "Molly Pitcher." Her work was not extraordinary. Thousands of women and children followed regiments and cared for soldier husbands and their comrades. That she is granted a pension is unusual, since few women receive them, but McCauley probably attracted more attention. A camp surgeon and others recall her as a warmhearted and brave woman who was also feisty, loud, and chewed tobacco.

— 1823 —

RELIGION

Betsy Stockton is sent to Hawaii to be a domestic servant for a white missionary family and to teach natives. She is among the first blacks, and one of few single women to work abroad. Most churches prohibit single women from missionary work, believing all women abroad need a husband's protection. Single women as evangelists abroad will not be common for another fifty years.

— 1824 —

WORK

Mary Jemison publishes her story, *A Narrative of the Life of Mary Jemison*, describing her life with the Indians. In 1758, when Jemison was a young girl, the Shawnees captured her family, killed her parents and siblings, but saved her and later adopted her. She found happiness and a good life with them, and later she married a Delaware. Now widowed and a naturalized American citizen, she farms and raises cattle in New York.

Since she is illiterate, she tells her tale to schoolteacher James Seaver, who writes the book. Seaver takes liberties with her story. He glosses over her happiness and portrays a survival tale of how a brave and moral woman can overcome hardship. Wanting readers to remember the Indians' brutality, he depicts them in racial stereotypes. Captivity narratives are exciting reading, and Indians are a uniquely American theme. The book will be reprinted twice and become a best-seller in America and England.

ARTS

Lydia Marie Francis publishes *Hobomok: A Tale of Early Times*, a novel set in Puritan Massachusetts. It portrays a marriage of a European and Indian, a favorite theme for Americans, who are endlessly curious about native life and culture. This novel establishes Francis's literary reputation, and she will become one of the nation's most prolific authors. It is so popular that the Boston Athenaeum offers her a membership and free access to their library, although they will later withdraw this privilege when she publishes an abolitionist tract.

JOINING FORCES

Two hundred women at a Pawtucket, Rhode Island, mill join male employees in a short, spontaneous strike to protest pay cuts and longer hours. Because of competition from other mills, and to increase stockholders' profits, factory owners periodically cut employee wages, speed up machines, and force employees to work more hours. Some women join men's demonstrations, while others initiate their own. Most of the female early protests are short-lived, since there is little female solidarity. Most women need to work for their family's survival and cannot afford to protest. Others, trained to be obedient, hesitate to participate in a public display. Strikes do little good, as disgruntled employees are easily replaced. Thousands of immigrants are also seeking jobs.

— 1825 —

WORK

Rebecca Pennock Lukens, recently widowed, takes over her family's ironworks business in Pennsylvania. The company is floundering, facing lawsuits and heavy competition. Lukens learns good business techniques. She manages the company with a firm hand, buys supplies carefully, sets standard prices for her products, and deals with customers personally. In the evenings she studies legislation affecting her business. Foreseeing the development of steam power, she will later reconfigure the factory to manufacture boiler plates for ships and wood-burning locomotives. These will be well made and earn a good reputation. The new railroads will transport her products across the country quickly, solving earlier transportation problems of rough or muddy roads and icy rivers. At Lukens's death, her company will be worth more than $100,000.

RELIGION

The Memoirs of Catharine Brown, a Christian Indian of the Cherokee Nation, is published posthumously, based on her diary and letters. Born in Alabama, **Catharine Brown** was baptized while attending a mission school. She urged friends and family to convert, founded a women's missionary group, and taught in a Indian school. In printing her memoirs, the church shows how Indian women can be fulfilled through Christian faith.

JOINING FORCES

Fifteen Massachusetts women establish a female temperance society to encourage abstention. They find women with drinking problems, warn them of the consequences of drinking, and ask them to sign abstention pledges. This early temperance group will inspire other organizations, and women will

American cartoon caricaturing Scottish-born reformer Frances Wright, 1829. (Library of Congress.) That year Wright had begun a lecture tour in the United States. Wright was both fascinated and repelled by American culture. She spoke forthrightly about her abhorrence of slavery, her strong opposition to organized religion, and the need for human rights for women. Not only were these topics controversial, but current mores forbade women to speak in public. Her audiences jeered, critics called her a "female monster," and newspaper reporters ridiculed her viewpoints. This illustrator portrays her as a "goose" that "deserves to be hissed." The young man who stands demurely holding her hat also looks foolish and helps illustrate the fallacy of crossing gender boundaries.

eventually dominate the movement. Men have formed temperance societies too, but they often bar women from membership and prohibit their speaking at conventions.

Frances Wright, a Scottish reformer visiting America, is horrified by slavery. She writes a plan for gradual emancipation and sends it to Congress. Getting no response, she puts it into action herself. She buys 640 acres in Tennessee for a colony, Nashoba, where slaves can live, farm, and sell crops to buy their freedom. She purchases slaves and relocates them to Nashoba, where they are instructed to clear and cultivate the land. The colony is unsuccessful. The colony's neighbors think her plan is crazy, and they shun her and the ex-slaves. The land is hard to clear, the crops fail, and her debts mount. She abandons her project and frees the remaining slaves, sending them to Haiti.

— 1826 —

EDUCATION AND SCHOLARSHIP

Editors of the new *American Journal of Education* announce that women's education is important and that they will publish articles and letters on the topic. Many readers and writers can continue the dialogue on female education, on what kind is best, and on how much schooling women should have. While this debate continues, more female seminaries are being built in New England and in western territories, to which thousands are immigrating.[48]

ARTS

Writer **Jane Johnson Schoolcraft** and her husband, ethnologist Henry Schoolcraft, found *Muzzinyegun*, a literary magazine. Jane's mother, an Ojibway, is fluent in her language and knowledgeable about tribal history. Jane and her mother write poetry and recount tribal legends, folktales, and chronicles for the publication. The journal, widely distributed on the East Coast, will earn a good reputation for fascinating and well-written Ojibway lore. The Schoolcrafts will entertain many American and English visitors in their Sault Sainte Marie home.

JOINING FORCES

Alcohol has always been part of American life. Ale and rum were imported in colonial days; people used it for medicine and even children drank it. Now, with increase in per capita consumption it is a growing problem. Women are particularly concerned; many have fathers, sons, or brothers who drink to excess, and families are often left destitute when husbands spend all their wages on drink. The American Society for the Promotion of Temperance is formed, a middle-class organization. Men run it, and women support it through fund-raising and volunteer work. They publish tracts on the dangers of drinking and urge people to abstain. Meetings often are like religious revivals, with participants offering emotional personal testimonies about their overindulgences. Their work is successful. The group will spawn some 5,000 state and local temperance societies, and they will persuade a million people to sign abstinence pledges. National alcohol consumption will gradually decline.

— 1827 —

DOMESTICITY

New Hampshire minister Charles Burroughs gives a speech on women's education. Affirming that training should emphasize domestic skills, he then speaks on the familiar topic of home. He describes home as the place where love is found and honor and virtue exist. Women, he emphasizes, can make the home an oasis for men who are adjusting to a changing business world. Many workplaces are now impersonal; there are hierarchies, jobs are specialized, and employers are distant from their employees. Like others who emphasize the importance of domesticity, Burroughs want the poor conditions of the workplace tempered by the tranquillity of home.

EDUCATION AND SCHOLARSHIP

Matilda sends a letter to the editor of the *Freedom's Journal*. She pleads with readers to support education for black women. She states that women need to know more than just how to cook. They have "minds that are capable and deserving of culture.... There is a great responsibility resting somewhere, and it is time for us to be up and doing."[49]

The journal, published in New York, is one of several newspapers for African Americans that are available in northern cities with large black communities. Some wealthy donors fund these publications, and others are supported by local churches. They are an important forum for literate blacks, since mainstream publications rarely offer news about African Americans.

RELIGION

Philadelphian **Sarah Allen** founds the Daughters of Conference. This group of women helps care for ministers in the African Methodist Episcopal (AME) Church by mending their clothing and cooking for them. Allen is the wife of Bishop Richard Allen. Attending a conference, she noted that many ministers looked shabby and decided that women should help. AME preachers are so appreciative that other chapters will be formed, and the group will eventually be an official part of the church.

English writer **Frances Trollope** is visiting the United States. While in Cincinnati, she hears nothing but talk of an anticipated revival. She is astonished by the excitement it generates among women, and later comments, "I never saw or read of any country where religion has so strong a hold upon the women, or a slighter hold upon the men."[50]

ARTS

Catherine Maria Sedgwick, who lives in Massachusetts, publishes *Hope Leslie*, a historical romance set in Puritan New England. Her characters are lively, strong, have good moral values, and are thoroughly domesticated, reflecting contemporary values. She is one of the first to use regional color, and her book adds to the growing body of literature about Americans. Reviewers praise it and the book sells well. She will write many more novels.

Literature is becoming dominated by women. Writing, once considered a dubious activity for women, is now a respectable occupation. Sedgwick's novels emphasize marriage, families, and daily life, popular themes with the American public. Such works contribute to the ongoing discussion of women's roles. Although some still frown on novel reading for women, morality tales are acceptable. More New England women, who attend the new female academies, are literate, and as the birthrate for upper- and middle-class white mothers declines they have more time to read.[51]

Ann Hall paints miniatures on ivory. She showed artistic talent at age five, when she cut paper figures and modeled in wax. Her physician father noticed her talent, encouraged her, and later paid for private lessons. Hall has had many displays, and she gets commissions from wealthy New York families. Critics have acclaimed her work for its delicacy. This year she is elected an artist in the National Academy of Design, and she will later become a full member. Decorum dictates that women not fraternize with men, so she will only attend a meeting when a quorum is needed.

LAW AND POLITICS

Cherokee males write a new constitution based on the American Constitution. Women are now prohibited from sitting on the council or voting, privileges they had enjoyed under the old laws.

— 1828 —

WORK

Boston minister John Blake founds the *Ladies Magazine* and appoints writer **Sarah Josepha Hale** as editor. She will fashion it into a popular publication, and her style will set the standard for the magazine industry. Unlike most editors, Hale publishes only original materials. She writes her own copy and hires many women authors and illustrators. The journal's mission is to help women become better wives and mothers. While Hale believes women should be educated, their domestic responsibilities take priority. The most "praiseworthy" work for women, she asserts, is "to make a happy home for her husband and children." Because she is widowed and the sole support of five children, she does not live the lifestyle she promotes.[52]

Nine out of ten textile workers are female. Most are young and single white native-born women. Although women dominate the textile industry, it is not their major occupation. Most females work in traditional trades: sewing at home, running boardinghouses, and working in small businesses, or as domestic servants.[53]

New Yorker **Sarah Johnson** advertises in the *Freedom's Journal*. She states that she is a dressmaker, can do other sewing, and will clean, repair, and refit leghorn and straw hats. As urban free black communities expand, more services are needed and women like Johnson find it profitable to start businesses.

ARTS

Jane Stuart, age sixteen, opens an art studio in Boston. Her father, Gilbert, has just died impoverished, and she is the sole support of her widowed mother and older sisters. She learned to paint while assisting her father mixing paint, doing backgrounds for his works, and cleaning brushes. He refused to train her and barred her from his art classes; nonetheless, she hid behind the door to listen to his teaching. Stuart does miniatures and portraits, and she copies her father's famous Washington likeness. She develops a style unlike her father's and will get some commissions. Her income will remain low, but she is an engaging figure. She later moves to Newport, Rhode Island, and as she ages she will become a beloved eccentric of Newport society.

JOINING FORCES

Reformer **Frances Wright**, who is again visiting the United States, begins a lecture tour. Her agenda is varied: she condemns slavery, attacks organized religion as harmful to women, advocates egalitarian marriages and free love, and suggests that racial intermarriage will solve prejudice. She is among the earliest women to lecture to large audiences of men and women. That she speaks in public is bad enough, but most people find her ideas scandalous and newspaper editors attack her as immoral.

— 1829 —

WORK

Americans can apply for job referrals at New York's Society for the Encouragement of Faithful Domestic Servants, and the office reports on its applicants for the past four years. Seventy-four percent were white women, 10 percent white men, 9 percent black women, and 6 percent black men.

These figures reflect the structure of domestic employment. Nearly 80 percent of New York City's domestic servants are women, and most of these are Irish immigrants.[54]

Young colonial women commonly apprenticed as domestic servants, which was considered an honorable occupation. Now, proficiency in spinning and weaving is no longer needed, and work as a household servant has a lower status. As more unskilled immigrant women take these jobs, white native-born women turn to factory work or teaching, where they can work fewer hours at higher pay.

Lydia Marie Child publishes *The Frugal Housewife*, offering married women household advice. She includes recipes, medical lore, and suggestions for house furnishings and decorations, with a focus on cleanliness, efficiency, and frugality. Child has a friendly and colloquial style that women find appealing, and her book will have many printings. Books are produced more easily today because of innovations and improvements in printing, and they are distributed more rapidly via the new canals, roads, and railroads that are linking parts of the country. Child's manuals are needed for the many women who emigrate west, leaving behind mothers and aunts who traditionally gave advice on running a household. More women are migrating west, and since 1810 the populations in Indiana, Illinois, and Missouri have increased nearly fourfold.[55]

EDUCATION AND SCHOLARSHIP

Almira Hart Lincoln, who teaches at the Troy Academy, publishes her text *Familiar Lectures on Botany*, which will be in print for fifty years and is the first of her many science texts. Later works will help students in geology, chemistry, and natural philosophy. Lincoln's contributions to science will earn her election into the American Academy for the Advancement of Science.

Four Haitian refugees and a French priest establish the Oblate Sisters of Providence in

Baltimore. They will establish a boarding high school for black girls. **Elizabeth Lang,** the order's superior, who taught in Haiti, heads the school. She plans an extensive curriculum, including French, Spanish, geography, history, spelling, and art, as well as practical courses in washing, ironing, cleaning, and child care. Most pupils are from the South, but some will travel from the North as far away as Canada to enroll. The school will gain national fame for its high standards.

JOINING FORCES

A citizen writes a letter to the *American Monthly Magazine* suggesting that married women should be allowed to own property, pointing out that the current system makes women deceitful and men greedy. This early plea for legal rights for married women will be addressed again by a later generation of female reformers.

Quaker writer **Elizabeth Margaret Chandler** publishes an "Appeal to the Ladies of the United States." She implores them as mothers to support abolition. They must look at their baby sons, she urges, and imagine the child being taken and enslaved forever. Would a mother not rather her child be dead? This technique of appealing to sentimentality and maternal instincts will be commonly used by abolitionists and will help persuade many white women to join the abolitionist movement.

LAW AND POLITICS

Many prominent leaders are concerned that immigrants have such large families, while the birthrates of native-born white women are falling. They fear that the "Saxon stock" is declining. This year, New York legislators revise state laws. They impose strictures on abortions: anyone who helps a woman abort a child will be jailed or fined. Other states follow New York's example and pass similar laws.

— 1830 —

WORK

Writer **Anne Newport Royall** publishes *Letters from Alabama*, the last of her ten volumes on American life. Royall loves travel and has spent the last ten years touring the nation by stagecoach and boat and writing about what she sees. Her books are successful and are appreciated by Americans who want to read about their country.

RELIGION

Officials of the New York Sunday School Union send members **Rebecca Cromwell Rouse** and her husband to Cleveland, Ohio. There they distribute religious tracts and spread the gospel. The Rouses have worked with religious reformer Arthur Tappan and have been inspired by his ideals. They want people to convert to Christianity, hoping this will stabilize lives in a rapidly changing society. Rebecca will organize a tract society and gospel union for women, and she will be active in benevolence for the next thirty years.

ARTS

Artist **Ruth Henshaw Bascom** paints a self-portrait — her profile in pastel. Married to an iterinant minister, she usually travels with him throughout New England. While he preaches, she paints. She is self-taught and specializes in portraits and landscapes, usually in pastels. Like other folk artists, she often adds paper cutouts, foil, or other decorations to her works. Considering herself an amateur, she does not charge for her art.

— 1831 —

WORK

Females now comprise 68 percent of cotton industry workers in the northern textile

A camp meeting in the West, lithograph, 1829. (Library of Congress.) Revival meetings were an American tradition. Because the church and state were legally separated, religious leaders worried that church membership might decline. They organized mass meetings to convince people to accept the faith. Ministers and exhorters would preach, read the Bible, and lead prayers. They guaranteed universal salvation to converts. Settlers would travel for miles to attend these camps and, as this photo shows, pitch tents anticipating a few days' stay. Women — the majority of attendees — were considered "naturally" pious and converted more frequently than men. Several females in this illustration have become believers. Some raise their arms and shout; another is overcome with emotion and faints; two others kneel on the ground, having thrown aside their bonnets in the excitement.

mills.[56] Most are young, unmarried New England girls with an average age of sixteen. They usually work for several years, then resign to marry or take another job. Because mill owners want to avoid slums like those in industrial districts in London, England, they build boardinghouses for their employees. This reassures parents that their daughters are living respectably and gives the girls a sense of community.

EDUCATION AND SCHOLARSHIP

Black middle-class women in Philadelphia form the Female Literary Association to educate and improve themselves. They meet in members' homes to read and discuss books and essays and to hear guest speakers.

Black women need to create their own educational programs. Because of racism they are generally unwelcome at public lectures. They believe education and self-improvement will help fight prejudice, and many women form groups like this one.

ARTS

Ornithologist and artist John James Audubon visits friends in Charleston and meets a houseguest, **Maria Martin**. She is interested in art and the natural sciences, and eventually he will become her mentor. He critiques her sketches, shows her painting techniques, and encourages her to develop her talents. She later works for him, painting flower and plant backgrounds for his watercolors of birds. Thanks to his support and help, she becomes a proficient nature painter and will illustrate many nature publications. Martin and Audubon remain lifelong friends, and he later designates a bird subspecies as Maria's woodpecker (*Picus martinae*).

Joining Forces

Thousands of immigrants have been arriving in New York, looking for jobs. Sewing is a skill many newcomers have, but the oversupply of workers keeps seamstresses' wages low. While male tailors are organized and fight for better pay, their unions prohibit female membership.

This year, **Lavinia Waight** and **Louise Mitchell** found the New York United Tailoresses Society. They hold meetings, adopt a fair wage schedule, and request public support. Waight, the secretary, speaks publicly about the exploitation of female workers. A *Boston Transcript* reporter who hears her speech writes that it is true that women should earn higher wages, but he rebukes Waight for her "clamorous and unfeminine [public] declarations."[57] Later, members strike for higher pay but are unsuccessful.

During the next decade, female seamstresses, shoe binders, tailors, and corset makers will organize unions in Boston, Philadelphia, and Baltimore, continuing to strike for higher wages, but most will be unsuccessful. Employers, of course, are more interested in profits and expansion than in fair working conditions, and employees are easily replaced. These early groups are the forerunners of future national women's unions.

Philadelphia black women organize the Colored Females' Free Produce Society. They call for a boycott of cotton, rice, sugar, molasses, tobacco, and all other products of slave labor. They give publicity to shops that refuse to carry produce from the labor of slaves, and they ask the public to patronize only these stores. Other women in northeastern cities are forming similar groups in order to hurt the southern economy. Although their efforts have little economic impact, they do offer moral support to the abolition movement.

Widowed Bostonian **Maria Stewart**, a black woman and former schoolteacher decides to initiate a public crusade against slavery and racism. She writes an essay, "Religion and the Pure Principles of Morality, the Sure Foundation on Which We Must Build," and William Lloyd Garrison, a white abolitionist and founder of the *Liberator*, a new antislavery publication, prints it. Her message is direct: she tells black people to be strong and courageous, fight racism, and educate themselves. She charges black women with finding better work than cooking and cleaning. "Possess the spirit of independence," she urges. "Possess the spirit of men, bold and enterprising, fearless and undaunted. Sue for your rights and privileges…. Weary them with your importunities. You can but die if you make the attempt, and we shall certainly die if you do not."[58]

Seventeen-year-old **Sarah Louisa Forten** writes an essay on slavery, "The Abuse of Liberty," which is published in the *Liberator*. This begins her career as an abolitionist. Forten's family is prominent and politically active in Philadelphia's black community. With her mother and two sisters, Forten will later help found the Philadelphia Female Anti-Slavery Society.

White Americans have used more birth control during the last thirty years, causing a decline in the birthrate.[59] Contraception is a private matter, and rarely discussed in public, but a few radicals address it. One is Robert Dale Owen, who publishes *Moral Physiology, or A Brief and Plain Treatise on the Population Question*. Maintaining that women have a right to limit family size, he advocates sex education, birth control, and abolishment of the sexual double standard. These issues will be addressed again by later female reformers.

— 1832 —

WORK

Charleston writer **Caroline Howard Gilman** founds *Rose-Bud, or Youth's Gazette,* an early children's publication and a place for her fiction, poetry, and prose. She will later publish more stories for children and books on household management and travel.

ARTS

Self-trained artist **Deborah Goldsmith** completes a watercolor portrait of the prominent New York Talcott family. Goldsmith works as an itinerant artist to support her impoverished parents, traveling through New York. She advertises in local newspapers and stays with the families she paints. Although many male artists travel, it is considered improper for a woman to journey alone.

JOINING FORCES

Many men have organized abolitionist groups, but they often deny women membership. Some females form fund-raising auxiliaries, but others want a direct voice in voting and making policy. A group of free black women in Massachusetts organize the Female Anti-Slavery Society of Salem to raise money for lectures, publications, and petition drives. This group will eventually admit white members, but most antislavery groups will be segregated or have separate seating at meetings. Many whites work for emancipation as their Christian "duty" but maintain racist attitudes.

Black abolitionist **Maria Stewart** speaks to a crowd in Boston's Franklin Hall. She gives a fiery delivery on racial and sexual equality. She challenges stereotypes of African Americans as lazy and inferior, insisting that they need only the education and opportunities available to whites. She attacks the stereotype of women as delicate and frag-

ile, since black women have always done heavy work. She tells blacks they must improve themselves and demand fair treatment. Stewart is one of the first women to address an American audience of both sexes. Many are incensed at her impropriety and at her radical message. Newspaper critics denounce her speeches, and crowds often jeer her. Stewart will later move to New York City, where she will join the black intellectual community and continue to crusade for abolition and women's rights.

— 1833 —

DOMESTICITY

The American Tract Society in New York publishes John S. C. Abbott's *The Mother at Home; or the Principles of Maternal Duty, Familiarly Illustrated.* Abbott, a Protestant minister, pleads with women to be good mothers. "When our land is filled with pious and patriotic mothers, then it will be filled with virtuous and patriotic men," he beseeches. "O that mothers could feel this responsibility as they ought!"[60]

The continuing writings on domesticity are in part a response to uncertainty and change in a nation in transition. Population growth, westward expansion, growing urbanization, and industrialization are altering the nation's character. Since 1800 the population has more than doubled, and immigration has more than tripled.[61]

While writers like Abbott beseech women to stay in their homes, opportunities for females outside the house are increasing. More young women work in mills and factories and express public discontent through strikes and protests. Hundreds of middle-class white girls graduate from the new academies, then take teaching jobs, often traveling west for work. More women are expressing themselves publicly through writing.

Woodcut illustration, Ladies Whipping Girls, *from a book on slavery in America, 1834. (Library of Congress.) A woman has tied her young female slave to a post and whips her.*

While slaves were legally the property of the male head of the household (and it was men who administered the most severe punishments), wives commonly whipped or boxed slaves, especially those who worked under their management. Young slaves learned that dawdling, disobedience, insolence, stealing food or even the bad mood of their mistress would bring swift punishment, and many came to expect a daily whipping.

WORK

Texas is part of the Mexican Republic, and to encourage growth the Mexican government has offered large land tracts to Americans who will settle, bring friends, and convert to Catholicism. The state's population has increased as pioneers move west; within a few years, nearly 35,000 Americans will live in Texas.[62]

The American government also wants westward expansion, as do the railroad and industry leaders. To encourage this, many people are writing promotional tracts. **Mary Austin Holley**, a cousin of Texas settler Moses Austin, is a forty-seven-year-old widowed teacher and writer. She publishes *Texas: Historical, Geographical, and Descriptive, in a Series of Letters, Written during a Visit to Austin's Colony, with a View to Permanent Settlement in That Country, in the Autumn of 1831*, one of the earliest tracts written in English for prospective Texans. She praises the area: the climate is pleasant and mild, she enthuses; and the soil is so fertile that pumpkins and corn grow with little labor; and it is easy to breed cows and horses. She points out the friendliness and hospitality of Texans, and encourages people to settle there. Women settlers appreciate her publication, which offers practical advice about what goods to bring, how to cook over an open fire, and how to decorate a log cabin. Although there are many American publications on household management, few proffer advice to pioneer women.

EDUCATION AND SCHOLARSHIP

Christian reformers found Oberlin Collegiate Institute in Ohio, which accepts women and men of any race. This early experiment in coeducation follows society's typical gender roles. There are separate classes for males and females, and some, like rhetoric, are closed to women. Students work to keep tuition low. Chores reflect society's roles: the men work outdoors, and the women do housekeeping, including darning the socks of the male students. Because the school is one of few that accept women, many future female leaders, especially blacks, will be Oberlin graduates.

Quaker **Prudence Crandall** heads the Canterbury Boarding School, a female academy in Plainfield, Connecticut. She admits her first black student, an aspiring teacher. This outrages white parents, who threaten to withdraw their daughters unless she dismisses the black student. As a humanitarian, Crandall is shocked by their hostility and decides to dismiss her white students permanently. She reopens the facility to black pupils only, advertising for "Young Ladies

and Little Misses of Color," which further inflames members of the community who believe only white females can be called "ladies."[63] Crandall's teaching reputation is good, and her advertisement gets a response from black parents in nearby states. Fifteen new students enroll. The townspeople, horrified, try to close the school. Some refuse to deliver supplies, others fill the school's well with manure, and many riot and threaten to burn the building. Local lawmakers fine the students as nonresidents and pass an ordinance prohibiting teaching nonresident blacks. They eventually arrest Crandall and close the school. Fifty-two years later, the Connecticut legislators will apologize, offering Crandall a pension and the return of her schoolhouse.

ARTS

Maria Turner publishes *The Young Ladies' Assistant in Drawing and Painting*. She explains how to paint on velvet and how to create theorem or stencil art, a popular technique for depicting still lifes of fruits or flowers. Because most art academies do not accept females, these manuals are popular.

JOINING FORCES

In Lynn, Massachusetts, a common job for women with families to support is shoe binding, which they can do at home at piecework rates. Employers often cut pay, and a group of workers decides to protest. One thousand workers form the Female Society of Lynn and Vicinity for the Protection and Promotion of Female Industry. They select officers, initiate dues, and pledge not to undersell each other. Their first strike the next year will be successful. They boycott the manufacturers, get public support, and earn a wage increase. After this first victory the organization falters. Like other early unions organized around one issue, interest often wanes when the problem is solved. It is also difficult for women who work isolated at home to maintain solidarity. Some impoverished members will again accept lower rates, and as others fail to attend meetings or pay dues the society eventually collapses.

Quaker abolitionist **Lucretia Mott** travels to Philadelphia to help organize the American Anti-Slavery Society, but when it is established the men decide it will be an all-male organization. Mott joins with other female abolition leaders to form the Philadelphia Female Anti-Slavery Society. Their goals are abolition and better education for African Americans. Founders of this group include black educator **Margaretta Forten,** who will hold office, help make policy, and represent the group at conventions. Beginning with forty-two charter members, the group will grow and become a powerful abolitionist society. They will raise thousands of dollars, build their own meeting hall, publish antislavery literature, and organize petition drives. They support schools for African Americans by funding teachers and books, and they assist fugitive slaves with food, clothing, and temporary shelter. Many friendships will be formed across color lines, and the society will be an ideal of cooperation and solidarity. After emancipation they will disband.

— 1834 —

EDUCATION AND SCHOLARSHIP

Educator **Susan Paul**, who teaches at a elementary school for black children in Boston, organizes a public concert featuring music students. By exhibiting her young pupils' talents and skills, Paul hopes to lessen racial prejudice. Many Bostonians attend the concert, which was advertised in the *Liberator*, and enjoy the performance. Paul's work is respected by black and white male abolitionists, who appreciate her deferential manner. Women of all races are expected to respect society's limitations, and teaching is within appropriate guidelines.

RELIGION

Anti-Catholic sentiment, brought to America by early English colonists, is on the rise. Many believe that the religion is anathema to American ideals of individual liberty. They oppose the church and suspect Catholics of a higher loyalty to the pope. As Irish Catholic immigration increases, nativist sentiment grows stronger. The newcomers enter an overcrowded labor market where wages are already too low. Many Americans, suspicious of single women unattached to a traditional family, dislike nuns. Some Protestant ministers preach against the pope's followers, and some bigots pass out anti–Catholic pamphlets accusing nuns and priests of being the Devil's agents.

Rebecca Reed, a young Boston women who wanted to become a nun, is judged an unsuitable candidate and dismissed from the order. Angry, she spreads false information about convent life. An enraged anti–Catholic mob burns the Boston Ursuline Convent and school. Other mobs during the next few decades will steal from cloisters, desecrate Catholic cemeteries, and burn several parochial schools.

ARTS

Ruth Shute, an itinerant portraitist, announces her arrival in New York's *Plattsburgh Republican*. Like other traveling artists, she stays at a hotel where clients come to be painted. Shute is self-trained, as are most contemporary female artists, and this frees her to experiment. She often pastes foil designs and paper cutouts to her watercolors and oils, giving her work an individual flavor. Her husband, also a painter, accompanies her. They collaborate on numerous portraits, although as the primary artist, she signs the work. Her clients are chiefly middle-class people who want portraits but are unable to afford a professional painter.

James Akin Draughtsman & Lithographer N.º 10 Prune Street Philadelphia.

"*Born to good luck," by "Scene-shifting in Fortunes Frolicks,"*
or the English beggar Girl's elevation to a Butler's Lady !!!

Fan "Puddledock," a Beggar low!
From England came to join the Show;
She long secur'd in British "Fa-me", ✢
A brag about her Family "Na—me"; ✢
Which "Jon'than" heard, shell'd out his mite,
To give poor "Puddledock" a bite ;
But she preferr'd to Pit or Boxes,
A "Call-boy's" Butler's—Orthodoxies ;
And now a Wife she damns all Stages,
Returning Jon'than "Pains and A-ches", ✢
By publishing loose tittle tattle,
Of stage flirts vulgar coarse lewd prattle ;
All what she saw heard lov'd or hated,
Two Volumes fill'd, of gossip prated ;
Hence the Proverb trite and known well,
A Beggar hors'd soon rides to

✢ *Family appellation Journal Vol.1.page 16 .*
✢ *Vide John P. Kemble's vile pedantic pronunciation*
for which he was very properly hissed.!!!

Entered according to act of Congress, in the year 1835, by James Akin, in the Clerks Office of the District Court .
of the Eastern District of Pennsylvania. ——

Drawing and verse, "A Frontispiece for a Journal," 1835. This satirizes the life of Frances Kemble, a British actress and writer. Kemble's Journal, published that year, was a harsh indictment of American society, and angry reviewers attacked her book. This critic depicts Kemble as a beggar. He writes that she came to America to find a rich husband. After her marriage to the wealthy Pierce Butler, she left the stage to become a writer. The gossip she publishes, "loose tittle tattle," and "coarse lewd prattle," will lead her to Hell.

Kemble, from a prominent but impoverished British acting family, sailed to the United States in 1832. She earned acclaim for her theater performances in New York City, Boston, and Philadelphia. Several years later she married Pierce Butler, who was heir to his grandfather's slave-holding fortune. It was a poor match. His family rejected her; like most Americans, they considered acting akin to prostitution. She was so appalled by the treatment of slaves on her husband's plantation that she became an active abolitionist. They later divorced and she eventually returned to London.

JOINING FORCES

A group of New York women establish the American Female Reform Society. Their first director, **Lydia Finney**, is the wife of Charles Finney, a prominent evangelist who supports their work. The group wants to improve America's morality. They believe values have declined since the waning of revivals, and as Christians they want to address the growing urban poverty, crime, and vice. First targeting prostitution, they ask women in the profession to give it up and to become Christians. They then relocate the women, many of whom are homeless. They will purchase a building where the women can live while learning job skills. The reformers also expose the hypocrisy of the double standard by publishing the names of the prostitutes' clients. Their newsletter, *Advocate for Moral Reform*, is circulated nationally and encourages others to start auxiliary groups. Within six years, women will form hundreds of local groups.

Many of these female organizers were previously active in revival work, where they learned to organize large groups, raise funds, persuade people to convert, and write religious tracts. They apply these skills to form new organizations, using evangelistic language and values to solve secular problems. Because reform is linked to Christianity and women's "natural" sphere, this work receives society's approval.

Female mill workers in Lowell, Massachusetts, strike in response to a 25 percent wage cut but are unsuccessful in getting wages restored. Two years later their boarding costs will be raised, but another strike will be fruitless. As working conditions worsen, the young female workers will gradually be replaced by immigrants and others who need work and will endure poor working conditions.

— 1835 —

WORK

Amelia Shad, who lives in the black middle-class section of Philadelphia, opens a boardinghouse and advertises it for "genteel persons of color."[64] Her wording assures the public of her respectability, since brothels are often billed as boardinghouses. Like most black women, Shad needs to support her family. Those with skills and capital like Shad can establish businesses, avoiding the drudgery and low pay of domestic work. However, women's ability to find any work often allows a family to survive. Although their husbands may have more skills, black men are frequently perceived as violent and are unable to find work.

JOINING FORCES

White women organize the Ladies' New York City Anti-Slavery Society to work for emancipation and give financial support to the black community. As evangelicals they view slavery as sinful and immoral, but their beliefs do not extend to racial equality. Wanting to stay segregated, they set dues too high for most blacks. As more white women form antislavery groups, integration is a controversial issue. Sometimes members quit if black women are included, whereas others leave if African Americans are excluded.

— 1836 —

DOMESTICITY

Several northeastern male crafts and trades unions have founded an umbrella labor group, the National Trades Union, to promote better conditions for working men. They are concerned that because women earn such low wages, the competition might decrease everyone's pay. They suggest that the solution is for women to stay at home. They publish a report proposing that women be barred from all factory work because of their delicate nature and "moral sensibilities." Because she earns lower wages, a wife working to support her family is "actually the

SLAVE MARKET OF AMERICA.

THE WORD OF GOD.

"ALL THINGS WHATSOEVER YE WOULD THAT MEN SHOULD DO TO YOU, DO YE EVEN SO TO THEM, FOR THIS IS THE LAW AND THE PROPHETS."

"AND THEY SIGHED BY REASON OF THE BONDAGE, AND THEY CRIED, AND THEIR CRY CAME UP UNTO GOD BY REASON OF THE BONDAGE, AND GOD HEARD THEIR GROANING."

"THUS SAITH THE LORD, EXECUTE JUDGMENT IN THE MORNING, AND DELIVER HIM THAT IS SPOILED OUT OF THE HANDS OF THE OPPRESSOR, LEST MY FURY GO OUT LIKE FIRE, AND BURN THAT NONE CAN QUENCH IT, BECAUSE OF THE EVIL OF YOUR DOINGS."

THE DECLARATION OF AMERICAN INDEPENDENCE.

"WE HOLD THESE TRUTHS TO BE SELF-EVIDENT,—THAT ALL MEN ARE CREATED EQUAL, THAT THEY ARE ENDOWED BY THEIR CREATOR WITH CERTAIN UNALIENABLE RIGHTS, THAT AMONG THESE ARE LIFE, LIBERTY, AND THE PURSUIT OF HAPPINESS."

THE CONSTITUTION OF THE UNITED STATES.

CONSTITUTIONS OF THE STATES.

DISTRICT OF COLUMBIA.

"THE LAND OF THE FREE."

READING OF THE DECLARATION OF INDEPENDENCE.

PART OF WASHINGTON CITY.

"THE HOME OF THE OPPRESSED."

CAPITOL OF THE UNITED STATES.

RIGHT TO INTERFERE.

PUBLIC PRISONS IN THE DISTRICT.

JAIL IN ALEXANDRIA.

FACTS.

JAIL IN WASHINGTON.—SALE OF A FREE CITIZEN TO PAY HIS JAIL FEES!

FACTS.

VIEW OF THE INTERIOR OF THE JAIL IN WASHINGTON.—FANNY JACKSON.

FACTS.

PRIVATE PRISONS IN THE DISTRICT, LICENSED AS SOURCES OF PUBLIC REVENUE.

SLAVE HOUSE OF J. W. NEAL & CO.

VIEW OF A SECTION OF ALEXANDRIA, WITH A SLAVE SHIP RECEIVING HER CARGO OF SLAVES.

FRANKLIN & ARMFIELD'S SLAVE PRISON.

"CASH FOR 200 NEGROES."

Published by the American Anti-Slavery Society, 144 Nassau-street, New-York; 1836.

An abolitionist broadside, with wood engravings, 1836. (Library of Congress.) This poster pleads for emancipation and the prohibition of the slave trade in the District of Columbia. Abolitionists targeted the District as a likely area for anti-slavery legislation. Debates in Congress over emancipation were prolonged by southern senators who argued for states' rights. But because D.C. was under federal control (and not a state) this argument would not apply. Yet Congress did not ban slavery in D.C. for nearly thirty more years.

The poster is designed to appeal to the viewers' emotions. Anti-slavery arguments bring in God and the Declaration of Independence. Pictures include an imprisoned slave mother and her children, and chained slaves led from an auction house. The American Anti-Slavery Society of New York published the broadside. Although women helped organize this group, they were denied membership.

same as tying a stone around the neck of her natural protector, Man."[65] Male union members often use domestic rhetoric when arguing against women as wage earners. Rather than advocating high wages for all, they maintain that if all men earned a "family" wage, women could afford to stay home.

JOINING FORCES

Eleven-year-old **Harriet Robinson**'s father has died, and the family moves to Lowell, Massachusetts, to find work at a mill. Harriet is employed as a bobbin doffer, and her salary helps support the family. The mill employees strike over a wage cut, and Robinson persuades the younger employees to join the walkout. The strike is unsuccessful and Robinson later leaves the mill, but this experience inspires her to become a labor reformer.

Abolitionist **Angelina Grimké** moved from Charleston to Philadelphia several years ago to live with her sister Sarah, also an abolitionist. Angelina joins the Philadelphia Female Anti-Slavery Society and begins work. She writes "An Appeal to the Christian Women of the Southern States," a letter to the *Liberator*, which is now published by the American Anti-Slavery Society. She asks southern women to get involved with emancipation, read the literature, talk about it, pray for emancipation, and circulate petitions. We can overthrow "this horrible system of oppression and cruelty," she insists. "There is something in the heart of men which *will bend under moral suasion.*"[66] Because her family is socially prominent and owns slaves, her campaign arouses much public interest and controversy. Her parents are shocked and become alienated from both daughters. Some southern postmasters destroy the publication. Friends in Charleston warn the sisters against returning home, where they might be harmed. Angelina becomes well known from the publicity and accepts a job with the American Anti-Slavery Society in New York.

Ernestine Potowski Rose grew up in a Jewish family in Poland, where she enjoyed an education and degree of freedom unusual for a girl. After her mother's death, her father arranged Ernestine's marriage to a wealthy man, which she rejected, preferring independence. She left Poland, traveled through Europe, and married an American. Now she lives in New York City. She has worked for reform in Europe and has a passion for justice. A new state law giving married women property rights has been debated in the legislature. Rose prepares a petition supporting it. She gets only six signers but submits it anyway. The law is not enacted, but Rose begins to work for women's equality.

A group of Ohio women send Congress a petition requesting abolition of slavery in the District of Columbia. Many abolitionists target the District because it is under federal rule, allowing debates on slavery to bypass filibusters of southern lawmakers.

LAW AND POLITICS

Antislavery petitions have been flooding the nation's capital. The majority of these are from women, since the petition is one way they can express political values. Southern lawmakers, angry and irritated, argue that women should not meddle in politics. They decide to pass a gag rule, which would automatically table all antislavery petitions. Massachusetts representative John Quincy Adams argues against the rule. True, it is women's job to be wives and mothers, but they can do more than just domestic work. They "are not only justified, but exhibit the most exhaulted virtue [in addressing] ... the concerns of their country, of humanity, and of God, and when their motives are pure and their purpose is virtuous."[67] Congress passes the gag rule, and it will take eight years to repeal it.

— 1837 —

DOMESTICITY

Bostonian **Eliza Farrar** publishes *The*

Young Ladies Friend, a manual of practical advice. She emphasizes, "A woman who does not know how to sew is as deficient in her education as a man who cannot write…. Have a piece of needlework always at hand."[68] Linking sewing with women is so common that sewing almost functions as a metaphor for women.

A Massachusetts Congregational minister heard that the Grimké sisters are speaking on abolition in public. Horrified, he publishes an official statement. "The appropriate duties and influence of women are clearly stated in the New Testament," he proclaims. They can teach Sunday school and conduct prayer meetings at home, but should never speak in public, and certainly not participate in reform. A woman's power is in her "dependence," he explains, and her job is to "form the character of individuals and of the nation."[69]

Many Americans agree with him, including educator **Catharine Beecher**. She publishes *An Essay on Slavery and Abolitionism, with Reference to the Duty of American Females*, cautioning women against public speaking, which could arouse public anger. A woman can best help the cause, Beecher writes, by remaining in her home and discussing it privately with family and friends, "quietly holding her own opinions and calmly avowing them." Her role is to "win everything by peace and love … [and] this is all to be accomplished in the domestic and social circle."[70]

WORK

A panic caused by careless business speculation shuts down many banks and initiates a three-year depression. Businesses fail, hundreds of factories and mills shut down, and wages are low. Workers in the industrial Northeast are especially affected. Women who sew at home are no longer guaranteed work, and many New England female mill workers lose their jobs, since most mills now operate part-time. To produce more cloth while keeping costs low, mills initiate speed-ups, setting machines at a faster speed, or stretch-outs, where each employee must operate several machines. Protests are ineffective, since dissatisfied employees are easily replaced. Wages are so low that often whole families need to work.

A published report lists the most common jobs held by black women in Philadelphia: laundress, dressmaker, tailoress, milliner, seamstress, cook, domestic workers, live-in servant, and "raggers and boners." A separate listing of skilled jobs held by these women includes: boardinghouse keepers, oyster house managers, schoolteachers, shopkeepers, cake bakers, and rug makers.[71]

Louis Godey, a Philadelphia publisher, buys the *Lady's Magazine* and renames it *Godey's Lady's Book*. He wants to build it into a leading publication and asks **Sarah Josepha Hale** to continue as editor. Godey will allow no politics or controversy, and he wants the magazine to reflect middle- and upper-class values, emphasizing the home as women's focus. Godey and Hale work together to expand the magazine's scope. They introduce engravings of styles and fashions and include more fiction, as well as social, moral, and historical essays. They print recipes and offer household advice and consumer information. Hale hires many female writers, pays them well, and allows them to sign their work. Believing that married women's work is domestic, she portrays this through stories, poems, essays, and editorials. Hale will edit *Godey's* for more than forty years and make it the nation's leading women's publication.

EDUCATION AND SCHOLARSHIP

Mt. Holyoke Female Seminary opens in South Hadley, Massachusetts, with eighty students. Founder **Mary Lyon** has traveled to raise funds, and women and middle-class families donated most of the school's endowment. Mt. Holyoke's mission is to train teachers, though students attend for various reasons. Many alumnae will teach, others will do church work, some want a good education, and still others social status. Students are seventeen or older, and as at other female seminaries, the curriculum includes work at both the high school and college level. Lyon wants a balance of piety and learning, and Christian values are taught. Tuition is low, and students do housekeeping to keep costs down. Many visitors praise the facility. Mt. Holyoke's reputation will grow, and it will eventually become a college. Lyon will head the school for twelve years. Like other female academy founders, she wants women to be useful citizens and encourages them to take themselves seriously. Later, many of the graduates will challenge society's expectations.

New York educator **Sarah Mapps Douglass** moved to Philadelphia to open a private high school for African American girls. The city's public education system is segregated, and black schools are overcrowded and poorly funded. Middle-class black parents appreciate the school, and forty girls are enrolled. Reverend Samuel Cornish, editor of the *Colored American*, a Boston publication, is in Philadelphia and visits Douglass's academy. He is impressed and writes a glowing report. Her students are *"interesting, improving scholars,"* he praises, "selected from our best families."[72] He commends Douglass's teaching, especially her knowledge of the sciences and her extensive and well-organized shell and mineral collection.

RELIGION

African Methodist Episcopal women in New York organize a fair to raise money for their church. Black women are the prime support of churches, which are an important institution in the black community. The buildings are also used for schools, social events, and political meetings and as a refuge for fugitive slaves.

JOINING FORCES

Nearly two hundred females attend the first antislavery convention of American women in New York. Delegates are members of local abolition societies, and the conference is interracial. Black abolitionist **Sarah Forten** reads a poem, that urges sisterhood for all women.

Sarah Grimké publishes an essay in the *Liberator*, in which she responds to the clergy's disapproval of women in public reform. She questions the male interpretation of the Bible, arguing that were women allowed to study Greek and Latin, they might prepare a different interpretation. She insists that Jesus did not divide work into separate spheres, but wanted both to do "good works." She writes, "Men and women were CREATED EQUAL; they are both moral and accountable beings and whatever is right for man to do, is right for woman to do."[73] This early call for women's rights generates strong public reaction. Critics attack her as impertinent, un–Christian, and certainly unladylike. Her writings will be influential for a later generation of activist women.

British writer **Harriet Martineau** publishes the third volume of *Society in America*, based on her extensive travels in the United States. In this volume she comments on American women. Their intellects are confined through restricted education, she writes, and their vocational choices are so limited that few can support themselves. If women are considered naturally religious, she wonders, why are they barred from studying theology? She denounces the chivalry and reverence men offer as "a substitute for justice." In their treatment of women, Martineau insists, Americans have "fallen below, not only their own democratic principals, but the practice of some parts of the old world."[74] Many Americans are offended by the work.

— 1838 —

EDUCATION AND SCHOLARSHIP

Georgia Female College opens in Macon. Spread on a four-acre campus, the school has a chapel, a dining room, classrooms, and a dormitory. Modeled after male four-year colleges, the curriculum is broad and includes math, sciences, French, and Latin. Girls can enroll at age twelve, and those not ready for college work can take preparatory classes. The school will flourish, enrollment will increase, and administrators will later change the name to Wesleyan Female College. It fills a need for southern females, who have traditionally attended northern schools. With the growing tension over slavery, many parents prefer to keep their children close to home.

RELIGION

Philadelphia Jewish philanthropist **Rebecca Gratz** wants children to have religious training and has taught them Judaism in her home. Now, inspired by the Christian Sunday school movement, she initiates a similar program. Under the sponsorship of Philadelphia's Female Hebrew Benevolent Society, a Sabbath school opens for local Jewish children. Gratz is appointed director, a position she will hold for another twenty-six years. The school will continue well into the twentieth century and will be a model for coeducational Sabbath instruction.

Gratz's work is part of a larger trend of giving Jewish women a wider role in the community. This reform was inspired in part by German Jewish immigrants who were active in European intellectual life. In their new home in America, they want to avoid the traditional isolation of Jewish women. Some have introduced choral and instrumental music into synagogue services, and others have founded women's organizations. But not all agree that Jewish women should be active in the synagogue. Many orthodox women, especially Russian and eastern European immigrants, prefer the traditional roles.

JOINING FORCES

The second Anti-Slavery Convention of American Women takes place in Philadelphia. **Sarah Smith**, a convention official, speaks on behalf of the business committee. She affirms women's right to fight slavery and asks them to be generous with their time, talent, and money. While she is speaking, an angry mob outside disrupts the meeting. The rioters are furious because the meeting is integrated, which they consider immoral. They block the doors, shout, throw stones, and later burn the building. Undeterred by the violence, the delegates meet the next day and pass a resolution. They condemn racial prejudice as sinful and resolve that white abolitionists must greet African Americans in public, visit and worship with them, and invite them to their homes. Not all vote for the resolution. Some women are unwilling to befriend a woman of another race. Black women who are friendly with whites risk being snubbed by other blacks, and whites who are friendly with blacks risk being ostracized in white society.

While some white abolitionists view emancipation as their goal, many blacks have a broader perspective. They want to assist fugitive slaves and support black communities. Because there is disagreement on how money should be spent, some blacks organize separate groups. Black women in Philadelphia form a Female Vigilance Association, an auxiliary to the city's Vigilance Committee, headed by a group of distinguished black men. These women help in Underground Railroad activities and raise money to feed and clothe fugitive slaves.

LAW AND POLITICS

Kentucky lawmakers are among the first to authorize partial suffrage. They pass a law allowing widows with taxable property and school-age children to vote in school elections. Before women are fully enfranchised, many states grant partial suffrage.

— 1839 —

EDUCATION AND SCHOLARSHIP

Two normal schools in Massachusetts

are built with public funds and private donations. One, in Lexington, is for females;
the second, in Barr, is coeducational. Students must be at least sixteen, have good
health and morals, and agree to teach after
graduation. There is no tuition, but students
must pay for books and housing. Visitors to
the new schools consider the training excellent; the students are respectful and well-
mannered, and the teachers offer good instruction. These Massachusetts institutions
are among the earliest normal schools.

Joining Forces

Attendees at the third annual anti-Slavery Convention of American Women in
Philadelphia are encouraged to keep preparing and circulating petitions. Women are a
major force in antislavery work; they raise
thousands of dollars, and some speak in public. They continue to overwhelm Congress
with petitions, despite the gag rule which tables all antislavery documents.

Angela Grimké Weld, who lives in New
Hampshire, is now married to abolitionist
Theodore Weld. This year she publishes
*American Slavery as It Is: Testimony of a
Thousand Witnesses.* The book is written
from slave narratives, escaped slaves' testimonials, clippings from southern newspapers, and reports of those who have observed
the treatment of slaves. The book, with its
horrifying reports, helps gain northern sym-
pathizers. Hundreds read it, including Harriet Beecher Stowe, who will use it in her research for *Uncle Tom's Cabin.*

Law and Politics

Married women are gradually gaining
more legal rights. In Massachusetts and
Maine, women deserted by husbands can
now legally sell property. This year, Mississippi legislators enact a law giving married
women the right to sell or give away the
slaves they owned before marriage. Lawmakers in other states are debating married

women's property rights, and they will pass
more laws in the next decade. The recent depression has stimulated this reform. Since a
wife's property can be taken by her husband's creditors, revised codes can help protect families against destitution and protect
wealthy women's inheritance.

— 1840 —

Domesticity

Ohio senator Benjamin Tappan complains to Congress that he has been getting
too many abolition petitions from women.
He angrily denounces these petitioners, accusing them of interfering with matters of
state, which is not their proper sphere of activity. He declares to his colleagues that it is
up to the men to deal with the "storms of
life" and for women to have the "calm and
sunshine of domestic peace and quiet to
enjoy." He announces he will not even present the petitions to the Senate.[75]

Work

Immigration has increased 260 percent
in the past decade, and 47 percent of this
year's newcomers are from Ireland. Many are
young single women who flood the cities,
looking for work in factories or as domes-
tics. Jobs are hard to find, and as the newcomers compete with the native-born, anti-
immigrant sentiment increases.[76]

Nearly 10 percent of all women over the
age of ten work for wages. They are mostly
young, single white women, widows of all
races, black women, and poor and immigrant
white women. Nearly 70 percent are domestic servants, and another 25 percent labor in
factories or manufacturing. Others teach,
bind books, and set type.[77]

Most married women of all races need
extra income. Few married white middle-
class women take jobs outside the home, but

they earn money as their mothers did. They take in laundry, sewing, or boarders, sell homemade cheese, butter, or eggs, or bind boots.

Margaret Fuller and Ralph Waldo Emerson found the *Dial*, a quarterly journal of transcendentalism. They will print essays on self-reliance, human freedom, and individualism. They announce that the publication will be "a cheerful, rational voice amidst the din of mourners and polemics."[78] Editor Fuller will shape it into a stimulating and thoughtful journal, offering criticism, literature, poetry, and essays on art, religion, and society. The journal will last for four years.

JOINING FORCES

A group of Americans, including reformers **Elizabeth Cady Stanton** and **Lucrecia Mott**, are in London to attend an antislavery conference. They are shocked when officials refuse to seat the women. The American party forces the issue. Finally, convention officials seat the women behind a curtain but warn them not to speak. Some of the American men join Stanton and Mott behind the curtain. In protest of the ruling, prominent abolitionist William Lloyd Garrison even refuses to address the convention. Mott and Stanton are so dismayed by this that they vow to begin work for women's rights.

school standards. Classes are high school and college level and include botany and geology, classical studies, music, arts, and languages. The school's mission is to train teachers as well as future wives and mothers. It becomes one of the South's finest schools and will be a popular choice for young southern women. In the South it is primarily elite white families who can afford to educate their daughters, the future plantation mistresses.

JOINING FORCES

Massachusetts abolitionist **Abby Kelley Foster**, who was raised a Quaker, resigns from the Society of Friends. She is impatient with the local group, which is unsupportive of abolition and prohibits using the meetinghouse for antislavery events. She moves to Connecticut and joins the lecture circuit, speaking on abolition and women's rights. She makes enemies by challenging the Christian church for its indirect support of slavery. Church officials attack her for being unladylike, and call her a "jezebel." When they ban her from speaking in churches, she lectures outside the buildings. Other women, inspired by her bravery, travel with her, and some become reformers themselves. An inspiring speaker, Kelley persuades many Americans to support abolition and also paves the way for acceptance of women's speaking in public.

— 1841 —

EDUCATION AND SCHOLARSHIP

Almira Lincoln Phelps and her husband, John, take over the Patapsco Female Institute in Ellicott's Mill, Maryland. She is the new principal and he the business manager. She is an experienced educator, having run her own school and taught at her sister Emma Willard's Troy Female Academy. The couple sets high standards for Patapsco and upgrades the curriculum to meet the Troy

— 1842 —

RELIGION

Henriette Delille and **Juliette Gaudin**, two black women in New Orleans, found the Sisters of the Holy Family. This order assists free black families and slaves. They build an orphanage and a school and will nurse the sick during a yellow fever epidemic.

Massachusetts cotton mill workers found a newspaper, the *Wampanoag and*

Juliann Jane Tillman, preaching in the African Methodist Episcopal Church, Philadelphia, lithograph, 1844. (Library of Congress.) Women were prohibited from preaching in this church, but Tillman found ways around the rules. Here she may have been a guest speaker.

Afro-Americans established the A.M.E. church in 1816. While its founders hated the racial prejudice in white churches, they accepted the traditional patriarchal structure. In this new black church, women were barred from administrative positions and denied the right to preach. During the 1800s, requests for female ordination were frequently raised but always vetoed. In 1900 male church leaders created a position of deaconess, but it would take nearly fifty more years before the approval of female ordination.

Operatives Journal, to publicize the poor working conditions and to air their grievances against management. Conditions have worsened in the mills. Employers demand longer working hours while cutting wages. This publication is one method of protest.

— 1843 —

DOMESTICITY

Some writers have become fascinated by women's brains, which they perceive as different from men's. By explaining how women's brains differ, they hope to show why the genders are different. In New York, Alexander Walker publishes *Women Physiologically Considered*, a work on the variations between male and female brains. He states that men's brains give them stronger reasoning power, as well as more courage and strength; women's brains, on the other hand, give them weaker reasoning ability, which is why they need male protection. He also elaborates on women's moral superiority, a popular viewpoint among Americans.

WORK

Boston doctor **Harriot Hunt** has a thriving medical practice treating women and children. Although prohibited from formal training, she studied with practitioners. Her medicine combines nursing, homeopathy, diet, psychological counseling, preventative medicine, and hygiene. She has observed the poor health of many urban women, and this year she founds a Ladies Physiology Society in Charleston, Massachusetts. She lectures twice a month, answers questions, encourages discussions, and invites guest speakers. She believes much of women's poor health is from an unbalanced diet, insufficient exercise, poor hygiene, constrictive clothing, and overheated homes. She addresses these topics and teaches basic female anatomy. Many find her series useful and adapt better health habits. Hunt will later apply to the Harvard Medical School for further education. Although she is rejected, Hunt requests permission to attend lectures, but the hostile reaction from the faculty and students results in a second denial. Years later the Female Medical College of Pennsylvania will give her an honorary degree, commemorating her pioneering work in Boston.

— 1 8 4 4 —

WORK

Gertrude Rapp lives in Economy, a cooperative religious community in Pennsylvania, where she has supervised silk manufacturing for nearly twenty years. Appointed to develop sericulture at age nineteen, Rapp did careful research on silk production. She studied, read, corresponded with experts, and experimented, keeping careful records. Economy now processes silk in all stages, beginning with planting mulberry trees, and manufactures more silk than other American companies. Rapp, who has already received acclaim and awards for her work, wins a gold medal from the American Institute of New York this year. They proclaim her silk the nation's best and even superior to most imported silk.

ARTS

The directors of the Pennsylvania Academy of Fine Arts (founded in 1805) already permit women to exhibit in annual shows. This year they allow female students to take a course in drawing, using nude plaster casts of males for study. Since knowing anatomy is essential for an artist, this is a great advance for women, although many Philadelphians condemn the idea. They believe women should not view male nude statues, and some irate citizens accuse the directors of corrupting young females.

JOINING FORCES

A group of Boston black women present a petition protesting the segregated school system to the Board of Education and Primary School Committee. The African Americans' schools are poorly supplied, buildings are neglected, and black teachers are rarely hired. Black parents want better schools, more black teachers, and better instruction. Other black women in New York, Boston, and Philadelphia are also crusading against racism in the school system.

— 1 8 4 5 —

DOMESTICITY

Sarah Josepha Hale's poem "Empire of Woman" is printed in *Godey's Lady's Book*, a leading women's publication. The "empire" refers to the home, and the verse honors the pious, gentle, and submissive wife and mother: the ideal woman. Some disagree with this portrait of the model woman, and most wage-earning American women are unable to live up to the standard.

Hale's poem reflects two trends in writings. One is content. Earlier articles frequently addressed the husband's role as family patriarch or the value of obedience and discipline for children, but now there is more emphasis on women's purity and "moral superiority" and their domestic joys and sorrows. The style of language has also changed, from a didactic tone to the sentimental and flowery. A writer addresses these trends in the *Mother's Assistant and Young Lady's Friend*, a popular Boston monthly. In "The Influence of Female Literature on Female Character," the essayist praises the popular writings about women, claiming that they will help women become more caring and sentimental, create loving homes, and, in turn, influence the world's morality.[79]

WORK

Dorothea Dix publishes *Remarks on Prisons and Prison Discipline in the United States,* which concerns her work in prison reform. She began her campaign when teaching religion to jailed women in Cambridge. Dix was horrified at the unsanitary conditions and was also shocked to discover many insane people imprisoned with criminals. Her appeals to local officials brought about improved conditions. She then spent eighteen months investigating incarceration facilities in Massachusetts, and her report to state lawmakers initiated change. She then moved to New Jersey for similar work, and will later travel throughout the nation inspecting prisons. Her work will inspire improvements in the housing and treatment of criminals and lead to the founding some thirty state mental hospitals. She is one of the first Americans to initiate prison reform.

EDUCATION AND SCHOLARSHIP

Massachusetts schoolteachers organize a state teachers association with a largely female membership. Hundreds of graduates of females academies now teach, and they are gradually replacing male instructors. New England school boards prefer females, since they are often better qualified than men and can be paid less. Female teachers usually make one-third of male teachers' wages.[80]

Frances Caulkins, a Connecticut schoolteacher and writer who likes local history, publishes *A History of Norwich*. Her work is well researched; she has consulted old newspapers, city, court, and genealogy records, and other primary sources. She will receive local acclaim and will later be elected the first female member of the Massachusetts Historical Society.

RELIGION

Evangelist **Phoebe Palmer** publishes *The Way of Holiness*, in which she recounts her religious experiences. Palmer believes in Perfectionism — the possibility of universal salvation — and her leadership and work have stimulated its revival. She leads a popular weekly prayer meeting, edits the movement's journal, and leads revivals in the United States, Canada, and Europe. She believes women should preach in public, and urges them to reclaim spiritual power. Her book sells well and will be followed by others. Palmer's leadership anticipates a greater role for women in mainstream religion.

Ellen Harmon, age eighteen, begins a traveling ministry in New England, in which she prophesies Christ's return. Her visions and trances reveal Christ's imminent return, and she wants to share the message. She later co-founds the Seventh-Day Adventist Church, with a creed based on her scriptural interpretations, and will publish thousands of tracts, books, and articles on her life and beliefs.

ARTS

The Hutchinson Family Singers are touring England, and they perform in London under the patronage of Charles Dickens. This well-known American group from New

Hampshire includes **Abigail Hutchinson** and her four brothers, Asa, Jesse, John, and Judson. Their repertoire includes hymns, patriotic and popular tunes, and songs that Abigail composed and arranged on abolition, temperance, and women's rights. The siblings have many rehearsals and are popular for their style and energy, though some of the songs are controversial. They tour the nation via the new canals, steamboats, and locomotives. The Hutchinsons are part of a new trend. Musicians are becoming professionals, and groups need managers, agents, and publicists.

Joining Forces

Sarah Bagley weaves in a Lowell, Massachusetts, cotton mill. Last year she helped found the Lowell Female Labor Reform Association to protest working conditions. This year they address hours. Some employees work thirteen-hour days, and the group wants this reduced to ten hours. They print and distribute leaflets requesting public support, and circulate petitions that more than 2,000 employees sign. After receiving the petitions, the Massachusetts legislature appoints an industrial commission, and Bagley is among those who testify. The lawmakers also listen to the mill owners' report. They recommend no changes.

Margaret Fuller, now a *New York Tribune* reporter, has been revising an essay she wrote several years ago. This year she publishes the enlarged work, *Woman in the Nineteenth Century*, a critique of American women's lives and a blueprint for change. She calls for equality between the sexes, insisting that women and men are not so different. She wants women to think for themselves and to learn self-reliance before marriage and motherhood so as to lessen their dependence on men. She advocates college for women and argues that they should be able to choose any occupation. The book is widely read and is circulated abroad. Although conservative critics denounce the book as "immoral and foolish," it will be popular. It is one of the early critiques on American women's lives, and later reformers will find it inspiring.[81]

— 1846 —

Work

Catharine Beecher's new book, *Miss Beecher's Domestic Receipt Book: Designed as a Supplement to Her Treatise on Domestic Economy*, is published. In this new housekeeping guide for middle-class married women, Beecher writes that women's most important work is in the home. As vocations such as medicine are becoming professionalized, requiring special skills and training, Beecher wants household management, which she calls domestic science, to be women's vocation. She instructs the reader how to run a household using modern and efficient techniques. She assures women that their job is critical to America's moral future. Her work is available in the new urban bookstores. Widely distributed throughout the country via the new canals and railroads connecting America, it helps spread her ideas throughout the nation. Beecher's fame and writings help strengthen the concept that women belong in the home.

Oregon has become such a popular destination that pioneers preparing for the journey are said to have "Oregon fever." Missionaries in the Northwest brag to friends about Oregon's fertile soils and abundance of game. **Ellen Smith** and her family leave Missouri with a party of several hundred to journey to Oregon. Misfortunes along the way include the deaths of Smith's husband and one daughter, but she continues on with her nine other children. In Salem, Oregon, she takes up a land claim of 640 acres, and she and her children clear the land, build a house, and begin to farm.

Mexican **Maria Gertrudes Barcelo**, who is wealthy, flamboyant, and fashionable, owns

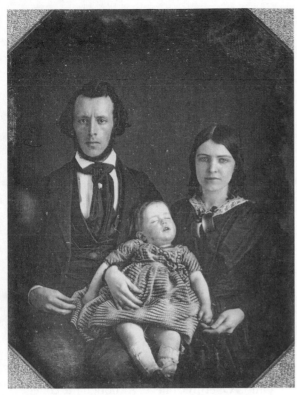

Portrait of Henry Joseph Adams, his wife Abigail Ridley Gibson Adams, and their daughter Anna, daguerreotype, 1846. (Library of Congress.) Abigail's dress reflects a new style, more subdued and dignified. Darker colors and heavier cloth replaced the lighter hues and fabrics of the early 1800s. Skirts were longer and sleeves tighter. Fewer frills and jewelry were worn, and Abigail wears only lace and a ribbon around her neckline. Even hairstyles became demure, with hair pulled back from the face and curled in ringlets in the back. The thinking behind this new style was that beauty came from the inner person and need not be reflected in dress.

The daguerreotype (a single photographic image) was invented by Louis-Jacques-Mandé Daguerre in 1839. During the next decade, Americans thronged to photograph studios. Middle-class families who lacked funds for a painted portrait could now acquire their likeness at a fraction of the cost. Having one's portrait done represented social status and helped preserve family history. Daguerreotypes became treasured family heirlooms that parents willed to children.

a Santa Fe gambling casino. The United States has declared war on Mexico, and American troops occupy the city. Barcelo befriends the soldiers and helps them. She informs them of conspiracies she has overheard and loans them money for supplies. When the U.S. government acquires New Mexico and other western territories in the Treaty of Guadalupe Hidalgo (1848), Barcelo will be among thousands of new American citizens.

Elias Howe patents his sewing machine. The invention will revolutionize the garment industry with greater production and profits, but it will change employment patterns for women. Since the machine works six times faster than a hand sewer, women who sew without machines will eventually be put out of business.

Alexander Turney Stewart opens the nation's first department store in New York City, billed as a Marble Dry-Goods Palace. The facility provides a new kind of shopping for female consumers and will eventually be another source of employment. While males are the first clerks, employers later hire females as a cost-saving measure.

RELIGION

Memoirs of the Life, Religious Experiences, Ministerial Travels and Labours of Mrs. Zilpha Elaw, an American Female of Colour; Together with Some Account of the Great Religious Revivals in America is published in London, recounting **Zilpha Elaw**'s work. Elaw, a Methodist, attended a camp meeting. She went into a trance and believed she was told to preach the gospel. Her church and her husband disapproved, and when she was widowed she became an itinerant preacher. She traveled throughout the country even in southern states where there was a risk of being captured and enslaved. Elaw implores people to follow God's law and to accept people of all colors. She asserts that her race and gender have given her spiritual and moral insight into God's word. Elaw is one of the first black women to write an autobiography, and her book sets a precedent for future narrations by black women.

ARTS

Connecticut writer **Lydia Sigourney**, age fifty-five, publishes a poetry book, *The Voice of Flowers*. Written in the popular sentimental style, her verses emphasize the home, family, motherhood, and religion, familiar themes her readers like. Before writing, Sigourney taught school, then married a widower with a hardware store. When his business declined, she began to write for magazines to support them. She is now well published, and her work emphasizes women's domestic sphere. She is among the earliest American women to have a successful writing career — so well known that Louis Godey pays her for the use of her name on his magazine's title page, and Edgar Allan Poe solicits her work for *Graham's Magazine.* Her readers call her "the Sweet Singer of Hartford."

JOINING FORCES

New Yorkers have called for a constitutional convention. On the agenda is female suffrage, which has long been under debate. A group of women send a petition demanding the vote, using the "taxation without representation" argument. The lawmakers ridicule this approach and again deny women suffrage.

Sojourner Truth, a former slave, starts a career as a traveling preacher and lecturer. She recently lived in the Northhampton Association, an interracial settlement in Massachusetts. There she met many abolition leaders, whose work inspired her to work for emancipation. She leaves the settlement and travels through the state, lecturing on abolition and women's rights, and preaching. As a former slave, her personal experiences are a powerful testimonial, and her speeches are lively, witty, and blunt. Her passionate style attracts large crowds, and abolitionist leaders advertise her appearances. She will later become one of the best-known speakers for abolition and for women's rights.

— 1847 —

WORK

The potato famine in Ireland has led to mass immigration to America, and this year 70,000 Irish arrive in New York. More than half are women, who compete with native-born women for jobs as domestic servants and seamstresses.[82]

Maria Mitchell, a librarian at the Nantucket Athenaeum, discovers a comet and is awarded a gold medal for her finding by the king of Denmark. Mitchell taught herself astronomy by reading widely and studying with her father, who is an amateur astronomer. Her award and subsequent fame will lead to jobs. She will be hired by the United States Coast Survey to compute tables of planetary positions. Later, when Vassar College is founded, she will be hired as an astronomy professor. At Vassar she will inspire many students and build a strong research program.

EDUCATION AND SCHOLARSHIP

Lucy Stone graduates with honors from Ohio's Oberlin College. Although the college is one of a few coeducational schools, women have a separate program and many restrictions. Most frustrating to Stone was the prohibition against public speaking to audiences of both sexes, since she wanted to learn and practice oratory skills. Although asked to write the commencement speech, she refused since she would be forbidden to deliver it. Growing up in a large family on a Massachusetts farm, Stone was aware of social injustices toward women even as a child. She noted her mother's hard life with long hours of household labor, her father's preferential treatment of his sons, and his ridicule of her desire to study Greek and Latin and attend college. She also sympathized with the antislavery movement, read the *Liberator,* and attended lectures. After graduation she is hired by the American Anti-Slavery Society as a lecturer, and her eloquence and sincerity will attract large crowds. Later she will be prominent in the women's rights movement.

Elizabeth Blackwell is admitted to Geneva Medical College in New York. She has been rejected by nearly thirty other

Lucy Stone, daguerreotype, mid–1850s. (Library of Congress.) Even as a young girl in Massachusetts, Stone resented the injustices dealt to women and hated the notion that they were inferior. While her father ridiculed her dream of studying Greek at college, Stone determined to become educated. She taught school, saved and borrowed money, and in 1847 she graduated from Oberlin College. Stone spent her life working for women's rights. She helped establish the American Woman Suffrage Association, and she founded and edited the Woman's Journal, *which stayed in print for fifty years and was considered the "Suffrage Bible."*

medical schools, despite extensive private study with doctors and excellent recommendations. The Geneva administrators were dubious about admitting a woman. They decided to give the students a voice, and thinking it was a prank, the student body voted to admit her. After graduation and further studies in England, Blackwell will return to New York City, but it will take her nearly a decade to establish a practice. She will be ignored by most doctors, barred from working in hospitals, and regarded suspiciously by the public. Eventually she will found and run a hospital for women and children, and help to establish a medical school for women. Her speeches and writings will inspire many American and English women to become

doctors. Blackwell will be among the earliest American women to earn a medical degree.

ARTS

Artist **Sarah Peale** moves to St. Louis at the urging of a family friend. She establishes a studio and will become the city's leading portraitist. Peale has worked in Baltimore and Washington, D.C., and is well known for her portraits of Thomas Hart Benton, Daniel Webster, and Lafayette. She and her sister Anna, a miniaturist, were admitted as academicians to the Pennsylvania Academy of Fine Arts in 1824 as the first female members. Her successful career is unusual for a female and is due to her talent, energy, and family help. She is the youngest daughter of portraitist James Peale, who encouraged her talent and allowed her to paint backgrounds for his portraits. Her uncle, painter Charles Wilson Peale, encouraged her, shared his studio, introduced her to associates, and helped her find patronage.

— 1848 —

DOMESTICITY

Angered by the agitation for women's rights in Boston and New York, a Philadelphian sends a letter to the *Public Ledger and Daily Transcript*. Women already influence and rule their families, he states, and "a mother is, next to God, all powerful." They need nothing more. He then praises Philadelphia females: "Our ladies glow with a higher ambition. They soar to rule the hearts of their worshippers, and secure obedience by the scepter of affection … and maintain their rights as Wives, Belles, Virgins, and Mothers, and not as women."[83]

EDUCATION AND SCHOLARSHIP

None of Boston's three medical schools accept female students. This year physiologist

Samuel Gregory founds the Boston Female Medical College, the nation's first for females. His school will remain open for nearly three decades, but with limited success. Gregory has no medical training (only an honorary M.D.), the school's admission requirements are low, and the classes are mediocre. The school will be hampered by internal problems and lack of funding, and most local doctors ignore the facility. Although some graduates will find teaching jobs, few will build successful private practices.

Sarah Worthington Peter, a wealthy Philadelphian, is concerned with the welfare of poor women who lack job skills. Envisioning women working in the decorative arts, she opens the Philadelphia School of Design in her home, employing the teachers with her own funds. The curriculum includes lithography, furniture carving, wood engraving, design, and illustration. Publicized and endorsed by Sarah Hale, editor of *Godey's Lady's Book*, this pioneering school will expand to train thousands in industrial and commercial art and will offer instruction to aspiring professional artists. The teaching is excellent, and the work of successful graduates helps lessen prejudice against female artists. It will thrive for nearly ninety years and then merge with Philadelphia's Moore Institute of Art, Science, and Industry.

The New Orleans Couvent School opens, a Catholic school for black children. The land for the school was provided sixteen years ago by **Marie Bernard Couvent**, a freed slave, who specified in her will that a school for orphaned black children be built. The school attracts a distinguished faculty and will continue into the twentieth century.

Elizabeth Ellet publishes her three-volume *Women of the American Revolution*, the first full-length study of females during the war. She interviewed descendants of well-known women and used both published writings and primary materials. Ellet was discouraged to find many women's papers burned or destroyed and urges people to keep family papers. Her book includes both the famous and lesser known, anticipating social history. Critics praise her clear style, and she has a wide readership. The work will be reprinted several times, and Ellett will write more. Later historians will praise her as among the first to write on American women's history.

RELIGION

John Humphrey Noyes founds a socialistic utopian community in Oneida, New York, based on Perfectionism. Members farm, log, and make silver utensils. The women are freed from society's conventions. They work outdoors with men and dress for practicality, with short skirts, bloomers, and short hair. Child care is communal. The group endorses women's right to sexual pleasure and voluntary motherhood. The members practice birth control. Oneida flourishes for thirty years but later gives up this lifestyle as neighbors become hostile and suspicious.

ARTS

Composer **Augusta Browne** publishes "The Warlike Dead in Mexico," a song dedicated to Henry Clay. Critics praise her unusual rhythms. The popular piece is one of about 200 Browne will compose. Like other female composers, she writes most mostly parlor and popular music. Acceptance of the work of these early women artists paves the way for a later generation to compose more serious pieces.

JOINING FORCES

Quaker **Lucretia Mott** and reformer **Elizabeth Cady Stanton** organize America's first women's rights convention in Seneca Falls, New York. Nearly 300 attend, including 40 males. Delegates write and adopt a Declaration of Sentiments, based on the Declaration of Independence. They claim full legal and political rights for married women, freedom from religious and educational dis-crimination, and full citizenship for all women. Press coverage is extensive — and so hostile that the story is picked up by news-papers around the country. The national publicity this small gathering generates in-spires women in many states to campaign for their rights.

Frederick Douglass, editor of *The North Star*, an abolitionist publication, supports women's crusade for equality and attends the Seneca Falls convention. He reports that " in respect to political rights, we hold women to be justly entitled to all we claim for men ... all that distinguishes man as an intelligent and accountable being is equally true for women.... We therefore bid the women en-gaged in this movement our humble God-speed."[84]

LAW AND POLITICS

Women's legal rights are being ex-panded through state legislation. This year New York legislators pass the nation's most comprehensive married women's property act. The law permits married women to keep property they had before marriage or re-ceived as gifts during marriage, and it allows that their property is not subject to their hus-band's creditors. This law expands wealthy women's rights and paves the way for further change.

— 1849 —

WORK

Women and men are moving west, at-tracted by opportunities and a chance to start a new life. Migration to the Pacific territories increased from 4,000 last year to 30,000.[85]

Ah Choi, a single Chinese woman, sails from Hong Kong to San Francisco and sets up a brothel for the thousands of men who are in California to pan for gold. Most of the gold seekers are single, and there is a market for prostitutes. Ah Choi's business prospers, and next year she will expand it.

Boston writer **Eliza Farnham**, whose husband is traveling in California, hears news of his death in San Francisco. She trav-els to California to settle his estate, and likes the area so much she decides to stay. She moves to Santa Cruz, builds a house, and buys land for farming. Like other frontier women, she adapts her dress to the new sit-uation. Long skirts drag in the mud, attract dirt and garbage, and are impractical for out-door work. Farnham finds an old school gym outfit of tunic and trousers and wears it reg-ularly for outdoor work. Other pioneer women also adapt more practical clothing, paving the way for later dress reform.

Thousands of blacks immigrate to Cal-ifornia, where slavery is prohibited. One is **Mary Ellen Pleasant**, a former slave. She moves to San Francisco to open a boarding-house. There are many single men who need room and board, and her business thrives. Later, as the black community grows and there is more discrimination, Pleasant will crusade for equality, such as the right of blacks to ride streetcars.

RELIGION

Preacher **Jarena Lee** publishes *Religious Experience and Journal of Mrs. Jarena Lee, Giving Account of Her Call to Preach the Gospel: Revised and Corrected from the Orig-inal Manuscript, Written by Herself,* a second version of her autobiography. She writes her story to show blacks how religion can offer freedom and self-authority even in a racist and sexist society. Lee distributes copies of her book at gospel meetings, hoping to con-vert nonbelievers to Christianity.

ARTS

English immigrant **Frances Palmer**, a new staff artist at Nathaniel Currier's New York firm, completes one of her many

A woman holding a book, "Sons of Temperance Offering for 1851," daguerreotype, early 1850s. She may have been in the auxiliary group, the Daughters of Temperance, whose membership exceeded 30,000.

In the early 1800s some Americans were troubled by the prevalence of alcoholism, which could drive whole families into poverty. It was men who formed and led the early clubs promoting temperance or abstinence; they gave female members little voice in policy. By the mid–1850s, female reformers wanted more power and formed separate groups. They eventually dominated the crusade. By 1920, membership in the Women's Christian Temperance Union (established in 1874) reached 800,000.

watercolors, *The Higher Bridge at Harlem, N.Y.* Workers engrave it, and it will be among the best-known prints, reproduced in many publications. Palmer had studied art in England, and after coming to America, she ran a lithographic and publishing firm with her husband. At Currier's she develops and improves techniques, including a new procedure for background tinting. She will remain one of the most valued and productive staff members for two more decades.

Artist **Lilly Martin Spencer** moves with her husband and thirteen children from Cincinnati to New York for better patronage and a wider audience. Within two years she will exhibit at the National Academy of Design and will be elected to honorary mem-

bership. Spencer is best known for her domestic scenes, and her work is often reproduced in lithographs. She showed early artistic talent, and her parents sent her to New York for instruction. By age eighteen she had completed fifty oils, and the next year she had her first public exhibition. Her husband is supportive of her work, and he keeps house and helps with her art.

JOINING FORCES

Writer Richard Henry Dana has been traveling throughout the nation ridiculing the demands of women's rights activists. Dana insists that the ideal woman is pure, innocent, and submissive and is exemplified in some of Shakespeare's plays. He says he is always courteous to women and he reveres them. He queries, what more do they want?

While local newspapers praise Dana's speeches and his message, Philadelphia liberals are particularly inflamed. They ask **Lucretia Mott** to respond, and she speaks at Philadelphia's Assembly Hall. Mott explains that a woman wants to be "acknowledged a moral, responsible being … not to be governed by laws the making of which she has no voice."[86] Countering Dana's claims of tender fictitious females, she cites heroic women in history and argues that contemporaries did not view them as unfeminine. Mott outlines American women's limited rights and opportunities and enumerates needed reforms. Her popular address will be published next year in America and England.

Amelia Bloomer, a temperance worker in Seneca Falls, New York, founds *The Lily: A Ladies Journal Devoted to Temperance and Literature.* The publication will later address suffrage and dress reform. A popular journal, it will last for six years, and its circulation will grow from a few hundred subscribers to nearly 6,000.[87]

Fourteen black women establish the Women's Association of Philadelphia, devoted to race elevation, self-help, and abolition. They are responding to Frederick

Douglass's call for African Americans to organize their own abolition groups. Douglass and other black abolitionists are tired of racism within white groups and suggest that while blacks should cooperate with whites, working within the black community will give them greater self-sufficiency.

LAW AND POLITICS

Tennessee legislators debate an act that would give married women property rights. They conclude that because married women do not have free and independent souls, they should not be allowed property ownership. **Amelia Bloomer** responds in *The Lily*, "Wise men these and worthy to be honored with seats in the halls of legislation in a Christian land."[88]

— 1850 —

WORK

More New England women are remaining single. This year, 17 percent of native-born women in Massachusetts are unmarried.[89] There are more jobs available for single women in the growing cities; they can write, teach school, or work as a seamstress, governess, or maid. The ideal, however, is for women to marry, and those who do not risk derision.

Although women are employed in more than 200 occupations, a new survey indicates they are concentrated in several vocations. Fifty-nine percent are in domestic service, 21 percent in cotton or textile factories, 7 percent teach, and 6 percent bind shoes.[90]

Immigration to the United States has increased 340 percent during the past decade, and 44 percent of this year's arrivals are Irish, many of them females.[91] Because of increasing prejudice against them, the Irish Catholic newcomers have trouble finding jobs. Most can only find low-paying jobs as mill workers or maids. In colonial times household servants were considered respectable, but this is changing. Many native-born women refuse to compete for these jobs with the Irish, and domestic service has a lower status.

A Mormon woman who moved to Utah to escape persecution for her religion records the work she has done this year. She taught school for four months, spun yarn, wove cloth, sewed clothing, knit socks, gathered maple sap for sugar, and picked cherries. She also worked for the church's relief society, making quilts and clothing for the poor, organized a Sunday school, and cared for her children and those of her husband's other wives. This woman, like some others in polygamous marriages, is pleased with the system. Living near other women gives companionship in isolated areas, and it is practical since child care is communal.

EDUCATION AND SCHOLARSHIP

The Cherokees, whose nation is now in Indian Territory, are a strong and well-established tribe. They have a constitution, publish newspapers and books, and have a good public education system. This year they open a boarding and day school for females at Park Hill, with teachers who are graduates of the eastern academies. The new institution is one of the first all-female schools west of the Mississippi.

Harriet Bishop has graduated from a female academy in New England. This year she travels to Minnesota to open St. Paul Seminary, a teacher training school. She encourages her students to move further west, where they can establish schools and teach Protestant values. Bishop and other educators are concerned about the increase of Catholic schools in the West and want to balance this with more Protestant-run schools.

ARTS

New Yorker **Susan Bogert Warner** starts a writing career to support her family.

This year she completes her first novel, *The Wide, Wide World*, the story of a young woman as she grows up. Reviewers like Warner's realistic portrayal of family life in an industrial society. The book sells more than one million copies, a record for an American publication. She will write nearly thirty other books, though none will be as successful as her first. Most native-born Americans are now literate and enjoy reading books on American domestic life.

JOINING FORCES

Abolitionists **Emily Robinson, Elizabeth Jones**, and **Josephine Griffin** organize a women's rights convention in Salem, Ohio. State lawmakers will gather this year to revise the state constitution, and the women want their rights to be addressed. The women decide to exclude males from speaking or leading, since they want to become self-sufficient. They pass twenty-two resolutions on political, economic, and human rights. Their report to the state lawmakers denounces common law as unjust, and they request full political and legal rights for all Ohio women.

LAW AND POLITICS

Congress passes the Fugitive Slave Act. It abolishes slavery in the District of Columbia and establishes procedures for returning escaped slaves. The act makes it illegal to help fugitive slaves and provides that law enforcement officers must assist southerners in catching runaways. Slaves who are identified as property are prohibited from testifying on their own behalf.

Harriet Hayden, who owns a Boston boardinghouse, has been sheltering many fugitives while arrangements are made to smuggle them to Canada. The new law's harsh penalties make her work more difficult and dangerous. She will have even more refugees to house and will face a greater risk from federal officials, who search her boardinghouse looking for runaways.

The Oregon Land Donation Act is passed this year to encourage westward settlement. It offers 640 acres to a married couple and allows the wife to hold her half separately. It also offers 320 acres to single women.

— 1851 —

WORK

New York inventor Isaac Merrit Singer patents a foot treadle for the sewing machine, making it easier to use. This and later improvements will lead to widespread use of sewing machines in factories. As sewing machine operators replace hand sewers, fewer employees will be needed and job competition will allow employers to keep wages low. Women who hand-sew at home will lose their jobs unless they buy or rent machines.

Tired of low wages and oppressive factory conditions, a group of 6,000 seamstresses in New York City organizes a Shirt Sewers Cooperative Union. They write to newspapers asking readers to give them work, since many are the sole support of their families. The public responds generously. Some donate money for office rent and sewing machines, and others order shirts. The seamstresses are soon ensconced in a building sewing shirts. They hire a business manager who directs their affairs efficiently, and orders and profits are split evenly among the members. The company will last for several years and is one of several sewing cooperatives being set up in urban areas.

Margaret Frick moved from Indiana to California several years ago to profit from the gold rush. A hotel she owns in Sacramento flourishes, since thousands of single men are moving west and need lodging. This year she decides to invest in another business. She sells her hotel and buys a dairy farm. Frick's success is unusual; most single women who migrate west work as servants or teachers.[92]

newspaper. Readers will follow the install-
ments avidly, and some find it so gripping
they write to the editor demanding to know
the story's end.

The next year *Uncle Tom's Cabin* is published as a book in Boston. It is an instant
best-seller, selling 300,000 copies in nine
months and more than a million in the next
two years. Many playwrights will adapt it for
the stage, and it will be translated into in
German, French, Polish, and Chinese.
Beecher now has fame and will continue to
write, supporting her husband and seven
children. Southerners hate the book; they denounce Beecher's portrayal as specious, and
many writers will publish books justifying
slavery.[93]

*A woman at a sewing machine, daguerreotype, c. 1853.
(Library of Congress.) The sewing machine revolu-
tionized the clothing industry. Business owners introduced it into factories and its efficiency allowed mass
production of ready-made clothing. Industry leaders
increased their profits by exploiting female machine
operators. They charged seamstresses exorbitant machine rental rates, plus costs for thread and fines for
broken needles. All these were deducted from already
low paychecks. For other women the sewing machine
was a boon and a miraculous labor saver. Middle-class
married women who sewed their family's clothing
were saved hours of hand stitching, as were those who
lived in rural areas that lacked access to factory-made
clothing.*

JOINING FORCES

Since the Seneca Falls gathering three
years ago, many women in northern states
are holding similar conferences. In Ohio,
local writer and reformer **Frances Dana
Gage** presides at a meeting in Akron. One
speaker is **Elizabeth Cady Stanton**, who calls
for women to be courageous and self-reliant.
She urges all women to learn a trade or profession to support themselves. "Women have
relied too much on the needle," she exclaims,
branding it a "one-eyed demon of destruc-
tion."[94]

Elizabeth Smith Miller, daughter in a
prominent New York family, enjoys gardening but feels restricted by her long dress that
drags in the dirt and hampers movement. She
designs and sews a short dress and trousers
(to be worn underneath) that are comfortable and suitable for outdoor work. Friends
admire it, and when **Amelia Bloomer** publicizes it in her reform journal *The Lily*, readers dub the costume "bloomers." Miller is not
the first to dress this way. Others wear similar garb for farming, travel, or hiking, for better health, or as a fashion protest. The style
is unpopular with most Americans, who condemn it as too masculine and against biblical teachings on how women should dress.

ARTS

Massachusetts writer and teacher **Harriet Beecher Stowe** has become a passionate
abolitionist. She reads slave narratives and
newspaper accounts of captures and is appalled by the passage of the Fugitive Slave
Act. Stowe wants to persuade Americans to
demand emancipation, and she begins a
novel about slavery, writing it in the popular
sentimental style, emphasizing home, mothers, and children. This year she completes
the first chapter and submits it to the *National Era*, a Washington, D.C., abolitionist

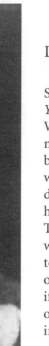

Harriet Beecher Stowe in her sixties, c. 1875. (National Archives.) Stowe's 1852 best seller Uncle Tom's Cabin, *brought her international recognition but not wealth, and money problems plagued her family. Her husband Calvin, a Biblical literature professor, suffered from poor health and depression, and he was unable to provide a steady income. When her children were young, Harriet earned money from teaching and writing. When Calvin retired 1861, she became the family breadwinner. Between 1862 and 1884 she published nearly a book a year. Of her seven children, four died: one as an infant, the others in young adulthood. In spite of all this she remained optimistic and energetic.*

Some women's rights leaders initially affect the dress, loving its comfort and the freedom of movement. But because wearing it in public causes ridicule, they will later return to traditional dress, fearful of alienating the public and detracting from more serious reform issues. Within the decade, bloomers will become unfashionable.

— 1852 —

DOMESTICITY

A women's rights convention is held in Syracuse, New York. An editorial in the *New York Herald* states: "Who are these women? What do they want? … Some of them are old maids whose personal charms have never been very attractive … [and others are] women who have been badly mated." They deride the male attendees as "hen-pecked husbands" who "ought to wear petticoats." The editor continues that it is "natural" for women to be subordinate to men. They want to vote, he complains, and fill posts already occupied by men. Would it not be laughable if a female preacher gave birth in the pulpit or a female legislator had a baby while making a speech?[95]

WORK

Shoe factory owners in Lynn, Massachusetts, buy sewing machines that will sew leather. This new technology causes many women who sew shoes by hand at home to lose their jobs. Females have traditionally stitched shoe uppers by hand at home, but the more efficient machines will produce more shoes in less time.

Mary Ann Shadd, a black writer and teacher from New England, has immigrated to Windsor, Canada. She established an integrated school, where she teaches, and she also writes. Shadd feels comfortable in Canada, where slavery was outlawed twenty years ago, and she wants to encourage black migration. She publishes *A Plea for Emigration or, Notes on Canada West, in Its Moral, Social, and Political Aspect*. Her guide includes statistics on agriculture and climate, describes employment prospects, and extols the advantages of country living. The publication is timely and read by many prospective emigrants. Since passage of the Fugitive Slave Law and the possibility of capture and enslavement, thousands of African Americans are fleeing the

Sister Mary Joseph, of the Sisters of Mercy, c. 1860. (National Archives.) Mary emigrated from Ireland to the United States in the mid 1850s. Shortly after her arrival in Charleston, South Carolina, a severe outbreak of yellow fever paralyzed the city. There were no hospitals, and no nurses other than the Sisters, since nursing was considered a vulgar occupation best left to slaves. Mary and other nuns trudged thorough streets with baskets of medicine and food and cared for the sick. During the Civil War, Mary worked in a military hospital in Beaufort, North Carolina, and tirelessly nursed Union and Confederate soldiers. The humanitarian war work of Catholic nuns earned them much respect and helped lessen anti–Catholic prejudice.

United States. During the next decade more than 15,000 black American families will settle in Canada.[96]

EDUCATION AND SCHOLARSHIP

While more normal and public high schools are being built in the North, many prohibit black students. **Myrtilla Miner**, a white educator who lives in Washington, D.C., believes black female teachers are needed to staff black schools. This year she founds a normal school for African American girls. Her institution will be successful and will later expand and thrive under black leadership, educating thousands of future teachers.

The National Board of Popular Education runs a program to help "Americanize" and "Christianize" the West. Prospective female teachers are recruited and trained, then sent west to teach pioneer children reading, writing, prayers, and morals. **Ellen Lee**, a program alumna on the Indiana frontier, reports her progress to the board. Her school is the first in the area. Many parents, illiterate themselves, were initially dubious about a female teacher, but they have accepted her. She teaches fifty students, ages fourteen through twenty-two. While she is happy to be doing "God's work," Lee feels isolated and lonely, and reports, "I am entirely deprived of sympathy and good society."[97]

RELIGION

Mary Joseph and **Mary Peter**, recent Catholic Irish immigrants, have joined the Sisters of Mercy in Charleston. There is a yellow fever epidemic in the city, and the Sisters care for the sick. The order has no hospital, so they travel through streets and alleys with baskets of supplies, food, and medicines. Immigrant nuns are among the few white women who will do public nursing. Although respectable white women are expected to care for sick family members, nurs-ing the public is viewed by most middle-class Americans as distasteful and vulgar work, suitable only for unskilled males and blacks. This Catholic sisterhood and their counterparts in other urban areas win respect for their nursing, and their work helps lessen local anti–Catholicism.

ARTS

Harriet Hosmer is a young sculptor in Watertown, Massachusetts. Her father, a prominent physician, encouraged her talent, paid for lessons, and even arranged for her to have private anatomy lessons. She is now ready for advanced training. The year she travels to Rome, where sculptors who want success go to study. She will have a productive stay, studying with English sculptor John Gibson, who offers her work space in his studio. Her friendship with Charlotte Cushman, a wealthy arts supporter, will introduce Hosmer to local patrons, and her subsequent commissions will pay for several years of study. Upon her return to the United States she will have exhibits, get many commissions, and become well known. Hosmer is among a small group of female sculptors who have successful careers. Because there is no long-established tradition of male sculptors in the United States, the public is willing to accept women in this art.

Writer **Alice Cary**, who grew up in Ohio, has moved to New York City. This year she publishes *Clovernook, or Recollections of Our Neighborhood in the West*. The book contains sketches and stories about the western Ohio frontier, based on her difficult childhood with a distant father. Readers like her sober portrayal of farm life hardships and the frustrations of being female in a male world. It becomes a best-seller in America and England. People are fascinated with the American West and find Cary's realistic account more absorbing than the typical romantic portrayals of the region. She will publish three sequels.

The Benjamin family, daguerreotype, early 1850s. (Library of Congress.) From left: Cornelia, her father Zina, sister Frances, brother Samuel, and mother Joanette. The Greek revival style in architecture and interior furnishings was fashionable in antebellum America, as seen by the column around which the Benjamins pose. The daughters are fashionably dressed in outfits of rich fabrics, and their off-the-shoulder necklines were in vogue for formal eveningwear.

Although Cornelia and Frances' young adulthood will be shadowed by the Civil War, the next generation of women will have greater opportunities. Frances will marry, and her daughter Frances Benjamin Johnston will become a prominent photographer, known for her pictures of notable Americans and of the nation's minorities.

JOINING FORCES

Cincinnatian **Elizabeth Aldrich** founds *Genius of Liberty*, a magazine for women. She wants readers to work for full political and civil rights, better wages, and dress reform, and she envisions America as "a nation of sensible, natural, free women."[98] The publication will last two years and then fold from a lack of subscribers. Most American women prefer mainstream publications such as *Godey's Lady's Book*. Other potential readers either lack the funds to subscribe to these publications, or have little time to read. Several similar journals are founded, and these early publications, although short-lived, keep alive the issue of gender inequality.

Physician Martin Delany, a prominent black abolitionist, publishes *The Condition, Elevation, Emigration, and Destiny of the Colored People of the United States Politically Considered*. He addresses the issue of black women's work, insisting that they are capable of more than domestic work and should be educated and have serious careers. He asks his readers to respect women, whom he believes are equal to men. Delany is among a few prominent black men who support women's rights. The stance is an unpopular one. Men who champion such reform are condemned as traitors to their sex, often jeered at in public and denigrated as "Aunt Nancy men" or "man-milliners."

Quaker **Susan B. Anthony** grew up in a household where distinguished reformers were frequent visitors, and she heard many discussions of politics, abolition, and social reform. Interested in temperance, she has joined a New York branch of the Daughters of Temperance; but she is frustrated at the treatment of women, who were denied permission to speak at a convention. This year she persuades her friend **Elizabeth Cady Stanton** to help organize a female temperance group. Five hundred attend the first meeting of the new group, the New York State Women's Temperance Society, and they elect Stanton president. A conflict develops when Stanton wants the group to campaign for additional reforms such as divorce law liberalization and female suffrage. These issues are too radical for most members, and next year they depose Stanton as president. Anthony resigns in solidarity; this begins their long partnership working for women's rights.[99]

— 1853 —

DOMESTICITY

Horace Mann, president of Ohio's new interracial and coeducational Antioch College, publishes *A Few Thoughts on the Power and Duties of Women*, in New York. He warns women against vocations of preaching or politics, explaining that they can influence public opinion in their homes and communities. If women "open fountains of purity and honor ... at the fireside, in the village circle," their morality will extend to the "voting booth," he promises.[100]

RELIGION

New Yorker **Antoinette Brown** completed theology course work at Oberlin three years ago, but she was denied both a degree and a preaching license by college officials. While seeking a ministerial position she traveled through the Northwest lecturing on women's rights and temperance, but she still wanted a ministry. This year she is finally offered a post at a Congregational church in South Butler, New York, and is ordained locally. Because her interpretation of Scripture is more liberal than her parishioners can accept, conflicts arise, and Brown later resigns as the church's minister. She will later become a Unitarian and found a church in New Jersey, where she will serves as pastor emeritus. Despite her struggles, her successes inspire women of the next generation to become ministers.

ARTS

African American singer **Elizabeth Taylor Greenfield**, known as "the Black Swan," performs in New York City's Metropolitan Hall to an appreciative all-white audience. Later she will apologize to African Americans, who were barred from attending the performance; she will give another concert and donate the profits to a home for the aged in the black community. Next year her tour of England will include a command performance for Queen Victoria. Greenfield, born a slave, was freed as a baby and raised by her former owner in Philadelphia. A neighbor was impressed with the child's natural singing ability and gave her music lessons. She has toured the northern United States, singing popular songs in many concerts. Some reviewers criticized her for a lack of professional training, while others praise her soprano-through-baritone range. She later settles in Philadelphia, teaches music, and organizes a troupe of black musical performers. This early famous black singer will inspire younger African American women to pursue careers in music.

Bostonian **Sarah Payson Willis Parton** left an unhappy marriage. Her work as a seamstress paid too little to support her family, so she turned to writing. Using the name Fanny Fern, she wrote for Boston magazines, and her articles were often reprinted in newspapers. James C. Derby, a New York publisher, admires her writings and decides to represent her. He brings out a book of her work, *Fern Leaves from Fanny's Portfolio Collection*. It is an immediate success and becomes a best-seller in America and England. Later Parton will become a popular columnist for the *New York Ledger*. She writes on controversial subjects such as the limitations of women's roles and the shortcomings of organized religion, and on taboo issues like divorce, prostitution, and venereal disease. Many readers and critics alike are tired of the pompousness and wordiness of most writers, and they praise Parton's direct and chatty style.

JOINING FORCES

As more Americans move west, many women who follow gold-seeking husbands are abandoned or widowed and need help. A group of wealthy San Francisco women organize the Ladies Protection and Relief Society. They find temporary housing for widows and their children, as well as employment for the women. The group appeals to the state legislature and wealthy private citizens for funds, and they are successful in getting donations. Using business contacts, they find jobs for young boys and teach girls housekeeping skills. Some members even take orphans into their own homes, teaching them values and manners. The group is well respected in the community and will continue to flourish into the twentieth century. Many other women moving west take the spirit of benevolence with them and establish similar organizations.

Paulina Kellogg Wright Davis, a wealthy socialite and women's rights crusader in Providence, Rhode Island, founds *Una*, a new women's publication. Davis is tired of the popular magazines on the ideal woman. Wanting to address practical topics,

she writes on marriage reform, suffrage, religion, poverty, health, and jobs. Her journal has limited appeal, but it will last for three years before financial problems force its closure.

— 1854 —

WORK

Most female printers like their work. Although they make half the salary of male printers, they earn more as printers than as factory workers. While many women wish they could be admitted to the male printers' unions, the men want to bar women from the occupation. They consider printing a "manly art" requiring both "intellectual and manly labor." Men fear that wages and prestige will decline, as more women are hired, and members of the National Typographical Union often strike when a female typesetter is hired. The local Philadelphia printers' union sends a letter to the *Philadelphia Daily News* stating their opposition. Men and women were created as different beings, they point out, and women belong at home. "The purity of women should be guarded with care ... and surely contact with the world would have a very pernicious effect on her morals."[101]

EDUCATION AND SCHOLARSHIP

New York City's Cooper Institute of Design for Women opens. Since most professional art schools still bar women, this early vocational institution will help train a new generation of artists.

ART

Black writer and abolitionist **Frances Ellen Watkins** brings out *Poems on Miscellaneous Subjects*, printed in Boston and Philadelphia. Her poems address slavery, women's rights, temperance, and religion, and the book will be acclaimed and reprinted several times. Called the "Bronze Muse," Watkins is admired for her writings and for her eloquent speaking style. Watkins's parents died when she was three, and relatives in Baltimore took her in and later paid for her education at a prestigious academy. She began writing early, and after graduation she had a local reputation as a good writer. Like most black women, however, she could find work only as a domestic servant and seamstress. She now works as a traveling lecturer for the Maine Anti-Slavery Society.

Massachusetts writer **Maria Cummins** publishes her first novel, *The Lamplighter*. It concerns a young orphan who is mistreated by her guardian. A kindly lamplighter takes her in, and his piety inspires her to become a virtuous adult. Readers applaud Cummins's detailed character portrayals and grim depiction of urban life. The novel sells 40,000 copies in two months and 100,000 more during the decade. It is printed in England and will be later translated into French, German, Danish, and Italian. Cummins will write more, but her first novel will be the most successful. Her work foreshadows realism in American literature.[102]

Writer Nathaniel Hawthorne is sojourning in Liverpool, England. Already irritated by the popularity of so many novels by American women, he is outraged by the success of Cummins's book. Next year he will contact William Ticknor, his New York publisher. "America is now wholly given over to a damned mob of scribbling women," Hawthorne writes in disgust, telling Ticknor that he plans a new work, but it would not have a chance while "public taste is occupied with their trash."[103]

— 1855 —

DOMESTICITY

An article in *The Lily* expresses the power of mother and home. Without them

"the world would be a chaos, without order ... patriotism or virtue.... "Not in the whole world ... is there a character as heroic as the home mother."[104] Domestic imagery continues to be popular and is used even by reformers, who hope a familiar theme might attract more readers.

WORK

This year 200,000 immigrants arrive in America. Many of the females have few skills and will accept any available work. In New York City, two-thirds of all dressmakers, shirt and collar makers, seamstresses, and artificial flower makers are foreign-born. Sixty-nine percent came from Ireland, and 14 percent from Germany. As immigrants continue to flood the eastern cities looking for work, they dominate the sewing industry in big cities. This oversupply of workers helps create the sweatshop system, where workers are exploited with long hours, poor working conditions, and low pay.[105]

Thirty-seven-year-old slave **Elizabeth Keckly**, a dressmaker in St. Louis, buys freedom for herself and her son. A skilled seamstress, she has many appreciative customers who loaned her the money. As a free women, she now has learned to read and write. Later she will move to Washington, D.C., where First Lady Mary Todd Lincoln will become a favored customer, friend, and traveling companion. Keckly will later recount their relationship in *Behind the Scenes: or Thirty Years a Slave and Four Years in the White House.*

ARTS

Josiah Gilbert Holland includes **Lucy Terry Prince**'s poem "Bar's Fight" in his book *History of Western Massachusetts*. Her work recounts the 1746 Deerfield Indian raid and is praised as accurate. Prince wrote it shortly after the incident, but as a black women she was unable to get it in print earlier.

— 1856 —

WORK

Many owners migrating west take their slaves, some of whom later buy or win their freedom. Many female slaves also travel west as cooks or laundresses for military expeditions or for fur traders. Most female slaves who become freed in the West settle in urban areas, where (like their eastern counterparts) they can find work only in low-paying jobs as domestic servants or as agricultural laborers.

A few have skills like midwife **Bridget Mason**, a Mississippi-born slave, who wins her freedom this year. She belonged to a Mormon family who first took her to Utah but then were told to found a colony in southern California. Mason drove the cattle and sheep and cared for the children, and she walked the whole way. She and the other slaves had been promised emancipation at the trip's end, but then she discovered that her owners had decided to take her to Texas. A black friend pleads her case to a California judge, who frees Mason and her three children. Since Bridget is a skilled midwife, she finds work with a local doctor. Later she will buy a home and become a leader and organizer in her new community.

— 1857 —

DOMESTICITY

White male slave owners commonly use female slaves as breeders. Then, to deny responsibility for the mixed-race children, they promulgate the idea that black women are promiscuous. This image is offensive to African Americans. Some replace it with another myth: black women are delicate and submissive woman, and their lives center on their husbands and children. They promote this image in writings and sermons, hoping

to gain the respect of whites who portray their women this way. One such writer is black educator **Mary Still** of Philadelphia, who urges women in her church to become "ideal" women. She writes, "The moral or degraded condition of society depends solely upon the influence of women." She who is "virtuous, pious, and industrious, [with] her feet abiding in her own house ... extends in her neighborhood a healthy influence, and all men call her blessed."[106]

RELIGION

Black preacher **Rebecca Cox Jackson**, who lives in a New York Shaker community, is disappointed at the lack of proselytizing among African Americans. She travels to Philadelphia this year to found a black Shaker community. The group, primarily female, will flourish for twenty-five years after her death. Like many other women, Jackson found autonomy and empowerment in religion, but she was frustrated by the lack of leadership roles for women. She took up Perfectionism, attended holiness groups, and preached as an itinerant minister before joining the Shakers. Later she will write her autobiography, *Gift of Power*.

— 1858 —

EDUCATION AND SCHOLARSHIP

Sarah Mapps Douglass, who heads the Girl's Department at Philadelphia's Institute for Colored Youth, also finds time for adult education. She knows that most grown women have no idea how their bodies work, and believes that such knowledge will lead to better health. She takes classes at the local female medical college, then prepares anatomy and physiology classes which she teaches in her home. The classes are so successful that she is asked to offer them to women in New York City. Most Americans consider such knowledge improper for women, and Douglass is a pioneer.

JOINING FORCES

The University of Michigan's charter called for a female department, but when the school opened the state legislature failed to appropriate the funds, and the student body is all male. Twenty-one-year-old **Sarah Burger** wants to enroll. She and eleven other prospective female students petition the board of regents, but administrators defer their requests. After three more postponements, Burger decides to attend a local normal school instead.

Burger's decision to petition the university was sparked five years ago when she attended a Cleveland, Ohio, women's rights convention. Speakers Susan B. Anthony, Lucretia Mott, and Lucy Stone urged women to work for greater rights. Many reformers have been traveling through New England and the Midwest, encouraging women to take action. Audiences are generally small and interest is scattered, but many who never heard a female speak in public before are inspired to action.

— 1859 —

WORK

Harper and Brothers publish William Sanger's book *History of Prostitution: Its Extent, Causes, and Effects Throughout the World*. Sanger lives in New York City, where there are nearly 6,000 prostitutes, and he decided to study them. He interviewed 2,000 jailed women to discover why they became prostitutes. Most had worked at jobs whose pay was so low that they were unable to support themselves. Nearly half had been domestic servants, another 25 percent seamstresses or milliners, and others worked in tobacco or paper box factories. In these jobs

50 percent of the women earned only one dollar or less weekly. Other became prostitutes after being deserted or abused by their husbands. More than half were immigrants. Sanger ascertained that more than half catch syphilis and that most die young. He writes that women need greater job opportunities and that employers should pay them "living" wages. Sanger also advocates legalizing prostitution and providing the women with medical care. Little attention is paid to his study; thirty-one years later there will be 40,000 prostitutes in New York City.[107]

ARTS

Sixteen-year-old soprano **Adelina Patti**, a daughter of Spanish immigrants, makes her operatic debut at New York City's Academy of Music. She sings selections from *Lucia di Lammermoor*, earning rave reviews in New York City's *Tribune*. A child prodigy, Patty sang operatic airs at age four and performed in public at eight. She will later tour England and Europe, and Queen Victoria will weep at Patti's rendition of "Home Sweet Home." She will have a successful career as a prima donna in Europe and American.

Harriet Wilson, who was born in New Hampshire, publishes *Our Nig; or, Sketches from the Life of a Free Black, in a Two-Story White House, North, Showing That Slavery's Shadows Fall Even There*. The work is semi-autobiographical and concerns Frado, the daughter of a black man and a white woman. Abandoned by her parents, Frado is indentured to a cruel mistress. To improve herself she attends church, learns to read, and earns financial independence as a milliner. She then marries a fugitive slave who abandons her and their son. Wilson wanted to show that racism exists in the North, and she surmised that a fictional work would be less offensive to white abolitionists. Privately printed in Boston, her work sells but is ignored by the press. Wilson's novel is among the earliest by an American black writer.

The Hidden Hand, a novel by **Emma Dorothy Eliza Nevitte Southworth**, is serialized in the *New York Ledger*. The melodrama tells of Capitola, a young woman who was kidnapped at birth and has many adventures before finding her home and claiming an inheritance. She wears male clothing and is outspoken and independent. Her story involves murder, a duel, carriage accidents, sightings of ghosts, and lunatics. The wealthy and prominent Southworth is a member of the Washington, D.C., literary circle. She began writing to support her family after being deserted by her husband, and will publish nearly sixty more novels. Believing all women need a profession, she encourages young writers and writes many books featuring abandoned wives who find strength and prosperity. The *Hidden Hand* is acclaimed by critics for its fast pacing and good character descriptions, and it will remain her most popular book.

JOINING FORCES

Harriet Tubman rescues a captured fugitive slave in Troy, New York. The arrested man is being interviewed at the U.S. Commissioners' office, and a huge crowd has gathered. Tubman instructs several young boys to yell "fire," and when the alarm bells ring, the crowd grows. As the manacled slave leaves the building, Tubman shoves his guards to the ground. She then grabs the slave, and when they are pushed down by the excited mob she slaps her bonnet on his head and shouts for friends to drag them to the river. Crossing it, the slave is put in a wagon and arrives safely in Canada the next day. Tubman began rescuing slaves a decade ago, after her own escape from a Maryland plantation. She is a notorious Underground Railroad conductor with a price on her head. When she travels south she dresses as an old man or a crazy woman; she carries a pistol for protection, as well as paregoric to quiet crying babies. Known as "Moses," Tubman will never lose a slave, and this fugitive is one of hundreds she rescues.

Sarah Parker Remond is from a prominent black abolitionist family in Salem, Massachusetts. While growing up she met many distinguished reformers who visited the Remond household, and she learned from her mother to stand up for her rights. She has accompanied her brother, antislavery lecturer Charles Lenox Remond, through New York and has decided to become an abolitionist speaker herself. She travels to England to lecture on slavery's horrors, often moving her audiences to tears. She will remain abroad for three years, and her speeches are widely publicized. Remond hopes the English will pressure Americans to emancipate all slaves.

— 1860 —

WORK

Fifteen percent of all adult females are in the census as part of the paid labor force. Most of them work in factories or as domestic servants. Another 15 percent, not listed as part of the paid labor force, work in family businesses or farms. The remaining 70 percent of all adult females are slaves and single and married white women.[108]

In Lawrence, Massachusetts, the Pemberton cotton mill collapses and catches fire. Of the 900 employees, who are mostly women, 88 die and 116 are seriously injured. While an investigation determines that the building's pillars were too weak, the final report finds the construction engineer innocent. The lack of concern for employee safety is common in factories employing unskilled workers of either gender.[109]

A study of the Chicopee, Massachusetts, paper and cotton mills discloses differential salaries by gender. Males receive 91 cents per day, and females doing the same job earn 66 cents. The continuing notion that married women belong at home and do not need wages allows employers to pay them less.[110]

There are more than two million African-American women, and 89 percent are enslaved.[111] Many work in cotton and woolen factories. Others labor in turpentine camps, sugar refineries, tobacco processing plants, or saltworks, or they cut trees and dig ditches. These workers have insufficient food, ragged clothing, substandard housing, and little or no medical care. Many southern employees would rather rent slave labor than hire employees who might organize, strike, or quit.

British nurse **Florence Nightingale**'s book *Notes on Nursing* is published in the United States. Nursing has been considered inappropriate work for women in America and Europe, and Nightingale is trying to change this concept. She believes that if professional training were available to nurses, nursing might become an acceptable vocation for women. Nightingale's personal integrity and her nurses' exemplary work during the Crimean War has won much public support. The book's American printing is timely, bringing limited acceptance of female nurses, who will be needed during the Civil War.

EDUCATION AND SCHOLARSHIP

Boston Transcendentalist **Elizabeth Palmer Peabody** is a well-known author who also owned a bookstore well stocked with foreign and radical writings. Like most women, she has also taught school. She is concerned with how children are educated, believing this is important to the development of an ideal society. Peabody learned of Friedrich Froebel's German kindergarten movement and became fascinated with his principles. This year she opens the nation's earliest formal kindergarten in Boston, basing its curriculum on Froebel's teachings. She will later produce a newsletter, *The Kindergarten Messenger*, and form a national organization promoting Froebel's ideas. Peabody will become a leader in incorporating kindergarten into the American public education system.

Fanny Jackson, born a slave in Washington, D.C., was bought by her aunt. At age fourteen she worked as a maid in a wealthy Newport, Rhode Island, household and attended the local segregated school. Her ambition was to become educated and then devote her life to educating blacks. "This idea was deep in my soul," she later explained.[112] She has graduated from the Rhode Island State Normal School, and this year she moves to Ohio to enroll at Oberlin Collegiate Institute. She will do well academically and be appointed Oberlin's preparatory department's student teacher. While putting herself through school, she devotes evenings to teaching in the local black community.

Education, a high priority for many African Americans, is part of racial uplift, which they define as bettering oneself, then helping others improve. While many white parents discourage their daughters from too much schooling, blacks frequently encourage females to become well educated. Jackson is among a group of pioneer black female college graduates who devote their lives to education.

LAW AND POLITICS

The New York legislature passes a married women's property act that permits women to own and sell property, run a business, own their wages, sue or be sued, and be a joint legal guardian of their children. Through petitions and resolutions, women have campaigned for decades to get this reform. Fourteen other states have enacted similar economic reforms, but the New York law is the nation's most comprehensive.

— 1861 —

DOMESTICITY

The shots at Fort Sumter have been fired, and the Civil War begins. As southern women send husbands and sons off to battle, many feel left out. Some write in their diaries or tell friends how useless they feel. Others write to newspapers asking how they can support the Confederacy. A common reply is that women's moral influence, example of unselfishness, and role as mothers are invaluable. In Georgia, an *Augusta Weekly Constitutionalist* editor pronounces, "Great indeed is the task assigned to women … not to make laws, not to lead armies … but to form those by whom laws are made and armies led."[113]

WORK

Southern women found groups to support the Confederate army. In Alabama women have established 91 relief societies. Some sew tents and uniforms, others knit socks, and still others hold concerts and bazaars to raise money. Females in South Carolina have organized more than 100 relief groups. A Petersburg, Virginia, sewing group meets daily. Women in Canton, Mississippi, have converted a mansion into a sewing workshop. Many have never before worked with a group of women, and the fellowship and feelings of usefulness gives them self-confidence. This relief work is needed because the southern economy is agricultural, and few factories exist to manufacture uniforms, army supplies, or weapons.

Virginian **Judith Brockenbraugh McGuire**, a minister's wife, helps her neighbors provide clothing and food for the troops. She writes in her diary, "We do what we can for the comfort of our brave men. We must sew for them, knit for them, nurse the sick…. All ages, all conditions, meet now on one common platform. We must all work for our country."[114]

Juliet Opie Hopkins, wife of an Alabama judge, travels to Richmond, Virginia, to set up a hospital for wounded Alabama soldiers. She serves as superintendent and matron, managing the kitchen, pantry, and laundry. She is an efficient organizer and manager, having learned administrative skills in her youth, while helping oversee her father's Virginia plantation. In appreciation, Alabama officials will put her picture on the state currency. Hopkins is among many upper-class southern women who organize makeshift hospitals. Although few of these women have worked in public, the demand for medical care is so great that need often overrides tradition. Women's wartime activities will strain customary gender roles in both the North and the South.

Sarah Emma Edmonds, from New Brunswick, Canada, has taken male dress and lives as Frank Thompson, a traveling Bible salesman. She now lives in Michigan, and when the war starts she joins a local volunteer regiment. She will serve for two years in the Army of the Potomac, fighting in battles, nursing soldiers, spying, and serving as a colonel's aide. Her memoirs, *Nurse and Spy in the Union Army*, which she will publish after the war, will include vivid battle accounts woven with themes of maternal devotion, religion, and sacrifice. Readers will like it, and it will be reprinted several times.

Edmonds is among some 400 northern and southern women who enlist in armies as men.[115] They join in a spirit of patriotism or adventure, to be with their husbands, or to receive food and pay. Passing as males causes few problems at first. Soldiers are needed, and officers rarely require medical exams or proof of identity. Since modesty is part of Victorian culture, few soldiers ever undress completely, and ablutions done privately raise no suspicions. Discovery often comes when they are wounded; some doctors reveal nothing, and others have the women discharged for "sexual incompatibility." Many whose gender is discovered upon capture are sent home.

President Lincoln calls for volunteers, and thousands respond. In Cleveland, women establish a Ladies Aid and Sanitary Society to collect and distribute clothing and medical supplies. In Troy, New York, women organize a soldiers' aid society and arrange with the government to sew army uniforms. In Bridgeport, Connecticut, females organize a soldiers' relief society. Other sew uniforms, knit socks and scarves, make bandages, can fruits and vegetables, and collect medical supplies. In some already-established benevolent groups, the new goal becomes helping the war effort.

Physician **Elizabeth Blackwell** is in New York City drafting plans for a female medical school and nursing college, but now she postpones this work. She wants to establish a central agency to coordinate the state's volunteer war work, and she also envisions a program to train women as nurses. Blackwell calls a meeting at the city's Cooper Institute, and nearly 3,000 prominent women and men attend. They form the Woman's Central Association of Relief (WCAR), whose goal is to coordinate women's relief work and to recruit, train, and place female nurses in military hospitals.

New York Unitarian minister Henry Bellows, who dominated the WCAR organizing meeting, is pleased with the group, believing that coordination of war work is vital. "Without … a clear idea of common goals," he says, "these devoted women might waste their zeal and produce as much harm as good from their excitement."[116] He now wants to form an official larger umbrella group to coordinate all northern war work. He persuades government officials to authorize it, and President Lincoln signs an order creating the United States Sanitary Commission (USSC). Bellows is the group's president, and the all-male directors include physicians, medical officers, and clergymen. Their job is to coordinate all northern relief work and to distribute all goods to the military.

Nurses and officers in the United States Sanitary Commission, Fredericksburg, Virginia, May 1864. (Library of Congress.) Male clergymen and physicians founded this organization to centralize northern war relief efforts. Women in many states had established local relief groups; they raised money for medical supplies, sewed uniforms, and canned and baked food. USSC agents traveled throughout the country urging women to provide goods for the troops. While the commission did establish an efficient organization, there were continuing tensions. Some women were unwilling to trust a distant agency. Others heard about corruption and fraud and decided to allocate their own supplies. Another sore point was that while USSC officers and agents received salaries, women were urged to volunteer their time to show patriotism. Many women were already straining to support families, had little time for extra work, and resented their loyalty being questioned.

The program hinges on women's volunteer work, and officials travel through the nation, encouraging women to form organizations, sew, bake, can, raise money, and send everything to the USSC. Many conflicts arise between women and USSC leaders, who assume that women have the leisure time for unpaid war work. Most have little free time for volunteer labor; they teach, work in mills, and are busy at home with families, farms, or businesses. They are also frustrated by the fact that males earn wages as agents, contractors, soldiers, and officers while women are expected to provide free labor.

Some WCAR members are dismayed to be under USSC jurisdiction, and Blackwell loses control of the nursing training program. Many women who have organized local groups want control over the fruits of their labors, and reports of fraud and corruption within the USSC make many women uneasy about sending their goods and funds to the central organization.

Prison reformer **Dorothea Dix** travels to Washington, D.C., to volunteer her services and is appointed superintendent of army nurses. Her job is to appoint, train, and supervise military nurses, who are given governmental commissions and will earn forty cents a day. Dix's appointment is controversial. She lacks medical training, has had no hospital administration experience, and is selective about who qualifies as a nurse. She accepts only females who are over thirty, "plain" looking, and of good moral character, and rejects applications from qualified nuns. She argues with hospital supervisors over job duties, fires nurses she did not appoint, and protests loudly when medical facilities fail to meet her high standards. Writer Louisa May Alcott, who volunteers at hospitals, comments, "She is a kind old soul, but very queer and arbitrary."[117] After many complaints, Dix's authority will be undercut by disaffected bureaucrats.

New York physician **Mary Edwards Walker** travels to Washington, D.C., seeking an appointment as military surgeon. She has an M.D., has been in practice for six years, and brings favorable letters of recommendation. Military physicians are needed; the surgeon general commands only thirty surgeons and sixty assistants for an army that is rapidly growing well beyond its prewar strength of 16,000. Yet no female physician had ever received a military commission. The idea is shocking and unorthodox; even female nurses are only grudgingly accepted by the military. Walker's initial application is denied, and while appealing she will work as a volunteer doctor in battlefields and hospitals.[118]

EDUCATION AND SCHOLARSHIP

Traditionally, schoolteachers in the South have been men, but since most are now on the battlefield, women are needed as instructors. The subject is controversial. While most upper- and middle-class southern parents think it is improper for their daughters to work in public, school administrators, newspaper editors, and clergymen declare that schools must be kept open in wartime and that females would make good teachers. In North Carolina, where less than 7 percent of teachers are female, there is a campaign to persuade women to teach. Some colleges add a teaching division, many college presidents urge their graduates to teach, and newspaper editors write articles on why women make good instructors. Many women get positions at schools, and they like the work despite the low pay. Next year Calvin Wiley, school superintendent of North Carolina, will praise this trend, asserting that women need employment and are well suited for "the business of forming the hearts and the minds of the young."[119]

RELIGION

Sarah Doremus, an active member of New York's Dutch Reformed Church, establishes the Woman's Missionary Union Society of America. This ecumenical group will support and encourage female missionaries and address the needs of native women and children. This early national group will be followed later by similar organizations. War needs preclude extensive missionary work, but when the conflict ends women's evangelical activity will flourish. They will organize societies to encourage female missionaries and the founding of more hospitals, schools, and orphanages for native women and children. A motto of many societies will be "Woman's Work for Woman."

ARTS

Many Americans traditionally view women who perform in public as immoral, but as they hear visiting European female singers their attitudes soften. One influential vocalist is the Swedish **Jenny Lind**, who toured America during the 1850s. She is lovely to see and sings superbly, and her agents shrewdly bill her as virtuous and pure. Her well-attended concerts have helped lessen prejudice against females on the stage, and her singing inspires many young American females to become divas.

Young **Clara Louise Kellogg** was inspired by Lind. As a talented eight-year-old singer and pianist, Kellogg attended a Lind performance and was confirmed in her resolve to sing professionally. Her family moved to New York, where she had the opportunity to study voice. Now, at age nineteen, the soprano makes her New York debut as Gilda in *Rigoletto*. She will become a leading diva in Europe and America, and her popularity will help diminish American suspicion of female vocalists.

The *Atlantic Monthly* publishes **Rebecca Harding Davis**'s *Life in the Iron Mills*, a story about impoverished laborers in Wheeling, Virginia, where she grew up. Raised in a middle-class family, she nonetheless observed the oppressive lives of local workers. Reviewers praise the work, and Davis gains fame and acceptance in the New England literary community. She will publish many more stories and articles depicting the harsh consequences of industrialization. She is among the earliest American writers to show sensitivity to class, race, and gender and to introduce realism and naturalism into fiction.

Harriet Ann Jacobs's autobiography, *Incidents in the Life of a Slave Girl, Written by Herself*, is printed in Boston under the pseudonym Linda Brent. Born a slave in Edenton, North Carolina, Jacobs was only six when her mother died, but her owner was kind and taught her to read, write, and sew. At her mistress's death, Jacobs expected freedom but was instead willed to the woman's three-year-old niece. Life in the new household became unbearable. The child's father wanted Jacobs as his mistress; angered at her refusal, he sent her to a plantation. Jacobs escaped and hid in swamps and with friends until she reached her grandmother's house in Edenton, where she lived in an attic crawlspace for seven years. She later fled to New York, where she was befriended by abolitionists who helped her evade capture and later bought her freedom.

Jacobs is among the earliest female ex-slaves to write an autobiography and is one of the first to portray slave owners' sexual oppression. These personal testimonies are a powerful tool for antislavery crusaders, who help the writers get published. Abolitionist Lydia Marie Child edited Jacobs's work and wrote the introduction. Next year it will be printed in England.

Like many wives of prominent southerners, **Mary Boykin Chesnut**'s life has been turned upside down. In the past few months her husband, James, resigned as United States senator from South Carolina, and shortly thereafter the state seceded from the Union. "...one's breath is taken away to think what events have since crowded in," she exclaims in her journal.[120] Her husband will be a Confederate congressional delegate and aide to General Beauregard, and Chesnut will travel with him throughout the South. In an articulate style, Chesnut will

THE SISTER OF CHARITY

HOME TIDINGS

OUR WOMEN AND THE WAR.—[See Page 570.]

Drawing, "Our Women and the War," published in Harper's Weekly, c. 1862. (National Archives.) This illustration shows how Civil War chroniclers portrayed women's work. A nun is praying with a hospitalized soldier; another woman is writing a letter for a dying veteran; others are knitting socks and scarves and doing laundry for officers.

Most contemporary writers and artists showed women's war work as limited to the traditional domestic sphere. Females were considered delicate, with little strength or ability for work outside the home. While women did indeed do the jobs shown here, they also did much more. Wartime needs upset the status quo of American society. Females were needed in arsenal factories, in government offices as clerks, and as copyists for congressmen. Many traveled far from home to supervise hospitals or establish medical clinics. Some founded or took paid positions in war relief organizations. Others managed family businesses or farms, operated tractors and harvesters, worked in the fields, or supervised slave labor. This shift in work by upper- and middle-class white women was difficult for everyone, but war chroniclers ignored the hostilities, conflicts, and disapproval that resulted. Because most Americans were unwilling to accept radical change in women's roles, they preferred to believe that the war had no effect on gender boundaries.

recount in her diary observations and comments on Confederate politics and leaders, southern society, and wartime's horrors. She will bequeath the journal to a friend who will publish it seventeen years after Chesnut's death.

Thousands of other southern women also write to express patriotism for the Confederacy and anguish about the war. Some, like Chesnut, confine their thoughts to private journals or correspondence; others send poems, stories, articles, and letters to newspapers and journals. Editors need submissions to stay in print, and

they praise this outpouring of female prose. While in prewar days it would be scandalous for a woman's name to appear in print, public exposure is now gradually accepted.

— 1862 —

WORK

With their husbands away at war, thousands of northern women travel to the cities to

seek employment. At the war's beginning cotton mills often closed because of
insufficient raw cotton, but as some southern
states are now captured and sheep are being
raised in New England, northern clothing industries are once again booming. Other factories manufacture shoes, boots, and army
supplies and are hiring women. Females also
work as clerks in government offices, stores,
and telegraph offices. Others cut paper collars, make hoopskirts, and mount photographs. Because of the oversupply of female workers, employers lower wages. These
cuts and price inflation result in many living
at starvation level.

Writer and former teacher **Mary Ash-
ton Livermore** wants to contribute to the
war effort. She hires a housekeeper and governess to care for her family and volunteers
to work for Chicago's Sanitary Commission,
a local branch of the United States Sanitary
Commission (USSC), which she will later
head. Livermore will spend three years working full-time. She will travel through the
North to speak on behalf of the USSC, encouraging women to donate money and collect supplies and food for the troops. Later
Livermore will plan and help run a fair that
earns nearly $100,000 for the Union army.
Her work with the commission gives her an
appreciation of women's capabilities. Previously opposed to women's being enfranchised, she will later support it and become
a leading suffragist.[121]

Mary Ann Bikerdyke, an energetic
forty-three-year-old Ohio widow, volunteers
to work with the Chicago Sanitary Commission. She is an excellent administrator and
has nursing skills. She is sent to Cairo, Illinois, to inspect military medical facilities
and is shocked to see the tent hospitals
unorganized and filthy. She takes over as
matron and supervises the cleaning of bed-
coverings, food and drink preparation, pro-
curement of clean clothing and bandages,
and distribution of medical supplies. Her
efficiency earns her an appointment as field
agent, and throughout the war she will travel

to the front to examine medical facilities, organize makeshift hospitals, supervise personnel, and collect supplies. She befriends
the northern commanders, some of whom
appreciate her no-nonsense approach. She
will not tolerate inefficiency, red tape, or de-
lays of any kind.

Eliza Woolesey Howland, a well-to-do
young New Yorker, and four other women
volunteer to work on the ship *Daniel Webster*, which carries wounded soldiers from
Virginia to military hospitals. They supervise the work of forty male nurses, load food,
linen, and medical supplies onto the ship,
and cook for the staff and patients.

There is still much conflict about female
nurses both in the North and the South.
Public reaction ranges from viewing them as
"angels," to grudging tolerance, to outright
hostility. Military doctors have much ill will
toward nurses, viewing them as a threat to
their authority, and are often more civil to
the female hospital volunteers who read to
soldiers, serve meals, and take dictation for
letters home. Nurses' duties vary among
hospitals; many are forbidden to assist in
surgery and can do little more than wash
wounds and feed patients. Although more
than 3,000 women in the North and the
South will nurse, the majority of Civil War
nurses are men.[122]

Fourteen women in Union Point, Georgia, set up a clinic for wounded soldiers who
are returning home and need food, rest, and
medical attention on the way. The facility
will serve more than 20,000 servicemen. Because of its success, other southern women
found similar facilities. A Georgia newspaper
editor praises the clinics as "one of the best
institutions which the war has developed in
our country."[123]

Virginian **Mary Greenhow Lee**, a young
widow, volunteers at the local hospital in
Winchester. Initially dubious about this
work, she wants to ensure that southern soldiers get good care. She finds food for the patients by foraging the countryside and asking
local farmers to donate crops, and she tries

to obtain medical supplies. She reads prayers to the soldiers and dresses their wounds. She enjoys the work, feels useful, and will remain in Winchester even when Union troops invade, at which time she will nurse northern as well as southern soldiers. She will remain there for three more years until the Union captures the city.

Although there is an urgent demand for workers in hospitals, Lee is one of few elite southern women who will do this work. Most upper- and middle-class white southern women believe hospital work is unsuitable, too laborious, and even dangerous. While some will read the Bible to patients, pray with them, or prepare food in their own homes, most cannot face the grubby job of caring for the wounded and bleeding. Those who do work as nurses or matrons are primarily widows or unmarried women with no other domestic responsibilities. Most southern nurses are male and female slaves who are hired out or captured to cook, clean, and care for the southern troops.

To encourage women to work in hospitals, the Confederate congress passes a hospital act. It authorizes positions for women in several matron categories, spells out duties and salaries, and specifies that nurses are to be hired only by surgeons.

South Carolinian **Phoebe Yates Pember**, a widow living with relatives in Georgia, accepts a job as head matron at the Chimborazo Hospital in Richmond, Virginia. She oversees housekeeping, care, and food for hundreds of patients. She is the hospital's first female administrator, and this displeases the doctors, who believe women belong in their homes. She is beset with problems. She faces continuing ill will of the senior staff and of the uneducated and inattentive workers, some of whom frequently raid the whiskey barrel, which is used for medicine only and is under Pember's charge. Resourceful and courageous, she manages the facility well and remains at her post until the Union captures Richmond, forcing her departure.

EDUCATION AND SCHOLARSHIP

Mary Jane Patterson, a young black whose family boards college students, graduates from Oberlin. She has taken the "gentlemen's course," a four-year program, and earns a B.A. She will devote her life to educating blacks, first as instructor at Philadelphia's Institute for Colored Youth, and later as principal of a new Preparatory High School in Washington, D.C., where she will promote high standards for students and add courses in teacher training. She is among the earliest African American female college graduates.

Union forces have captured South Carolina's Sea Islands, and after the Confederate planters fled the islands, nearly 100,000 slaves remained. Treasury Secretary Salmon Chase has persuaded President Lincoln to employ agricultural supervisors to oversee the cotton crop harvest and to hire teachers to prepare the freed slaves for citizenship. They name this mission the Port Royal Project and recruit workers. One of the first teachers hired is **Charlotte Forten**, a young black woman from a prominent New England family. She travels from Philadelphia to St. Helena Island, and with two white female instructors she will hold classes in a Baptist church. In the daytime she teaches children to read and write, and in the evenings she instructs adults. She offers additional sessions on black history to encourage the freed slaves.

RELIGION

Barbara Kellison, a member of the Iowa Christian Conference, publishes *Rights of Women in the Church*. In this forty-four-page pamphlet she quotes and then refutes biblical citations that "prove" women are unfit to preach. Women's right to preach will be addressed again by reformers after the war, but some progress has been made. Many women already offer sermons outside the church, and female Quaker clergy are common. Some Congregationalists, northern Baptists, Unitarians, and Universalists allow women to be ordained in individual churches. More women will be ordained by the century's end, but the controversy over female ministers will continue into the twentieth century.

ARTS

When writer **Julia Ward Howe** of Boston visited Washington, D.C., last year, she felt inspired by patriotism and wrote a poem, *Battle Hymn of the Republic*. The *Atlantic Monthly* publishes it this year, and it receives little attention until someone sets it to music. Now nearly everyone knows it, and it becomes the most treasured song in the North.

Writer and Unitarian minister Thomas Wentworth Higginson publishes an essay in the *Atlantic Monthly* calling for talented young writers to submit work. **Emily Dickinson**, a solitary young poet who lives in Amherst, Massachusetts, has been writing for the past decade but is unpublished. She sends Higginson a few poems and asks if he thinks they could be published. Perplexed by her work, he discourages her from publication but offers his friendship. They will become lifelong correspondents, and after her death he will help get her poems published.

The Carreño family has moved from Venezuela to escape political instability. They settle in New York City so that their young daughter **Teresa Carreño**, a talented musician, can take lessons. This year, at age ten, she makes her debut. Her performance gets such praise that the well-known pianist Louis Gottschalk takes an interest her. Her gives her occasional lessons and will influence her style. Carreño will become a prominent pianist and perform throughout Europe and the United States, inspiring other young women to become professional pianists.

LAW AND POLITICS

The Confederate army is shrinking from deaths and desertions, and President Jefferson

Freed slaves in front of Foller's house, Cumberland Landing, Virginia, May 1862. (National Archives.) This group has escaped behind federal lines. They are considered freed and designated as "contraband." They will be given jobs with the Union army for the war's duration.

After the war one urgent task was to find spouses, parents, children, and siblings. A second was to get an education. Slaves had been forbidden even a rudimentary schooling, and they were eager to attend schools founded by the Freedman's Bureau and churches. Economically, life was harsh for the freed people. They lacked money to buy land or farming equipment, and most who stayed in the South sharecropped, which kept them in poverty and under white control. Life became worse after Reconstruction. When federal troops were withdrawn from the South, white congressmen enacted Jim Crow laws, denying civil rights to blacks, and violence increased. Between 1870 and 1920, more than a million blacks migrated north searching for a better lifestyle.

Davis signs a conscription law drafting all white males between eighteen and thirty-five. This affects many middle and upper-class southern wives, who now head their households and face the formidable task of supervising slaves. In non-slave households, women will have to manage farms and work in the fields. Many are unwilling to accept this responsibility and move in with relatives.

Union soldiers have conquered New Orleans, and the citizens are enraged. Many disobey military orders. People form mobs, some local shopkeepers refuse to serve Union troops, and several ministers refuse to lead prayers for the United States. The city's administrator, Major General Benjamin Butler, punishes the men for infractions. Many women, believing their gender will protect them, are also disrespectful. They cross the street to avoid soldiers, spit at northern officials, and lean out of windows to dump the contents of chamber pots on the Yankees. In response, Butler decrees and posts copies of General Order Number 28: any woman who treats soldiers with contempt or hostility will be regarded as and treated as "a woman of the town, plying her vocation." Most of the female offenders — young, attractive, and from well-to-do families — are so shocked at the implications that they obey the regulations.[124]

Birthrates of native-born whites have decreased faster than those of nonwhites during the past twenty years.[125] Immigrant families are also large, and many fear that the children of immigrants and of African Americans will soon dominate the American population. Ohio passes a law barring contraception and abortion and prohibiting the publication of any contraceptive literature.

— 1863 —

DOMESTICITY

During the war approximately 300,000 women (in both the North and South) are new to the labor force. Because their husbands or fathers are in the army, most need the income. Northern male laborers react in various ways. Some are supportive, knowing that women need to feed their families, while others are dismayed at the increase of women in the job market. *Fincher's Trades Review*, a northern labor publication, prints an article lamenting this trend. The writer calls it a "most unnatural invasion of our firesides by which the order of nature is reversed, and women, the loveliest of God's creatures reduced to the menial conditions of savage life."[126]

In the South many wealthy white women who work find it difficult to accept a paycheck. While volunteer work is traditional for them, a paying job violates the cherished ideal of southern womanhood. Nor do most husbands want their wives to accept jobs or do household chores. As the war drags on, however, women have little choice.

There is also another pressure put on southern women. A new southern woman is needed, one who is patriotic and will sacrifice for the Confederacy. Magazines and newspapers advise married women to send their men to battle with pride and happiness, and they urge single females to befriend soldiers. Newspapers caution women that only soldiers deserve good mates. Poets glorify the Confederate troops, as do composers. A popular song, "I Would Like to Change My Name," concerns a young woman seeking a husband — "But he must be a soldier, a veteran from the wars / One who has fought for Southern rights beneath the Bars and Stars."[127]

WORK

Amanda Worthington, who lives in Mississippi, needs to fish to supplement her family's scanty diet. Frustrated with fishing in her hoopskirts, she makes a more practical bloomer costume. Other southern women, doing household chores in the absence of slaves, devise similar garb or even wear trousers. Those whose former slaves had fixed their hair are unable to arrange the elaborate hairstyles and now cut it short. Traditional ideas of southern women's apparel are being eroded as southern women learn to care for themselves and their households.

The *Charleston Mercury* reports that **Amy Clarke**, who dressed as a male to fight alongside her husband at Shiloh, fought on even after he was killed. Although few other southern women fight in battles, many form military units and drill with guns. Students at Georgia Female College have formed a unit, and women in Harrisonburg, Virginia, write to the secretary of war for permission for their regiment to bear arms. The bemused secretary denies them permission.

Seventeen-year-old **Susan Bradford** lives with her parents on Pine Hill Plantation in Florida. Her parents care for wounded soldiers in their home, with Susan's help. She also sews and knits, and she writes in her diary, "We are busy spinning, weaving, sewing and knitting, trying to get together clothing to keep our dear soldiers warm this winter."[128]

Many northern seamstresses are suffering because lower wages and inflated prices for goods make it difficult for them to feed their families. Before the war home sewers were paid directly by factory owners, but now the government employs contractors to organize and manage the sewing of military clothing. These contractors deliver fabrics, needles, and thread to the women, then pay them for the completed garments. They can make better profits if they pay the women less, so they keep wages low and sometimes fail to pay them at all.

In response, sewers in Brooklyn organize the Sewing Woman's Beneficial Association. They share work and profits, and are successful. Other seamstresses in Detroit, Baltimore, Chicago, and Buffalo also organize such groups. Some succeed, but others are short-lived.

EDUCATION AND SCHOLARSHIP

Clemence Lozier is a well-to-do physician with a thriving practice in New York. She began her practice late in life, having left an unhappy marriage at age thirty-seven to get a medical degree. She believes that women deserve better health care and that more women should become physicians. She establishes the New York Medical College and Hospital for Women, a homeopathic facility. This year it opens with seven students and nine professors. She will contribute operating funds from her own income and will run it as the dean for twenty years. The college will gain a national reputation and remain open for fifty years.

RELIGION

Olympia Brown is ordained as a Universalist minister at the denomination's assembly meeting in Malone, New York. It has been a struggle for her to get this far. Growing up as a Unitarian, she always wanted to be a minister. After graduating from Antioch College she entered theology school at St. Lawrence University in Canton, New York, but with a warning from Ebenezer Fisher, the school's president, that he disapproved of female preachers. Although Brown did well in courses, Fisher refused to recommend her for ordination. She will be a well-liked minister, in part owing to her informal style—she often preaches with no lectern, preferring to address her congregation directly. After having several parishes in New England she will eventually settle in Wisconsin, where she will encourage young women to become ministers.

JOINING FORCES

Hundreds of women and children in Richmond, Virginia, riot in the streets to protest the food shortages. Armed with knives and pistols, they smash storefronts, march into stores, and help themselves to bread and food. They are tired of the war and of the food shortages. There is already a lack of salt, coffee, and vinegar. Merchants hoard goods and then sell them at inflated prices. Although laws prohibit violence, enforcement is unsuccessful. Local officials are embarrassed by the mob's unladylike behavior and ask the newspapers not to report the riots. Other women riot in Savannah, Mobile, and Petersburg, Virginia, protesting food shortages.

The United States Congress passes a law drafting all white men between the ages of twenty and forty. There is a loophole for the rich, who can pay the government in lieu of serving or hire a replacement soldier. Already frustrated by insufficient wages, wartime shortages, and inflated prices, women and men in New York City riot to protest the loopholes for the rich. They demand that all men with families be exempted from service. They riot for six days until police finally quash it; more than 100 die and 300 are injured.[129]

Many northern women are founding loyal leagues to support to the Union. Reformer **Susan B. Anthony** calls a meeting in New York City to form a Women's Loyal National League. She tells the group that the war is being fought to free slaves, although the president and Congress do not admit this. She announces that it is time for women to demand immediate emancipation. She urges them to "Forget you are women and go forward in the way of right.... Rise up with earnest honest purpose ... speak the true word and do the just work." The group passes two resolutions: that all citizens of African descent and all women need civil and political rights, and that members will pledge their time, money, talent, and even their lives for a new Union that will include universal freedom. They defer the question of women's rights for the war's duration, and they petition Congress demanding a constitutional amendment to abolish slavery.[130]

— 1864 —

WORK

Rebecca Lee Crumpler receives a medical degree from the New England Female Medical College and sets up a practice in Boston's black community. After the war she will return to her birthplace, Richmond, Virginia, to practice and will accept as patients many ex-slaves. She will specialize in women's and children's health care and will later write a book on medical care. As one of the earliest black physicians, she inspires others to enter medicine. She herself was inspired by the aunt who raised her, who was the community healer.

Iowan **Annie Wittenmeyer** is a volunteer whose work with wounded soldiers was so successful that she was appointed a paid agent for the state's sanitary commission. When the state commission was subsumed under the national commission, Wittenmeyer lost her job, but she still wanted to work. This year she drafts a plan for military hospitals to add kitchens where freshly cooked food can supplement army rations. The United States Christian Commission, a group devoted to the spiritual and material welfare of soldiers, helps fund this work. Her first kitchen, in a hospital in Nashville, Tennessee, is so successful that eventually kitchens will be made standard in all military hospitals.

Physician **Mary Edwards Walker** receives a commission as assistant military surgeon for a hospital in Chattanooga, Tennessee, becoming the only female doctor with a military commission during the Civil War. However, most of the troops are healthy, so she works in the community. Before her appointment she was examined on her medical knowledge. The examiners were irritated by the odd and sharp-spoken woman wearing trousers, and they failed her, but she got the appointment anyway. For her work, Walker will be awarded the Congressional Medal of Honor, but it will later be withdrawn. After the war she will leave medicine and retire to her family farm in Oswego, New York. She will work for suffrage and dress reform but is ignored by the townspeople, who view her as an eccentric old women.

Because of northern blockades, few manufactured goods are available in the South — most noticeably clothing. President Jefferson Davis asks women to make and wear homespun to show their patriotism, but his request is not fulfilled. Many women do not have spinning or weaving skills, since this has traditionally been the work of servants or slaves. Nor is the equipment available. Some retrieve spinning wheels from their attics, but many believe the work is beneath them. One who makes homespun is **Elizabeth Neblett**, mistress of a Texas cotton plantation and eleven slaves. She writes to her husband, Will, who is in the army, about her new chores. He replies that having his wife do this work is "mortifying," but she responds that she has no choice; the children and slaves need to be clothed.[131]

Many southern females who need work petition the Confederacy for government positions. They are hired as post office clerks, as seamstresses at the Richmond Clothing Bureau, as arsenal workers sewing cartridges, and as war clerks. A desirable post offered to women of higher social standing is a clerk in the Treasury Department, where salaries are high. Twenty-year-old **Adelaide Stuart** works here signing and cutting Confederate banknotes. Although she had never expected to work for pay, she enjoys it and feels more healthy. "I have not had the time to be giving up to such lady like ailments as nervousness," she comments.[132]

EDUCATION AND SCHOLARSHIP

More southern well-to-do parents are sending daughters to schools. Many girls are bored due to the lack of friends and potential beaus, and with military troops in cities their safety is a concern. Enrollment has increased at some schools. At Hollins College in Virginia, the number of students has almost tripled in the last three years, and this year there are 103 students. Some schools are being disrupted by war needs. The tin roof of Georgia's Baptist Female College was needed by the Confederacy, and then the entire building was converted into a hospital. In these cases, classes are often held at the students' homes.[133]

ARTS

Richmond publishers bring out **Augusta Jane Evans**'s new novel *Macaria; or, Altars of Sacrifice*. It is a war story, and she dedicates it to the Confederate army. It concerns Irene, an independent young women who decides to choose useful work in a local hospital rather than pursue romance. It reflects Evans's own frustrations and conflicts about serving her country. This best-selling novel boosts southern morale, although some readers insist that Irene is not a good role model for southern womanhood.

Northern writers are also writing about women. **Mary Eastman** composes "Jenny Wade of Gettysburg," a poem based on a true story. Jenny baked bread for the Union army. She is so dedicated to this task that when Confederate troops arrive at her door and ask her to leave, she continues to bake and gets shot. Poet John Greenleaf Whittier writes of Barbara Frietchie, an eighty-year-old Maryland citizen who refuses to take down her Union flag when Stonewall Jackson's troops march into her city. She tells them she will defend her flag even if it means they kill her, and the general, who could not order the killing of an elderly woman, spares her. These portrayals of women becoming heroes for baking and for cherishing a flag help set the stage for later histories of the Civil War. Many historians will describe women's main contributions to the war as work in their homes.

JOINING FORCES

Seamstresses and other female wage earners in Philadelphia are becoming impoverished. While inflation has increased the cost of lodging and food 75 percent, their pay has been cut 30 percent. Twenty thousand working women petition Edwin Stanton, Lincoln's secretary of war, for fair wages to match the cost of living. "Let this be done without delay," they plead, reminding him that they are not beggars, but working women who are nobly serving their country. Lincoln asks Stanton to look into the situation, stating that women should not have to accept pay cuts.[134]

In New York City nearly 30,000 seamstresses are looking for work.[135] Many are immigrants who need to support their families, while others are widowed or have husbands in the war. Because the contractor system dictates work and pay, many are worse off than ever. They work fifteen-hour days for low wages and sometimes receive no pay. This year a group of sewing machine operators organize a Working Women's Union. The charter members, 100 strong, pledge to campaign for shorter working days, and they raise money to give members sick benefits. Other seamstresses organize in Boston, Philadelphia, and Detroit, and some have public support since their work is for the war effort.

Members of the Women's Loyal National League circulate petitions for a constitutional amendment emancipating all slaves. Women travel throughout the North, and people sign the petitions on "fenceposts, plows, the anvil, the shoemakers' bench." The signers are from all walks of life: "women of fashion and those in the industries ... in the parlour and the kitchens ... statesmen, professors, editors, bishops, sailors, soldiers, [and those] building railroads and ditches." As signatures are obtained, women send the petitions to Congress. By next year they will have obtained nearly 400,000 signatures. Their campaign

gets much publicity, and New York's *Tribune* praises them: "The women of the Loyal League have shown great practical wisdom in restraining their efforts to one subject ... and great courage in undertaking to do what has never been done in the world before, to obtain one million names to a petition." The petitions will help persuade congressmen to pass the Thirteenth Amendment.[136]

— 1865 —

WORK

Josephine Griffing, a prominent Ohio abolitionist, moves with her three daughters to Washington, D.C., to work with freed slaves. She is appointed a general agent for the National Freedman's Relief Association. She helps find food, temporary housing, and jobs for slaves who have fled north, even sheltering some in her own home. As the war draws to an end, she envisions a large central program to help ex-slaves. She and others lobby senators and the president for such an organization, and their efforts lead to the establishment of the Bureau for the Relief of Freedmen and Refugees. Hundreds are hired to provide food, shelter, medical care, and education for emancipated slaves. Griffing accepts a bureau post. Five years later, when Congress fails to renew the bureau's status as a government agency, she will continues this work on her own.

Many northern women have been managing family farms, and agriculture is flourishing. Grain commands high prices from the American government and is in demand in Europe. New technology and mechanization have made the work easier, and in the last five years there has been a threefold increase in the number of harvesters and reapers being used.[137]

Southern women running farms and plantations have more difficulties. Many slaves have escaped, and with a smaller workforce the cotton crops are diminished. On smaller farms work is laborious because so many mules and horses have been requisitioned by the army.

Twenty-two-year-old **Malvina Black Gist**'s life has been turned upside down. Her young husband died in battle, and Union troops burned her hometown of Columbia, South Carolina. Now staying in Richmond, Virginia, she works in an improvised Confederate Treasury Department in a hotel. She likes her job, the excitement of the war, and the presence of handsome army officers in town, but she struggles with the absence of slaves. Bemoaning her lack of practical skills, she writes in her diary, "Wish I had been taught to cook instead of how to play on the piano."[138]

EDUCATION AND SCHOLARSHIP

Vassar, a women's college in Poughkeepsie, New York, opens, based on the Mount Holyoke model. Matthew Vassar, a retired brewer, has founded the school, and he gives it the largest endowment ever offered a female academy. Vassar is convinced that if more Christian women would become schoolteachers, the country's morality would be improved. The curriculum emphasizes teacher training, but many courses are offered and the school will develop strength in physics and astronomy.

JOINING FORCES

Cincinnati seamstresses who make army clothing and tents under the contract system cannot survive on their wages. The women petition President Lincoln. They are honest workers, most of whom have husbands in the war, and are paid little while the contractors make huge profits. They write, "The contractors are paid one dollar and seventy-five cents per dozen for making gray woolen shirts, and they require us to make them for one dollar per dozen."[139]

Other sewing women in big cities have the same problem. Some organize coopera-tives to bypass the contractors. A group of Detroit seamstresses organize a protective association to improve working conditions and standardize wages. They agree on a rate scale and persuade employers to adhere to it.

In January, Congress passes the Thirteenth Amendment, which frees the slaves but fails to address their citizenship or voting rights. Abolitionists are concerned, and the American Anti-Slavery Society has regrouped to work for another constitutional amendment to enfranchise black males. They are joined by the Republicans, who want the votes of the future two million freedmen to join their party, keeping the South under Republican control.

Wendell Phillips, the society's president, endorses only black male suffrage. Because of the extensive opposition to female suffrage, Phillips fears that linking the two causes would defeat them both. Yet women deferred work for female suffrage during the war and now expect to be enfranchised. When Phillips tells them they will have to wait — that it is now the "Negro's hour" — many women are shocked and embittered. An enraged **Elizabeth Cady Stanton** queries Phillips about his "apparent opposition" between slaves and women. "My question is this," she writes: "Do you believe the African race is composed entirely of males?"[140]

LAW AND POLITICS

Lee surrenders in April, and the Confederacy has been defeated. In December, Congress ratifies the Thirteenth Amendment, prohibiting slavery or involuntary servitude in the United States and lands under its jurisdiction.

— 1866 —

WORK

Alfred Bloor, a United States Sanitary Commission official, sends a report on the commission's work to Congressman Charles Sumner. Bloor writes that work was "exceedingly well done by the women and comparatively ill done by the men." He reports that women provided nearly $15 million in goods and services. This is one of the first times that women's domestic work has been publicly acknowledged and given a dollar value. Bloor also comments that when female suffrage is debated, their war contributions should count.[141]

During the war, government administrators were pleased with women's work as clerks copying documents and speeches for congressmen. They decide this is suitable employment for them and give hiring preference to war widows. They also set a wage scale with different rates for male and female clerks. Women will be paid $900 a year, but men will earn between $1,200 and $1,800 a year.[142]

ARTS

Artist **Lilly Martin Spencer** paints *The War Spirit at Home, Celebrating the Victory at Vicksburg.* The work depicts a family. The mother is reading news of the triumph in the newspaper while holding a baby; small children are marching around wearing celebratory paper hats, and one beats a makeshift drum; the father sits in the background. Spencer is a popular artist, and her works are loved by the American public. Hundreds are reproduced in lithographs or etchings, although she makes no money from these copies. As photography continues to supplant portraiture and European art becomes preferred to American paintings, her works will seem dated. She will die impoverished.

George White teaches music at Fisk, an all-black school in Nashville, Tennessee. This year he initiates a new group, the Fisk Jubilee Singers. The singers are five women and four men, and some are former slaves. Several years later, when the school is ready to close from lack of funding, White takes his group on the road to raise money. The singers have a wonderful style, and their repertoire includes slave songs. After a successful American tour, they perform in Europe. Their concerts are so popular that they will raise $150,000 within seven years. They introduce gospel music to the United States and Europe and bring the need for education for blacks to the public's attention. Later Fisk will become a college.[143]

Congress commissions eighteen-year-old sculptor **Vinnie Ream** to make a full-size statue of Abraham Lincoln, who was assassinated last year. She had already completed a bust of him last year, for which he modeled personally. Ream first makes a plaster model in her studio and then travels to Rome render it in marble. She will complete it five years later, and it will be placed in the Capitol Rotunda. Reaction is mixed. Some dislike the work thinking Ream was too young to get the commission and considering her "untrained." Others praise it, such as a Wisconsin senator who declares it "Abraham Lincoln all over."[144]

JOINING FORCES

Few freed slaves in the South are able to find good jobs. Most women work as sharecroppers, agricultural laborers, or servants. For many, the work is so hard and pay so little that they move to the city to find work as laundresses. This allows them to work in their own homes and control schedules, but wages are still low. Black washerwomen in Jackson, Mississippi, organize for better wages. They write to the local newspaper, setting specific rates for their work and asking that their customers honor these rates.

The wording of the proposed Fourteenth Amendment is being debated, and women hear that the word "male" will be used to define voters. In response to this, **Elizabeth Cady Stanton** and **Susan B. Anthony** send Congress a petition for women's suffrage with 10,000 signers. Although women have sent hundreds of these petitions to state lawmakers, this is the first directed to Congress.

At a Boston meeting of the American Anti-Slavery Society, **Lucy Stone** and **Susan B. Anthony** propose that the group merge with women's rights groups. The mission would be to work for universal suffrage and women's rights. The group's president, Wendell Phillips, who maintains that black male suffrage must be won first, does not allow members to vote on this proposal.

Stone, Anthony, and others call women's rights leaders to meet in New York City, where they form the American Equal Rights Association (AERA). Their goals are universal suffrage and women's rights. They will work for enfranchisement on the state level, and members lobby and petition to eliminate sex and race restrictions from state constitutions. Members include those who were active in abolition and women's rights, as well as some of their spouses. Considerable tensions arise because of different priorities. Member Frederick Douglass, despite his advocacy of women's rights, now states that while female suffrage is "desirable," black male suffrage is "vital" and should come first.[145] Although the AERA is a large group, with many prestigious members, their inability to agree on goals weakens the organization.

LAW AND POLITICS

Congress passes the Fourteenth Amendment. It defines American citizens as all people born in the United States, therefore giving black people citizenship, but it excludes women from suffrage by specifying that state lawmakers who deny "male inhabitants" voting rights will have reduced representation in Congress. This is the first time gender is specified in the Constitution, and the word "male" is repeated three times. Many are unhappy with the amendment. Some women are insulted and view it as a betrayal. White male southerners, who want to keep black men out of power, are furious and initiate anti-black riots. Because the language is ambiguous, Republicans fear southern states

might still prevent black men from voting, and they make plans to propose another amendment enfranchising black men.

— 1867 —

WORK

More women want to become physicians, and there are now three female medical colleges; they are in Boston, Philadelphia, and New York City. This alarms many male doctors. This year the Philadelphia Country Medical Society passes a resolution forbidding their members from consulting with female doctors; they also state that women should not become physicians. Women should take their domestic duties more seriously, they suggest, because "the home influence of woman is one of the greatest benefits growing out of Christian Civilization." Fulfilling her domestic role properly would not allow a female doctor time to practice.[146]

Stoves have been replacing the open hearth for cooking in many middle-class homes, and women are eager for even better kitchen technology. This year, fifty-seven-year-old **Elizabeth Hawks** of Troy, New York, designs and patents a stove with a separate chamber for baking bread. This will allow loaves to be baked thoroughly and will give the top and sides a nice crust. Her improved stove will become popular, and she will earn royalties on nearly 4,000 stoves.[147]

EDUCATION AND SCHOLARSHIP

The Freedmen's Bureau establishes Howard University in Washington, D.C., to give former slaves advanced education. Howard offers high school and college courses, and it will later add law, divinity, and medical schools. It is coeducational, giving black women — who are barred from most white colleges — a chance to get professional degrees. One prominent graduate will be **Mary Ann Shadd Cary**, who will get her law degree from Howard and set up a successful practice in Washington, D.C.

Writers Linus P. Brockett and **Mary C. Vaughn** publish *Women's Work in the Civil War: A Record of Heroism, Patriotism, and Patience*, in Philadelphia. Brockett is affiliated with the United States Sanitary Commission (USSC), and the book is considered an official history. They include stories of hospital nurses and volunteers, women who sewed, baked, and canned, and those who bravely cared for wounded or dying husbands, fathers, and sons. The authors portray the women as self-sacrificing, patient, courageous, and cheerful, making no mention of gender conflicts or rivalries in hospitals or within the USSC. In the introduction they affirm that women's war work did not change them and that now they can return to benevolent work within their communities.

ARTS

New York sculptor **Edmonia Lewis**, of Chippewa and African-American heritage, is studying in Rome. To commemorate Emancipation she creates *Forever Free*, a marble sculpture of male and female slaves, wearing broken chains. This is one of many works she will create to honor African Americans. Lewis, who is self-taught, finds acceptance among the Italians and the Americans in Rome and gets many commissions. While her work will become well known in Europe and America, attention frequently focuses on her exotic heritage and striking looks rather than her art. As the neoclassical style is replaced by more modern forms, her works will fade from public attention by the late 1880s.

JOINING FORCES

Two referenda are on the Kansas ballot: female suffrage and black male suffrage. The American Equal Rights Association supports both, and members **Lucy Stone**, **Susan B. Anthony**, **Olympia Brown**, and **Elizabeth Cady Stanton** are in Kansas speaking at rallies and distributing literature. Stanton, working in sparsely populated areas, travels in a mule-drawn carriage and addresses crowds in log cabins, train depots, schoolhouses, barns, hotels, and churches.

The Kansas Republicans wage a strong battle against female suffrage, and the state's Democrats support neither ballot. Abolitionists and Republicans who campaign for black male suffrage are silent about the women, not wanting to link the two causes. Democratic financier George Train, an outspoken racist with presidential ambitions, offers to support the female referendum, viewing it as good publicity. Stanton and Anthony accept his offer, to the dismay of Lucy Stone and others who abhor Train's blatant racism. Despite the intensive campaigning, Kansas voters defeat both referenda.

— 1868 —

DOMESTICITY

A new journal, *The Household*, is founded for rural American women. A traditional publication for wives and mothers, it offers advice on cleaning, cooking, child care, house decorating, and gardening, as well as essays, short stories, poetry, and book reviews. The editors view women as the "central light and animating spirit of every True home" and urge readers to "let woman then accept the high position and important work assigned her. No sphere can be more exhaulted, no work more honorable.... Let her be satisfied to be woman and act her part." Ten thousand will subscribe the first year and in two years this will increase to 50,000.[148]

Lily Dale, a *Household* subscriber, writes to the editor. She has heard about the clamor for women's rights and certainly supports rights, but she defines them in her own way. "You my married friend," she explains, "have the right of counseling and advising your husband ... and the exclusive right of so adorning his home." Those who have children, she continues, have the right to educate them. They do not need the ballot box, she tells women, since their influence will be far greater than their vote if they "teach your sons to be thinking, honest men."[149]

WORK

Mary Evard is a milliner who also likes to tinker. She has been experimenting with cooking stoves and invents a movable partition to create two cooking sections, one with wood and the other coal. This offers the flexibility of moist and dry cooking so that meats and cakes can be baked simultaneously. She patents her invention, and her husband manufactures them as Reliance Stoves. Sales are large at first, but as companies with more capital imitate her appliance the Evards will be driven out of business.

EDUCATION

Sarah Woodson, a black Oberlin College alumna, has been teaching English and Latin at Ohio's Wilberforce University. When she hears of emancipation she decides to teach former slaves, and she accepts a position at a black girls' school in Hillsborough, North Carolina. The school is among thousands that the Freedmen's Bureau will found, and Woodson is among 9,000 instructors hired. Black and white northern benevolent societies will pay for teachers' salaries and provide school supplies. By the early 1870s, more than 4,000 schools will be founded, and teachers will educate nearly a quarter million children and thousands of adult freedpeople.[150]

JOINING FORCES

New Yorkers **Elizabeth Cady Stanton** and **Susan B. Anthony** found *Revolution*, a women's rights journal, with the motto "Principle, Not Policy — Justice, Not Favors — Men Their Rights and Nothing More — Women Their Rights and Nothing Less."[151] They support suffrage, better working conditions and pay, more vocational choices, more education, abortion rights, sex education, and the abolition of the double standard. They reprint essays by past and present notable women, as well as fiction, poetry, and book reviews. The journal gives women's suffrage a strong voice and is one of few reform publications to address issues of the working class. But it is controversial. Many consider sexuality an inappropriate topic for a public forum, and the editors are uncompromising in advocating radical social change. It will last for two and one-half years, but then financial backer George Train will withdraw support. Insufficient subscriptions will force its sale to another publisher.

Lucy Stone, **Julia Ward Howe**, and other prominent women organize the New England Suffrage Association to work for getting female suffrage amendments in every state constitution. They form the group in response to the new publication *Revolution*, which they believe too radical. The women want a conservative suffrage voice and view voting rights for women as separate from other social and economic oppression. They support the proposed Fourteenth Amendment, accepting the idea of black men being enfranchised before women.

Susan B. Anthony establishes the Working Women's Association in New York, the first national group to address working-class female wage earners' concerns. Anthony wants to improve their working conditions and gain a new constituency for suffrage. Membership includes wealthy and working-class women, and conflicts arise from divergent viewpoints between the social classes. Most wage earners' priority is higher wages and membership in the male unions. Many wealthy members, however, idealize the poor and fail to understand the realities of wage-earning women's life. Their priority is to offer educational and cultural activities to the working women, and they often support employers instead of members who are on strike. Eventually most working-class members will resign, leaving the group's leadership to educated middle-class women. The failure to gain support for suffrage among working-class women will result in suffrage having a middle-class constituency.

LAW AND POLITICS

The Fourteenth Amendment is ratified.

U.S. Congressman George Washington Julian, who is from Indiana, proposes legislation to enfranchise all women in the territories. Some male reformers and lawmakers like the idea, and they speak for it to congressional committees. It could test the impact of women voting, and since territorial residents only vote in local elections, it would not give females a strong national voice; it might even encourage more women to move west. Legislators discuss the bill, but no action is taken.

— 1869 —

WORK

New Yorker **Sophronia Bucklin** publishes her memoirs, *In Hospital and Camp*, on her nursing work in the war. Many Americans have criticized women for accepting wages for their war work, and Bucklin addresses this. She explains that she and others needed to support themselves, but they did nonetheless have national loyalty. Bucklin and other nurses who persisted in their work despite hostility and difficulties have helped Americans accept the idea of nursing as a suitable female profession. During the next few decades, more programs will be founded in hospitals and schools and more women will enter this vocation. Bucklin, however, is

unable to find a nursing position and has returned to her former job as a seamstress.

Irish immigrant **Kate Mullaney**, a collar maker in Troy, New York, helps establish a Laundry Union and Cooperative Collar Company. They advertise for shareholders to fund the group and earn interest in their investments. For a year the cooperative prospers as the women sew, wash, and iron men's shirt collars, but then business will decline. Competing manufacturers run a successful boycotting campaign, and need for the service declines as paper collars are introduced.

EDUCATION AND SCHOLARSHIP

Fanny Jackson Coppin, a teacher and administrator at Philadelphia's Institute for Colored Youth — a college-prep high school — is promoted to principal, a position she will hold for thirty-two years. She will add college graduates to the faculty and strengthen the curriculum, especially in sciences. Believing that black youth need vocational as well as academic study, she adds industrial and vocational courses, with dressmaking, millinery, and cooking for girls and printing, shoemaking, and carpentry for boys. The school, already renowned, will acquire an international reputation under Coppin's leadership.

RELIGION

Boston Methodist women organize a Woman's Foreign Missionary Society. One of their first recruits this year is **Isabella Thoburn**, an Ohio schoolteacher. They send her to Lucknow, India, where she will work for thirty years. She will begin by teaching six young Indian girls in a rented room in a bazaar. As enrollment increases, the society will buy a former royal palace for the school building. Boarding facilities will be added for out-of-town students and to provide a Christian environment. Thoburn, who is selfless in her work as teacher and evangelist, wants to foster a Christian spirit and encourages her girls to disregard caste divisions among them. She also teaches religion to impoverished children and supervises evangelical work of local Christian women. The school will expand, offering high school instruction and then college courses, becoming Lucknow Woman's College. After Thoburn dies, it will be renamed Isabella Thoburn College.

New Yorker **Maggie Van Cott** passes an examination for a local preaching license from the Methodist Episcopal Church. A church member for nearly ten years, she has been conducting prayer meetings and Bible study groups and has led revivals where she attracted huge crowds with her dramatic style. Three years later, Bishop Gilbert Haven, editor of a church publication, will proclaim her as "without doubt today the most popular, most laborious, and most successful preacher in the Methodist Episcopal Church." Before retirement Van Cott will convert nearly 75,000.[152]

ARTS

Harriet Morrison Irwin, a Charlotte, North Carolina, mother of five, designs and patents a hexagonal house. She dislikes the typical Victorian houses with their dark kitchens, poor ventilation, and inefficient use of space. Although she lacks professional training, she has studied architecture texts and histories, and her plan improves earlier hexagonal structures. It includes an interior with three hexagonal-shaped rooms and two with diamond shapes. Construction costs are low since fewer materials are needed than for square homes. Her plan provides for good ventilation and makes efficient use of lighting and heat. The lack of corners makes housecleaning easier. Irwin has one house built for her family, and her husband and brother-in-law form a company to advertise and construct them. Her house plan receives acclaim, and a Missouri writer celebrates her design as beginning "a new era in architecture."[153]

JOINING FORCES

Elizabeth Cady Stanton and **Susan B. Anthony** found the National Woman Suffrage Association (NWSA). Their goal is an amendment to the U.S. Constitution that would enfranchise women. Stanton believes this would take less time than persuading state legislators to amend their constitutions. The time for reform is now, she believes, predicting that after Reconstruction there will be political apathy. An additional goal is obtaining full civil rights for all women. Men can join, but the officers must be women. Members meet weekly in New York City, and leaders travel throughout the country to encourage women to form local groups.

The group opposes the proposed Fifteenth Amendment because it enfranchises only black men, and Stanton uses racist arguments in her crusade against it. She speaks from a privileged upper-middle-class white position. She is angry that immigrant males (many who have a low social standing) can vote and that all black males might be enfranchised before educated white women. Many suffragists use this racist and elitist rhetoric, alienating many other suffragists.

Lucy Stone, her husband, Henry Blackwell, **Julia Ward Howe**, and others convene in Cleveland to organize the American Woman Suffrage Association (AWSA). This group is formed from an earlier New England suffrage group. Their goal is female suffrage through amendments to state constitutions. They remain allied to male abolitionists and to Republicans, believing that men will eventually help women get the vote. They endorse the proposed Fifteenth Amendment. Membership includes both genders, and Henry Ward Beecher is the first president. They have no timetable for their goal.

LAW AND POLITICS

Congress passes the Fifteenth Amendment, which states that American citizens cannot be denied the vote on the basis of race, color, or previous condition of servitude.

Legislators in Wyoming Territory pass an act granting all resident women over twenty-one full suffrage and the right to hold office and sit on juries. The women who worked for this are jubilant, although its passage was easy from lack of strong or organized opposition. It brings the territory national attention, which is good public relations. Wyoming leaders want more Americans to move there, especially those with capital to invest. They also want more women: of the 9,000 Wyoming residents, only 1,200 are female.[154]

Iowan **Arabella Babb Mansfield**, a college graduate, has worked as a law office assistant and now wants to establish her own practice. Despite passing the bar with excellent scores, she was denied admission since the state's code admits only white males. She appeals to the Iowa Supreme Court, and they admit her to the bar. The next year lawmakers will delete "white male" from the code.

A black woman, **Josephine De Cuir**, brings a case of discrimination to the United States Supreme Court. While traveling on a Louisiana steamboat, she was forced out of a section reserved for whites. Her lawyer argues that a Louisiana Reconstruction law prohibits racial discrimination in public transportation. She loses her case. In *Hall v. De Cuir*, Chief Justice Waite rules that the Louisiana law violates the U.S. Constitution's commerce clause. If each state were to regulate its own transportation, he opines, it would be too confusing when conveyances pass through other states. Mrs. De Cuir's case will be cited in other suits to claim Reconstruction laws invalid, and will set a precedent for denying civil rights to African Americans.[155]

— 1870 —

WORK

Women are joining the labor force in record numbers as industrial expansion cre-ates more jobs, yet their occupational choices are still limited. Of the 1.3 million females working in non-agricultural jobs, 70 percent are domestic servants and 24 percent work in clothing, shoe, and textile factories. Working conditions are poor, since few women are organized, and competition keeps wages low. The oversupply of labor is compounded by increasing immigration, which in the last decade rose 250 percent.[156]

Many Americans are concerned about the increased of single white native-born women in the labor market. They believe overwork might weaken women's ability to have children, thus endangering the nation's future. Others are troubled about young women living alone in big cities, exposed to immorality and corruption. Different solutions are offered. Many conservatives believe women belong at home in their "proper sphere." Some reformers acknowledge the need for women to work, and they endorse protective labor legislation to guard the health of these future mothers. Still others think more occupations should be available to women. There is a great interest in facts and statistics on working women, and many studies are being done.

Virginia Penny has been investigating working women, and she publishes the results in *How Women Can Make Money: Married or Single*. She found 533 jobs open to women, but most pay subsistence wages. She urges more vocational training for females and blames the paucity of vocational choices on the widespread notion that all women belong at home.[157]

New Yorker **Susan McKinney Steward**, who grew up in an elite black family, receives a medical degree from the New York Medical College for Women, a homeopathic facility, where she is class valedictorian. Steward's practice will include patients of all races and will flourish as her reputation grows. She will be active in the local and state medical societies, work for suffrage, and preside over the local temperance society. Steward and other black female physicians are often more accepted in their communities than their white counterparts, since black women are expected to hold jobs.

Margaret Knight has mechanical talent and likes to make things. As a young mill worker she invented a device to prevent a shuttle from sliding out of a loom. She has repaired houses, done upholstery, worked with daguerreotypes and photographs, and engraved on silver. Now she works for a Massachusetts paper bag company. For several years, in her free time, she has been designing a machine to make flat-bottomed paper bags, bypassing tedious hand work. She patents the device, and international attention will bring her wealth and fame. She will later establish her own company, the Eastern Paper Bag Company in Hartford, Connecticut.

EDUCATION AND SCHOLARSHIP

The majority of high school graduates are women: this year they earn 56 percent of the 16,000 diplomas. This trend will continue well into twentieth century.[158]

More female high school graduates are attending college, and this year women earn 15 percent of all bachelor's degrees.[159] Some attend women's schools and others enroll in state schools, which more states are establishing under provisions of the 1862 Morrill land grant. As more public colleges are built, women are demanding admission. Universities in California, Indiana, Iowa, Kansas, Michigan, Missouri, and Minnesota now admit females. Many administrators, however, are uneasy about this trend. They fear women might become the majority. They impose constraints: at some state schools only resident females can enroll; at others, course selection is limited and library access restricted. When Wisconsin admitted women during the war, females were required to stand in the classrooms until all male students were seated; they have now closed the school to women. Some administrators will later establish separate colleges

for females to keep them isolated from the main university.

Ada H. Kepley receives a degree from Chicago's Union College of Law, becoming one of the first women to earn an accredited degree. Other females who want to apply to law school are unsuccessful. A comment by a male trustee of Columbia University College of Law reflects the typical attitude. When the school denies three women admission, he proudly announces, "No woman shall degrade herself by practicing law in New York, especially if I can save her."[160]

JOINING FORCES

Spiritualist, reformer, and entrepreneur **Victoria Woodhull** is from a large and eccentric family who ran a traveling medicine show. Victoria, her second husband, James Harvey Blood, and her sister Tennessee Claflin now live in New York City, where they run a prosperous brokerage firm funded by railroad magnate Cornelius Vanderbilt. Victoria now seeks new endeavors. Her friend Stephen Andrews, a lawyer and radical philosopher, persuades Victoria that society needs reform. She announces plans to run for president of the United States. She and Tennessee found *Woodhull and Claflin's Weekly*, a radical publication endorsing free love, legal prostitution, diet and dress reform, and world government. They condemn the double standard of morality and expose business corruption and Wall Street fraud. The newspaper will run for six years.

Lucy Stone and Henry Blackwell found the *Woman's Journal* in Boston, a forum for their American Woman Suffrage Association (AWSA). The publication has a moderate tone. They offer news on American and European suffrage activities, notices of women's rights conventions, biographical sketches of prominent women, and commentary on politics. The journal includes a children's column, poetry, and short stories. Among the many distinguished contributors will be **Mary Livermore**, William Lloyd Garrison, and **Julia Ward Howe**. Although circulation remains small, it is one of the best-known women's rights publications and will last (under several names and different editors) until 1920. Readers call it "The Torchbearer of the Woman Suffrage Cause."[161]

LAW AND POLITICS

Utah Territory's governor and legislative assembly pass an act enfranchising women twenty-one years or older who have lived in the territory for at least six months. Unlike Wyoming's female suffrage law, this one arouses much controversy. One problem is that there are too many Utah women. While only 2,000 women are in Wyoming, 43,000 live in Utah, comprising almost half the state's population. Moreover, many are in polygamous marriages, a custom that arouses suspicion and disapproval among most Americans.[162]

The Fifteenth Amendment is ratified. Abolitionists and Republicans hail the victory, as do **Lucy Stone**, Henry Blackwell, and other AWSA members, who believe that the Republicans will now help women get the vote.

— 1871 —

WORK

Mary Virginia Terhune lives in New Jersey with her family. Well-known for her writings, she publishes under the name Marion Harland. While assisting her husband in parish activities, she continued to write. Now age forty-one, she decides to write a book on running a household, etiquette, and entertaining — something she wishes had been available to her years ago. There is a market for such a book. Since the war, many men have become wealthy, and they and their wives, who hope to advance socially, would be receptive to such a book. This year Terhune publishes *Common Sense in the Household*, which becomes a national best-seller and will be translated into French, German, and Arabic. She will write many more articles, newspaper columns, novels, and books on various topics. A highly energetic women, Terhune will publish her last book at age eighty-nine.

EDUCATION AND SCHOLARSHIP

Fourteen-year-old **Martha Carey Thomas** of Baltimore is the daughter of a Quaker physician and his wife. An avid reader and independent thinker, she has been influenced by her mother's support of women's rights. Thomas was chagrined by a recent conversation between her cousin and a dinner guest who claimed it was futile to educate women since their primary function is to sew, cook, and entertain husbands. Carey writes to a friend: "[When I grow up] my *one* aim and consecrated purpose *shall* be and is to show that a woman *can learn can reason can compete* with men in the grand fields of literature and science and conjecture." Thomas will later become the second president of Bryn Mawr College.[163]

Sarah Allen, a white teacher from Illinois, has been instructing black children at a Freedmen's Bureau school in Cotton Gin Port, Mississippi, for six weeks. Early one morning, costumed and armed Ku Klux Klanners knock at her door. They order her to leave the state because whites should not educate blacks, and they caution that this is her only warning. Frightened, Allen leaves her post and later testifies about it to a congressional committee. Allen is among hundreds of female teachers who staff the Freedmen's Bureau schools. The KKK wants to close these schools; their campaign of terror includes ordering white female teachers to leave, as well as whipping, raping, and even killing black instructors. With other white southerners, the KKK helps to destroy many Reconstruction programs and succeeds in closing many schools.

ARTS

The Vienna Ladies Orchestra makes its first American tour. Organized several years ago by musician **Josephine Weimlich**, it began as a string quartet and then grew to nearly twenty members. They perform light classics and popular works for appreciative American audiences. Later, American musicians will form their own all-female groups. More women are studying music, but few jobs are available in orchestras or bands. Traditional prejudice holds that women lack the strength, skill, or dedication to be professional musicians. Women's orchestras will be a source of employment.

JOINING FORCES

Abigail Scott Duniway, a widowed Oregon pioneer who runs a notions and millinery store, has taken up the cause of women's rights. Hearing her customers discuss the lack of legal rights for married women inspired her to action. This year she moves to Portland and establishes a weekly newspaper, *The New Northwest*, endorsing suffrage and other reforms. She is a skillful editor and lively writer, and her publication will last for sixteen years. She will later help found the Oregon Equal Suffrage Society.

— 1872 —

WORK

Chicagoan **Jane Wells** invents and patents a baby jumper. This device has a child-sized seat suspended on flexible cords from a freestanding frame. By touching its feet to the floor, the seated baby can swing, turn, and jump. The jumpers are made at the Occidental Manufacturing Company, which her husband, Joel, manages. With some variations and improvements, the contraption will be popular well into the twentieth century.

EDUCATION AND SCHOLARSHIP

Alice Freeman, who lives in Windsor, New York, has graduated from a local female academy and wants to attend college. She has chosen the University of Michigan, which now admits women. Her parents have been saving for their son's education but are reluctant to finance college for a daughter. They loan her the money when she promises to repay it; Alice will also help finance her brother's education. Upon graduation four years later, she will be among eleven women in a class of seventy-five. After a decade of teaching, she will be appointed Wellesley College's second president. At Wellesley she will raise academic standards, improve the library, hire faculty with graduate degrees, and help transform it into a prestigious women's school.

Alice is typical of the young women from middle-class families who pursue higher education. These pioneering women want to improve society. Most do not choose a full-time domestic life, but they remain single or marry later and have few children. Many teach or become administrators at women's colleges; a few enter law or medicine; and others enter the new vocation of social work. Others volunteer on school or college boards or work for charity. They help inspire younger women to go to college and pursue careers.

RELIGION

Twenty-two-year-old Sister **Blandina Segale**, an Italian immigrant, has joined a Catholic order, the Sisters of Charity. She is sent west to Colorado and New Mexico, where she will found missions and hospitals and teach school. Particularly important will be her work establishing and running a hospital for the indigent of Santa Fe. She is a capable fund-raiser and will persuade the territorial government to help support the facility.

JOINING FORCES

New Yorker **Louisa Lee Schuler** served on the executive committee of the Women's

Central Association of Relief during the Civil War. She learned to be an efficient administrator, gained confidence in her leadership skills, and now wants a peacetime career. Deciding that state charitable and correctional facilities need reform, she establishes the State Charities Aid Association. The organization oversees female visitors who investigate conditions in institutions and advise on improvements. The association then lobbies for reform legislation. Schuler is among many elite women who enjoyed the responsibilities and challenges of their war work and now seek full-time careers in charitable or educational work.

Susan B. Anthony, who lives in Rochester, New York, decides to vote, claiming her rights as an American citizen under the Fourteenth Amendment. She persuades her sisters and others to join her, and sixteen women register to vote. On election day Anthony votes for Ulysses S. Grant for president and for several congressmen. Three weeks later she is arrested at home by a U.S. marshal, since New York's constitution forbids women to vote. The other women are also arrested. Anthony and her group are not the first women to vote; many others have tried it and most were not arrested. Because Anthony is so prominent, her arrest makes national headlines.

LAW AND POLITICS

Victoria Woodhull, who has already announced her candidacy for president of the United States, now forms the Equal Rights Party, dedicated to social reform. Five hundred join and select her as their candidate. She chooses Frederick Douglass as her candidate for vice president but neglects to get his consent. During her campaign she is ridiculed for her support of free love. Minister Henry Ward Beecher denounces her publicly, and when she learns of his love affair with a married women she is angry at his hypocrisy and prints news of the affair in *Woodhull and Claflin's Weekly*. She is promptly arrested for sending "ob-

scene" materials through the mail, and election day finds her in jail. Her political party disintegrates, and she loses many supporters. While in jail she reads the election results: Republican Ulysses S. Grant wins with more 3.5 million votes, and Horace Greeley is second with than 2.5 million. The paper fails to report the 3,000 votes won by Woodhull.[164]

— 1873 —

DOMESTICITY

Edward C. Clarke, a retired Harvard Medical School professor, believes women do not belong in college and is alarmed at the number of females pursuing higher education. He publishes *Sex in Education: or, A Fair Chance for the Girls* in New York, describing case studies of college women who ruined their health by excessive studying. Some were unable to bear children, others became crippled or lived with constant headaches and pain, and still others died. To show that women should not exert their brains, he draws upon the Spencerian model of limited energy in a closed system. He explains that too much studying causes excessive blood flow to the brain, leaving insufficient energy for the internal organs, thus weakening the reproductive system. He also points out that women need extra rest during menstrual periods and should be in bed rather than in class. His book is popular; it will be discussed widely and regarded seriously enough to be reprinted seventeen times.[165] His thesis however, arouses much controversy. Some parents and educators accept his thinking, but others dismiss it. Many parents want their daughters to become educated in order to have better job opportunities, and they ignore his opinions. Others claim he has insufficient proof of his thesis. The *Woman's Journal* reviews Clarke's work critically, and many people will publish books and reports refuting his argument.

WORK

Writer **Louisa May Alcott** publishes *Work: A History of Experience*, a novel based on her own search for work. It concerns Christie Deven, an orphan raised by her aunt and uncle. At age twenty-one Deven leaves to become independent. She finds work as a governess, teacher, domestic servant, factory worker, nurse, actor, and seamstress — the jobs open to women. Though cheerful and competent, Deven finds each position unsatisfying; wages are inadequate, and employers are demanding and mean-spirited. When a employer refuses to pay her wages owed, the destitute Deven feels suicidal. A friend rescues her and takes her to Cynthie Wilkins, a compassionate laundress who offers Deven friendship and temporary shelter. Deven helps with chores and child care. She later works as a domestic, marries, and is widowed during the Civil War. After the war she manages her late husband's greenhouse business, raises their daughter, and joins a women's rights organization, where she finds happiness with a circle of female friends. In the book Alcott shows that the ideal of true domesticity is impossible for most women and that women's lives are more complex than usually is portrayed.

Everyone has difficulty finding jobs this year, and thousands have lost work due to a bank failure that causes a panic. Businesses and railroads in the North and West grew rapidly after the war and became overextended, with insufficient markets. Triggered by the bank failure, thousands of other businesses fail and by next year some three million people will lose jobs. The depression will last for five years.[166]

Amanda Theodosia Jones, a former Chicago schoolteacher, invents and patents a food canning method that preserves flavor. The Jones process involves removing air from a container of food, heating the liquid, and then sealing the can. Later Jones will establish the Woman's Canning and Preserving Company, run and owned by women, and they will use Jones's process to can lunch meats, fruits, and puddings. The corporation will prosper and expand, opening branches in Aurora, Illinois, and Montello, Wisconsin.

EDUCATION AND SCHOLARSHIP

A group of former slaves in Greensboro, North Carolina, open a coeducational school in the basement of a Methodist Episcopal church. Lyman Bennett of New York helps them get started, and the local Freedmen's Aid Society helps with operating expenses. The school will grow, and in the twentieth century it will be a women's college, supported by the church's Woman's Home Missionary Society. Bennett College will be eventually be known as the Vassar of the South for its well-educated and socially polished graduates.

RELIGION

Susan McBeth, a Scots immigrant and teacher, accepts an appointment with the Presbyterian Board of Home Missions to work with the Nez Percé in Idaho. She is experienced with Native Americans, having taught Choctaw girls in Indian Territory. This new assignment will begin her life's work with the Nez Percé. She teaches at the mission in Lapwai, Idaho, for a year, then helps prepare Indian men to be ministers. She believes, as do most missionaries, that Indians must become Christian and adopt American values to assimilate successfully into American culture. She tries to persuade the Nez Percé to reject their traditional customs and beliefs. She will remain in Idaho working with them for another twenty years. Among her accomplishments will be a dictionary of the Nez Percé language.

LAW AND POLITICS

Myra Bradwell, who has studied law with her husband and edits the *Chicago Legal*

News, has passed the Illinois bar exam. As a female, however, she is denied permission to practice. She appeals to the United States Supreme Court, arguing that under the Fourteenth Amendment she is an American citizen and cannot be denied privileges and immunities. The Court rules against her in *Bradwell v. Illinois*. As a married woman she has no separate legal identity, it is subsumed under her husband's in traditional common law. Therefore she is not included in the amendment's equal protection clause. Justice Joseph Bradley attests that married women belong at home and that having a career is incompatible with the harmony, identity, and interests of family life. "The paramount destiny and mission of women [is] to fulfill the noble and benign offices of wife and mother.... This is the law of the creator."[167]

Susan B. Anthony, arrested last year for voting, is on trial in a New York circuit court. She has publicized the case, claiming her rights as a citizen to vote, but is forbidden to speak during her trial. Judge Ward Hunt, presiding over his first criminal case, has already decided the verdict, and he instructs the male jurors to find her guilty, which they do. In *United States of American v. Susan B. Anthony*, Judge Hunt rules that for a woman to vote is "against the peace of the United States of America and their [the women's] dignity."[168] Anthony is fined $100, which she refuses to pay. Charges against the other female voters are dropped.

Reformer Anthony Comstock opposes birth control, abortion, and expressions of sexuality in art and literature, all of which he judges obscene. He wants the government to regulate morality and has been lobbying for national legislation addressing this. Congress passes the Comstock Law, which forbids mailing any obscene materials, including contraceptive devices and birth control instructions. Several states also enact laws prohibiting advertising, publicity, or any information about birth control. Despite these laws, birthrates continue to decline.[169]

— 1874 —

JOINING FORCES

New Yorker **Jennie Willing**, a Methodist college professor, organizes a women's gathering to discuss forming a national temperance society. She believes the time is right. Last year reformer Dio Lewis spoke to a crowd in Fredonia, New York, asking women to promote temperance. Local women were inspired, and they marched to saloons and ordered them closed, and they urged people to sign abstention pledges, sang hymns, and prayed loudly in public for prohibition. Females in a nearby town initiated similar activities, and as news of the crusade spread via newspapers, letters, and travelers, thousands of American women have been roused to action.

Although many Americans have already been promoting temperance, this movement will be national. More liquor is available because of industry expansion since the war, and there is much corruption, with state regulations often flaunted. More saloons have opened — in Ohio alone, there is nearly one bar for every twenty people.[170] Women married to alcoholics often live in poverty, as husbands use their wages for drink. Wives have little legal recourse, since in most states husbands own all property, children, and even their spouse's wages. Men who lose their jobs from excessive drinking have difficulty finding new work, since the depression has caused widespread unemployment.

Representatives from Jennie Willing's group gather in Cleveland, Ohio, and establish the Women's Christian Temperance Union (WCTU). They elect **Annie Wittenmeyer** as president and **Frances Willard** as secretary. Both are efficient and devoted leaders. They travel through the United States speaking on temperance and convince many women to organize local groups. They lobby Congress for prohibition and petition lawmakers to investigate liquor industry corruption. They will later mount a large reform program to improve society; they will build kindergartens, schools, and health clinics and will lobby for protective legislation. The WCTU will become the century's largest national women's movement. In five years there will be nearly 1,000 local groups, with a total membership of 26,000; by 1920 membership will be 800,000.[171]

Women have been responding to Edward Clarke's book on why women should avoid college. One critique is *Sex and Education: A Reply to Dr. E. H. Clarke's "Sex in Education,"* edited by **Julia Ward Howe** and published in Boston. Contributor **Maria Elmore** wonders why Clarke is only concerned about college women's health. Does he assume all other female occupations allow monthly vacations, daily rest periods, and little use of the brain? She describes the demanding work and long hours of seamstresses, store clerks, schoolteachers, mothers, and factory workers. "Has Dr. Clarke written a book on 'Sex in Manufacturing Establishments,' or 'Sex in Sewing?' If he hasn't, he ought to," she reports.[172]

— 1875 —

DOMESTICITY

Orson S. Fowler, a phrenologist, publishes many works on motherhood and marriage, advising women on pregnancy, child care, and running a household. In a new work, *Sexual Science*, he cautions women against joining the women's rights movement, whose leaders he characterizes as grouchy spinsters and dissatisfied wives. Very few males seek independent women, he warns, and "this clamor [for suffrage] drives men from you.... It will destroy your prospect of marriage which is the only 'sphere' in which you can ever be happy."[173]

WORK

Although the first writing machines

(predecessors to the typewriter) were invented in 1714 by an Englishman, typewriters are not yet commonly used in businesses. Among the many Americans to design a typewriter was printer Christopher Latham Sholes of Milwaukee, Wisconsin. He constructed a machine eight years ago, and last year he signed a contract with E. Remington and Sons, a New York gun company, to manufacturing his machine. Only 400 were sold, but they are promoting it. An advertisement for a Remington typewriter appears this year in *The Nation* as a possible Christmas gift. The company promises that their machine could provide employment for women as a copyist or clerk, and that "Mere girls are now earning from $10 to $20 dollars per week with the 'Type-writer.'" In eleven years, typewriter factories will be manufacturing a thousand machines yearly. Their introduction in businesses will revolutionize office work and open a new vocation to women.[174]

EDUCATION AND SCHOLARSHIP

Wellesley Female Seminary, chartered five years ago, opens in Massachusetts with several hundred students. Harvard alumnus Henry Fowle Durant and his wife, **Pauline Durant**, want to give women a Christian education to strengthen their bodies and minds. They model the school on Mt. Holyoke, where Henry serves as trustee. They are generous with funding and provide an extensive library and a laboratory with the latest scientific equipment. They hire only female faculty and set high standards. A preparatory department is added, since most new students are unqualified for college work. Later students and faculty will rebel against the religious and highly structured environment, and the female seminary will be transformed into a college.

Sophia Smith, who died five years ago, was a pious and well-read Massachusetts woman who inherited a family fortune. She often wished she had a chance for a college education, and against the advice of male educators she left her bequest for a women's college. Smith was idealistic about the benefits of college. "By the higher and more thoroughly Christian education of women," she wrote, what are called "their 'wrongs' will be redressed, their wages will be adjusted … [and] their influence in reforming the evils of society will be greatly increased as writers, as mothers, as members of society." Smith College, built in Northampton and based on the Mt. Holyoke model, was chartered in 1871 and opens this year.[175]

ARTS

In New York City, painter **Helena de Kay Gilder** helps found the Art Students League, a center offering classes with progressive teachers and a gathering place to discuss new trends. Gilder has been dissatisfied with the National Academy of Design, a conservative and male-oriented school that sets standards for American art by selecting juries to appraise exhibits. The new league welcomes female students, and women serve on the board of directors. Many future female painters, including Georgia O'Keefe and Isabel Bishop, will study here. Other advances in art education during this decade are the founding of art academies in Cincinnati, St. Louis, and Chicago, and all will admit females.

JOINING FORCES

Young Women's Christian Associations have been established in many big cities. Their purpose is to help young women who have moved to cities seeking work. Concerned with protecting morality, YWCA members establish boardinghouses for them and offer job placement and cultural and educational programs. The members are primarily upper- and middle-classes white women who reject black members and prohibit young African-American women from attending their programs. In response, many black YWCA women form their own groups

to help young black women adjust to urban life.

Despite the disapproval of many male clergymen who believe the money would be better spent within the Young Men's Christian Association, the YWCA has expanded and flourished. Twenty-eight associations have been founded, with 8,000 members and total assets of three-quarters of a million dollars.[176]

LAW AND POLITICS

Wisconsin lawyer **Lavinia Goodell** wants to practice law but is denied admission to the bar. Her appeal to the state supreme court is unsuccessful. Chief Justice Ryan rules that women have no business practicing law because they are "modeled for gentler and better things"; dealing with criminals and hearing crude language would threaten their "innocence." Goodell will appeal again, and win, five years later. Since the war more women are studying law, but because most states admit only white males to the bar, women must appeal to the courts or legislators for permission. Most states lack consistent policies on female attorneys, and rulings and decisions are often arbitrary.[177]

Several years ago, **Virginia Minor**, who lives in St. Louis, addressed a state women's suffrage meeting. Her lawyer husband, Francis, had formulated an argument for women to vote under provisions of the Fourteenth Amendment: since women are citizens as defined in the amendment, they cannot be denied privileges and immunities, and they already have suffrage. She suggested that women try to vote, and that those who are denied permission appeal in court. She herself attempted to register but was denied permission. She and her husband (since married women cannot act as a legal entity) sued the registrar, Reese Happersett, for denying her constitutional rights. She lost her case and also lost an appeal to the state supreme court.

This year she appeals to the United States Supreme Court. In *Minor v. Happersett*, Chief

Justice Morrison Waite upholds the earlier decisions. He rules that while women are indeed citizens, they have been historically viewed as a "special class of citizen," and their lack of suffrage rights does not hamper their rights as citizens, since the Constitution's framers did not intend to give all citizens suffrage. After this ruling, suffragists will no longer attempt to vote but will instead campaign for an amendment to the Constitution establishing female enfranchisement.[178]

— 1876 —

DOMESTICITY

Forty-six-year-old **Mary Holywell Everett**, a physician with a large practice, receives a letter from her mother asking her to return home and help nurse her sick sister. Traditionally, family members have a "claim" on adult female relatives, but Everett is unwilling to leave her patients. She turns to her former mentor, New York doctor Samuel Lilienthal, who reminds her that if she is needed at home, she must go. He advises, "Even at the risk of losing your practice entirely, duty commands you to remain by the side of your old mother and help her carry the burden … certainly I would not leave your sister to the care of strangers."[179]

ARTS

Photography is a growing business in California, and it offers employment to women. Many work in darkrooms, others color and retouch photos, and still others own galleries or take the pictures. One photographer is fifty-one-year-old **Eliza Withington**, who owns a studio in Ione City, California. She does ambrotype portraits and also travels to shoot landscapes and the mining industry for stereographs. In "How a Woman Makes Landscape Photographs," in

The Philadelphia Photographer, she describes traveling to a shooting site in a stagecoach, private carriage, or fruit wagon, packing the cumbersome and heavy equipment, and carrying it over rough terrain. She makes a portable darkroom from a thick skirt and develops the glass plates on location. Because photography is a new art form with no tradition of male dominance, women who enter the field are accepted.

Americans are organizing the Philadelphia Centennial Exposition to celebrate life, art, and culture in the United States. There will be displays of art and of practical inventions like typewriters, lamps, and sewing machines. Some females want a separate display of items made by women, and the male organizers approve of this provided they can find the funds. **Elizabeth Gillespie**, a granddaughter of Benjamin Franklin, agrees to head a committee, and they raise the funds. The organizers then announce that there is insufficient space in the main hall for women's displays; the committee must raise more money to pay for construction of a separate building, which they do. The Woman's Pavilion causes controversy; some female artists would rather show in the main hall, while others think the proposed exhibits are too conservative and should include copies of unjust American laws, as well as goods made by factory women.

Many female artists exhibit — some in the separate building, others in the main one — and several are awarded medals. There are sculptures by **Vinnie Ream** and a likeness of Cleopatra by **Edmonia Lewis**. Paintings shown include works by **Emily Sartain** and **Cornelia Fassett**. **Imogene Robinson Morrell** exhibits some large historical paintings, which critics praise for their strength and power. **Susan Stuart Frackelton**, who paints china, shows a portable gas kiln which she invented. Also displayed are women's inventions, including furniture, appliances, clothing, and sewing machine and laundry washing improvements.

A black church congregation in Washington, D.C., woodcut, from the Illustrated London News, *November 18, 1876. (Library of Congress.) This fashionable black congregation is from a middle-class black community in Washington, D.C. After the Civil War thousands of blacks fled the South for the District, the city of Lincoln and freedom.*

African American churches were central institutions. Before emancipation they served as refuge for fugitive slaves. They were also used for schools, community gatherings, and political meetings. Black women were prominent in founding and supporting churches. It was primarily the women who raised money to build the churches, taught Sunday school, directed choirs, cooked for social gatherings, and helped clothe and feed the ministers.

JOINING FORCES

Susan B. Anthony wants the National Woman's Suffrage Association included in the Centennial program. When her request is denied, the members prepare "A Woman's Declaration of 1876." It is based on the Constitution's Bill of Rights and proclaims, "We declare ... our full equality with man in natural rights ... we deny the dogma ... that woman was made for man.... We ask [for] justice [and] ... equality ... [and] that all the civil and political rights that belong to citizens of the United States be guaranteed to us and our daughters forever." Their declaration describes the injustices toward women since the nation's beginning and calls for American leaders to be impeached because they have conducted an unjust government. They print copies and distribute them to the entire Centennial program audience.[180]

— 1877 —

WORK

Nurse **Clara Barton**, well known for her compassionate war work, begins a campaign to establish an American Red Cross Society. Barton became aware of the International

Red Cross on a trip to Switzerland during the war, and she admired their work as a neutral group helping those in need. She writes newspaper articles, travels and lectures, publishes a pamphlet explaining the organization's work, and lobbies Congress and the White House. Within several years the United States will affiliate with the international group, and Barton and others will organize an American Association of the Red Cross. By 1900 the United States will have a federal charter for a national Red Cross.

EDUCATION AND SCHOLARSHIP

Della Irving Hayden, a freed slave, wanted to become educated. She attended a Virginia public school, then transferred to the state's Hampton Normal and Agricultural Institute, a school Union officers founded to educate freed slaves. Living conditions are rough: students sleep in barracks, the roof leaks, and there is not enough food. Like many other students, Hayden often took a leave of absence to teach in local schools to earn tuition for the next semester. This year she graduates with honors. She will become a superb educator and will later found the Franklin Normal and Industrial School. Education is important to black women; it may lead to a teaching position, which is one of few jobs open to them besides domestic service or agricultural work.

ARTS

Artist **Mary Cassatt** has been studying abroad and is now settled in Paris. An outspoken and independent painter, she is impatient with the Paris Salon's jury system and their conservative definitions of good art. Although they have accepted some of her work, two recent pieces were rejected as too avant-garde. She vows to bypass the jury system and never to accept prizes, medals, or commissions. Edgar Degas invites her to join his group of independent painters, called impressionists by the critics. These artists reject traditional historical and sentimental themes, preferring everyday reality, and they paint the countryside, urban streets, and cafés, with people posed informally. They have created a new painting technique that breaks down color into tones that reflect light. Cassatt accepts his invitation. She is the only American in the group, and this begins their close forty-year friendship. Cassatt will have a productive career and will be known for her informal portraits of mothers and children. She will be highly respected by the French but less known in the United States, where she nonetheless helps introduce impressionism. Her parents, who disapproved of her plan to study art, later move to Paris, where Casatt will support and care for them.

Writer **Elizabeth Stuart Phelps** publishes *The Story of Avis*, about a talented artist who marries a ne'er-do-well and is forced to become the family's sole support. When she tries to reclaim her talent years later, her creativity has vanished. Phelps's message is that a married woman cannot be an artist. It is based on the life of her mother, a talented writer whose duties as a minister's wife and mother of three ruined her health and prevented her from having a successful writing career. She left many unfinished manuscripts when she died at thirty-seven. Phelps has vowed to stay single in order to write.

JOINING FORCES

Boston physician **Harriet Clisby** is concerned about poor women, and especially immigrants who need jobs. With several friends, Clisby found the Women's Education and Industrial Union. It is housed in a large building on Boylston Street where women can learn dressmaking, millinery, and needlework, get free legal advice, and learn English. Later, the facility will provide training in retail and domestic work and offer a job-finding service. They will later establish a women's credit union. The Women's Education and Industrial Union will serve thousands and exist well into the twentieth century. It functions much like the earlier houses of industry and foreshadows the later settlement houses.

Irish immigrant **Mary Harris Jones** has had a difficult life. She lost her husband and children in a yellow fever epidemic, and later she lost all her possessions in a Chicago fire. She has taught and has also worked as a dressmaker for the wealthy. Aware and resentful of the gap between her clients and most Americans, Jones vows to change this. She has joined the Knights of Labor and decides to devote her life to labor reform. This year she travels to Pittsburgh to support striking railroad employees who are in danger from mobs who blame the nation's economic problems on the workers. This starts her long career as a labor activist. She has no permanent home but travels where she is needed. She encourages and helps organize strikes, speaks on unions, and encourages people to join or form them. Nationally known as "Mother Jones," she will continue her work into her nineties. She is unsupportive of women's suffrage, insisting, "You don't need a vote to raise hell."[181]

— 1878 —

EDUCATION AND SCHOLARSHIP

Olive San Louis Anderson publishes *An American Girl and Her Four Years in a Boy's College*, a novel based on her student days at the University of Michigan. A strong theme is the tension between male and female students. Wilhelmina Elliot, the heroine, wants to become a new kind of woman, but she discovers that society's gender roles are rigid. She is viewed as either a lady or a student, but not both. Her tutor develops a crush on her, and male classmates, who view her as an intruder, are hostile. Despite her difficulties, Wilhelmina prefers coeducation to women's schools, believing the larger schools

offer more intellectual and social freedom. Her novel reflects the experience of many female students at coeducational universities.

Kate Douglas Wiggin, who lives in Santa Barbara, California, has attended a training school for kindergarten teachers. After graduation she is offered a position in San Francisco to teach a class sponsored by city's Public Kindergarten Society. The school, in the slums, has more than fifty students from working-class families. These children, who were previously considered disobedient, become model students under Wiggin's guidance. She later becomes an expert in early childhood education and will write and lecture on the topic and visit many schools to offer advice. Later, widowed and in poor health, she will write books for children; among her best-known stories will be *Rebecca of Sunny Brook Farm*.

Californian **Angustias de la Guerra Ord** is from a prestigious Spanish family. Her father was a captain at the Santa Barbara Presidio, and her husband was the secretary of state and acting governor of Monterey. She has witnessed many changes from Spanish to Mexican rule, then to American statehood, and believes the history of the power struggles, rebellions, and daily California life should be preserved. She dictates her memoirs to Thomas Savage, an employee at Berkeley's Bancroft Library, who transcribes her recollections for the library's collections. It will be later translated into English and published by the Academy of American Franciscan History in 1956 as *Occurences in Hispanic California*.

ARTS

Catharine Ann Drinker, an aspiring artist, writes to George Corliss at the Pennsylvania Academy of Fine Arts. She is taking a class for "amateur ladies" and wishes the school would offer life-drawing classes for "serious women students."[182] Drinker eventually completes her training through private study and becomes a respected artist.

She will later be invited to the academy to lecture on perspective. As one of the earliest female art instructors, she will inspire younger women.

Joining Forces

Susan B. Anthony and **Elizabeth Cady Stanton** have drafted a constitutional amendment for national suffrage. At their request, California senator Aaron Sargent presents it to Congress as the Anthony Amendment. Legislators take no action, but it will be introduced to Congress annually until it becomes the Nineteenth Amendment.

— 1879 —

Education and Scholarship

Rosaline Cunningham, a black schoolteacher, has been working in the Mississippi public schools for nearly a decade, supporting her family. Their situation changed when federal troops were removed from the South and white Democrats took control of the state. Her wages were cut so severely that her family is unable to survive. She writes to the Kansas governor explaining her situation, adding that many other black families are in the same plight. She asks if there is public or private money to fund travel for her family and neighbors.

Since Reconstruction ended, conditions have worsened in the South for African Americans. The Democrats want to close all public schools for blacks. White farmers and landowners exploit black workers by paying subsistence wages. Whites want to reclaim control of the South, and they terrorize African Americans. Gangs roam the South, fighting and killing blacks, and armed men guard polling places, barring black men from voting. Thousands of African Americans are fleeing north, many to Kansas. Called the Exodusters, they seek a new home where they can live peacefully. This year 6,000 blacks will immigrate to Kansas.[183]

Religion

Martha McWhirter, who lives in Belton, Texas, feels restricted by her husband's demand that she account for all money she spends. Deciding to earn her own income she sells milk, butter, and eggs. Talking with her neighbors, she discover many who have similar problems. Under McWhirter's guidance they establish the Sanctificationists, a cooperative and religious work community. They live by the Bible and discuss their religious experiences and dreams. They work as laundresses and earn money from selling butter, eggs, and cloth they weave, putting the money into a common fund. As the savings grow they buy a house, then a hotel and farm that they will manage. Within a decade more than fifty members will join the community. Work is divided among the members, and each works four hours daily, devoting the rest of the day to reading, music, or painting.

Arts

May Alcott publishes *Studying Art Abroad and How to Do It Cheaply* in Boston. A talented artist, Alcott has studied in Europe, supported by her sister, writer Louisa May Alcott. This is a timely guide; hundreds of young women are traveling abroad to study art. Alcott critiques the schools that allow women, warning the reader that some offer inferior instruction yet cost more than the all-male schools. She recommends that women study privately rather than attend low-quality schools; and more teachers now accept female students, especially in Paris.

Artist **Alice Barber** is commissioned by the Pennsylvania Academy of Fine Arts to commemorate the school's introduction of life-drawing classes for women. She completes *Female Life Class*, which shows artist Susan Macdowell painting from a live female model. Barber has studied privately with the famous painter Thomas Eakins and has trained in Paris and Rome. She will later marry art instructor Charles Hallowell Stephens and become well known, winning many medals and prizes. In her Philadelphia studio she will earn many commissions for portraits and landscapes. She will also be noted for her realistic book and magazine illustrations.

Portraitist **Cornelia Adele Fassett**, who lives in Washington, D.C., with her photographer husband, completes an oil painting, *The Electoral Commission in Open Session.* When the outcome of the Tilden-Hayes 1876 presidential election was unclear, Congress chose a commission to decide. There was much excitement in town about who would be chosen, and emotions ran high. Fassett wanted to commemorate the event and has been working on it for several years. The work shows a commissioner speaking to a large audience that includes prominent Americans. She painted some of the faces from life and others using her husband's photographs. The government later buys the work for the Capitol. The piece continues to attract attention, and nearly twenty-five years later a critic in *Pearson's Magazine* comments, "The likeness of nearly all [the faces] are so faithful as to be a constant source of wonder and delight."[184]

JOINING FORCES

Frances Willard, a former teacher and college dean in Illinois, is elected president of the Women's Christian Temperance Union (WCTU). She expands the organization's goals beyond temperance. She has boundless energy and wants members to reform society; she frequently tells them "to do everything." To incorporate her broader goals, the group's slogan becomes "For God and Home and Native Land." She will organize the group into thirty-nine departments, including education, health, welfare, labor reform, prison reform, social purity, and peace. Members in the departments will educate the public and lobby for legislation. Willard expands the work internationally, sending missionaries to organize in Asia and Europe; she will later form a World's Women's Christian Temperance Union. Each year she will travel thousands of miles throughout the United States to promote temperance. Under her leadership the group will become the largest reform movement of American women. She will remain president for twenty years, until her death, when the group's focus will narrow to prohibition and total abstinence.

The WCTU is primarily a white, middle-class Protestant group, and members have little interest in organizing immigrants or African Americans. Because Willard wants the support of southern women, she allows groups to be segregated. Although some black women form local WCTU groups, they deplore the segregation policies and often prefer to support temperance through their own churches and clubs.

LAW AND POLITICS

Lawyer **Belva Lockwood** is a member of the Washington, D.C., bar and has a successful practice. Several years ago, when one of her cases came to federal court, she was denied permission to speak. Outraged at this injustice, she has been lobbying and persuading congressmen to allow female lawyers the right to practice in federal courts. Due to her persistence, Congress passes a bill allowing this.

— 1880 —

WORK

As American industry expands, more people leave farms to seek urban employment. In the past twenty years the number of workers in transportation, construction, and manufacturing has increased 300 percent. As corporations grow and oil, steel, railroad, and finance conglomerates are formed, the volume of record keeping and correspondence increases, causing changes in office work. In prewar days several male clerks could handle a small business's records, which were handwritten. Now more businessmen buy typewriters, which are more efficient for the increasing volume of paperwork. Women learn to type and use office machines in high schools and business institutes, and they are replacing male clerks, who now work as supervisors or administrators. During the past decade the number of employed stenographers and typists increased from 154 to 5,000, and the percentage of women in these jobs grew from 5 to 40 percent. Since the typewriter is new in American businesses and there is no tradition of male typists, females are accepted and sought out by employers, who pay them less than men. Women like office work; it is considered respectable work, it pays more than factory jobs, and it is less restrictive than teaching, where personal lives are regulated and marriage forbidden. Most typists are young, white, and single.[185]

Americans continue to move west, and more women are making the trek. Ten years ago almost 4,000 women went west; this year nearly 7,000 do. One is **Nelly Cashman**, a prospector who follows the booms. While awaiting her fortune, she supports herself by providing fellow migrants lodging and supplies. She ran a restaurant in Nevada and a boardinghouse in British Columbia, and now she has relocated to Tombstone, Arizona — site of a silver boom. She opens a hotel and a store selling clothing, boots, and groceries. She will eventually make her fortune, getting $100,000 from a claim.[186]

EDUCATION AND SCHOLARSHIP

The number of American teachers has increased from 85,000 to 153,000 during the last decade. Women make up 68 percent of all teachers.[187]

More women are pursuing higher education; they comprise about one-third of all college students and will earn 19 percent of all baccalaureates. The 28 percent who attend women's colleges appreciate the close community, female professors, and feeling of belonging. Many of these alumnae will become settlement house founders and Progressive Era reformers.[188]

JOINING FORCES

Sarah Winnemucca, daughter of a Paiute chief, has witnessed trouble with corrupt Indian agents and land-hungry white settlers. Her tribe was removed from their home in Nevada to an Oregon reservation and later exiled to Washington Territory amidst hostile tribes. Because Winnemucca speaks fluent English she is the tribe's spokeswomen; she often travels, speaking on injustices they have endured. This year she is invited to Washington, D.C., to meet President Rutherford Hayes and Secretary of the Interior Carl Schurz. The leaders are sympathetic and promise that the tribe can return to Oregon and will receive land allotments. But an Indian agent prevents this, fearing trouble from white settlers. Winnemucca later publishes her autobiography, *Life among the Paiutes: Their Wrongs and Claims.*

— 1881 —

DOMESTICITY

Secretary of the Interior Carl Schurz wants Indians to become assimilated into American society, and this includes accepting traditional Victorian gender roles. Schurz, like many reformers, misunderstands the tribal division of labor by gender, since it is different from American customs. Schurz is aware that Indian women are farmers and that they often carry tepees and other equipment while traveling. He comments,

"The Indian woman has so far been only a beast of burden."[189] Schurz and other reformers want Indian women to make the household the center of their lives. They send Indian children to government schools and strip them of all tribal identity. They are put in Western clothing, taught English, and forbidden to speak their native tongue. Boys learn to farm, and girls are taught sewing, cooking, and housekeeping and often placed with local families as domestic servants.

An article in *Scribner's*, "A Mother's Duty to Her Girls," concerns the lack of domestic training for girls in many schools. The writer urges American mothers to teach their daughters the importance of domestic life, reminding the reader that "in spite of the efforts of the strong-minded to eliminate the womanhood from our women, every true woman will continue to find her fullest development and her serenest happiness as wife and mother."[190]

EDUCATION AND SCHOLARSHIP

Sophia Packard and **Harriet Giles**, white Baptist missionaries from New England, travel to Atlanta. Disturbed by the segregated education and the lack of facilities for black youth, they decide to found a school for black females. With money from local black ministers, they begin classes in a Baptist church basement. Within a year there will be 200 students, ages fifteen through fifty-two, whom they train to teach, become missionaries, or do church work. The school will expand, later be named Spelman Seminary, after a generous donor, and eventually be supported by the Woman's American Baptist Home Missionary Society. A nursing program and other vocational courses will be added, and Spelman will eventually become a four-year liberal arts college for women.[191]

Booker T. Washington and **Olivia Davidson**, graduates of Hampton Institute, establish a coeducational normal school for African Americans in Tuskegee, Alabama. It opens in a log house with thirty pupils, later expanding to include more buildings and a farm where students can work to fund their education. Davidson contacts abolitionists and other potential donors, and she raises thousands of dollars for supplies, books, maps, and clothing. The school, later called Tuskegee Institute, will be famous for its extensive academic and vocational curriculum.

Marion Talbot, a recent Boston University alumna, feels isolated and uncertain about her future. Her mother, Emily, an active reformer, suggests creating a group of female college graduates, and they establish the Association of Collegiate Alumnae. They contact women throughout the United States, and soon many local branches are formed. Members exchange ideas and information about careers and encourage younger women to attend college. The organization flourishes and eventually becomes the American Association for University Women.

Susan B. Anthony, **Matilda Joslyn Gage,** and **Elizabeth Cady Stanton** publish the first two volumes of the *History of Woman Suffrage*. They have been collecting materials for several years, and the work is based on speeches, letters, pamphlets, testimonials, resolutions, and other documents. Clergyman William Ellery Channing praises the work in a London newspaper, and the *New York Sun* also compliments it. Stanton later recalls that reaction was more favorable than she expected.

ARTS

Amy Fay, who could improvise on the piano at age four, trained at the New England Conservatory and later traveled to Berlin for advanced study. It was a wonderful environment for a young musician. Many prominent conductors and performers lived in Germany; she took classes with Franz Liszt and attended concerts by Clara Schumann, Anton Rubinstein, and Hans von Bülow. During the six-year stay she wrote to her parents with glowing praise about her studies and about the excitement of hearing famous musicians. This year she publishes her letters as *Music Study in Germany*, in New York. The book is popular with Americans and will inspire thousands of young women to follow in her footsteps. It will be reprinted many times and translated into German and French.

JOINING FORCES

Southern black women who work as sharecroppers or field laborers face conditions little better than slavery. Their wages are at subsistence level, usually half of male earnings, and employers deduct for sickness or lateness. Many women move to the city to work as cooks, laundresses, and child care nurses for white families. In these jobs too they are exploited.

In Atlanta laundresses are tired of low wages and call a mass meeting for collective action. Three thousand women attend, including other domestic workers. They form a union, elect officers, and demand higher wages. The public ignores them, and the workers strike. The white community is outraged. Strike leaders are arrested, landlords raise workers' rents, and the city council proposes to increase the laundresses' license fees. The *Atlanta Constitution* calls them the "Washing Amazons." The strikers eventually return to work at the old rates. Black women in other cities are also unable to improve working conditions. In response they migrate north, hoping to find better work. Between 1870 and 1910, two hundred thousand African Americans will leave the South.[192]

Susette La Flesche Tibbles, daughter of an Omaha chief, presents a paper, "The Position, Occupation, and Culture of Indian Women," to a meeting of the Association for the Advancement of Women. Through her writings and speeches, Tibbles, a well-known spokeswoman for the Omaha and Ponca tribes, is educating the public on the injustices done to the tribes. Several years ago she toured the East Coast, speaking to civic groups and literary clubs and testifying before Congress. Known as "Bright Eyes," she has gained much sympathy and support for Indians' rights.

Colorado writer **Helen Hunt Jackson**, who respects Native Americans and believes they were treated badly, publishes *A Century of Dishonor: A Sketch of the United States Government's Dealings with Some of the Indian Tribes*, in New York. Having done extensive research at New York's Astor Library, she describes the unfairness of American policies, explaining how the Poncas and others were cheated out of land and treated badly by agents. She sends a copy to all officials involved in Indian affairs but receives no official response. Later she will write *Ramona*, another novel on Native Americans, which will sell well. Jackson's work is influential in getting the Dawes Act passed, giving land allotments to the tribes.

— 1882 —

WORK

In Salt Lake City, the Women's Relief Society founds the Deseret Hospital and appoints Mormon physician Ellen Ferguson as director. At leader Brigham Young's suggestion, the facility also offers classes in nursing and obstetrics. Young encourages women to become nurses and doctors and sends many Mormons to women's medical colleges in the East. By the early 1890s Utah will have one of the highest proportions of female doctors in the West. Because there are fewer physicians on the frontier, women are more easily accepted as doctors than are their colleagues in eastern urban areas.

ARTS

Philadelphia's art academy has been adding more classes for women. They first offered a life-drawing course with plaster casts of nude male statues, although a fig leaf was discreetly placed over the genitals. Later they allowed women to draw from live nude females, and five years ago male nudes modeled in female drawing classes. The public shock still reverberates. An irate Philadelphian scolds the academy's director and tells him that young ladies from "refined and godly" households have no business studying nude males or females, that this will ruin their innocence and corrupt females' "chaste and delicate thoughts."[193]

JOINING FORCES

Indian reformers have been meeting to discuss how the tribes can be best assimilated into American culture. Most believe that Indians must become Christians and accept Victorian gender roles. A noted spokeswoman is Philadelphian **Amelia Stone Quinton**, who has formed a committee of prominent Philadelphia women, later called the Women's National Indian Association. Quinton has already traveled throughout the United States urging Americans to improve conditions for the Indians. She has circulated several petitions that were sent to Congress. This year she drafts another petition calling for a new policy that gives education, legal rights, and land allotments to Indians. Nearly 100,000 people sign it, and Massachusetts senator Henry Dawes will present it to Congress.

— 1883 —

DOMESTICITY

Publisher Cyrus Curtis's newspaper, *The Tribune and Farmer*, includes a women's column. His wife, **Louisa Curtis**, thinks it can be improved, and he assigns her to write it. Readers like the new column so much that the Curtises expand it as a supplement to the *Tribune*, the *Ladies' Journal*. By the year's end

circulation of the supplement is at 25,000, and they devote themselves to it full-time. With a goal of improving standards in American homes, they will hire prominent writers, famous illustrators, and leading experts to advise on fashion, child care, home decorating, and cooking. Within two years the publication, renamed the *Ladies' Home Journal*, will see circulation increase to 270,000.[194]

WORK

Californian **Isabel del Valle**'s Rancho Camulo, like many other ranches owned by Hispanic families, is in decline. Before the Americans settled in California, most ranches were self-sufficient; they had dairies and vineyards, and the owners raised cattle. They were popular spots for travelers and visiting friends, and ranch owners were noted for their hospitality. As Americans took power, many Hispanics lost their land in title disputes, to white squatters, or because they were unable to pay the increased taxes. Writer **Helen Hunt Jackson** visits Rancho Camulo to get a flavor of Spanish California for her novel *Ramona*. Jackson's novel will be published next year; it will be reprinted many times, bringing fame to del Valle's ranch. By providing lodging for the hundreds of curious tourists each year, she will be able to keep her property.

Physician **Katharine Layne Curran** is appointed curator of botany at the California Academy of Sciences. In medical school she had studied botany, which was important because doctors need to use plants in order to prepare medicines. After receiving her M.D., Curran was unable to establish a successful practice and worked for the academy's herbarium curator. She will keep her new job for ten years and bring higher standards to the facility by adding new specimens, classifying them, and improving the academy's publication.

Melvil Dewey, a founder of the American Librarian Association and of the *Library Journal*, has long urged women to enter the field. Dewey advocates librarianship for educated women as a good alternative to teaching, pointing out that the quiet and uplifting atmosphere will offset the low pay. Dewey is now Columbia College's chief librarian, and to the dismay of trustees at the all-male school, he hires several Wellesley graduates to help him organize the library. Later he will insist that women be admitted to his library training program; when denied classroom space, he will teach in a storage room. Dewey's strong stance on women's suitability as librarians helps establish it as a female-dominated profession.

EDUCATION AND SCHOLARSHIP

Fifty-seven-year-old **Martha Lamb** writes children's stories and magazine articles and also enjoys history. Six years ago she published a book on colonial New York that was praised by historian George Bancroft, and she belongs to several local historical societies. This year she purchases the *Magazine of American History*, a respectable journal with financial trouble. With energy and a flair for editing, she develops it into a professional publication with a national focus. She writes many articles, solicits others, includes book reviews, and prints many original documents. She will edit the publication until she dies ten years later.

ARTS

Julia Britton Hooks, who formerly taught music at Kentucky's Berea College, was one of the college's first black instructors. She now lives in Memphis, where she teaches school. Active in the black community, she wants to promote classical music. This year she founds the Liszt-Mullard Club to introduce people to serious music and raise money. Her goal is to provide scholarships for young aspiring black musicians. She will later establish the Hooks School of Music, an integrated facility. Students will include future prominent composers like W.

C. Handy, who will be called the "father of the blues."

Writer **Ella Wheeler**, who has been in print since age fourteen, submits *Poems of Passion* to a Chicago publisher, but they reject the work as "immoral." Newspapers pick up the story, and another firm eagerly offers to publish it. Because of the intrigue and hint of scandal, people rush out to buy the book, and 60,000 copies will be sold, making Wheeler famous. She will publish much more poetry, which the public will love. Critics, however, will never take her work seriously, which will embitter her.[195]

Artist **Mary Hallock Foote** writes and illustrates *The Led-Horse Claim*, a story about the silver boom in Leadville, Colorado. It is serialized in the *Century*, then later published as a book, and is the first of nearly sixteen books on western life and culture that she will write and illustrate. Because she accepts her editor's insistence on happy endings, she gets little attention from critics. A later generation of reviewers acknowledges her realistic portrayals of western mining families.

New Yorker **Emma Lazarus** is a well-published Jewish poet. Recently her sympathy has turned to the Jews who are fleeing Russian and German pogroms and immigrating to the United States. More come each year, and by 1890 there will be 80,000 Jewish refugees living in New York City.[196] Many are illiterate, have few job skills, and live in poverty. Her compassion aroused, she now writes on Jewish history and oppression.

Frédéric Bartholdi's Statue of Liberty has arrived in New York City from France. Congress will finance erection of the statue, but not the base. The Bartholdi Statue Pedestal Campaign is formed to raise money. Among their activities is a contest for writing an inscription to be engraved on the pedestal's base. When the Bartholdi contest is announced, Lazarus decides to compete. Those who enter the competition include prominent writers Walt Whitman, Mark Twain, and Henry Wadsworth

Longfellow, but it is Emma Lazarus who wins. Her sonnet "The New Colossus" describes the statue as the "Mother of Exiles" who lifts her torch to welcome the oppressed, the homeless, and the poor to America.

Fifty-six-year-old artist **Candace Thurber Wheeler** leaves her job with painter and glassmaker Louis Tiffany, where she created embroideries and designed textiles for the homes of prominent Americans. Wanting more women work as designer and interior decorators, she founds the Associated Artists, an all-female firm in New York City. The artists will have a large patronage. Working for American homes, they will design and manufacture textiles, create patterned wallpapers and carpets, and make murals with themes from American literature. They will experiment with bold colors and different textures. Wheeler helps popularize American designs and helps bring about the art nouveau movement.

LAW AND POLITICS

Suffragists in Washington Territory have been working for female enfranchisement for thirty years. Many bills introduced to the legislators have been rejected, but this year's bill passes. The female voters take their responsibility to bring morality to the populace seriously and will help defeat a corrupt administration in Seattle. The advocacy of many women for prohibition, however, will lead to disenfranchisement. Four years later a gambler indicted by a grand jury will charge that it is unlawful for women to sit on juries or vote, and the territory's supreme court overturns the law.

— 1884 —

WORK

The Massachusetts Bureau of Statistics of Labor publishes a report, "The Working Girls of Boston," the results of a study done four years ago. The investigators found that 20 percent of the city's females held jobs, and nearly half of these were domestic workers. They studied a sample group of 1,032 women who were employed in work other than domestic service. Eight percent worked as carpet sewers, in restaurants, or in laundries; 12 percent were bookkeepers, clerks, or saleswomen; and the remaining 80 percent worked in manufacturing. These jobs included sewing clothing, making or binding books, processing tobacco, packing foodstuffs, and working in factories making furniture, musical instruments, paper, boxes, rubber, straw, or elastic goods. They discovered that most of the workers lived in undesirable housing, which was often factories with air pollution, and in cramped and dirty apartments with inadequate toilet facilities. Most women were in poor health from standing or sitting long hours and from breathing dust or chemicals. Wages were low, and the average income was $5.17 per week, which often supported whole families. Most earned less than men in the same jobs.[197]

EDUCATION AND SCHOLARSHIP

Methodists in Baltimore, inspired by the opportunities for men at Johns Hopkins, establish the Women's College of Baltimore, which will later become Goucher College. Other southern educators are also founding seminaries for girls. There is Mary Baldwin in Virginia, Judson in Alabama, and Agnes Scott in Georgia; all will later become colleges.

The Mississippi State Normal and Industrial School is founded for white females. Other normal schools are being built in Texas, Oklahoma, and the Carolinas. American teachers are needed for the growing urban populations and in the West. Most normal schools have lower tuition than colleges, and teaching is a good occupation for the thousands of women widowed by the war.

Mt. Holyoke's reputation is being challenged as other eastern female schools are founded, and there is a movement to expand and improve its academic standards. New trustees are elected, and **Elizabeth Blanchard** is appointed the new principal. She starts a college department, adds more courses, including sciences and laboratory study, and hires faculty with college degrees.

Joseph Taylor, a Quaker doctor and businessmen, has left his fortune for a women's college with the same high standards as Haverford (a men's school). Bryn Mawr is founded, whose goal is to train teachers and educate future mothers.

RELIGION

Ursuline nun **Sister St. Angela Abair** travels to Montana Territory to establish a mission for the Northern Cheyennes. The facility will include a girl's boarding school where Cheyenne girls will be educated and converted to Christianity. It will begin as a one-room schoolhouse but later expand to a boarding school. Although the girls do learn to read and write, many are unhappy with the rules forbidding tribal dress or language, and punishment is harsh for those who fail to learn Christian prayers.

LAW AND POLITICS

Ida Wells, a young black Tennessee teacher, commutes to Fisk University at night, hoping to qualify for a job in the Memphis public schools. While taking her usual seat on the train, she is told by the conductor to sit in the second-class smoking section, now reserved for blacks. She refuses to move, and the conductor shoves her off the train. Wells sues under the 1875 Civil Rights Act, which prohibits segregation in public facilities. She wins and receives $500, but several years later the state's supreme court reverses the decision.[198]

Last year the U.S. Supreme Court ruled in *Civil Rights Cases* that the American gov-

Ida B. Wells

"I'D RATHER GO DOWN IN HISTORY AS ONE LONE NEGRO WHO DARED TO TELL THE GOVERNMENT THAT IT HAD DONE A DASTARDLY THING THAN TO SAVE MY SKIN BY TAKING BACK WHAT I HAVE SAID." --1917

Ida B. Wells, age 25, engraving, 1887. (Library of Congress.) Wells taught school in Memphis, Tennessee. She also attended college at night, joined the local lyceum, and taught Sunday school. She had family responsibilities as well: at age 16 her parents died from yellow fever and she undertook the support of her five younger siblings.

Wells later became a newspaper publisher, writer, and prominent reformer for black civil rights. She refused to compromise on vital issues. The quote below the photo is her retort to secret service men who threatened to arrest her for treason during World War I when Wells spoke out against an incident in Houston, Texas. Black soldiers were stationed at a camp waiting to be sent overseas. A riot had erupted, several whites were killed, and the blacks blamed, although they were defending themselves. Several were court-martialed, hanged and thrown in a common grave. Wells protested the government's action, and her outspokenness probably prevented her arrest.

ernment does not have to protect people from discrimination in public places — that blacks can be limited to "separate but equal" facilities — thereby invalidating the 1875 act. Southern lawmakers are enacting Jim Crow laws that permit separate facilities and seating for blacks in schools, restaurants, theaters, buses, and hotels. They use the Court's ruling to uphold these laws. Wells, like most blacks, deplores the ruling, and she is among the first to challenge it. Her case against the railroad initiates her long career in fighting for justice for blacks.

Lawyer **Belva Lockwood** accepts the nomination as presidential candidate for the National Equal Rights Party at a California convention. She does not expect victory, but believes women have the right to run for public office. Her party supports equal rights for all, universal peace, uniform marriage and divorce laws, and protection of industrial workers. She is an excellent speaker, witty and knowledgeable. Although the press ridicules her campaign, she wins 4,000 popular votes, mostly from New York, California, and Illinois. She also carries the entire Indiana electoral vote and one-half of the Oregon electorate. Democrat Grover Cleveland wins the election.[199]

— 1885 —

DOMESTICITY

Magazine publishing has expanded since the war. Twenty years ago only 700 journals were in print, and this year there are more than 3,000. There is increasing specialization in American society, and many new publications address specific interests or occupations. A new one is *Good Housekeeping*, put out by Clark Bryan in Holyoke, Massachusetts, for the "Interests of the Higher Life of the Household." He offers articles for wives and mothers on household management and decoration, child care, fashion, and beauty, and publishes fiction and poetry. Later the magazine staff will establish a laboratory to test household products and appliances, rating them for consumers. Readers love it, and within a decade circulation will be at 55,000.[200]

WORK

Writer **Gertrude Bustill Mossell**, from

a prominent black Philadelphia family, is well known for her writings on the rights and the history of black women. Her articles have appeared in newspapers in New York City, Indianapolis, and Philadelphia. Editors of the *Freeman*, a New York African American publication, ask her to become a columnist, and she accepts the job. In her first piece she addresses women's suffrage, telling her readers to become informed about politics so that they can vote intelligently when they get enfranchised. Later columns will address employment; Mossell encourages women to train for a profession, insisting they do not need to choose between the home and work.

ARTS

Many women who work as organists or choir directors in Protestant churches have composed hymns or written verses for traditional music, but these are generally unknown outside the church. Composer **Eva Munson Smith** has collected religious compositions and lyrics by women, and she publishes them. Her book includes 2,500 verses and more than 50 hymns.[201]

Violinist **Jeanette Thurber** establishes the National Conservatory of Music in New York City. Thurber studied music in Paris at a government-funded music school, and she thinks Americans deserve public music education. Unable to get government support, she finances the school herself. She welcomes male and female students of all races and includes women on the faculty. She also creates a scholarship program for talented African Americans. The school attracts attention and good staff; for several years it will be headed by composer Antonín Dvořák.

— 1886 —

EDUCATION AND SCHOLARSHIP

Lucy Craft Laney, a black educator, opens a girls' school in Augusta, Georgia.

A pregnant woman and her family on their land claim in Guthrie, Oklahoma Territory, 1889. (Western History Collections, University of Oklahoma Library.) In the 1830s, American government officials set aside most of present-day Oklahoma for the resettlement of eastern Indian tribes. This region was called Indian Territory. Later, as settlers moved west, there was more demand for land. In 1889 the government opened part of Indian Territory (later designated as Oklahoma Territory) to non–Indian settlement. This family is among 50,000 who claimed homesteads. Their temporary house, a tent and lean-to, marks their claim. This woman will give birth in rough conditions, but thousands like her were willing to endure hardships for land ownership and a new life.

With financial support from the local Presbyterian church and the black community, she begins classes in a church basement. She takes no salary, but uses donations to run her school. She later rents a two-story house, and the next year the school offers teacher training and industrial study. By the turn of the century the facility has expanded and will include a kindergarten, a nursing training program, and classes in printing. Known as the Haines Normal and Industrial Institute, it will be considered the equal of the well-known Tuskegee Institute.

New Orleans's economy has been racked by the Civil War, and many buildings are in ruin. Educators' priority is to rebuild and found schools so that the city's youth can be educated locally. Merchant Paul Tulane has given money to upgrade a private university for white men, and it has been renamed for him. The wife of a Tulane trustee asks Josephine Newcomb, a local philanthropist, to finance a women's college. Newcomb agrees and stipulates that it be named for her daughter who died. The Sophia Newcomb Memorial College is founded, as part of Tulane University, for young white women.

RELIGION

Methodist **Lucinda Helm**, who lives in Macon, Georgia, wants more authority for church women. While attending a conference of southern churches she persuades officials to establish a Woman's Department of Church Extension, whose main goal will be to raise money to build and repair parsonages. Appointed the group's secretary, Helm uses her position to expand their responsibilities. Four years later she persuades officials to change the group's name to the Woman's Parsonage and Home Missionary Society.

Male church leaders in many denominations doubt the value of home missions, maintaining that funds should be directed overseas. Women, aware of local poverty and problems, want to help American communities as well, and they will eventually establish a powerful network of women's home missions.

ARTS

Artist **Emily Sartain** is appointed principal of the Philadelphia School of Design, a women's school for professional and commercial artists. Wanting to offer more advanced work and tougher classes, she improves the curriculum by introducing classes in perspective and design and by hiring new faculty, including some avant-garde artists. She also hires live models for life-drawing classes. She will head the school for more than thirty years, and her pioneering advances help many female artists get a solid training.

Julia Ettie Crane founds the Crane Normal Institute in Potsdam, New York, where women can study for careers as music teachers. More American women are becoming trained musicians, but they are still barred from most orchestras and bands. Teaching is one alternative, and by 1910, 60 percent of all music teachers will be female.[202]

JOINING FORCES

The Knights of Labor is a union that admits women and men of all races. Currently nearly 50,000 females belong, representing about 10 percent of the union's total membership. **Leonora Berry**, a widowed Irish Catholic hosiery worker, is a long-standing member who has served as representative and delegate. At this year's convention she is appointed general investigator of women's conditions, a new position. She will help organize women and encourage labor reform. She will visit hundreds of cities, inspect

An African American family outside their dugout near Guthrie, Oklahoma Territory, 1889. (Western History Collections, University of Oklahoma Library.) The family is dressed in their best, and the woman's clean white apron is an attempt to look elegant. Copies of this photo would be sent to friends and relatives back home. The family's dugout, with a timbered front, is built into a hillside. Pioneers commonly built these until money could be found for a better home. Dugout living was primitive. Such dwellings were difficult to keep clean; dirt would often fall from the ceiling, walls might leak in a rainstorm, and bugs, snakes, and small animals often moved in.

To help freed slaves, Congress passed the Southern Homestead act in 1868 offering public domain lands in the South to ex-slaves and white southern loyalists. The project, however, was unsuccessful. The Freedmen's Bureau, which was to provide money to the families for resettlement, did not get the necessary funding. When the Act was repealed in 1876, many black families moved further west, to Oklahoma, Texas, Kansas, and Colorado. Some black families joined new western black towns; others homesteaded in more isolated rural areas.

factories, help organize unions, testify to Congress on reform, give speeches, distribute literature, and answer correspondence. It will be difficult work. Many women refuse to join unions, others decline leadership positions, and factory managers often refuse her permission to inspect their facilities. The church will attack her as a " lady tramp" for doing this public work, and while traveling she will have to leave her sons with relatives. Remarrying four years later, she will resign her position but not be replaced. The Knights of Labor, now at peak membership, will decline and lose power from internal problems, leadership battles, and conflicts with other unions.[203]

— 1887 —

DOMESTICITY

The debate on female enfranchisement continues in publications and speeches. Most Americans are against it, fearing that it will destroy family life. One forceful opponent is Senator George Vest, a Missouri Democrat. Addressing Congress, he proclaims that universal suffrage will destroy the county. Women are too delicate for worldly pursuits like politics, he warns. Voting would remove them from their pedestals at home, where they guide their families "toward the good and pure." Women, he insists, with their great moral sensibilities, make "the name of wife, mother, and sister next to that of God himself."[204]

WORK

There is much public concern about the increasing number of women in the labor force. Some Americans are distressed by the gap between the "ideal" woman (the wife and mother at home) and the reality — the thousands who need to earn a living. Others deplore the wretched conditions and low wages

of industrial workers, and many fear for the morality of young urban working women. Because of wide-spread interest, journalists are writing on the topic. An editor at New York's *Tribune* assigns journalist **Helen Campbell** to write a series on wage-earning women. Campbell, already known for her work on employment and poverty in the United States, interviews female servants, garment makers, and department store clerks in New York City. Her series is published as a book, *Prisoners of Poverty: Women Wage Workers, Their Trades and Their Lives.* Campbell and others who investigate the wretched conditions of many female wage earners help publicize the problem and encourage reformers to action.

RELIGION

Lucy Rider Meyer and her husband established a training school for missionaries in Chicago several years ago. She is now interested in the deaconess movement. This originated in Germany in the 1830s, when a Lutheran pastor began a school to train church women for social service work. Methodists want to create a similar program in the United States, and this year Meyer opens a Methodist Deaconess home in Chicago. Several women rent rooms in the city, preparing for careers in which they advise, support, and help convert the urban poor. Although they do not take vows, the women dress alike in black dresses with white collars and cuffs and receive a small stipend. Conflicts will arise later as more facilities are built and various groups compete for authority over the women, but by late 1930s the deaconesses will be ruled by a single church board of directors. The movement gives females employment and brings more laywomen into official church positions. By 1900 there will be more than one hundred such American homes representing many Protestant denominations. Women will train as deaconesses through the early 1900s, but their numbers will decline after the 1920s, with the increasing availability of secular jobs such as nursing and social work.

LAW AND POLITICS

Women in Utah Territory lose their right to vote. Many American lawmakers are repelled by polygamy, a common practice among Mormons in the territory. An earlier bill forbidding it failed to pass Congress, and now a stronger bill, the Edmunds-Tucker Act, which prohibits both plural marriage and female suffrage in Utah Territory, is enacted into law.

In Washington Territory females have often served as jurors. Several years ago, **Mollie Rosencrantz** appealed her indictment by a territorial grand jury on which married women served, claiming that their presence made the decision unconstitutional. She lost her appeal in *Rosencrantz v. Territory of Washington*, but dissension was strong. Judge Turner declared his "repugnance" for having married women on juries, since their "life theater is and will continue to be and ought to be ... primarily the home circle." Now the same territorial court reverses its earlier decision. *Harland v. Territory* prohibits women in Washington Territory from being jurors. Most American territories and states already ban females from jury duty, and by 1942 twenty states will forbid it.[205]

— 1 8 8 8 —

WORK

Red Cross founder **Clara Barton** gives a Memorial Day speech, addressing women's work during the Civil War. The need for women's labor forced them to gain self-confidence, develop skills and use their talents, she explains; their accomplishments forced American men to recognize their value as workers. After the war, she suggests,

American women were "at least fifty years in advance of the normal position which continued peace ... would have assigned [them]."[206]

EDUCATION AND SCHOLARSHIP

Several years ago, New Yorker **Annie Nathan Meyer** entered Columbia University's program for women. She was outraged that the female students were tested on the contents of lectures they were forbidden to attend, and after marrying she left the program. Reflecting on her experience, she believes women deserve a college with the high standards of the all-male Columbia. She and several friends draft a letter proposing that a female annex to Columbia be founded, supported by funds from private individuals. Many distinguished New Yorkers sign the letter, which they send to the Columbia trustees. Meyer then publishes an article in *The Nation* outlining plans and asking for endorsement and money. New Yorkers respond favorably. The new school will be called Frederick A. P. Barnard College, after a former Columbia president who supported coeducation. Meyer chairs the planning committee and heads the fund-raising drive. She recruits the first trustees and will later serve on the board for nearly fifty years. Proud of her Jewish heritage, she wants "desirable" Jewish women to enroll and also recruits worthy black candidates. The school will develop an excellent academic reputation, especially for its anthropology program. In the late twentieth century it will merge with Columbia University. Meyer will have a successful writing career, but she will be ambivalent about women's role in American society and will become a prominent anti-suffragist.

Because female professors are rarely hired at coeducational universities, employment at women's colleges is a good option, and Vassar and Wellesley prefer them to male faculty because they are good role models. Many of these women stay single and devote

Creek women in Okemah, Indian Territory, doing the Ribbon Dance, 1880s. (Western History Collections, University of Oklahoma Library.) This traditional dance affirmed the role of women in the Creek Muskogee tribe. When government agents and missionaries who worked with the tribes tried to convince them to relinquish native customs, Native American women were particularly resistant. The white way of living, with the male as household head and most valued family member, held little appeal.

their lives to scholarship, teaching, and the college.

Lucy Maynard Salmon's career exemplifies this lifestyle. She has a master's degree in history from the University of Michigan and is appointed the first history professor at Vassar College. She will introduce courses in modern historical methods and techniques and offer advanced senior seminars. Salmon mentors many students, encouraging them to go on to graduate school and to find jobs other than high school teaching. As the history department chair she will allow her faculty freedom in teaching methods. She will also improve and expand the college library, help develop a flexible curriculum, and help the faculty gain more power in college policies. Active professionally, she will publish several books, help found the American Historical Association, and organize a regional association of history teachers. Remaining at Vassar until retirement, she will be among those early scholars who build the school's excellent reputation.

RELIGION

Fifty-six-year-old **Sarah Gorham**, a member of the African Methodist Episcopal Church, is appointed missionary to Africa. Several years ago she visited relatives in Liberia and saw the need for churches, schools, and health clinics. She will work in Freetown and Sierra Leone, establishing a mission school for religious training and vocational study. More American single women missionaries are being sent abroad, and like Gorham, many blacks feel a kinship with Africans and request assignment there.

ARTS

Bostonian **Clara Kathleen Rogers**, a famous retired opera singer, organizes a

A southern middle-class family in their parlor in the South, c. 1900. (North Carolina Collection, Pack Memorial Public Library, Asheville, N.C.) The parlor was the heart of the family home; the fireplace was the focus, and family photos and memorabilia were displayed with pride on the mantle. The mother's rattan rocking chair was becoming common in American homes. Mass-produced items were inexpensive and could be ordered from catalogs. The photograph is conventional for the era: the father reads the Atlanta Constitution, and the mother, the family Bible. The daughter wears a dress with fashionable leg-o'-mutton sleeves, and the son does schoolwork. A black female servant stands behind the family.

manuscript club for young composers to encourage them, help them get published, and have their works performed. Rogers sympathizes with the difficulties of beginning composers. As a young music protégée at the University of Leipzig in Germany her first choice was composition, but it was forbidden to her as unsuitable for females and she trained in voice instead. After retirement she began to write music, and although she has published several chamber pieces, she maintains that had she been allowed to study composition while young, she would have produced longer and more serious pieces.

Violinist and conductor **Caroline Nichols** founds the Fadette Women's Or-chestra of Boston. Her goal is to employ female musicians, who are barred from the Musicians Union and unable to find jobs in orchestras or bands. Beginning with six players, the group will increase to twenty. They will perform throughout North America, playing symphonies, overtures, light classics, and salon pieces and performing in parks, resorts, and theaters. The Fadettes will develop an excellent reputation as a serious women's orchestra and give employment to hundreds of female musicians. It will last through the early twentieth century.

American-trained artist **Celia Beaux**'s painting *Les Derniers jours d'enfants* has been accepted at the Paris Salon, and she takes her first trip to Europe for advanced study. There she will visit museums and study in Paris and England with noted artists, improving her style. When she later returns to Philadelphia, her career will flourish. She will accept many commissions, have solo exhibits, and receive awards and critical acclaim. By the turn of the century she will be considered one of America's leading portraitists, often compared to John Singer Sargent. Like other prominent female artists, she remains single.

JOINING FORCES

The American Federation of Labor, a national trade union, was established in 1886 to organize and protect craftsmen and skilled workers. Although their priority is organizing white, native-born, skilled male laborers, in time they do charter several women's unions. One successful group formed this year is the Chicago Ladies Federal Labor Union No. 2703. The union's organizer and secretary is **Elizabeth Morgan**, an English immigrant and former mill worker. Members include clerks, bookbinders, typists, dressmakers, music teachers, and laundresses.

— 1889 —

DOMESTICITY

Publisher and writer Edward Bok, a Dutch immigrant, is appointed editor of the *Ladies' Home Journal*. He has written a popular newspaper column for women and has a good sense of what women like to read. He will expand the magazine, adding the latest house plans, tips on home decorating, stories by famous American authors and advice columns on courting, marriage, and motherhood. Bok promotes the domestic ideal in advice columns, where the ideal woman is gentle, sweet, and self-sacrificing, and in sto-

ries where working women are generally unhappy but find love and marriage as the solution to their problems. These messages encourage readers to be satisfied with traditional lifestyles and to disregard new ideas on women's rights. Women love the updated publication, and circulation, now at 400,000, will double in eleven years.[207]

As more women work as typists and stenographers, there is a public outcry about women in offices. Newspaper editors insist that women are taking jobs from men and that office work is incompatible with female "sensibilities." Many cartoonists ridicule female clerks by portraying them spilling ink, styling their hair, and reading fashion magazines in the office. One outspoken opponent is Marion Harland, who publishes "The Incapacity of Business Women" in the *North American Review*. "Men conduct all branches of what is known as business ... more systematically and successfully than women," he reports. While female stenographers will "giggle," have "tiffs" with coworkers, and "sulk" if reprimanded, office boys are quick, punctual, and respectful. It is unwise to hire women, he warns, since they are temporary workers and will quit when they marry. This debate on female wage earners will continue well into the twentieth century, and opponents' arguments help keep women's wages and status low.[208]

WORK

As more women pursue higher education, they want more challenging employment. Other than teaching, there are few accepted vocations for female college graduates, who traditionally return home to help with domestic chores or do charity work until marriage. **Jane Addams**, a graduate of the Rockford Seminary in Illinois, is among this early generation of college graduates with few prospects for a good job. Unwilling to return to her parents' home, Addams does not want to become a missionary, and poor health has disrupted her medical school plans.

Lou and Minnie Irwin milking cows, Indian Territory, 1880s. (Western History Collections, University of Oklahoma Library.) As this photo shows, women usually did the milking on family farms. Other female chores were planting vegetable gardens, canning the produce, raising poultry, and making butter whose sale to neighbors supplemented the family income. Between the late 1860s and 1910 most Americans lived on farms. National leaders and officials in the U.S. Department of Agriculture viewed the family farm as an ideal unit to balance the nation's growing urbanization and industrialization.

On a recent trip to England, Addams was appalled at the poverty and despair in east London slums and also impressed by the work at Toynbee Hall, a settlement house run by college men, in assisting the poor. She is inspired to found a settlement house in the United States. Returning home, she and her former classmate Ellen Gates Starr find and rent the Hull mansion, a run-down building in an impoverished section of Chicago. They furnish it, move in, hire female college graduates, and begin programs for neighborhood residents, who include thousands of central and southern European immigrants. Hull House programs include medical advice, job training and placement, clubs for all ages, teas and lunches, classes and discussion groups in music, English, literature, and American customs, and lectures on politics, history, and economics. They will later provide recreational activities, a health clinic, a kindergarten, a nursery for infants of working mothers, a library, and a meeting space for unions, reform groups, and other civic activities. The Hull House program expands and will be a great success, benefiting the urban poor and giving employment to many educated women. The staff will have close ties with faculty at the University of Chicago, many prominent women in civic clubs, local government officials, and state reform groups. As the program and facility expand they will become self-supporting, raising thousands of dollars — much of it from generous and wealthy Chicago women. There are other settlement houses in the United States, but Hull House is among the most successful. The work of Addams and her staff ushers in social work, a new career for educated women that will grow in popularity.

Susan La Flesche, who grew up on the Omaha Indian reservation in Nebraska, graduates first in her class from the Women's Medical College in Pennsylvania. Her scholarship in high school at Virginia's Hampton Institute was so superb that the Women's National Indian Association awarded her a full scholarship for medical school. She will later return to Nebraska as a physician for a government school for Omaha Indian children. She will be active in community affairs, help organize a county medical society, and chair the local board of health. Because of her skills as a physician and her dedication to civic affairs, Omahas will view her as a tribal leader, an honor rarely accorded to a female.

ARTS

Boston artist **Lilla Cabot Perry** is in Paris attending an exhibit of impressionist paintings. She likes the new style so much that she visits Claude Monet, with whom she will establish a close friendship. Although he does not accept private students, Monet encourages her and spends hours with her discussing new techniques. During the next decade she will bring her family each summer to Giverny, where they rent a house next to his. By adapting some of his techniques, she improves her work as a portraitist. Perry also introduces impressionism to Americans. She lectures on the new style at public forums and art institutes and encourages art patrons to buy these new works. This unusual painter, who began painting at age thirty-six, lives in Boston with her husband and children, and her work supports the family. She has frequent exhibitions, and later she will help found the Boston Guild of Artists.

JOINING FORCES

New York journalist **Jane Cunningham Croly** founded the Sorosis Club twenty years ago, when female journalists were banned from the New York Press Club. It offers professional women mutual support, intellectual improvement, and socialization. She has noted that as members moved from New York they founded new clubs. Believing that many women in a single group can have a powerful voice, she decides to build a national umbrella organization to represent women's clubs. At the Sorosis anniversary celebration, members establish a General Federation of Women's Clubs (GFWC). They return home, promote the umbrella group, and encourage other clubs to join the national group. They will hold their first convention next year, when the GFWC will represent 200 clubs, with a membership of 20,000 women. Club delegates attend biennial meetings to share progress, ideas, and goals. The local clubs are active in their communities and states. They lobby for better schools and playgrounds, establish kindergartens, libraries, and health clinics, fund scholarships for needy girls, and offer classes in typing, domestic skills, and child care. They form legal aid societies and public art associations and lobby for legislation to improve factory conditions and regulate child labor. By 1920 nearly a million women will join. Members are primarily conservative white middle-class women who discourage the participation of Jewish or black women.[209]

— 1890 —

WORK

Employment in the United States has increased during the past decade from 17 million to nearly 23 million. Women comprise 17 percent of wage earners, and 86 percent of the female workers are single. Many are war widows; in the South alone more than 60,000 women lost husbands and now need to support families.[210]

More white women have entered several growing professions. Since the Civil War's end the number of stenographers and typists has increased from 154 to 33,000, and females in these jobs increased from 5 to 64 percent. Women are 92 percent of all trained nurses, and the number employed has nearly tripled. Women continue to dominate teaching, holding 71 percent of the positions, which have increased in number threefold.[211]

A new census indicating race shows nearly a million black women in the labor force, many of them newly freed slaves. Thirty-eight percent work in agriculture, 31 percent are domestic servants, 16 percent are laundresses, and 3 percent work in manufacturing.[21]

EDUCATION AND SCHOLARSHIP

In the past twenty years more colleges have been built, stimulated by the passage of a second Morrill land grant, which gives states federal lands which they can sell to establish colleges. Since 1870 the number of coeducational facilities increased from 29 to 43, and women's colleges have increased from 12 to 20.[213]

College graduates are primarily whites, and far more black men get degrees than do black women. Although many young black women are encouraged to attend college, most have neither the opportunity nor the finances to do so. This year, 2,500 white women hold baccalaureate degrees, contrasted to only 300 black men and 30 black women.[214]

ARTS

New York amateur photographer **Catharine Weed Barnes** joins the staff of the

Students at the Cherokee Female Seminary, Tahlequah, Indian Territory, c. 1890. (Western History Collections, University of Oklahoma Library.)

Education was important to the Cherokees. After their forced resettlement from Georgia to Indian Territory during the 1830s, they developed an extensive public education system. The first female seminary, built in 1850, was one of the earliest female high schools west of the Mississippi. Teachers were college graduates from the eastern women's colleges. Administrators set high standards and the seminary gained an excellent reputation. The building burned down in 1887, and the new one, seen in this photo, was in the Cherokee Nation capitol.

American Amateur Photographer as associate editor. In her column "Women's Work" she encourages females to become photographers. Barnes is a pioneer and helps set a trend for women. Many wives or daughters have traditionally worked in family portrait studios, where they would arrange subjects, advise on hairstyle and dress, or help process photos. Some later inherited the family business and decided to learn how to use the camera. Photography, as one of the arts, is becoming a more acceptable career for women who must earn money.

JOINING FORCES

Ida Van Etten, a delegate from the Working Women's Society of New York, speaks at the American Federation of Labor's national convention in Detroit. She discusses the importance of getting women into unions. Most labor leaders, she states, are against it because they believe that single women are transient workers and that married women should stay home. And most employers oppose women's unions because they want low-cost employees who are convenient as strikebreakers. Unionization, she warns, is the only remedy against inhumane sweatshops, and if women fail to organize they will become a permanent lower class of workers. Van Etten urges the AFL to create a staff position for a women's union organizer.

Since the Civil War's end, many Americans have newly strengthened feelings of patriotism, and some are establishing groups to honor their heritage. Last year men organized the Sons of the American Revolution, but women were barred from membership. In response, **Ellen Hardin Walworth**, **Eugenia Washington**, and other Washington, D.C., women form the Daughters of the American Revolution. They ask First Lady **Caroline Scott Harrison** to be president-general, and she agrees, giving the group prestige and authority. Membership is limited to direct descendants of males who fought or worked in the Revolution. Their goal is historic preservation, education, and encouragement of patriotism. They will raise money for shrines, monuments, and memorials to honor past leaders and will establish a genealogy library and a museum. Believing in the superiority of their white Anglo-Saxon heritage, they bar black women until the 1970s. Their conservative attitudes will cause a loss of some prominent members. **Jane Addams** will be expelled because of her pacifist stance during World War I, and First Lady **Eleanor Roosevelt** will resign over their refusal to allow a prominent black singer to perform in their Constitution Hall in Washington, D.C.

Bostonian **Alice Stone Blackwell**, the daughter of women right's leaders **Lucy Stone** and Henry Blackwell, is active in reform and edits *Woman's Journal*, a suffrage publication. She and many other reformers want to strengthen the suffrage movement, and they believe that the current two groups, the National Woman Suffrage Association, and the American Woman Suffrage Association dilute women's power. Blackwell helps their merger into a new organization, the National American Woman Suffrage Association. Their goal is full enfranchisement of women in every state. Ambitions of earlier activists to obtain broader civil and human rights for women are dropped. They publicize differences between the genders, emphasizing that women are morally superior and that women's getting the vote will eliminate corruption in American society. Younger women take over leadership and develop political skills. Membership is primarily white, middle-class, and conservative. They wish no connection with radicals, rebels, or people with a questionable lifestyle. Northern members do not welcome blacks; hoping for strong southern support, they informally allow those state chapters to ban African Americans. Other American suffrage groups exist, but this national organization is the largest. In three years membership will be at 13,000, and by 1910 around 75,000.[215]

LAW AND POLITICS

Some women become involved in local politics. In Minnesota women can vote in school elections and may run for school boards and other school offices. **Sarah Christie Stevens**, a college graduate and former teacher, is a local figure in politics. She is nominated for Mankato County's superintendent of schools, and both the Populist and Prohibition Parties endorse her. Her husband, William, is a farmer, and the family is well regarded in the community. Stevens is knowledgeable about school issues, and her public speaking is lucid and eloquent. Her supporters include prominent local men and the local Civil War veterans group, who applaud her nursing work during the war. She wins the election and will run again in four years.

— 1891 —

WORK

Ohio journalist **Julia Ringwood Coston** founds *Ringwood's Afro-American Journal of Fashion*. Since most American women's magazines are for whites, this pioneering publication fills a need. Coston offers articles and illustrations on fashion, stories and essays by black writers, an advice column, art and literature departments, and biographical sketches of prominent black women. She hires other African American women as editors, illustrators, and writers. She keeps subscription costs low, attracting several thousand subscribers. The magazine is so successful that several years later Coston publishes a second journal, *Ringwood's Home Magazine*.

Halle Tanner Dillon, daughter of a prominent Pittsburgh black family, graduates with high honors from the Women's Medical College in Philadelphia. At the same time, Booker T. Washington has been searching for a doctor for Tuskegee Institute. Dillon's dean recommends her for the job, which she accepts. Her duties are extensive. She treats the school's students and staff, their families, and the local black community, personally preparing all medications. She also heads the school's health department and teaches courses. Feeling a duty to the black community, she will later establish a program for

Women and children by their sod house in Oklahoma Territory, 1890. (Western History Collections, University of Oklahoma Library.) The sod house, of hardened bricks of soil, was the typical structure pioneers built on the treeless plains. These houses stayed warm in winter, cool in summer, were fireproof, and offered protection against high winds. They also offered hazards: In heavy rains mud forming on the roof could collapse it; they were dark, with often only one window; insects and snakes took up residence; the dirt floors were impossible to keep clean. Many of these families were unable to prosper and moved back East. Others who succeeded would build new wooden houses, and convert the old sod structure to a root cellar or a place to house animals.

training nurses at Tuskegee and a clinic for the school and local residents. Her work is typical of many pioneer black female physicians. They see the need for health care for African Americans, who are usually barred from white medical facilities. Some work at black schools, and others establish free or low-cost medical clinics or found programs to train black women as nurses.

While more white women are graduating from medical schools, discrimination bars most African American females from this training. Of the nearly 7,000 female physicians in 1900, less than 100 will be black. When Dillon passes the state medical exam, the *New York Times* announces on its front page that she is the first woman in Alabama to pass the state medical examination, which they depict as "unusually severe." For the white male medical establishment, this is indeed front-page news.[216]

EDUCATION AND SCHOLARSHIP

Alice Morse Earle, who lives with her family in Brooklyn Heights, New York, has always liked history. Her parents have strong Massachusetts roots, and they treasure family heirlooms and collect antiques. At her father's request, Earle wrote a magazine article on her ancestors' church in Vermont, then a longer piece on New England meetinghouses for the *Atlantic Monthly*. Expanding on the theme, she now publishes her first book, *The Sabbath in Puritan New England*. Americans have a renewed interest in their history, and her book is popular. Reviewers praise the work, and it will be reprinted in twelve editions. For the next decade Earle will publish many articles, book reviews, and a book each year. She will write on American eighteenth-century morals, manners, and lifestyles, with details on colonial gardens, sundials, china, and costumes. She researches carefully, using public records and documents as well as private materials in American historical and antiquarian societies and in the British Museum. As she becomes well known, readers will send her their family documents, letters, and photographs. Since most contemporary historians are writing political history, Earle is a pioneer in social history.

RELIGION

More American women are preaching. Several years ago, reformer **Frances Willard** investigated this and found nearly 1,000 women in the pulpit, including Quakers, ordained ministers, and more than 500 evangelists. She reported that the Methodists, Baptists, Free Baptists, Congregationalists, Universalists, Unitarians, and the Society of Friends allow women to become ministers. As more females become spiritual leaders, conservative Americans claim this contradicts biblical authority. Presbyterian Robert Dabney, who lives in Richmond, Virginia, is particularly angry. In an article in a church publication, "The Public Preaching of Women," he denounces female clergy as "infidels" who defile "the sanctity of scripture."[217]

ARTS

Twenty-three-year-old **Sophia Alice Callahan**, a high school teacher in Muskogee, Indian Territory, publishes her first novel, *Wynema: A Child of the Forest*. It is about a southern teacher and her favorite student, Wynema, a young Creek woman. The work portrays Creek culture, showing the American government's injustices toward tribes and the difficulties of an Indian girl caught between her native world and white society. Callahan's book is among the earliest novels by a Native American. Younger Indian writers will later take up her theme of the struggle of Indians in American society. Callahan will die from pleurisy several years later, unable to realize her dream of opening a school for young Creeks.

Plans are under way for a World's Columbian Exposition in Chicago to honor the 400th anniversary of Columbus's arrival in America and to show progress in the United States. Because Congress included no females in the fair's governing commission, a group of prominent women petitioned Congress to include at least one. They refused this request, but a "Board of Lady Managers" whose job it will be to plan exhibits of women's contributions to American life has been appointed. These displays will be held in a separate building, to be designed by a female architect chosen in a contest.

Architect **Sophia Hayden** is a recent Massachusetts Institute of Technology graduate whose thesis was a blueprint for a neoclassical museum. She submits her plan for a Renaissance-style building and wins first prize; she will be the architect and oversee construction. The museum will be completed and dedicated two years later. It is magnificent, with a stately central hall surrounded by meeting rooms and a library, with a rooftop garden and restaurant. Some critics praise its beauty and elegance, and Hayden will win several medals for her work. Even chief architect Daniel Burnham, who opposed hiring a female designer, will admire her building and suggest she open an architectural firm in Chicago. Others will judge her more severely. A surly critic for the journal *American Architect* pronounces her building as "neither worse nor better than might have been expected" and describes the rooftop garden and restaurant as a "hencoop for petticoated hens, old and young." He then questions how women, with their "physical limitations," can succeed in such a stressful profession.[218]

Despite Hayden's successes, conflict and controversy surround the building for the women's exhibit. A female architect argues that women should not compete in a public contest. Some women artists object to segregated exhibits. No black women are appointed to the Board of Lady Managers, and a delegation of African American women is angered when their request for separate ex-hibit space for their race is denied. Other women complain that Hayden has been inadequately compensated; she receives an "honorarium" of $1,000, while the male exposition architects are paid $10,000.

JOINING FORCES

Writer and reformer **Francis Watkins Harper** speaks at a temperance symposium sponsored by the African Methodist Episcopal Church. She denounces drinking as a terrible evil and proclaims it the duty of all Christian women to campaign against alcohol. Her plan for prohibition is straightforward: "Consecrate, educate, agitate, and legislate."[219] Harper is national secretary of the Colored Section in the Women's Christian Temperance Union (WCTU) and is one of few black women active in this organization. Linking temperance to respectability and racial uplift, many black females crusade for prohibition, but because of blatant racism in the WCTU most eschew membership. While Harper is bitter about the group's racist policies, she encourages African American women to work for temperance, either in segregated WCTU chapters or in their own clubs and churches.

Josephine Lowell, who founded the New York Board of Charities, has turned to labor reform. She is concerned about working conditions of female store clerks. They are forced to work twelve-hour days, prohibited from sitting on the job, given insufficient bathroom facilities, limited to ten-minute lunch breaks, and paid poorly. Last year she established the New York Consumers' League. This group of middle- and upper-class women inspects stores and reports on working conditions. This year they compile their first "white list" of eight stores in the state that provide acceptable working environments. They print the list in newspapers and ask consumers to boycott all other department stores. League members close their accounts with unlisted stores and encourage the public to do so. Each year their

Two young women by a rock boundary marking the intersection of Colorado, Oklahoma Territory, and New Mexico Territory, c. 1890. (Western History Collections, University of Oklahoma Library.) These large geographic regions were sparsely settled. Colorado's population was around 400,000, Oklahoma territory about 260,000 and New Mexico, 160,000. There were few structured activities for young women, but the loneliness was offset by a freedom their eastern urban counterparts lacked. For example, after finishing chores, many were allowed to ride horses and explore their new homeland.

list of "white" stores expands as more store owners bow to public pressure. The group will also help clerks organize unions, support strikes, and work for protective legislation. It will later expand into the National Consumers' League.[220]

— 1892 —

EDUCATION AND SCHOLARSHIP

The University of Chicago, a private school, opens. President William Rainey Harper hires a strong faculty, many from prestigious eastern universities, and plans to build a strong graduate program that emphasizes research. The charter calls for co-education, and Rainey encourages women to enroll. The first undergraduate student body is 40 percent female.[221]

Harper hires as dean of women **Alice Freeman Palmer**, a former Wellesley College president. As she had transformed Wellesley from a girl's school to an excellent college, she now applies her administrative talents to

Chicago. She arranges better housing, sets up a fund-raising committee, and establishes a network of female faculty, prominent Chicago women, and Hull House leaders. Three years later Palmer's successor, **Marion Talbot**, will continue this work; she will improve women's housing, build a clubhouse with a pool and gymnasium for women, and add programs for female students. Chicago will be an attractive option for women, and within the decade 52 percent of the undergraduate student body will be women; they will have earned 56.3 percent of all Phi Beta Kappa honors. Their success will make Rainey fearful that Chicago might now be considered a women's school, and he will later retreat from his commitment to female scholars.[222]

Mathematician **Christine Ladd-Franklin** presents a paper on her theory of how we see color at an international Congress of Psychology in London. She has long been interested in vision theory and has done postgraduate research with professors in Göttingen and Berlin. Some aspects of her theory will be considered valid well into the twentieth century. Ladd-Franklin did graduate work at

Johns Hopkins as a "special student," since females were barred from enrolling as graduate students. She fulfilled all requirements for a Ph.D. in math and completed her dissertation in 1882, but was denied the degree because of gender. In 1926 the university will finally award the diploma to the seventy-nine-year-old scientist.

ARTS

Forty-one-year-old New Yorker **Mariana Van Rensselaer** publishes *English Cathe-* *drals*, a study of twelve churches she had examined while traveling abroad. Van Rensselaer is a well-known and respected critic who helps set trends in art. Although she did not attend college, her wealthy background, exclusive private high school education, extensive travels abroad, and wide reading have given her expertise in the arts and literature. Her writing is clear and lively and she is a frequent contributor to *Century Magazine* and *Harper's*. She will continue to publish articles and books on painters, architects, house and landscape design, social issues,

The Lady Macabees, Allegan, Michigan, c.1890. (Allegan County Historical Society.) The Lady Macabees, in ceremonial dress, face the camera proudly. They hold their scepters, symbols of power and authority. Their mortarboards indicate they are educated. This group's name probably came from the biblical mother of the Macabees, a model of female courage and heroism.

Their club was among thousands that American women founded. Most early groups had religious or charitable goals; later ones bonded for mutual help, intellectual improvement or civic betterment. Because most white, middle-class married women were not employed outside their homes, these memberships gave them a community and a purpose. So many clubs were founded during the 1890s that a General Federation of Women's Clubs was formed as an umbrella organization, linking clubs throughout America.

and the early history of New York City. *English Cathedrals* will remain one of her best-known works.

Chicago sculptor Lorado Taft receives a commission to create several large neoclassical sculptures for the Columbian Exposition. In need of assistance, he wants to hire some promising young women, his former students at the Art Institute of Chicago. Taft asks architect Daniel Burnham, the exposition's chief planner, for permission to hire them. Burnham replies that Taft can employ whomever can do the work — "white rabbits if they will help out."[223] One of Taft's assistants (who are dubbed the "white rabbits") is young architect **Janet Scudder**. She will later recall how thrilling it was to work with Taft, meet famous sculptors, learn new techniques, and even get paid. Scudder will become prominent in the early twentieth century for her commissioned bronze statues, fountains, and public monuments.

JOINING FORCES

The American Federation of Labor is the primary American umbrella labor group. President Samuel Gompers hires **Mary Kenney** as a national organizer of women, and she is the AFL's first paid female employee. Kenney, from a poor Irish immigrant family in Missouri, had to leave school in the fourth grade to help support her family. She is now a bookbinder in Chicago, active in labor politics, and has formed a local union. Her job with the AFL is to organize women. She will travel throughout the Northeast, helping New York garment and shirt makers and Massachusetts printers, bookbinders, shoe binders, and carpet weavers form unions. Despite her successes, in five months the federation cancels her position, citing insufficient funds. They will not appoint another female as full-time organizer until 1908. Membership in the AFL is increasing, and by 1897 will reach 265,000. Yet female wage earners, while increasing in number, remain mostly unorganized. In three years they will

comprise only 5 percent of all labor union members.[224]

Conditions for most blacks have not improved significantly since Emancipation. They struggle in the South as field laborers, and in the North as underpaid servants or industry workers. Blatant discrimination prevails throughout the United States. A small group of black women is protesting these injustices. These women — prominent, well educated, and well spoken — are representative of America's "New Woman"; they are educated, independent, self-supporting, and active in reform. Many are inspired by the leadership of their black abolitionist foremothers.

One leader is **Anna Julia Cooper**, the daughter of a slave and her master, whose mother taught her the value of education. Cooper, whose bachelor's and master's degrees are from Oberlin, teaches at a black public high school in Washington, D.C. During summers she writes and travels, lecturing on education, racism, and sexism. This year she publishes her first book, *A Voice of the South by a Black Woman from the South*, a collection of her essays and speeches. Her theme is education. She links freedom to education and insists that more black women must get college degrees, that their talents are untapped. She notes how few black women graduate from college, blaming this on society's apathy. She chastises black men for their lack of support and berates white female reformers for their elitism and for passively accepting racial prejudice. Cooper will continue to write and speak against injustices, and at age sixty-six she will earn a doctorate from the Sorbonne.[225]

Journalist **Ida Wells** lives in Memphis, where she co-owns and co-edits *Free Speech*, a black newspaper. She is enraged when three local black grocery store owners are arrested, then taken from jail and lynched. There is no protest from the white community. Wells organizes a boycott of the local trolley, which nearly closes the company down. She publicly proposes that the entire Memphis

African American community immigrate to Oklahoma, depriving Memphis of their labor. She writes scathing articles protesting lynching. Questioning the justification for lynching (that black men rape white women), she suggests that it might be the white women who favor black men. Reading this, furious white readers burn her newspaper building and threaten her life; she moves to New York City, seeking safety. She finds employment with a local newspaper and begins her anti-lynching campaign. After extensive research, she publishes a feature story in the *New York Age*, which is then printed as a pamphlet, *Southern Horrors: Lynch Law in All Its Phases*. White southerners are furious at her defamation of white southern men as cowards and liars, but her crusade gets little attention from white northerners, who rarely read the black press.

The next year Wells will travel to England and obtain support from the British, who will form a national anti-lynching society. International pressure, publicity, and exposure will finally force some white Americans to denounce lynching. While Wells's campaigns do not stop lynching, she has made more Americans aware of it.[226]

LAW AND POLITICS

More farmers are settling in the West, but this is a time of severe depression in agriculture. There has been drought in the Great Plains, causing failed crops; and while taxes have been rising, cotton and wheat prices are falling, driving many farmers to bankruptcy. This is a catalyst for a third national political party, one that gives farmers and other working people a voice. There have already been regional coalitions of farmers, but southerners and westerners have been unable to agree on a focus for one party. With this depression, the time is right for a new national party.

Mary Elizabeth Lease, who lives in Kansas, is well known for her dynamic speeches and writings supporting farmers and the labor movement. She attends a meeting in St. Louis to help establish a national party to represent farmers and laborers, and serves on the planning committee. The new Populist Party proposes reforms in money, public land, and transportation and wants to clean up corruption in business and industry. At the Populist convention in Omaha, Nebraska, Lease seconds the nomination of Iowan James Weaver as the Populist Party's presidential presidential Party candidate. Although the Populists will fail as a major reform party, some of their ideas will later be enacted. Lease will soon quarrel with Populist leaders and later resign her membership, but she continues to agitate for birth control, prohibition, and female enfranchisement.

— 1893 —

WORK

A severe depression has hit the United States. The Philadelphia and Reading Railroad has gone bankrupt, and others will follow. Thousands of businesses and manufacturers will overextend themselves and lay off employees, and hundreds of banks will fail. Not all Americans are affected. The gap between rich and poor has been widening— but millions face severe hardship. Nearly 20 percent of the labor force will lose their jobs, and 20,000 in New York City alone lose their homes. In many families, wives of unemployed husbands seek work. Many of these women are new to the labor force, and they help increase the number of female wage earner during the decade from 4 million to 5.3 million.[227]

The bicycle, which has been modified for safety, has become popular with middle- and upper-class Americans. Women like it, feeling freedom and independence. Many question the value of bicycling for women. Some claim it will damage their reproductive systems, make them reckless, and destroy their femininity; others insist it is healthy. In four years more than 10,000 businesses in the United States will sell bicycles.[228]

Bicycle riding also stimulates dress reform. Campaigns have been initiated for more comfortable and lighter clothing for women and for elimination of steel corsets. Decades ago bloomers were fashionable, but they have long been subjected to ridicule and are not worn by most women. Now dressmakers and inventors design outfits for women's cycling. Traditional dress is heavy, cumbersome, and gets caught in the wheels and pedals.

One inventor is **Margaret Hobbs Lawson**. She patents a comfortable bicycle garment that consists of trousers (padded in the crotch for comfort) worn under a long skirt, thus hiding the trousers, which are considered masculine. Many other women design clothing for bicycle riding and for other sports newly popular with women, such as ice skating, croquet, tennis, and golf.

EDUCATION AND SCHOLARSHIP

Johns Hopkins is forced to admit women to its new medical school because of a donor's stipulation. Wanting to build America's best medical school, University administrators began fund-raising several years ago. **Mary Garrett**, heir to a railroad fortune, offered $60,000 for a medical school. She stipulated that all students must first have a bachelor's degree (not commonly required), that women be allowed to enroll, and that their program be equal to that of the male students. The trustees declined Garrett's offer, but they were still unable to raise the funds. This year Garrett offers $307,000 with the same stipulations, and the college accepts her conditions. Currently, few prestigious medical schools accept women, and many females are delighted at this opportunity. In the early 1900s many distinguished female medical scientists will have Johns Hopkins degrees.[229]

RELIGION

Suffragist and writer **Matilda Joslyn Gage**, who lives in Fayetteville, New York, believes that Christian teachings are responsible for the slow progress in women's rights. She publishes *Women, Church, and the State*, a broad critique of Christian influence. She accuses church leaders and ministers of controlling women's minds and bodies and of promoting society's double standard. She insists that women are not inferior to men and rejects the concept of original sin. Although Gage is a churchgoing Baptist, she believes that reform must come from outside the church because attitudes about females are too deeply rooted in Christianity. Her book is widely read and harshly criticized by conservative Americans. Women have been critiquing Christianity for nearly seventeen hundred years, but because earlier studies are unknown, later scholars lack a general framework and must review the same arguments.

The Columbian Exposition sponsors hundreds of symposia, and a popular one is the World's Parliament of Religions. **Hannah Greenbaum Solomon** has been asked to organize a Jewish women's congress. Solomon asks prominent American Jewish women to participate, and the congress is the first large gathering of American Jewish women. At the meeting they form the National Council of Jewish Women and call for organizing local chapters. Their goals are reform and philanthropic work for new Jewish immigrants. This is important because thousands have fled pogroms in eastern Europe and settled in American cities. There is concern that that the newcomers, so different from Americans in dress and language, might kindle anti–Semitism, and they want to help the newcomers become more American. Leaders also encourage women's greater participation in the synagogue, establish study circles, and found more Sabbath schools. The group anticipates later organizations such as the National Federation of

Temple sisterhoods and the National Women's League of the United Synagogues of America.

ARTS

William Canby, the grandson of **Betsy Ross,** recounted the story of how she designed and sewed the American flag in a paper he presented to the Pennsylvania Historical Society in 1870. He heard the tale from his aunt, but he could find no contemporary documentation to confirm it. Nonetheless, his audience was charmed. *Harper's* later published the account, and it was soon included in American school books. Artist Charles H. Weisburger's painting of Betsy Ross is displayed at the Columbian Exposition. Entitled *Birth of Our Nation's Flag*, it portrays Ross showing her flag to George Washington and other leaders. The painting arouses much attention and excitement. Several years later women will form a Betsy Ross Association to restore the house where she sewed the flag, making it a national monument. The idea of a woman sewing the country's flag is important as a national patriotic myth, and it is easily accepted by Americans.

JOINING FORCES

The "city" created for the Columbian Exposition is called the "White City" for its neoclassical white marble buildings, but it represents little of black America. When black women requested separate display space, the Board of Lady Managers appointed a southern white woman to represent their interests. This and other racist behavior by the organizers so infuriated activist **Ida Wells** that she wrote *The Reason Why the Colored American Is Not in the Columbian Exposition.* The black community raises hundreds of dollars to print the pamphlet, and they sell thousands at the exhibition.

Chicagoan **Fannie Barrier Williams**, from a wealthy black New York family, is a former teacher and married to a prominent lawyer. Active in social and cultural affairs, she has joined the city's Women's Club, is on the library board, and is a spokeswoman for black associations. At the exposition she speaks at the World Congress of Women about African American women's progress and status. She lists their accomplishments as dedicated teachers and founders of benevolent and civic societies, and explains how difficult this has been amidst segregation and violence in the South. She then speaks angrily about the lack of jobs for them. Except for teaching in segregated schools and doing menial work, she states, "colored women can find no employment in this free America. They are the only women ... for whom real ability, virtue, and special talents count for nothing."[230]

African Americans need a strong voice to protest discrimination. In the South, Jim Crow laws deny blacks their civil and legal rights, and in the North discrimination runs rampant. Several upper- and middle-class black women in the Northeast form clubs for black women. Their motto is "lifting as we climb." Because many whites judge all blacks by the poorest and least educated, these groups first improve themselves, then help others who are in lower economic group.

Bostonian **Josephine St. Pierre Ruffin**, a black reformer and writer, establishes the New Era Club for middle-class black women. Members fight discrimination, encourage racial pride, and take on civic projects such as organizing kindergartens for black children. These women want to show white people that they are talented, skillful, and can develop power and leadership. Ruffin tries to get the New Era Club accepted as an affiliate of the General Federation of Women's Clubs, but it is rejected since it is a non-white organization.

Hallie Quinn Brown, the daughter of former slaves, has a college degree from Wilberforce University in Ohio. She has taught, has been the dean of women at Tuskegee, and now teaches elocution at

Wilberforce. She is well known in the United States and in Europe for her lectures on black American culture, music, and folklore and for her club activities. This year she helps organize the National League of Colored Women (NLCW) in Washington, D.C. It will be an umbrella organization representing local and state clubs. Her group is one of the first national black women's clubs.

LAW AND POLITICS

Suffrage for women in Colorado has been debated for thirty years. Women have submitted petitions to the legislature, organized speaking tours, and sponsored lectures by prominent eastern suffragists. Another referendum is put on the ballot this year, and the Populist, Republican, and Prohibition Parties support it. Colorado women's new strategy is to campaign among local people rather than bring in eastern speakers. They win, and Colorado becomes the first American territory to enfranchise women by popular referendum.

— 1894 —

EDUCATION AND SCHOLARSHIP

As more women seek higher education, many want to attend Harvard University, but the Harvard Corporation has insisted that the school remain male. Twenty years ago, in a program dubbed the Harvard Annex (later incorporated as the Collegiate Institute of Women), qualified women could take night courses from Harvard professors, but they could not receive a Harvard degree. Several years ago Harvard president Charles W. Eliot, who is sympathetic to women's education, suggested to a group of women that if they could raise $250,000 to cover costs, females would be permitted to attend and graduate from Harvard. Under the aegis of **Alice Freeman Palmer**, former Wellesley

president, they raise the funds, but the Harvard Corporation rejected the money — and the idea — as too risky. As a compromise, Radcliffe College is chartered this year, with a faculty to be selected by the Harvard Corporation. Graduates will receive a Radcliffe diploma, considered equivalent to a Harvard degree.[231]

Martha Carey Thomas, appointed president of Bryn Mawr College this year, has been persistent in her own education. After graduating from Cornell in 1877, she applied to Johns Hopkins for graduate work in Greek but was barred because of her gender. She then traveled to Germany to begin doctoral work at Leipzig, where she was allowed to take courses but not earn a degree. Transferring to the University of Zurich in Switzerland, she finally earned her doctorate, summa cum laude.

At Bryn Mawr, Thomas has been a dean since the school's opening in 1885. She had applied for the presidency and was told she was too young, but as dean she took on many extra administrative duties. Now president, she will build Bryn Mawr into a prestigious college with high standards. She raises admission and graduation requirements, she develops a broad curriculum, and requires foreign languages. She begins a graduate program with fellowships for students, and she seeks the best scholars for the faculty. She will oversee fund-raising for buildings, a lovely campus, and an extensive library. Thomas is a controversial president; some call her a tyrant, while others admire her drive, persistence, and successes. She will head the college until 1922.

Mathematician **Charlotte Angas Scott** publishes her text, *An Introductory Account of Certain Modern Ideas in Plane Analytical Geometry*. Scott, an English immigrant whose graduate work was at the University of London, is one of few women in the world to have a Ph.D. in math. M. Carey Thomas hired Scott in 1885 to build the mathematics program at Bryn Mawr College, and Scott heads the department for forty years. She will be an effective and influential professor and will publish extensively in international journals. Although she will discontinue using her text in her own classes after advances in algebraic geometry make her work outmoded, other instructors will use it much longer. Later editions will be published in 1924 and 1961.

RELIGION

Julia A. J. Foote, who lives in Cleveland, Ohio, is ordained as deacon of her African Methodist Episcopal Church. She has been religious since age fifteen, when she had an "awakening" and joined the Boston AME church. To the dismay of her husband and parents, she wanted to preach and church leaders expelled her from the church and threatened excommunication. She took on an itinerant ministry for thirty years, finally settling in Cleveland. Her persistence is rewarded, and she obtains official leadership at age seventy-one.

Attitudes of black church officials are similar to those in white churches: male leaders want to ban women from leadership roles. Although some black men have always upheld the "true womanhood" ideal, many black men have adopted the patriarchal attitudes of white society, hoping this will earn them respect.

JOINING FORCES

The Dawes Severalty Act had been passed in 1877. Its goal was to bring Indians into mainstream American society by providing for the dissolution of tribes as legal entities. It also authorized the division of reservation lands into individual allotments, after which Indians would be granted American citizenship. Implementation of the act is complicated and difficult. Many tribes are voicing objections. Hopi women in the Moqui Village in Arizona do not want changes. This year, twenty-two Hopi women petition the Bureau of Indian Affairs. They

write that while they respect Americans, they fail to understand their agricultural system. "None of us ever asked that it [the tribal land] should be measured into separate lots, and given to individuals, for this would cause confusion," they explain. Women own the fields and are assigned to them on the basis of family size. Men cultivate the fields and give the crops to the women, who then prepare the food and handle the surplus, sometimes bartering it for other goods.[232]

The act is unsuccessful in assimilating Native Americans into American society. Most reservation lands end up in the hands of white settlers. Nonetheless, the allotment program continues and by the mid–1930s Indian tribes will have lost 60 percent of the 138 million acres they once owned.[233]

Nearly two million immigrants have arrived in the United States since 1890, and as they crowd the cities and compete for jobs, nativist sentiment increases. Female suffrage leaders exploit the public fear of the immigrant "menace." They point out that millions of uneducated and "ignorant" foreigners have a voice in government, while well-educated native-born white women do not. Last year the National American Woman Suffrage Association passed a resolution suggesting a literacy requirement for all voters to ensure against "rule by illiteracy."[234]

Suffragist **Elizabeth Cady Stanton**, who formerly advocated universal suffrage, now uses nativist arguments. She writes to the *Woman's Journal* that all male immigrants should understand English and pass a literacy test before being granted full citizenship. This will keep the "ignorant and depraved" from voting, stimulate learning, and help the country become homogeneous once more. It is in the interest of all educated men and women, she affirms, "that this ignorant, worthless class of voters should be speedily diminished."[235]

LAW AND POLITICS

Ohio female citizens have gained some legal rights since the early 1880s. Married women can now sue or be sued, control their own property, and be appointed guardian. Less progress has been made for voting rights. Several full-suffrage amendments have been vetoed, as have three school suffrage bills. This year the legislators permit women to vote for school trustees, but when **Ida Earnhart** tries to register to vote she is turned away. In her appeal a court rules in her favor, but the decision will be later challenged and will be upheld by the state supreme court. The struggle of Ohio women is typical of females in many states.

Belva Lockwood, a Washington, D.C., lawyer and member of the local bar, wants to try a case in Virginia, but is forbidden to practice law there. A Virginia state codes allows a "person" who is licensed to practice law in any other state or Washington, D.C., to practice in Virginia. Lockwood appeals to the state supreme court, which rules that "a person" (in this case) means a male, thus disqualifying her. Her subsequent appeal to the United States Supreme Court upholds the Virginia ruling.[236]

— 1895 —

EDUCATION AND SCHOLARSHIP

Public education has increased since the end of the Civil War. In this era of progressive reform, schooling is considered a way to train young people to improve society. As more states enact compulsory education laws, more public schools are built, especially in urban areas where they are supported by tax dollars. More students enroll in elementary and high schools, and the number of high school graduates during the past five years has increased 64 percent. Because many young men can get jobs or apprenticeships in business or law without high school diplomas, more females graduate from high school. This year women make up 60 percent of all high school graduates.[237]

More Americans are enrolling in college. Since 1890 there has been a 55 percent increase in total degrees awarded, and this year women earn 18 percent of bachelor's degrees.[238] The protests twenty years ago questioning women's suitability for higher education have lessened, and more middle-class women attend college. Many students and alumnae view themselves as "New Women": those who are independent, educated, interested in sports, and wear comfortable and less restrictive clothing. The "New Woman" may also have a career, thereby rejecting the Victorian ideal of home as woman's sole concern.

Women are making progress in graduate education. In 1889, twenty-five women held doctorates, primarily from Syracuse, Boston, Wooster, Michigan, Cornell, and Smith College. Women who wanted to study at most other prestigious all-male institutions were informed there was "no precedent" for it. Although some supportive professors allowed particularly bright women to attend their classes, few were granted degrees, even after completing requirements.[239]

Now more Americans are aware of women's eagerness for graduate education. There are magazine articles on where to do graduate work, and professors at women's colleges encourage their students to pursue doctorates. Group such as the Association of Collegiate Alumnae fund graduate scholarships and fellowships. Six prominent universities now accept women into their doctoral programs: Yale, the University of Pennsylvania, Columbia, Brown, Stanford, and the University of Chicago. While in 1890 women were awarded 1.3 percent of all doctorates, this year they earn 9 percent.[240]

Florence Bascom received a doctorate in geology from Johns Hopkins. She was the first woman to receive the degree, in part because of family connections. Her work was superior and the faculty supported her, and a family friend knew Daniel Coit Gillman, the university's president. Bascom is offered a position at Bryn Mawr College this year.

She advances rapidly and will rise to full professor. She will build a strong department, organize a geology lab with rock, mineral, and fossil collections, and set up a geology library. Bascom is among a small group of female scholars and scientists who have satisfying careers at women's colleges. Here they teach small classes with bright students and serve as role models for the girls. There is intellectual discussion with other faculty members. Few other college teaching jobs are available; women are rarely hired at coeducational institutions.

RELIGION

At age eighty, **Elizabeth Cady Stanton** publishes *The Women's Bible*. She wants radical reform in the United States and sees church teachings as responsible for women's oppression. She hopes the work will encourage women to think for themselves. Having spent decades studying and reviewing biblical texts, she believes that the men who translated the Bible were biased against women. The book is authored by a committee of twenty women but written primarily by Stanton. She cites texts and chapters in the Bible, then revises them, giving women a greater role, and she adds more stories of historical women. Reaction to *The Women's Bible* is strong; religion has great importance in American life, and Stanton is viewed as a heretic. Few suffragists support her work, fearing it will hamper their cause. Next year the National American Woman Suffrage Association will pass a resolution disavowing any connection to Stanton's book. Because it is so controversial, and because Stanton is so well known the book sells well, going through seven printings in the first six months, as well as several translations. She will publish a second volume three years later.[241]

Rosa Sonneschein, a American Jew in Chicago, founds and edits *The American Jewess*, one of the first American Jewish magazines in English. She publishes fiction by leading female Jewish writers and offers social and political essays. Sonneschein encourages her readers to assimilate into American society but to still keep their faith and take on a more active role in the synagogue. She is a Zionist and one of the first Americans to promote a Jewish homeland in Palestine.

ARTS

Nampeyo, a Hopi woman in northern Arizona, is a potter. Her skills have a long tradition among Southwest Native American women, who created the large jars for carrying water to their villages. They often competed to create the most beautiful designs and patterns. Nampeyo learned to make pots from her grandmother, and she is interested in the older designs. Her husband works for archeologists who are excavating the nearby prehistoric village of Sikyatki. He finds an interesting pottery shard and gets permission take it home. Nampeyo copies the drawing and from it creates her own design, which she uses on her pots. Her patterns will be admired by the Hopi and by scholars of her tribe's history and culture. Anthropologists will later photograph her work and describe it in their reports, proclaiming it a symbol of Hopi culture.

JOINING FORCES

James Jacks, president of the Missouri Press Association, has written a letter portraying American black women as having no virtue, character, or morality. Copies of the document circulate, and activist **Josephine St. Pierre Ruffin** is enraged. She calls for a national conference, and delegates from black women's clubs meet in Boston. They resolve to end discrimination and restore civil rights. To do this, they form a new group, the National Federation of Afro-American Women (NFAAW). Ruffin inspires the delegates. Women work hard, as teachers, mothers, laborers, but are ignored by society and are denied admission to white women's clubs on the assumption that women are "ignorant and immoral." She insists, "[we must] declare ourselves ... [and] ... teach an ignorant and suspicious world that our aims and interest are identical with those of all good aspiring women."[242]

LAW AND POLITICS

Most Americans are against female enfranchisement. They believe women belong at home, not in public life. Despite decades of campaigns, women now have full suffrage in only two states, Wyoming and Colorado.

Massachusetts is a major hub of suffrage activity, and state lawmakers want to test public support. They hold a mock referendum on women's suffrage, allowing women who qualify for school elections to vote, although the election results will not be binding. Only 4 percent of eligible female voters vote.[243] The measure is defeated. This pleases those who oppose suffrage, and they promptly form two new anti-suffrage groups.

— 1896 —

WORK

Urban reformers are establishing cooking schools to teach working women and future wives to prepare nutritious meals. **Fannie Merrit Farmer**, a graduate and now head of the Boston Cooking School, publishes *The Boston Cooking School Cookbook*. As a former domestic servant, she wanted to improve her cooking by developing accurate measurements for ingredients (measurements are not generally given in other cookbooks). Farmer's publisher doubts that the book will sell well and forces Farmer to pay publication costs, but her investment is well recovered. It is a best-seller and will have twelve later editions. Farmer makes enough money to open her own cooking school in Boston, which will last through the 1940s. She will write other cookbooks, but her first is the most successful, selling four million copies in seventy years.[244]

Industrialization has lowered the physical quality of many published books, as more are put out by larger presses using mechanized processes. Much of the earlier craftsmanship and design has been lost, and cheaper paper, which deteriorates more quickly, is now commonly used. As a protest against industrialization and mechanization, English artists and artisans have developed an arts and crafts movement. They prefer handmade and individually designed objects, and they establish small cottage industries in pottery and furniture making, weaving, and printing.

The arts and crafts movement has spread to the United States. In Wausau, Wisconsin, Philip V. O. Van Vechten and his partner, William Ellis, found a printing press to publish their magazine *The Philosopher* and to produce limited editions of carefully crafted books. **Helen Bruneau Van Vechten**, Philip's wife, selects, edits, and designs the books. She develops careful printing methods ensuring quality work. She hand-feeds high-quality paper through the machine, giving an even spread of ink on each page. She chooses artists' illustrations and page designs and thoughtfully selects what to publish. Her books will include works by Lewis Carroll, Rudyard Kipling, Elizabeth Barrett Browning, and Robert Louis Stevenson. Book collectors around the world will value the publications, and Van Vechten gains an international reputation for her beautiful, high-quality books.

EDUCATION AND SCHOLARSHIP

Twenty-nine-year-old **Edith Hamilton** holds bachelor's and master's degrees in Greek and Latin from Bryn Mawr College. She has just returned from Germany, where she did graduate work at the universities of Munich and Leipzig, funded by a prestigious

Bryn Mawr fellowship. Upon her return to the United States, she is offered a position as head of the Bryn Mawr School, a private girls' college prep school in Baltimore, founded by **Martha Carey Thomas.** Hamilton, who has no administrative experience, has dreamed of becoming a classics scholar, but she reluctantly accepts the position. She needs the salary, believing she might someday need to support her mother and sister.

The school is floundering financially, and Hamilton begins a campaign to convince wealthy Baltimore parents to send their daughters to her school. She will expand the curriculum, raise standards, and build the school into a respected institution. She will head it for twenty-four years until tensions with Thomas prompt her to resign. Hamilton will have a second career as a respected author. She will publish her first book, *The*

Pageant, "The Old and the New," Allegan, Michigan, 1896. (Allegan County Historical Society.) This tableau contrasts women's traditional roles with new and expanded options for some Americans in the 1890s. The woman on the bicycle represents the "New Woman." Her starched shirtwaist blouse, small, tidy straw hat, and narrow skirt represent clothing reform, with greater physical freedom. Her bicycle symbolizes new interest in physical activity; many women took up sports, and gym classes were often required for female college students. The other women depict the traditional lifestyle: their cumbersome and heavy dresses have fuller skirts and are laden with frills and lace; some wear fussy decorated hairpieces and flowered hats. Several hover over a baby, showing that traditionally, motherhood was considered women's greatest role.

The "New Women" were usually from middle-class families. Many were college graduates — some from the new coeducational state universities and others from the elite women's colleges. They became typists or clerks, or worked in settlement houses, in labor reform, as teachers, or as professors in women's colleges. Others pioneered in medicine or law. Many opted to remain single. Those who married often opted for smaller families.

Greek Way, at age sixty-three, and her last at age ninety. She will have a devoted following of readers who praise her ability to capture the spirit of ancient Greece. She will receive many literary awards and honors, and in 1957 the Greeks will make her an honorary citizen of Athens.

ARTS

Writer **Sarah Orne Jewett** sold her first story at age eighteen and has been writing ever since. She publishes *The Country of the Pointed Furs*, a novel about a Maine fishing village. Her poetic descriptions of the landscape and realistic sketches of eccentric villagers are praised, and this work ensures her success as a writer. She will later be a mentor to younger writers Willa Cather and Kate Chopin.

Three well-known classically trained African-American singers perform together in Carnegie Hall. They are among the first blacks to sing here. One is operatic soprano **Marie Smith Williams**, known as Selika, who has performed in Europe and is known as the "Queen of Song" for her ability to sing difficult cadenzas. She is joined by **Flora Bateson**, another internationally famous concert singer, who has an extraordinary vocal range. The third is **Sissieretta Jones**, a leading American prima donna. She will later organize a group of traveling musicians, the Black Patti Troubadours. Their music will be a transition to blues styles, which younger black female singers will make popular.

JOINING FORCES

Chicagoan **Elizabeth Lindsay Davis**, who resigned her teaching job upon marriage, is now active in community work. This year she organizes the Phyllis Wheatley Women's Club, which she will head for twenty-eight years. Their goal is to help young black women who move to the city. They will open a home where the girls can rent rooms, and they will offer the girls recreational, vocational, and educational programs and help them find jobs. Chicago's YWCA offers similar services but permits only whites. Davis will later write and publish a history of the black women's club movement, *Lifting as We Climb*.

Another black woman in club work is **Mary Church Terrell**, the daughter of a prominent millionaire in Nashville, Tennessee. Her father allowed her to attend college, but when she insisted on a teaching career, he was so shocked at her rejection of the traditional upper-class lifestyle as a "lady" that he disinherited her. Terrell now lives in Washington, D.C., where this year the National League of Colored Women (NLCW) and the National Federation of Afro-American Women (NFAAW) are having conventions. Terrell and others believe that a single national group of black women would be more powerful than two groups. The NLCW and the NFAAW merge to become the National Association of Colored Women (NACW). This umbrella group represents hundreds of local and state clubs. Their mission is self- and community improvement. Members throughout the United States will found nurseries, kindergartens, mothers' clubs, and homes for the elderly. They will create job training programs and educational programs with thousands of dollars in college scholarships. A newsletter, *National Notes*, will link members by publishing local clubs' reports. Members are primarily Protestant, middle-class educated women. They will become a strong advocacy group for blacks as membership increases. In twenty years, 50,000 women will be members.[245]

LAW AND POLITICS

Utah residents want their territory to become a state, but the United States Congress, whose members despise polygamy, have previously denied them statehood. Mormons, whose members dominate Utah government leaders, now abolish polygamy and territorial lawmakers hold a constitutional convention in preparation for statehood. Utah women campaign for suffrage. This year they work for grassroots and bipartisan support and are able to convince the delegates to include full suffrage in the constitution. Utah finally becomes a state.

Idaho women recently organized a new female suffrage campaign. They campaigned locally and sponsored educational programs, emphasizing that females in neighboring states have voted for years with no drastic consequences. All state parties (Progressives, Democrats, Republicans, and Silver Republicans) support it, and a new bill is presented to the state legislature. It passes, making Idaho the fourth state where women have full suffrage.

— 1897 —

DOMESTICITY

The American Federation of Labor publishes the *American Federationist* for discussion of labor issues. Bostonian Edward O'-Donnell, a union secretary, contributes an article, "Women as Bread-Winners — The Error of the Age." He complains about the growing number of women in the labor force, which he views as a direct attack on the home. When women take jobs, it is like "the knife of the assassin, aimed at the family circle," he argues. Not only is it unnatural for women to earn wages, he writes, it will make them unfeminine. Since men support the family, they lose dignity if women work; and when employers hire women, they deprive men of jobs. Like O'Donnell, most labor union members think women do not belong in the labor force, and certainly not in unions. As these attitudes are publicized more, the notion that women belong at home is reinforced.[246]

In this age of experts and specialization, many middle-class white women meet in-

formally to discuss child rearing and attend lectures on being a successful mother. **Alice McLellan Birney**, married to a lawyer in Washington, D.C., and the mother of two daughters, believes all mothers should learn the new scientific principles of child rearing. While attending a Chautauqua summer school, she suggests forming a national mother's club to encourage women all over America to establish child study groups. Nearly 2,000 women converge in Washington, D.C., to form the National Congress of Mothers (NCM), and they elect Birney as the first president. The press covers the event enthusiastically, and prominent Americans endorse the new group. Although members state that all classes and races are welcome, most NCM members are middle class and white. In the 1920s the group will become the Parent-Teachers Association.

WORK

Little health care is available for most American blacks, and they have a high mortality rate. Many hospitals accept only white patients, and those facilities that admit blacks (in separate wards) often bar black doctors from visiting their patients. It is also difficult for prospective black nurses to get training. Charlestonian **Ann DeCosta Banks** wanted to be a nurse. The local hospital's program for training nurses prohibited blacks, so she traveled to Hampton, Virginia, to study at the Dixie Hospital and School of Nursing. Returning to Charleston this year, she discovers that Alonzo Clinton McClemman, an African-American physician, has founded a hospital for blacks; the facility includes a school for training nurses. Banks is appointed head nurse at the school and will spend her life improving health care for African Americans.

EDUCATION AND SCHOLARSHIP

Phoebe Apperson Hearst, a former teacher now married to a wealthy businessman, supports education. She funded kindergartens and libraries in San Francisco, and while traveling with her husband to villages in South Dakota and Montana she helped establish local schools. She is now widowed and has inherited her husband's fortune from mining, oil, and real estate. She is a longtime benefactor to the University of California, and this year she is appointed their first woman regent. Female enrollment is increasing, and by the turn of the century women will make up 46 percent of all students.[247] Noticing that women are uninvolved in campus affairs, Hearst begins a program to help them become more active. She will provide scholarships, create a work-study program, develop literary and athletic programs, and fund a new faculty position for a female physician to teach hygiene. Hearst also supports the college as a whole. She pays for new buildings, a theater, and an anthropology museum, and she will contribute to faculty raises and research grants. Hearst will remain a regent until her death in 1919. Her legacy includes making the school more supportive to women and helping transform it from a small provincial college to a major research institution.

Elizabeth Evelyn Wright, the daughter of an illiterate slave, was born in a three-room shack but has worked her way through school and is an alumna of Tuskegee Institution. Upon graduation she has decided to open her own vocational school, based on the Tuskegee program and the ideals of self-help. She has made many attempts to establish

Daughter of a rancher en route to school on a burro, Battlement Mesa Reserve, Colorado, 1898. (National Archives.) Education was important to Colorado settlers, and establishing a schoolhouse was a first priority in many communities. Students might be schooled in an abandoned cabin or dugout until a permanent structure could be built. Teachers were often paid by subscription, and the length of the school term would depend on community resources. Children would travel by foot, horseback, or donkey, often carrying old textbooks or slates that their parents had used.

In some western communities there was less emphasis on gender roles than in eastern urban regions; and boys and girls might share chores. When not in school, this little girl might have hauled water, fed cows, gathered buffalo chips for fuel, and helped take goods to market.

schools in her home state, South Carolina, but has been unsuccessful. In some communities white residents burned the building materials before a structure could be erected, and in others whites drove her out of town. This year she succeeds. She begins classes on the second floor of a store in Denmark, South Carolina. Enrollment increases and she decides to expand. She later receives money from a white benefactor, buys twenty acres of land, and builds a larger facility. The enrollment will increase and the institution will flourish despite continuing opposition from whites. Wright heads the school, now called Voorhees Industrial School after a benefactor. She will supervise teaching and continue to raise funds for expansion. By the 1960s Voorhees will be a four-year liberal arts college.

— 1898 —

DOMESTICITY

Harriot Hickox Heller speaks to the National Congress of Mothers in Washington, D.C. To promote motherhood as an important profession, she suggests, it must be "redefined, amplified, enriched," and we must "*discover* the lens that will focus all a woman's power upon her motherhood." Members of the congress — primarily white middle-class women who are not wage earners — hope to convince American women that they belong at home. They ignore the needs of working-class women who contend with motherhood and employment; many believe that the poor should not even have children.[248]

WORK

Congress has declared war on Spain for ignoring turmoil and revolution in Cuba, including the explosion of an American battleship in Havana harbor which killed hundreds. Congress also declares Cuba free and announces that the United States military will help drive the Spanish off the island. This begins the Spanish-American War, which causes much excitement as young men enlist to fight in Cuba. Young women want to be military nurses, and they inquire at government offices about applying.

Physician **Anita Newcomb McGee**, who lives in Washington, D.C., sees this war as an opportunity for jobs for nurses and a way to improve their image. She socializes with the Washington elite and knows many government and military leaders. She proposes to George Sternberg, the military surgeon general, that a committee be established to screen qualified nurses, after which they could be sent to bases and camps. Sternberg agrees to the plan and appoints McGee as acting assistant surgeon general. Under the aegis of the Daughters of American Revolution, a committee is appointed to interview nurses and submit a list of those qualified. Of 5,000 applicants, nearly 1,000 are sent to Cuba. Medical care is badly needed, since 93 percent of war fatalities are from malaria and yellow fever. McGee's program is so successful that after the war she helps establish an official Army Nursing Corps.[249]

ARTS

Harriet Powers, an ex-slave who lives on a Georgia farm, is a talented seamstress. Some of her quilts have been exhibited at local fairs and were praised for their beauty and artistry. This year a group of women commission her to create a quilt for the president of the Union Theological Seminary. Powers likes Bible stories, which she has memorized from church sermons, and she dramatizes the creation of the animals in this work. Using African motifs, she tells the story in fifteen cotton appliqués sewn with colored and metallic yarns. Some of her quilts will later be acquired by the Smithsonian Institution and Boston's Museum of Fine Arts.

Writer **Gertrude Atherton**, who was raised in San Francisco, has always been unwilling to accept society's strictures for women, and even as a child she refused to learn to sew. She found marriage dull and constrictive, especially since her wealthy husband was jealous of her writing ambitions. Atherton later left her daughter to be raised by her mother-in-law so that she could begin a writing career. A theme in her work is how women are limited in society, and many of her fictional heroines are unconventional. This year she publishes *The Californians*, a novel of three wealthy families in the 1870s. Although Atherton has lived in New York City and in London, her writings are set primarily in California, and her books offer its social history from the Spanish era through World War I. She will write nearly one book a year. Although she has a broad readership in the United States and England, some critics complain that she sacrifices quality for quantity. At age ninety she will complete her fifty-sixth work.

JOINING FORCES

Thousands of Mexican-born people have become American citizens since the 1840s. Many migrated north, seeking employment, and others' homelands were annexed by the United States. Nearly 4,000 native Mexicans now live in the southwestern United States. There is much discrimination against them, and most live in poverty. It is especially difficult for women, who have low-paying jobs in domestic service, food processing, or sewing or as seasonal agricultural workers.[250]

Seventeen-year-old **Sara Estala Ramírez**, whose college degree is from a Mexican normal school, immigrates to Laredo, Texas, to teach at the Seminario de Laredo. She becomes active in the Mexican-American community and joins the Partido Liberal Mexicano. She speaks against discrimination and encourages women to become independent and fight for their rights. She publishes in the local press articles on politics and also writes stories, plays, and poems. Her death at age twenty-nine will prematurely end her ca-

reer as a writer and a political leader, but later Chicana writers will take up her theme of Mexican-American solidarity.

Eighteen-year-old **Agnes Nestor** lives in Chicago and works as a glovemaker to help support her family. Conditions in the factory are deplorable, and following the values of her father, who was in the Knights of Labor, she decides to take action. She leads her female coworkers on strike, demanding elimination of machine rental, the right to have a union, and higher pay. They are supported by the men's cotton glove union, and after a ten-day strike they win. Nestor will later become active in the Women's Trade Union League and be appointed to public commissions for labor, education, and defense. When she is forty-nine, she (who left school in the eighth grade) will receive an honorary LL.D. from Loyola University.

Writer **Charlotte Perkins Gilman,** who is already well known for her stance on women's rights, publishes *Women and Economics*. This new book critiques the traditional American family. She suggests that it is unreasonable to insist that all women should be mothers and have no other job. If men can combine parenthood and work successfully, so can women, she maintains, emphasizing that the genders differ less than is commonly believed. She states that women's economic dependence on their husbands is good for neither, since it keeps women in a permanently subordinate position. She proposes that communities organize cooperative kitchens to provide meals for private homes and that they found day-care centers to help mothers who are wage earners. Some Americans praise her book for its lucidity and thoughtful arguments. It will be reprinted the next year, go through seven more editions, and be translated into seven languages. Gilman will publish many more books and articles proposing change in society's structure, and during the next decade she will be a leader in the feminist movement. But most Americans disagree with her call for radical change.[251]

A women sewing on her porch, western North Carolina, c. 1889. (North Carolina Collection, Pack Memorial Public Library, Asheville, N.C.) Note the windowsill, which has been brightened with flowers in containers. This woman may be mending her family's clothing or sewing for another family.

— 1899 —

WORK

Chemist **Ellen Swallow Richards** has two degrees from Vassar College. She has also earned a bachelor of science in chemistry from the Massachusetts Institute of Technology, where administrators were dubious about her presence on campus and classified her as a special student. She later did graduate work in chemistry at MIT and should have earned a doctorate, but the department chairman refused to grant its first doctorate of science to a woman. For several years she taught night classes in chemistry and mineralogy to local schoolteachers in a laboratory funded by a Boston women's group. Later, when the lab closed, MIT appointed Richards as instructor of sanitary chemistry,

and she worked in a new laboratory, developing procedures to investigate water, sewage, and air quality.

Richards wants to find a better niche in the academic world. She has already published two texts — *The Chemistry of Cooking and Cleaning* and *Food Materials and Their Adulterations* — that apply chemistry to everyday life. Expanding on this theme, she decides to found a new academic field to educate future wives and settlement workers. This year, with the encouragement of librarian Melvil Dewey, she calls for a conference at Lake Placid, New York. The eleven participants establish "home economics" as a new scientific discipline. They define it as the study of cooking and the household arts, whose goal is to improve home life. Members will meet annually, more will join, and in 1908 they will become the American Home

Economics Association. Classes in home economics, already popular in some high schools, will be added to more curricula.

The founding of home economics as a university subject offers a new kind of employment for women but also establishes a sex-segregated field. Many administrators in coeducational colleges are reluctant to have female faculty but are willing to hire them to teach home economics. To the dismay of many females in the humanities and sciences, an appointment to teach home economics is often the only position they can get. By 1911, 60 percent of all female college instructors at coeducational institutions will teach home economics.[252]

Maggie Lena Walker, a young black woman in Richmond, Virginia, has been a member of the Independent Order of St. Luke since age fourteen. Originally established in the late 1860s as a mutual benefit organization for blacks, St. Luke once flourished, but lately membership has declined and they are heavily in debt. Walker, a former schoolteacher and accountant, is appointed the new secretary. She will help the order pay its debts and will expand their program. She will oversee a new youth department that encourages education and offers loans and scholarships. Under her leadership, members will found a Penny Savings Bank, which offers mortgages. They will also open and run a cooperative department store and will publish a newspaper whose editorials protest discrimination. Walker sees both women and men as needed for community strength, and she will inspire Afrrican Americans to self-help and hard work. St. Luke will eventually have more than 100,000 members in twenty-eight states.[253]

EDUCATION AND SCHOLARSHIP

Lulu Ruth Faling, whose degree is from the Michigan State Normal College, accepts a job teaching Latin in a junior high school in Kalamazoo, Michigan. Choosing to remain single, she will have a long career as teacher and later as school principal. Faling has chosen the typical job of most white, middle-class young women who want a respectable profession. The need for teachers continues, as

Navajo women shearing sheep, 1890s. (National Archives.) Navajo women and men had separate roles, each considered important to the tribe's well-being. Processing hides was traditional women's work, and, as in this picture, was done communally with children playing under watchful eyes.

Women also owned the livestock. They cared for the sheep, oversaw grazing, helped with birthing of lambs, did the shearing, and butchered and distributed the meat. Livestock ownership gave women power and independence. Some became wealthy, but they had a moral obligation to share their riches; greed was a societal taboo.

Navaho families traced their descent through their female ancestors. Families lived in extended communities under the authority of a matriarch who controlled finances and had the final authority in family decisions.

more young Americans are being educated. Enrollment in public secondary and elementary day schools increased from seven million in 1870 to fifteen million this year. During this same period the number of teachers increased by 275 percent. Females have been the majority of public school teachers since the end of the Civil War, and will be 84 percent of all teachers by 1920.[254]

ARTS

Malvinia Fay Pierce organizes the Women's Philharmonic Society of New York, a women's orchestra whose members also support young female musicians. The members are musicians who perform or teach music, and the group offers four concerts each season in Carnegie Hall. They forgo paychecks for their performances, using admission fees for scholarships.

Widowed **Kate Chopin**, who lives in St. Louis, began writing in her thirties to support her six children. Well known for her short stories in national magazines, she hosts a salon of writers and intellectuals. She is liked for her readable and languid prose and for her authentic regional descriptions. Many of her stories take place in Louisiana, where she has lived, and she is familiar with bayou life and Creole culture. This year she publishes her second novel, *The Awakening*. Set in the New Orleans area, it concerns an unhappily married young woman who is searching for an identity. She leaves her husband for a lover and becomes awakened both sexually and artistically. Public response is negative. Reviewers castigate Chopin's portrayal of sexual longing, insisting that her themes are immoral and in poor taste. Her popularity declines, and her publisher cancels her last short story collection. Public reaction is so hostile that she writes little more and retreats into private life. A later generation of women in the 1970s will rediscover her works, praise them for their emphasis on women's issues, and reintroduce Chopin to Americans.

Alice Dunbar, who grew up in New Orleans, now lives in Washington, D.C., with her husband, poet Paul Dunbar. She is college educated, has taught, and also writes. At age twenty she published a book of sketches, stories, and poetry. This year her husband's publisher, Dodd, Mead, and Company, in New York City, brings out her second book, *The Goodness of St. Roque and Other Stories*. Dunbar writes of Creole culture and New

Mary Fry by her farmhouse in Allegan, Michigan, c. 1900. (Allegan County Historical Society.) Fry, in her early seventies, wears an elegantly embroidered apron that belies her difficult life. She bore seven children, five of whom lived, and managed the family farm since 1873, when her husband Jacob left for Nebraska, where he later died.

Fry had emigrated from Scotland with her family at age eight. She met Jacob in Ohio and after marriage they traveled west searching for good farmland. He was disabled in the Civil War, became restless, and wanted to move further west. Men often wanted to trek further west, and like Mary, many wives refused to leave their homes.

Orleans history in a lively style, but showing the sadness in people's lives. The work gets excellent reviews. Dunbar continues to write short stories (a new tradition among black writers), but her themes of oppression and violence make many publishers reject her works. An outspoken and energetic woman, Dunbar participates in the black women's club movement where she works against lynching and for suffrage, but she is also socially active and enjoys dressing fashionably and going to parties, concerts, and the theater. She will continue to write articles, newspaper columns, and poetry. During the Harlem Renaissance, many younger female writers who respect Dunbar as an older successful writer will ask her to read their works and judge contests.

JOINING FORCES

Recently, women have organized consumer groups in Chicago, New York, Brooklyn, and Philadelphia. Some believe a national consumer's group is needed, and reformers **Florence Kelley**, **Maude Nation**, and **Josephine Shaw Lowell** organized a National Consumers' League last year. They hope to improve labor conditions by investigating and publicizing conditions in industries with sweatshop conditions. They also want to put a union label on goods produced under fair labor conditions.

The union's president, former Unitarian minister John Garth Brooks, asks Kelley to serve as secretary. Kelley holds a law degree from Northwestern, is a longtime resident of

Little girl with dolls and tea set, Norman, Oklahoma Territory, early 1900s. (Western History Collections, University of Oklahoma Library.) She represents at this time an ideal female child: attractive and white, surrounded by miniature accoutrements of her future life.

Emma Coleman took this portrait in her studio in Norman, Oklahoma Territory. Coleman and her husband migrated from Iowa. Coleman first worked as a seamstress, then took up photography, a popular vocation for many western women. Through commercial photographs middle-class families could preserve their likenesses for posterity. As seen in this picture, gender and setting were important. Photographers carefully selected props, background drops, and even chairs for their subjects.

Hull House, and is prominent in Illinois reform; she has been a state factory inspector and is known for her investigation and publications on conditions in the Chicago slums. She advocates public intervention to prevent corruption, the abolishment of child labor, and protective legislation for working women. She accepts the position and moves to New York. Kelley will travel throughout the United States, speaking to labor unions, legislative committees, and women's clubs, urging reform in industry. She will help organize local chapters in twenty states and help to plan two international conferences. Her work will raise public awareness of labor problems, and will help get minimum wage laws passed in many states. Kelley will remain the union's secretary until her death in 1932.

— 1900 —

DOMESTICITY

Most white married women remain full-time homemakers, and this year less than 4 percent are employed outside the home. But as more young women graduate from college, many Americans criticize higher education as unnecessary for them. A woman who signs herself "An American mother" writes to the *Ladies' Home Journal*

Laundry hanging in the yard of a tenement, Park Avenue and 107th street, New York City, c. 1900. (Library of Congress.) The building is in Italian Harlem, which by the 1930s was the city's largest Italian settlement. Tenement buildings were jammed with units to maximize landlords' profits. The apartments were small with narrow windows that allowed little sunlight or fresh air. Most had sinks, but the few bathrooms were communal. The units were swelteringly hot in the summer and damp and chilly in the winter. Married Italian women did not commonly work outside the home; they earned money by taking in boarders. This involved extra cooking, cleaning, and laundry, especially arduous in such small living quarters. No space was wasted in urban areas, and on laundry day lines of clothing could be seen drying between buildings.

to express irritation at the increasing number of females in college. Insisting that most of them will marry, she questions the value of their education. The only training young women need, she believes, is one that "recognizes the differences between the sexes and trains a girl thoroughly for her womanly work."[255]

WORK

The nature of work has changed since the Civil War's end as the United States moved from an agricultural economy to an industrial one; now nearly two-thirds of all workers are in non-farm occupations. And more Americans hold jobs. During the past twenty years the total number of wage earners increased from 17 million to 29 million.[256]

During this same time, female employment increased from 2.6 million to 8.6 million, and women are now 17 percent of the labor force. Wage-earning women include almost 41 percent of all black women over age ten, and 16 percent of all white women over age ten, who are mostly native-born single, widowed, divorced women or immigrants. Nearly 17 percent of all female employees are the sole support of their families.[257]

Most females are unskilled laborers. Nearly 25 percent work in factories, mostly garment and textile, and another third work in domestic service. Others work in tobacco industries, make boots and shoes, serve as clerks in department stories, or labor in laundries. Most black women (who are barred from most clerical and factory work) hold poorly paid jobs in domestic service, as laundresses, or in agriculture. Women dominate some of the newer professions that have grown since 1870. Females are now 77 percent of all stenographers and clerk typists, 74 percent of all teachers, and 94 percent of all trained nurses.[258]

Alice Cunningham Fletcher, a former teacher who grew up in New York, is well read in ethnology and anthropology. She is interested in Native American culture and has befriended Susette La Flesche of the Omaha tribe, a prominent speaker on Indian rights. Fletcher has lived with the Omaha and Winnebago tribes in Nebraska, where she helped supervise the granting of individual allotments to tribal members. Her stay with the Plains Indians furthered her interest in their culture. She has already written and lectured on Indian music, and this year she publishes *Indian Story and Song from North America*. In this book she transcribes Omaha, Sioux, and Pawnee music, and Fletcher is among the first to record their music. She will continue to study Indian culture and will publish many articles on her work. Self-taught, Fletcher is a transitional figure in ethnology and anthropology. The next generation will have college degrees and professional credentials.

Pauline Hopkins, a playwright and singer in Boston, performed with the Hopkins Colored Troubadours for twelve years but has left the group to have more time to write. She supports herself as a stenographer and writes in the evenings. This year she helps establish *The Colored American*, a Boston-based magazine that promotes black heritage, culture, and pride. She begins as editor of the women's department but quickly gets promoted. Her editorial skills, incisive political columns, short stories, and biographical sketches of prominent African Americans help build the magazine's reputation. Four years later, when a more conservative black publisher buys the publication, she leaves her job and returns to stenographic work and writing. One of her best-known books is *Contending Forces: A Romance Illustrative of Negro Life North and South*, recounting the lives of black families from slavery through post–Reconstruction. Although she publishes many stories, books, and articles, she will remain unacknowledged until the late twentieth century, when a new generation will admire her perception and portrayal of racism and sexism.

Native Americans have been writing and publishing since the early 1820s, and the

Cherokees have a strong literary tradition. When the tribe was relocated from Arkansas to southeastern Indian Territory, the Park Hill Mission, founded in the mid–1830s, became known as the "Athens of the American South." It flourished for thirty years and was famous for its excellent schools as well as for its printing press, publishing house, and bindery, which put out many notable texts, books, almanacs, and religious tracts. Women as well as men wrote and published some of this material for the Park Hill Mission.

Cherokee **Ora V. Eddleman Reed**, who lives in Indian Territory, has followed her ancestors' tradition. This year she is appointed editor of *Twin Territories: The Indian Magazine of Oklahoma*, a publication founded by her sister and brother-in-law. Reed knows the business, having worked for her father's newspaper, the *Muskogee Evening Times*. For *Twin Territories* she will contribute fiction, poems, stories for children, and articles on Cherokee folklore, helping to preserve their native culture. She will later edit the Indian department of *Strum's Statehood Magazine*.

ARTS

Washington, D.C., photographer **Frances Benjamin Johnston** is well known for her portraits of the wealthy and famous and for her book on the White House interior. She recently turned to documentary photography, being influenced by her friend Jacob Riis, a journalist who investigates schools in urban slums. After visiting Washington, D.C., black public schools to photograph students and teachers, Johnston documented the African American youth who were learning vocations at the Hampton Institute in Virginia. Johnson skillfully captured her subjects' dignity and spirit. This year she exhibits the photos at the Paris Exposition. She is awarded a gold medal and receives international acclaim for her portrayal of American education. She will continue to document American society; she photographs more vocational school students and also shoots factory laborers and miners, capturing their individuality and the effects of industrialization. She will continue to work through the 1930s, photographing people, gardens, and buildings. Funded by Carnegie Foundation grants, she will complete several large projects on southern colonial architecture. Johnston will be remembered for her high standards, professionalism, and pioneering work in photojournalism.

JOINING FORCES

New York is becoming the nation's garment-making center; within the next decade, nearly 50 percent of the city's industries will be clothing factories. Many of these produce women's garments, and although some male tailors and cutters have organized, there is no general union for women's clothing makers. This year, the United Brotherhood of Cloak Makers Union calls a convention in New York City to form the International Ladies' Garment Workers' Union (ILGWU). They select officers, design a union label, and recruit women, who are 70 percent of the industry's workers. Many members are female Jewish immigrants from eastern Europe with a tradition of fighting for social justice. Because conditions in most factories are deplorable, they are glad to be unionized. Membership grows slowly, and the early male leaders are conservative and discourage strikes.

Nine years later, female ILGWU members will participate in a massive walkout of shirtwaist workers in New York City. They will withstand police brutality, imprisonment, and bitterly cold weather, and win. Their victory will attract new members. By 1916 the ILGWU will have more than 90,000 members, and half will be women. On the staff will be a female educational director and eight women organizers. The organization will be powerful in winning strikes and fighting sweatshop conditions.[259]

Many American anarchists are active in big cities. They call for radical change and envision a more rural and libertarian society, one not dominated or ruled by government, in which the people are self-sufficient and live simpler lives in villages. Some write or translate (from German or Russian) journal articles on socialism and reform, hoping to educate and persuade Americans. Others want to educate themselves on how best to reform American society.

Thirty-four-year-old anarchist **Voltarine deCleyre** lives in Philadelphia. Like other American revolutionaries, she hates industrial society and calls for radical change. She wants Americans to live more simply and frugally, and she distrusts big government. She is a libertarian and a pacifist; "I make war upon privilege and authority," she claims. She has recently become interested in socialism, having met several European socialist leaders she respects. This year she forms a reading group called the Social Science Club. Members meet weekly, read socialism tracts, and discuss political reform. Beginning with five, membership increases, and they will become the city's best-known anarchist group. Hoping to educate the public, they will hold outdoor meetings, sponsor lectures, write articles on anarchism, and print and sell articles they translate from German and Russian. The next year these radicals will become less public due to mass hysteria and fear after President William McKinley's assassination by an anarchist. Attendance at deCleyre's reading group will drop, but she will continue to agitate for reform. DeCleyre will die at forty-six, and because she has shunned publicity she remains unknown for her work. Her legacy will be a large body of writings, including articles, printed speeches, poems, and essays. Fellow anarchist Emma Goldman will later praise deCleyre as "the poet-rebel, the liberty-loving artist, the greatest woman Anarchist of America."[260]

— 1901 —

DOMESTICITY

Many white men are protesting what they perceive as the dominance of women in society. They insist that men need to reassert themselves and America needs to become more masculine. Some are angered at the increasing number of female wage earners, whom they think belong at home. In the *Independent*, a prominent national weekly, writer and social commentator Henry Finck expresses his viewpoint in "Employments Unsuitable for Women." He tells women to avoid jobs that might make them "bold, fierce, muscular, brawny in body or mind," warning them that such work might make them unmarriageable. Finck admits that while some women may need to support themselves, employment should be considered a temporary solution that must eventually be "cured … by marriage or some other way of bringing the workers back to their deserted homes."[261]

WORK

Nearly half a million immigrants sail to the United States this year, with 46 percent leaving central and eastern Europe. Nearly half of the newcomers are Jews, fleeing persecution. Arriving in America, they move to cities where earlier Jewish immigrants have settled. Many come to Milwaukee, Wisconsin, where there is a large German Jewish population.[262]

Lizzie Black Kander, a married Jewish woman in Milwaukee, wants to help immigrants adjust to life in America. She helped found a mission where newcomers can take painting, drawing, and sewing classes. Because of the great influx of Russian Jews this year, Kander and others enlarge the mission into a settlement house. Kander teaches cooking, and her classes are popular since she observes kosher dietary laws. She teaches the immigrants how to cook simple and

Italian immigrant women buying bread on Mulberry Street, New York City, c. 1900. (Library of Congress.) The Mulberry Street community, on the Lower East Side, was the city's oldest Italian settlement.

In 1900 most immigrants were from central and southern Europe, and 22 percent were from Italy. They were fleeing overpopulation and excessive taxes. Farmers were frustrated with the depleted soils and the decline in prices for their exports of olive oil, lemons, and oranges. New immigrants generally settled in established ethnic communities that offered a familiar language along with their own churches, traditional celebrations, and familiar foods.

nutritious American meals. This year she decides to print her recipes for the students, since many are struggling with English. The settlement house trustees deny her request to fund the project, so she and several others pay printing costs for her *Settlement Cookbook*. Surplus copies are sent to a local department store. One thousand copies are sold, and a later edition has even higher sales. Kander uses the profits for settlement house expenses. She will continue to revise and update the book, long after the settlement house closed and became a Jewish community center. Kander forms a company for the cookbook, and they used the profits for Jewish community activities. It will still be in

print in the 1960s, having gone through forty editions and sales of more than a million copies.[263]

EDUCATION AND SCHOLARSHIP

Thirty-year-old archaeologist **Harriet Ann Boyd** describes her recent fieldwork in "Excavations at Kavousi, Crete in 1900" in the *American Journal of Archaeology*. Boyd has become an archaeologist, despite discouragement and setbacks. After graduating from Smith College she spent four years in graduate study at the American School of Classical Studies in Rome. To her disappointment, the professors prohibited her from excavating and suggested she become an academic librarian. Eager to explore and excavate, last year she took off on her own, traveling to Crete at the suggestion of a British archaeologist. Turkish rule of the island had recently ended, and the region was little known by archaeologists. Traveling by mule, she discovered some tomb sites at Kavousi, an early Greek settlement she described in her master's thesis for Smith College. Next year she will return to Crete and discover Gournia, a 3,000-year-old Minoan town site which she believed to be a city in the *Odyssey*. She will direct its excavation for three seasons, supervising hundreds of workers. Boyd will later discover and excavate other Bronze and Iron Age sites in the Aegean region. While prejudice against females in archaeology will continue through much of the twentieth century, the pioneering work of Boyd and several others will be a wedge for a younger generation.

Mary Emma Woolley, an alumna of Wheaton Seminary and Brown, has been teaching biblical literature and history at Wellesley.

This year she begins a new job as president of Mt. Holyoke College. The school was chartered as a college in 1888, but earlier presidents kept the founder's tradition and encouraged students to prepare for a life of "Christian service." Woolley will turn the school into a prestigious college. She will recruit a strong faculty with graduate degrees, raise their salaries, give them teaching freedom, and establish a sabbatical program. She will create a more flexible curriculum, initiate the honor system for students, and abolish sororities. Broadening and strengthening the curriculum in academics, she resists adding home economics and will build a strong graduate program. Woolley believes in the importance of role models, and when she retires in 1937 she will be disappointed that her successor is male.

RELIGION

Thirty-nine-year-old **Alma Bridwell White,** who became a Methodist at age sixteen, has been preaching and leading revivals for eight years, despite church leaders' disapproval.

A southern black woman being baptized in a river, early 1900s. (Library of Congress.) Black women played a major role in religion since the slave days. Following the West African tradition, slave women often led prayers or informal services on the plantations. After emancipation, black women (like white women) were the majority of church members. It was their fundraising that helped many churches survive.

This year, living in Denver, she founds a new sect, the Pentecostal Union. She defines her sect as "pure" Methodism and encourages proselytizing, sanctification, and faith healing. Next year she will move to New Jersey, where she will establish headquarters and be formally ordained. Membership in her group (later called the Pillar of Fire Church) will grow. White will lead revivals throughout the United States and in England, write tracts, books, and pamphlets, have a missionary program, establish seven vocational and Bible schools, and buy two radio stations. By 1936 membership will be over 4,000, and her church will be worth nearly $4 million. Although White permits ordination of white women, her tolerance ends there. When the Ku Klux Klan regains strength during the 1920s, she will praise it as "the greatest moral and political movement of the generation."[264]

ARTS

Bostonian **Gertrude Bonnin**, who writes under her Sioux name, Zitkala-Sa, or Red Bird, publishes *Old Indian Legends*. The book is a collection of folk stories she heard from tribal elders while growing up on the Yankton Sioux Reservation in South Dakota. Bonnin believes native cultures should be preserved. At age eight she had been sent from her home to a boarding school in

Sewing class at the Riverside Indian School, near the Wichita River, Oklahoma Territory, c. 1901. (Western History Collections, University of Oklahoma.) The students look bemused and unhappy. They had been taken from their tribal homes to this boarding school, stripped of their familiar clothing, fed unfamiliar food, and taught a new religion. They were forbidden to speak their native language or follow any traditional customs. Discipline for disobedience was harsh.

This school was one of several dozen financed by the American government, whose goal was to assimilate Indian youth into American culture. Students were brought to the schools at age five or six, often without their parents' permission, and some remained there until their twenties. Their curriculum included Christianity, character development, citizenship, and vocational skills: boys learned carpentry, brick masonry, livestock raising, and farming, while girls learned to cook, sew, and clean. Racism was rampant; many teachers believed their pupils were inferior and treated them with hostility.

Nearly 3,000 Indian girls were educated in these schools. While the Indian reformers believed this education would improve the Indians' lives, most such attempts were unsuccessful. A minority assimilated into the wider American society, but most students returned to their tribal homes, having been trained for a non-existent situation. Many were left confused and unhappy, feeling neither Indian nor American.

Indiana, where she was forbidden to speak her language or keep her native dress. Though she is now successful in American society — she is a college graduate, has taught school, and is a well-regarded violinist who toured Europe — she remembers being stripped of her native heritage. She wants to help Native Americans regain their pride. Her book is well-received, and she will continue to publish sketches, stories, and poems on Indian life. She will also work for Native American rights, believing tribes should work together for a stronger national voice.

Asian immigration to the United States has nearly doubled in the last decade, and this year nearly half of the 14,000 Asians are from Japan and China. While there is prejudice against them, and quotas set on the number of immigrants, many Americans are fascinated by their culture, which they perceive as primitive, romantic, and exotic. New York novelist **Winnifred Eaton**, whose mother is Chinese, writes about Japan under the pen name Onoto Watanna. This year she publishes her second novel, *A Japanese Nightingale*. The work tells of the difficulties of a Japanese woman and her Anglo lover. Nearly 200,000 copies will be sold, and it will have three editions and be translated into several languages. It will be transcribed as a play and produced on Broadway. Eaton will write fourteen other romance novels with Japanese settings and characters, often lavishly illustrated with Eastern art, which will be widely read by the Americans, Canadians, English, and Japanese.[265]

— 1 9 0 2 —

EDUCATION AND SCHOLARSHIP

More women are attending coeducational colleges and universities, and at some state institutions there are as many female undergraduates as males, or more. College administrators are troubled, fearing that

their institutions will be considered "women's schools," lowering their prestige and making them undesirable to males. One solution is to limit or segregate the women; some set quotas, and others established separate undergraduate schools for females.[266]

At the University of Chicago, President William Rainey Harper has been alarmed by the female students' successes. Since the school's opening a decade ago, women have received 46 percent of all bachelor's degrees and 56 percent of Phi Beta Kappas.[267] Harper decides to establish a separate junior college for women. The proposal gains national attention, and although many disagree with the idea it is implemented. By 1907, women will be reintegrated but will have lost ground. Male enrollment has increased, and a new club has been founded for them. Rainey hires few new female faculty. The student newspaper will also change. There will be an emphasis on football and other male sports, women's activities will be relegated to a back-page column, and editorials will be addressed to college men.

Charlotte Hawkins, a young black college student, had accepted a job in Sedalia, North Carolina, teaching black children in a one-room schoolhouse. She also becomes helpful and active in community affairs. This year the American Missionary Society, who funded the school, close it but offer Hawkins another position. The townspeople ask her to stay and donate fifteen acres and an abandoned blacksmith shop for a new school. Hawkins is able to raise money for a new facility, which she calls the Alice Freemen Palmer Memorial Institute, after her mentor. It opens this year, offering agricultural and vocational training. She will continue to expand it, and her school will attract national attention and financial support from ordinary and prominent Americans. The institute will become a secondary school, one of few places in the region where black teens can take college-preparatory courses. Later, junior college classes will be added. Hawkins will be the institute's president for fifty years. She will become prominent in state educational

A pioneer family and Indian friends by their tent at the opening of Anadarko, Oklahoma Territory, 1901. (Western History Collections, University of Oklahoma.) As pressure grew for sparsely populated lands in the territory to be opened to non–Indian settlement, surplus lands outside the reservations were gradually made available. This family drew lots for homesteads in surplus lands outside the Kiowa-Comanche and Wichita-Caddo reservations. The family pitched a tent to mark their claim. They are posing with their new Indian neighbors.

While Anglo settlers and Indians often felt mutual fear, most encounters were peaceful. On the westward trail, accidents and disease killed more pioneers than did Indians. Unless the homesteaders were hostile, or Indian treaties were being violated, or there were previous unsettled grievances, relations were peaceful. Many Native Americans helped pioneers adjust to their new home, showing them how to build shelters and where to gather herbs and berries. They often traded wild game, robes, and baskets for coffee and flour. In some areas Indians worked for Anglos as servants and helped farm.

associations and in the black women's club movement, and she will earn a national reputation for her innovative work in racial cooperation in education and for her civil rights work. Hawkins will later earn a bachelor's degree from Wellesley College; additional diplomas on her wall will be honorary master's degrees and doctorates from prominent American black universities.

JOINING FORCES

Susan B. Anthony publishes "Woman's Half-Century of Evolution" in the *North American Review*. Enumerating progress in women's legal rights, she announces that in most states married women can now own property, make wills, transact business, sue, and initiate divorce. In one-fifth of the states, married women share legal guardianship of their children. She writes that women have made progress since rule under English common law, but that they will always lack equality with men until they can represent themselves by voting.

Woman doing laundry outside a tent, 1901. (Western History Collections, University of Oklahoma.) This family, waiting for the opening of Anadarko, Oklahoma Territory, has pitched a tent for temporary housing.

Doing laundry involved finding a water source in an arid region, lugging it in pots that could weigh more than 40 pounds, and then building a fire to heat it. Women made their own soap of ashes, fats, and lye. Cleaning the filthy garments involved intensive scrubbing while bending in an uncomfortable position. Rinsing, wringing, and hanging the wet and heavy clothing required strength. Laundry took a full day.

— 1903 —

DOMESTICITY

Debate continues about American female wage earners and the effect on their families. Writers and reporters investigate women in industry, and they publish conclusions in surveys, reports, and articles. Some even take factory jobs so they can give a firsthand account. New York journalist **Bessie Van Vorst** dressed as a laborer and traveled to Perry, New York, and Pittsburgh, Pennsylvania, to work in factories. She reported that women work harder than men and get fewer benefits, and that even the highest-paid women make less than the lowest-paid men. She concluded that this discrepancy is acceptable, since all men support

their families but few women do. She also claimed that most women spend their wages for clothing and extras and work temporarily while waiting for marriage. She suggests that since most native-born women do not need to earn a living, they should leave factory jobs for the very poor and accept employment only in "feminine" occupations such as lace making or bookbinding.

Her sister-in-law Marie worked with her, and their study was serialized in *Everybody's Magazine* last year. This year it is published by Doubleday, Page, and Co. as *The Woman Who Toils: Being the Experiences of Two Ladies as Factory Girls*. Since the book gives credence to the myth that most women are temporary workers and spend their wages on frivolities, it gets national attention. Even President Theodore Roosevelt reads it and approves of their conclusions. Roosevelt is concerned with the decline in white birthrates in the United States, and he fears that children of minorities and immigrants will eventually dominate American society. Calling this "race suicide," he wants white American women to leave their jobs, stay home, and produce big families. He writes to Van Vorst that women must "recognize that the greatest thing for any women is to be a good wife and mother."[268]

WORK

Journalist Arthur Vance, new editor of the *Woman's Home Companion*, wants to increase readership and attract homemakers. He hires writer **Gertrude Battles Lane** as household editor at twenty dollars a week. Lane views housewives as intelligent and thoughtful, with interests outside the household. She determines what readers want through questionnaires and will invite twelve readers annually to New York for a roundtable discussion. Lane will build the magazine into a leading publication whose circulation will lead all other women's magazines. She initiates a "Better Babies" column with the latest advice on prenatal and child care, and publishes articles on running a household efficiently. She will publish fiction by leading writers, illustrated with eye-catching art. Later, presidents Wilson, Coolidge, and Hoover and First Lady **Eleanor Roosevelt** will contribute columns. Lane will get promoted quickly and be appointed editor in chief in 1912. She will head the magazine until her death in 1941, when her annual salary will be more than $50,000. *Companion* publisher Joseph Knapp will call Lane "the best man in the business."[269]

EDUCATION AND SCHOLARSHIP

While more colleges for women are being built in the South, academic standards

Phoebe, a caretaker, sweeps the grounds at Magnolia-on-the-Ashley, in Charleston, South Carolina, 1901. (Library of Congress.) Like most blacks in the South, she had few job options other than work in the fields or menial labor. Phoebe might be a former slave. Female freed women had a lower status than male freedmen after the war. Black women were denied the status of white "ladies" (women whose primary duty was to care for home and family) because of race, and they were denied the right to vote because of gender.

are often lower than those of their northern counterparts. Many southern first-year college students received a less-than-adequate secondary education, and they are unprepared for college work. Nor do students view their female professors (mostly from the North) as role models. This first generation of southern female college graduates hopes to avoid the "family claim," but they also anticipate marriage and motherhood after graduation, rather than careers. As a result, some find themselves unqualified for graduate work or for a second bachelor's degree at a northern college.

A Sunday school group outside a schoolhouse, Pleasant Valley, Oklahoma Territory, c. 1902. (Western History Collections, University of Oklahoma.) The church was an important frontier institution. If churches were not yet built, services could be held in a schoolhouse, store, or even a train depot. The Sabbath was a needed day of rest from the week's labor of farming and a break in the isolated pioneer life. Families would travel miles to hear a sermon and socialize afterwards. It was women who organized the churches and taught Sunday schools. These youngsters and their parents are dressed in their best. Many lacked shoes but wore their pretty Sunday hats with pride.

One who faced this problem is **Elizabeth Avery Colton**, an alumna of Statesville Female College in North Carolina. She applied to Mt. Holyoke for a second degree, but needed to do preparatory work before being admitted. Colton begins a campaign to raise academic standards of southern women's colleges. This year she establishes the Southern Association of College Women. Members will survey courses and requirements in southern white women's colleges, seminaries, and normal schools and publish the results. While they will be unsuccessful in persuading state legislatures to set educational standards, their work will attract national attention. Some southern schools will broaden their curricula and raise graduation requirements. Later the group will merge with the Association of Collegiate Alumnae, becoming the American Association of University Women.

The University of Chicago publishes **Helen Bradford Thompson**'s dissertation,

The Mental Traits of Sex: An Experimental Investigation of the Normal Mind in Men and Women. Bradford is one of the first scholars to challenge the belief that biology causes differences in intelligence and personalities of men and women. She studied with psychologist James Angell, a young Chicago professor who wants to investigate human nature. He is skeptical of holistic theories of biological determinism and wants empirical research done, hoping to develop new theories. Angell supports female graduate students, and he encourages Thompson to pursue this research.

Thompson first analyzed the gender-differences studies done during the past twenty-five years. She found a general agreement that men are more analytical and have more variation in intelligence, while women are more emotional, have less variation in intelligence, and tend to be mediocre. The researchers concluded that these differences matched male and female roles in society.

Thompson found the studies inbred and formalistic. Even younger researchers failed to use the new experimental methods in measuring intelligence. Many of the writers' conclusions disagreed with their own findings, and Thompson found much faulty logic and inconsistency. None of the experts agreed on exactly how the sexes differ. Thompson then selected fifty Chicago undergraduates, twenty-five of each gender, and tested them in the laboratory. She measured differences in motor skills, personalities, sensory abilities, sensitivity to taste, touch, smells, and temperature, pain thresholds, and perception of color and weights. She found individual variation between and within genders but no pattern of consistent differences between the genders. She even concluded that women are not more emotional than men. The minor similarities within each gender she attributed to social conditioning. Her pioneering study questions conventional views on differences in men's and women's intelligence and inspires later studies which use more subjects and more sophisticated analytical techniques.

RELIGION

Margaret Seebach publishes "Shall Women Preach?" in the *Lutheran Quarterly*, and her answer is a resounding no. She first discusses practicality, pointing out that most women marry and will be needed at home for their "moral influence." She then raises the question of the male clergy who would have to take celibacy vows to avoid temptation of their co-workers. Her main justification is that women have lesser reasoning ability than men. "A woman ordinarily cannot convince a man of a thing by argument," she insists. "In logical presentation of truth, she is usually a failure." Therefore, how could a woman persuade men to embrace Christianity? If women preach, she maintains, men would leave the church.[270]

ARTS

Isabella Stuart Gardner, the wife of a Boston millionaire, is a flamboyant and eccentric trendsetter. She is known for her elaborate parties, fêtes, and Japanese tea ceremonies, attended by the Boston elite and prominent artists and intellectuals. Her main interest is art, and she has acquired masterpieces in her travels abroad. Twelve years ago a two-million-dollar inheritance from her father allowed her to augment her collection.

Deciding to build a museum to house her collections, she helped design a fifteenth-century-style Italian villa with a courtyard and glass skylights. This year, at age sixty-three, she opens her museum to an excited and eager crowd. She owns Italian Renaissance paintings and drawings, Dutch masterpieces, Asian treasures, and works by contemporary American and European artists. Her acquisitions also include tapestries, sculpture, artifacts, furniture, stained glass, choir stalls, and rare books, manuscripts, and correspondence of famous artists and writers. Few of the works have labels since she wants viewers to experience the art alone, undistracted by mention of the artists. She will leave the museum to the city of Boston in her will, with a large endowment, but will stipulate that nothing be rearranged, added, or deaccessioned so as to preserve her unique vision. The museum will flourish, and near the end of the twentieth century it will be visited annually by nearly 175,000.[271]

Writer **Mary Austin**'s first book, *The Land of Little Rain*, is published by Houghton, Mifflin in Boston. Here Austin portrays life in Inyo Country, a sparsely populated desert area between two mountain ranges in southeast California. Drawing upon what she has observed for fifteen years, she writes of Hispanics, Native Americans, and Anglos who are hunters, miners, ranchers, and artisans. Critics praise her lucid descriptions of the desolate yet beautiful landscape and her portrayal of people not often written about. Writer Ambrose Bierce calls the book "delicious," adding, "And what a knack of observation she has! ... if she is still young, she will do great work — if not, well she has *done* it in that book."[272] Austin will write much more, both fiction and nonfiction, emphasizing natural history and the people and environment of the western United States. She will develop a large circle of artist and writer friends in California, New Mexico, New York, and London. She will also be an activist, speaking at home and abroad for women's suffrage, birth control, protection of the environment, and Native American rights.

JOINING FORCES

The goal of the National American Woman Suffrage Association (NAWSA) is to get each state to amend its constitution to give females full suffrage. There has been tension with southern women, who want to prevent black women from getting suffrage, and southern legislators have already been disenfranchising black men. Although NAWSA members disagree about who should vote, the majority of the leaders want the support of the southern membership. This year, members adopt a states' rights policy, giving women in individual state chapters the right to decide who will be enfranchised in a proposed state constitutional amendment. This angers many black members, who turn to their own black organizations to campaign for suffrage. Although NAWSA members have been able to surmount some class and regional boundaries, they will be unable to overcome racial differences.

Unionist **Mary Kenney O'Sullivan** attends a meeting of the American Federation of Labor in Boston, where she and William English Walling, a wealthy New England reformer, found the Women's Trade Union League. Modeled after an English alliance, it is the first national American group whose goal is to organize women wage earners.

Membership cuts across classes and includes workers in industry and manufacturing, settlement house leaders, and middle- and upper-class reformers. In the first ten years, members help workers unionize by giving support, funds, money, advice, and publicity. They give similar help to strikers. Later, conflict will arise over leadership and goals. Unionists like O'Sullivan want to emphasize organizing, to improve workers' conditions, while others want to develop programs for workers' education and social uplift and to work for protective labor legislation. Membership will increase, with branches in many states, but within a decade the group's emphasis will be lobbying for protective legislation.

— 1904 —

DOMESTICITY

The Appleton Publishing Company in New York brings out psychologist G. Stanley Hall's new two-volume work, *Adolescence: Its Psychology and Its Relations to Physiology, Anthropology, Sociology, Sex, Crime, Religion, and Education.* Hall is a distinguished scholar with a Harvard Ph.D., and he is president of Clark University. He helped found the "new" psychology, concerned with human behavior and the mind.

Hall views adolescence as a crucial time in human development, and he writes that how our youth are educated will determine the course of civilization. He is among those who believe American society has become too soft from too many female teachers, college students, and wage earners. He maintains that boys are being raised to become "sissies," and he wants white men to reclaim control of society. He proposes that boys and girls need different kinds of education because the genders have evolved separately. Women are more primitive, being at an earlier evolutionary stage, while men are more modern, adaptive, and variable. Females should not be trained for careers, he writes, since excess learning might damage their reproductive system and cause them to rebel against their "natural" roles of wife and mother. In contrast, males need a rigorous college curriculum and should be exposed to sports, fraternity pranks, and roughousing as outlets for their "natural" toughness. Although some scholars are challenging Hall's viewpoints, he is beloved by mothers' groups and is respected by prominent educators and national leaders. His writings will educate and inspire several generations of psychologists and educators.

WORK

New York journalist **Ida Tarbell**, who writes for *McClure's* magazine, is already recognized for her writings on Napoleon and Abraham Lincoln. *McClure's* recently as-

signed her to investigate the Standard Oil Company, since she knows the oil business. Tarbell grew up in Titusville, Pennsylvania. When oil was discovered nearby, her father, a carpenter, founded a company making wooden oil tanks, but it later failed as Standard Oil grew more powerful and swallowed smaller concerns. Tarbell studied business documents and other writings and interviewed company leaders. Her series was published in *McClure's*, and this year it is published as a book, *A History of the Standard Oil Company*. It is widely read and acclaimed by a public eager to lambaste the excesses and corruption of big business. Tarbell will later write for *American Magazine*, exposing more corruption in American industry, and still later will support herself through lecturing on the Chautauqua Circuit. Despite her success, Tarbell later expresses resentment against women's rights in her 1912 book, *The Business of Being a*

Mrs. A. J. Blankenship and her daughter and their family restaurant and bakery, 1903. (Western History Collections, University of Oklahoma.) Their tent home is behind the business. On the frontier the labor of all family members was needed. It often took years for a farm to prosper enough to support the family. In the interim women took in boarders, sewed or cleaned for local families. Others, like this woman, opened businesses.

Woman. That business, she states, is marriage and motherhood.

EDUCATION AND SCHOLARSHIP

Mary McLeod Bethune, one of seventeen children of ex-slaves, was raised in South Carolina. Her dream was to become a missionary in Africa, but she was refused an appointment because of her race. She then decided to become an educator. Teaching for several years, she now moves to Daytona, Florida, where there is a growing black community but no public education available for them. This year she founds the Daytona Educational and Industrial Institute. It is at first a small school in a rented house, with six young students who use wooden boxes as seats, slivers from logs for pens, and the juice of elderberries for ink. Bethune envisions a larger facility to train black girls in nursing, cooking, teaching, and religion. While developing her school she becomes active in community affairs, establishes religions programs, and even founds a hospital for blacks. She earns respect from white and black Daytonans for her persistence and drive. Her school enlarges as she raises funds locally from white and black businesspeople, and nationally when Booker T. Washington publicizes her work in the black press. Her institute will expand into a large school with many buildings and a farm, and it will later become the coeducational four-year Bethune-Cookman College.

At age sixty-one Bethune will turn to government as a leader and spokeswoman for race relations and civil rights. She will resign the college presidency to serve on public committees and commissions. Developing a friendship with President Franklin and First **Lady Eleanor Roosevelt**, she will become their informal but influential adviser. Her "black cabinet," a group of government employees, will work for better employment opportunities for blacks and for reclaiming

Girls' basketball team, University of Oklahoma, Norman, Oklahoma Territory, c. 1905. (Western History Collections, University of Oklahoma.) In the center is Alice Boyd, daughter of the university's president, David Ross Boyd. The women are wearing blue serge gymnasium outfits, and their long hair is swept up in the fashionable pompadour style.

A Territorial Act of 1890 authorized a public university in Norman. The school opened in 1892 and, like many new institutions of higher learning, was coeducational. As the curriculum expanded, sports were added. A fitness craze had swept the nation, and exercise was urged for young women (some believed a strong constitution promoted fertility). In 1891 an educator for the YMCA had invented basketball, which became a popular college sport.

Anglo settlers and their Indian friends gathered for a sociable afternoon, 1905. (Western History Collections, University of Oklahoma.) Fiddle players were cherished in sparsely settled regions: music was an antidote to the drudgery and solitude of life. Neighbors often became cherished friends, and gatherings with music were eagerly anticipated.

their civil rights. Under her leadership they will be a strong voice in Washington and a powerful link to the White House during the New Deal.

ARTS

Architect **Julia Morgan** opens an office in San Francisco. She studied at the University of California's School of Engineering at Berkeley, where she received encouragement from noted architect Bernard Maybeck. She later earned a diploma in architecture at the Ecole des Beaux-Arts in Paris. Morgan will have a successful career. She will be helped by the wealthy **Phoebe Apperson Hearst**, who gives her commissions and recommends her to friends. Hearst will also introduce Morgan to her son, William Randolph, who will hire

her to design his castle, ranch, and newspaper offices in San Francisco and Los Angeles. His commissions will comprise one-third of Morgan's work. The 1906 San Francisco earthquake and fire will also help her build her practice, as new buildings are needed. She will be well known for helping shape the Bay-area cityscape. She will design more than 800 structures, which will include redwood shingle houses, the women's city club, the YWCA, the University's Greek Theater, churches in Berkeley and Oakland, Mills College buildings, and churches and hospitals. Her workload will increase in the 1920s, and she will have enough commissions to staff a full office during the Great Depression.

Morgan's success is unusual. The study of architecture, like other fields, is becoming

Members of a women's orchestra posed outside the home of Frank Barnes, Lampassas, Texas, c. 1905. (Western History Collections, University of Oklahoma Library.) Women formed these ensembles because most orchestra and band leaders refused to hire females. These novelty groups became popular in the United States after the 1870s and had successful tours. Note there are some woodwind and brass players. These instruments had long been considered taboo for women, who were thought too delicate to master them.

Females were admitted into the musicians' union in 1903, but prejudice was so ingrained that most were still unable to find jobs. They continued to establish all-female groups during the twenties and thirties. By the late 1940s, some small town orchestras hired women, but it would take decades before they were accepted into major orchestras.

specialized, with more required credentials. The American Institute of Architects (AIA), a professional organization, has tightened membership requirements. While they suggest that women could work as architects' assistants or in "domestic" architecture, they insist that females would be unable to supervise building construction or prepare large drawings. The editor of the AIA journal will later describe the ideal architect as a "gentleman of cultivation, learning, and broad sympathies ... who can inspire, organize and direct widely different classes of men."[273]

— 1905 —

DOMESTICITY

Women's membership in unions is declining. Five years ago 3.3 percent of all women in industry were organized, but in five more years their membership will be 1.5 percent. One reason for this is the persistence of labor leaders' belief that married women belong at home. This year a writer for the *Woman's Home Companion* interviews Samuel Gompers, president of the American Federation of Labor. When asked if he thinks married women should be employed, he replies, "No! ... generally speaking, there is no necessity for the wife contributing to the support of the family by work.... The wife as a wage-earner is a disadvantage economically considered, and socially is unnecessary."[274]

More American women are joining clubs. Five years ago the General Federation of Women's Clubs, which represents white middle-class groups, had 150,000 members, and the number is increasing. Some national leaders are concerned about club activities and ask women to retreat from public life. In a *Ladies' Home Journal* article, former president Grover Cleveland holds this view. While admitting that some religious and benevolent groups are harmless, he claims that many others are not, especially those that foster "intellectual improvement or entertainment." He charges that women are bored at home and join clubs to retaliate against their husbands. The aim of these clubs "directly menaces the integrity of our homes," he warns. He then pleads with women to follow their "Divinely appointed path of true womanhood."[275]

WORK

White middle-class households have become smaller as birthrates continue to decline, and technological conveniences are making home maintenance easier. More middle-class families have gas, electricity, running water, and bathrooms. The availability of packaged foods, ready-made clothing, hand-cranked washing machines, iceboxes, vacuum cleaners, and electric irons lessens the housewives' burden.

Two other trends balance these conveniences. Fewer women now work as domestic servants, as better-paying jobs in industry, offices, and stores are available. This has created a servant problem: the demand for maids is greater than the supply. Also, the public health movement, with its publicity about germs, has helped raise cleaning standards. The discovery of germs as a cause of

disease became public knowledge during the 1890s, and there has been much preoccupation with dirt and its consequences. Home economists have taken up the campaign to promote higher standards of cleanliness. They suggest that a thorough housecleaning, formerly done infrequently by housewives, should now be performed daily to keep homes pure and clean. Manufacturers are producing more cleaning products and equipment. In their advertisements they insist it is a moral necessity to have a clean house. Magazines join the crusade about cleanliness. The *Ladies' Home Journal* cautions, "We should be careful how we sweep and dust a room. Once the dust is set in motion there is no knowing where some of the spores contained in it will lodge."[276]

— 1906 —

EDUCATION AND SCHOLARSHIP

Economist **Edith Abbott**, whose doctorate is from the University of Chicago, is awarded a Carnegie fellowship to the London School of Economics and Political Science. Her studies and her acquaintance with socialists **Beatrice** and **Sidney Webb** will influence her entire career. She is inspired by their ideas and writings on reform and wants to found similar programs to eliminate poverty in the United States.

Several years later she will assist **Sophonisba Breckinridge**, who directs research at the Chicago School of Civics and Philanthropy, an independent facility that trains social workers. Abbott investigates Chicago's social problems. Believing that finding facts and figures is the first step toward solving problems, she investigates slums, poverty-stricken black, white, and immigrant families, children in factories, and conditions in industry and in jails. She will write more than one hundred books and articles on her research, suggesting reform programs. Her studies will become social work classics, used in formulating national policies.

Twenty-five-year-old **Lucy Sprague**, a Radcliffe graduate, moves to Berkeley, California, to become the University of California's first dean of women. The school is coeducational but female enrollment has increased, causing a backlash from campus males. Some professors warn students that if they study too much they will lose their femininity, and they denounce the female instructors as "unnatural." Cartoonists ridicule students as ugly and as "old maids" and they lampoon the suffrage movement in newspapers and yearbooks. The school publication devotes more attention to sports and male activities. Sprague is shocked at the hostility and vows to build a female community and increase its presence on campus. She will set curfews, guidelines for social behavior, and a code against cheating. She will plan programs linking women students with the female faculty and will ask faculty wives to give teas and poetry readings. Sprague will attend meetings of women's clubs and suggest ways to increase membership and projects to link the clubs. When she learns that 90 percent of female students plan to teach school, she takes groups to San Francisco to visits slums, jails, and asylums to show possible careers in civic work. She talks to university department heads about jobs for female graduates, interviews women in many professions, and presents a report to the university's president, Benjamin Wheeler. She will establish an annual pageant to be written, produced, and performed by students, thereby encouraging their artistic talents. Next year Sprague will report that that when she arrived 42 percent of female students were active on campus, and this has increased to 81 percent. Six years later she will leave California to marry; her successor, **Lucy Ward Stebbins**, will continue Sprague's work.[277]

ARTS

The grand piano, a costly instrument, was modified into an upright during the mid–1800s. The upright has become popular in America because of its availabity, and it is now found in hundreds of middle-class homes. Many young women play it, and some have turned to ragtime, which, though once considered immoral, is now fashionable. Some females are even composing tunes. Milwaukee pianist **Adaline Shepherd** publishes her first rag, "Pickles and Peppers." It is a jaunty tune, and two years later presidential candidate William Jennings Bryan will use it as a campaign song. This increases its sheet music sales to nearly 200,000. Shepherd will

Delia Reich at her piano, Michigan, c. 1914. (Richard D. Miles.) The piano was considered an instrument suitable for women, and by the turn of the century, nearly 90 percent of all pianists were female. The upright was common in middle-class homes, being less costly than a grand piano. Reich's instrument is elegant; note the carved panel in the front where the music rests. She covered its top with a tasseled bunting and decorated it with family photos and memorabilia. Pianos were replacing fireplaces as a parlor's center focus, as more families acquired central heating.

write two more rags, but then she will marry and retire from composing.[278]

Sculptor **Mary Abastenia St. Leger Eberle** completes her work *Roller Skating*, which she modeled after a girl in the streets of Manhattan. This bronze piece depicts a young girl skating happily, with her arms wide open and hair flying back. Eberle is among a group of artists who are tired of the popular stylized and elegant art portraying genteel society. They want to create more realistic art. Some depict urban life with its grittiness and vitality, celebrating it as one aspect of American life. Many work in bronze as a better medium than the traditional marble for showing wrinkled skin or sagging socks. Eberle will later establish her studio in New York City's Lower East Side so that she can observe ghetto children at play. Because realism is not yet in vogue, Eberle will earn few commissions, and art critics will dismiss her work as unattractive. Later she will gain recognition and respect and be elected an associate of the National Academy of Design.

San Francisco artists **Lucia Mathews** and her husband Arthur found a new magazine, *Philapolis*, to give readers ideas on furnishing new homes and businesses that will replace the ones devastated by the San Francisco earthquake and fire. This year they also open a furniture store. Lucia paints oil pictures, designs and paints furniture, and decorates screens, boxes, and picture frames. She uses many Japanese and floral motifs and art nouveau and Pre-Raphaelite designs. The Mathews' work helps popularize the Californian decorative arts movement, the western version of the arts and crafts movement. Their work sells well, but within a decade, as modernism replaces decorative arts styles, their designs become outmoded.

Richard Pratt, who founded the Carlisle Indian School in Pennsylvania in 1879, has resigned as superintendent, allowing some changes in the school's curriculum. Pratt's motto was "Kill the Indian, save the man." His goal was to assimilate Indian children into American society by forbidding them to retain tribal dress or customs. This year Winnebago artist **Angel DeCora** accepts a position to develop and head a native arts and crafts program at Carlisle. Teaching the traditional art forms, DeCora encourages her students to experiment with native designs. She is also concerned that many paintings on Indian life and culture have incorrect details, and she urges her students to portray native dress correctly.

JOINING FORCES

The National American Woman Suffrage Association plans this year's convention in Baltimore. They are discouraged that despite decades of work, women have full suffrage in only four states: Wyoming, Colorado, Utah, and Idaho. They think this is due to prevailing conservative attitudes. Many Americans still think women are inferior and that suffrage is too radical; even some prominent women are unsupportive or oppose it. To broaden support, they plan an active program featuring prominent Americans. A tribute to the eighty-six-year-old **Susan B. Anthony**, who is much loved, are held. They ask local leaders to participate. Ira Remsen, who is president of Johns Hopkins University, agrees to be the key speaker. Others at the podium are William Welsh, a former Johns Hopkins Medical School dean, **Martha Carey Thomas**, president of Bryn Mawr College, and **Jane Addams**. Hundreds attend the convention, and the movement acquires new supporters. Many Johns Hopkins faculty members publicly endorse it, as do more prominent female scholars and scientists. Thomas will found the National College Suffrage League, in which students, faculty, and alumnae will campaign for suffrage. These new constituencies will give the suffrage movement added strength.

LAW AND POLITICS

Congress passes the Pure Food and Drug Act. Many drug manufacturers add narcotics

Women trimming currency at the Bureau of Engraving and Printing, Washington, D.C., 1907. (National Archives.) Most are young, middle-class white women. They wear shirtwaists with high collars and ribbons, are well groomed, and have fashionable hairstyles. During the Civil War women were hired to staff government offices. They were good workers and could be paid less than men. This set a trend for office work as a female profession. Note the male supervisors by the walls.

and alcohol to their products and exaggerate claims about effectiveness. The act requires truth in advertising, demanding that labels must list all ingredients and that drug makers must prove claims of efficacy. Members of the General Federation of Women's Clubs have been working and lobbying for this legislation, and they celebrate its passage.

— 1907 —

RELIGION

Although Unitarians have allowed female ordination since the early 1800s, church leaders have discouraged it. The Harvard Divinity School, the alma mater of many male liberal ministers, still rejects female applicants. By 1890 only seventy women had been ordained as Unitarians or Universalists. Recently, church leaders have noted the decline in male theology students and are concerned that the denomination has lost prestige in the eastern United States. Samuel Eliot, president of the American Unitarian Association, wants the religion to become more "manly." He plans to train women as parish assistants, hoping this will deflect their desire to preach. The Joseph Tuckerman School in Boston opens this year with three students. The curriculum offers courses in Sunday school administration, mission work, nursing, teaching, and hygiene. The students are told their role will be a domestic one; they should not plan to do any public speaking or reform work, and they must certainly avoid the "folly of the women's movement." The skills they will need are "affection, friendship, support and kindness." The school will be unsuccessful. Many students will withdraw, feeling the program is too narrow, and will turn to secular social work. Few graduates will find jobs. Churches hesitate to employ them because ministers' wives and church women provide these services free. Those who do find jobs earn low salaries and work long hours. After fifteen years, the school will have only forty alumnae.[279]

ARTS

Musician **Frances Theresa Densmore,** a native of Red Wing, Minnesota, who teaches in Boston, has turned her attention to Native American music. Inspired by Alice Fletcher's book on Omaha music, she decided to visit tribes to hear their music herself. Two years ago she visited a Chippewa village where she heard and transcribed a religious ceremony; later she published her account in the *American Anthropologist.* This year she realizes that written transcriptions are insufficient to preserve native heritage. She borrows a phonograph so she can transcribe songs on wax cylinders. She will spend the next forty years — until well into her eighties — traveling and recording Indian music. She is partially supported by a grant from the Smithsonian's Bureau of Ethnology. To visit tribes inaccessible by car, she will travel in a boat or

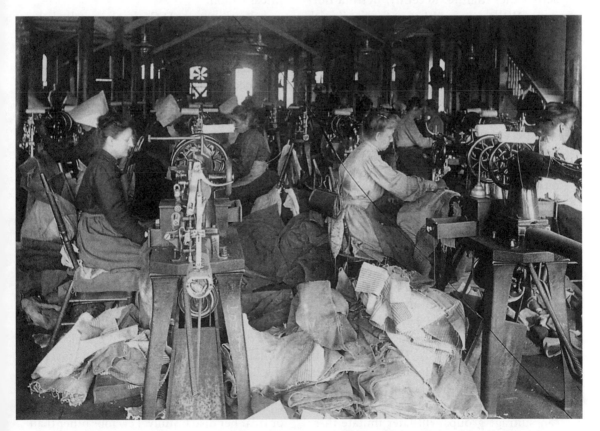

Female workers at the United States Post Office Department's mailbag repair shop, 1907. (National Archive.) These white, middle-aged women wear aprons to cover their street clothing. The male supervisors probably earned more than twice what the women did.

Working conditions were poor. Employees were often fined for talking, they were allowed few rest breaks, and toilet facilities were primitive and dirty. Shops were poorly lit and cramped; in this photo cloth scraps litter the floor, a fire hazard. Such conditions led reformers to agitate for industry regulation.

a birchbark canoe. The work is often frustrating: her bulky equipment sometimes fails, and often the only buildings available to work in are empty jails, shacks, or sheds with mice. Densmore will be respected for her writings on these declining cultures in monographs and articles, illustrated with her photographs of the musicians, and for the music of more than thirty tribes on nearly 2,000 wax cylinders.[280]

JOINING FORCES

British suffragists use militance to demand the vote, even at the expense of being imprisoned. Americans are eager to hear about their work, and there is much visiting across the Atlantic. Recently, **Bettina Borman Wells**, a member of the British Women's Social and Political Union, urges a New York City audience of suffragists to become more aggressive. They should demand rights in public outdoor meetings, have demonstrations, disrupt meetings, and announce boycotts. Because this behavior is unexpected of women, they will get better press coverage, she advises. "We must eliminate that abominable word 'ladylike' from our vocabularies," she insists "we must get out and fight."[281] Following her suggestions, New York librarian **Maude Malone** organizes the American Suffragettes. Members are left-wing reformers, egalitarians, intellectuals, writers, artists, and teachers. Twenty-three attend the first meeting in Madison Square and announce they will march in the city's first all-female parade. Later they have the parade, despite being denied a police permit, and attract huge crowds. They will speak in schools and hold outdoor meetings. Their activities win the support of socialists and many wage-earning women. Other American suffrage groups will later imitate these tactics.

Harriot Stanton Blatch, the daughter of **Elizabeth Cady Stanton**, has returned to New York from a twenty-year stay in England. A Vassar graduate, she wrote her thesis on poverty in England. She admires working-class women and wants to bring them into the suffrage movement, having them join forces with middle- and upper-class women. This year she forms the Equality League for Self Supporting Women. Members include industrial and manufacturing workers, seamstresses, milliners, settlement house workers, lawyers, physicians, writers, and reformers. Their goals are to improve conditions for workers and to campaign for suffrage. They hold rallies and outdoor meetings and organize parades. Members speak to legislative committees. Two hundred women join the first year, and in eighteen months membership will be at 20,000.[282] The group will later be renamed the Women's Political Union.

Washington, D.C., is often called the black middle-class capital. After the Civil War thousands of ex-slaves migrated there, viewing it as the city of Lincoln, symbolizing freedom. Since Reconstruction's end and the initiation of Jim Crow laws, thousands more southerners have fled to the capital, looking for education, jobs, and upward mobility. Yet there is much discrimination in the city, and some southern legislators are calling for even more restrictions. **Mary Church Terrell**, a distinguished educator and fifteen-year city resident, is embittered by the prejudice, and writes "What It Means to Be Colored in the Capital of the United States," for the *Independent*. While many call Washington, D. C., the "Colored Man's Paradise," this is far from true, she begins. Hotels and restaurants, unless black-owned, are closed to her. If she wants to travel to national monuments she is forced to travel in the back of the trolley. She is barred from most theaters and unwelcome in white churches. Department store clerks ignore her or treat her disdainfully. Few jobs other than menial labor are open to black women, no matter how smart or educated they are, she writes. And conditions have worsened. Even in the black school system, African Americans can no longer be superintendents or department heads. No art or law schools admit African Americans, and only one white university does. That such oppression based on skin color should exist in the capital of a country founded on freedom is "hideous and hateful," she declares. Many of the indignities Terrell and others endure will continue well into the twentieth century.[283]

— 1908 —

WORK

Rose Knox and her husband have formed a gelatin business in Johnstown, New York, where nearby tanneries provide the raw materials. Because gelatin is commonly used only in dishes for invalids, Rose develops recipes for everyday use. This year her husband dies and Knox takes over the business. She is an excellent administrator with a good business sense. She will demonstrate cooking with gelatin, publish more recipes, and write a newspaper column. She keeps the plant in good condition and gives her staff a five-day workweek and benefits, ensuring company loyalty. She will build an experimental kitchen and fund research for new gelatin uses. The Knox Company will expand physically and attain a larger market. They will eventually have 60 percent of all sales of unflavored gelatin and be worth $1 million by the early 1920s.[284]

A woman and her young children making artificial flowers at home, c. 1908. (Archives of Labor and Urban Affairs, Wayne State University.) Just as today, females needed to supplement their husband's inadequate wages. Many women would take in piecework. Some made artificial flowers or shelled nuts in their tenements, often recruiting their three- or four-year-olds to assist.

RELIGION

Mary Baker Eddy, who founded the Church of Christ, Scientist in 1879, publishes several journals and weeklies for her followers. This year the eighty-seven-year-old leader decides a daily newspaper is also needed and founds the *Christian Science Monitor*. She is tired of the yellow journalism and the overemphasis on crime in American newspapers, and she has often disapproved of the way her church business is reported.

The *Monitor* will become known for accurate stories and good international coverage, and it will be read by many who are not Christian Scientists. At the end of the twentieth century it will remain a respected American newspaper.

ARTS

Marian MacDowell studied piano at age ten and later traveled to Germany for advanced work, hoping to become a concert pianist. She abandoned this plan when she married composer Edward MacDowell, working as his secretary, copyist, and critic. This year Edward dies, and his fifty-one-year-old widow decides to implement his dream — to establish a rural retreat for artists. Friends and clubs have raised $30,000 for his medical bills, and this money was put in a memorial fund. She uses this to buy 135 acres in rural New Hampshire and founds the MacDowell Colony. Royalties from his music pay for operating expenses, and MacDowell raises more through lectures and recitals. She will gradually enlarge the facility to more than 700 acres. Many young artists nurtured there will later achieve prominence, including Aaron Copland, Willa Cather, Thornton Wilder, and Elinor Wylie. MacDowell will manage the retreat with a firm hand for nearly forty years, and she will receive several awards for her distinguished contribution to American arts.[285]

JOINING FORCES

Lugenia Burns Hope, who lives in Atlanta's black community with her family, wants to improve the neighborhood. This year she begins a reform campaign, organizing a group of women who raise funds to establish kindergartens and day care centers. Their projects are so successful that they expand their work and become the Neighborhood Union. They divide the black communities into districts and survey the needs of each. Hope is an outspoken advocate for black causes, and she gets the help of local college administrators, church leaders, and prominent Atlanta citizens. Her group will raise money for playgrounds, nurseries, and a medical clinic, and they will lobby to get streets paved and lighting and a public sewage installed. They will also be able to get an African-American high school in the city and the nation's first public housing for African Americans. The National Association of Colored Women, the Urban League, and other black organizations will later initiate projects using the Neighborhood Unions' methods.

Martha Franklin, a black nurse from New Haven, Connecticut, whose nursing degree is from the Women's Hospital in Philadelphia, wants to join a professional association, but she is barred from the all-white American Nurses Association. Deciding to establish a group for black nurses, she writes to nursing school graduates to determine interest. This year fifty nurses meet at a New York City church. They found the National Association of Colored Graduate Nurses and elect Franklin president. Their goals are to raise educational standards, fight employment discrimination, and improve blacks' health care. They will compile a national employment registry, establish a fellowship program for postgraduate training, and publish a newsletter. Membership will increase. Despite their work, discrimination in education and employment will continue through the late 1940s.

Members of the Asheville High School faculty, Asheville, North Carolina, 1909. (North Carolina Collection, Pack Memorial Public Library, Asheville, N.C.) At the top is Robert V. Kennedy, principal; second row: M. K. Weber, Mary E. Anderson, Sue F. Robbins, Mr. Rubins; front row: Mabel M. Robinson, Helen G. Robinson, Miss Russell, and L. Josephine Webster.

This photo reflects national trends in school employment. Most administrators were men, and most teachers, women. Male teachers earned more than their female colleagues . In most urban areas only single female instructors were hired. The percentage of female teachers in the United States who were 66 percent of all teachers in 1870, increased to nearly 80 percent in 1909. While most teachers in the antebellum South were men, by the turn of the century most were women.

LAW AND POLITICS

In *Muller v. Oregon*, the U.S. Supreme Court upholds an Oregon law limiting female laundry and factory workers to ten-hour days. Justice Louis Brandeis rules that since "healthy mothers are essential to vigorous offspring, the physical well-being of women becomes a object of public interest and care in order to preserve the strength and vigor of the race." Although female reformers have lobbied and worked for this and celebrate the victory, the ruling has negative long-term consequences for wage-earning women. It helps sets a precedent for gender bias in protective-

labor legislation; it upholds traditional views on gender roles; and it will limit women's job opportunities. The decision also initiates a period of increasing state legislation protecting female workers. By 1914 twenty-seven states will have laws regulating women's hours.[286]

— 1909 —

EDUCATION AND SCHOLARSHIP

Black writer and activist **Nannie Helen Burroughs** helped found the Women's

Convention, a women's auxiliary group of the Baptist Church and a voice for black women. As secretary, she crusades for social justice, better education, and better employment. Because most black women are wage earners, Burroughs wants better vocational education for girls from low-income families. She has convinced the Women's Convention to support a school, and this year the National Training School for Women and Girls in Washington, D.C., opens. Burroughs is president and will head it for nearly fifty years. Her curriculum includes training for missionary work and courses in dressmaking, domestic service, clerical skills, bookkeeping, barbering, shoe repair, and printing. Burroughs wants students to be proud of their heritage, and requires all students to take a course in African-American history. The school's motto is "Bible, bath, and broom," indicating that black women need religion, cleanliness, and housework skills to survive in the United States. During the school's first decades several thousand will graduate, including some students from the Caribbean and Africa. In the 1960s the school will be renamed the Nannie Helen Burroughs School.

Vivian Gordon Harsh, a black high school graduate in Chicago, accepts a job as a junior clerk at the city's public library. She will receive several promotions while she continues her education, and she will eventually earn a graduate library degree. Later, heading a branch library in Chicago's south side, Harsh will start a collection of writings by African Americans. She will buy books, journals, pamphlets, and documents with funds from grants, private donations, and her own salary. She will involve the community through library programs featuring black writers, and her branch library will become a meeting place for black artists and intellectuals, many of whom will donate their papers and typescripts. She will build the Special Negro Collections through the 1930s, despite opposition from library administrators. Eventually the collection will

include nearly 70,000 volumes, including many rare black newspapers and valuable archival materials on Illinois black history. In 1970, ten years after her death, the holdings will be renamed the Vivian G. Harsh Collection of Afro-American History and Literature.[287]

Since 1900, psychologists, geneticists, anatomists, and physiologists have been studying gender differences. Most researchers have concluded that intelligence and personality traits are unrelated to gender. This year, Franklin Mall, a respected anatomist at Johns Hopkins, publishes his research on male and female brains in the *American Journal of Anatomy*. He concludes that brain weight varies between genders and among races; that there is no correlation between a brain's weight and the person's intelligence; and that there is no such thing as a male or female brain. His work helps disprove earlier claims that intelligence differs by gender. Other scientists are doing similar work and reaching similar conclusions, and by World War I it will be unfashionable in psychology and other sciences to link gender with intelligence.

RELIGION

Frances Xavier Cabrini, an Italian immigrant and Catholic nun, becomes a naturalized American citizen this year. She has founded schools, convents, hospitals, and orphanages on three continents and has raised money to support them. After her death she will be the first American canonized by the Catholic Church.

Physician and Methodist missionary **Clara Swain** publishes *A Glimpse of India*, on her life as a missionary doctor. In 1869 a new American women's missionary society gave Swain the appointment to India. At that time few American women were medical doctors, and they were pleased to appoint her because women were needed to treat females and children. Swain worked primarily in Bareilly, a city in northern India. She provided medical care at the city's mission and in orphanages, and she often traveled to patients' homes riding on her elephant. She was permitted to treat women and children who were sequestered in zenanas and had no access to medical care. She also taught medical classes and trained hundreds of Indians as medical providers. Swain wanted to build permanent medical facilities in Bareilly, and she was given a gift of forty acres by the Nawab of Rampore. There she established a dispensary and a women's hospital, where patients of all castes could be accommodated. It was one of India's first hospitals for women, and the sick would travel from as far away as Burma to be treated. Later her hospital will be enlarged to provide health care for all Indians and will be renamed the Clara Swain Hospital.

ARTS

Writer **Gertrude Stein**, a Radcliffe alumna, has moved to Paris to live with her brother Leo, an aspiring artist. They both admire the new abstract art, and they have bought works by Cézanne, Monet, Matisse, and Pablo Picasso, whom Gertrude has befriended. The Steins hold a popular salon where Gertrude meets Alice B. Toklas, who is visiting from California. Toklas eventually moves in and becomes Gertrude's typist, proofreader, critic, and companion. Stein has been experimenting with an impressionistic writing technique: she uses words to convey a state of mind or impression, rather than developing a plot or characters. She uses this method in her book *Three Lives*, which she has privately printed this year. Reaction to her book is lukewarm, and although Stein continues to write she will not achieve fame in the United States until the publication of her 1933 work, *The Autobiography of Alice B. Toklas*.

Missourian Illustrator and cartoonist **Rose O'Neill** of Missouri is recently divorced and supports herself by contributing stories, poems, and illustrations to several leading women's magazines. This year, *Ladies' Home Journal* editor Edward Bok, who likes O'Neill's drawings, encourages her to fashion a new cartoon character. She creates the Kewpies, chubby-faced cupids with wings and wisps of hair. She uses them initially to illustrate her stories and poems. Kewpies become so popular that she sells the concept to manufacturers who produce Kewpie figurines, greeting cards, soaps, and dolls. O'Neill will earn nearly $1.5 million from royalties, enabling her to travel in Europe for many years. She later returns to her Connecticut estate, where she will write more poetry, take up sculpting, and entertain lavishly.

JOINING FORCES

Swedish writer and socialist **Ellen Key**'s book *The Century of the Child* is translated into English and becomes a best-seller in the United States. Key values the role of the mother, claiming that "not woman, but the mother is the most precious possession of the nation."[288] Key believes that if mothers would raise their children full-time they would produce a civilization of superior citizens. She suggests the mothers be paid for their work and that unmarried mothers be fully supported by the state. Key will write more books endorsing divorce, free love, birth control, and women's sexual fulfillment. She will be a popular but controversial figure in the United States. While her writings inspire much discussion among women's rights advocates, most Americans consider her program too radical.

The first American telephone exchange was established in 1879 in New Haven, Connecticut. By 1900 there were more than 1,000 exchanges and Americans had 1.3 million telephones. By 1920 they will own 13.3 million.[289] The phone company prefers to hire female operators since they will accept low wages, are considered more docile than men, and have pleasant voices As the industry expands, the job of operator has become a female occupation. Two years ago women were 96 percent of all telephone operators. Because the job is demanding, with strict supervision and uncomfortable working conditions, many operators wanted to join the International Brotherhood of Electrical Workers, the male telephone employees' union. This year they are finally admitted.

There are 500 shirtwaist factories in New York City employing more than 30,000 workers, many of whom are unorganized. Because of worsening conditions in factories, several shirtwaist shops are on strike. Members of the International Ladies' Garment Workers' Union (ILGWU) are supportive, and they meet in New York's Cooper Union to discuss a citywide walkout. After several officials speak, Clara Lemlich, a young Russian Jewish immigrant and a shirtwaist worker prominent in the ILGWU, takes the podium. She urges the crowd to strike, and they agree. Between 20,000 and 40,000 garment workers strike, and this shuts down the city's clothing production. Nearly 75 percent of the strikers are female, making this the largest mass walkout of women. The walkout shuts down the city's clothing production. Members of the Women's Trade Union League, the ILGWU, and the Socialist Party help the strikers. Some join the strike and others arrange for picket coverage, give food or relief money to strikers' families, generate publicity, and donate bail money. After four months the strike is officially called off. Workers in more than 300 factories get their conditions met, and thousands join the ILGWU, helping it become a powerful union. The strike inspires other walkouts and begins a period of militancy among female laborers.[290]

Last year a two-day race riot in Springfield, Illinois, left many dead. Reformer William English Walling was so appalled that he published an article in the *Independent* in which he insisted that if nothing is done to fight prejudice there may be a northern race war. Social worker **Mary White Ovington** responded to his call, and she and several others met with Walling to plan for a national organization. They then contacted sixty prominent black and white leaders, who meet this year in New York City. **Ida Wells-Barnett, Mary Church Terrell, Jane Addams,** and others meet to organize the National Association for the Advancement of Colored People (NAACP). Their goals are to fight segregation and lynching and to protect blacks' civil rights through legal and political action. They reject the style of accommodation that Booker T. Washington uses in dealing with racism, preferring the confrontational methods advocated by W. E. B. Du Bois (who is also a founding NAACP member). The early officers are white men, but African American males later dominate leadership. The organization will expand into a prominent one with branches in all states. In the late twentieth century membership will be more than 500,000.[291]

— 1910 —

WORK

Women comprise 21 percent of all wage earners. They continue to dominate several occupations that have grown. The number of stenographers and typists and of social workers has tripled since 1900; women comprise respectively, 83 percent and 93 percent of these employees. The number of trained nurses has increased nearly sevenfold during the past decade, and 93 percent are women. Women continue to dominate the teaching profession, comprising 83 percent of all teachers.[292]

Another growing vocation for women is librarianship. Americans established more than 3,000 public libraries in cities in the late 1870s; by 1900 this figure had increased to 8,000. Many were gifts from Andrew Carnegie, who will spend $39 million funding libraries. He stipulates that towns must raise local taxes for support. Because city administrators prefer to buy books and keep staff costs low, they hire women, who can be paid less and are already viewed as "guardians of culture." This year women comprise 79 percent of all librarians.[293]

The majority of African American women still work in menial and low-paying jobs. A survey shows that 52 percent of all black women work in agriculture as sharecroppers, farm laborers, or seasonal workers. Another 28 percent are employed as laundresses or cooks. There has also been a large migration of blacks from the South: since 1870 more than 200,000 have migrated north, where they find work as maids. Southern black women comprise the majority of domestic servants in the North.[294]

EDUCATION AND SCHOLARSHIP

Nurse **Lillian Wald** has already pioneered in public health. Fifteen years ago she established a nurses' settlement house in New York City's Lower East Side, offering health care to local residents. Her facility has expanded to provide convalescent care, first aid, and educational and social services. Wald has also called for better education for nurses for she believes her own training was inadequate. This year she helps establish a Department of Nursing and Health at Columbia Teachers College. Graduates of the program will later establish many nursing training schools and public health clinics in the United States.

RELIGION

Helen Barrett Montgomery, a prominent civic leader in Rochester, New York, is active in the Baptist Church. She has been commissioned by the Central Committee on the United States Study of Foreign Missions to report on the accomplishments of female missionaries. This year she publishes *Western Women in Eastern Lands: Fifty Years of Woman's Work in Foreign Missions*. The work

reviews what American women have done in Asia. They have converted hundreds to Christianity, taught women and children to read and write English, given medical care, and built hospitals, clinics, orphanages, and schools. Montgomery believes churchwomen should retain control of their own missionary organizations. She is uneasy about the trend of many Protestant church leaders to merge women's groups into the main church body. She will later serve on several national women's mission boards and help organize the World Wide Guild, a national Baptist group that encourages young women to enter missionary work.

ARTS

Musician **Emma Azalia Smith Hackley**, who now lives in Philadelphia, has had an active music career in Detroit and Denver. She has taught, performed in black groups and orchestras, directed church choirs, and organized city choruses. She also helped many young African American musicians find employment in southern black colleges. Hackley believes that knowing their musical heritage will help instill racial pride in young people. This year she tours the South, lecturing on and performing black folk music. The appreciation she receives inspires her to later organize a series of black folk music festivals. Many young black musicians attending these were unaware of the beauty of spirituals and gospels, and they will later incorporate the older melodies and rhythms into their compositions and performances.

JOINING FORCES

Members of the National American Woman Suffrage Association have collected 404,000 signatures on a petition requesting an amendment to the United States Constitution for full suffrage for women, which they present to Congress. There is much other suffrage activity this year. In New York City's Greenwich Village, socialist Max

Cartoon, "Election Day!" by E.W. Gustin, 1909. (Library of Congress.) This is typical editorialization of perceived role-reversal. A woman dressed to go out to vote glances at her husband with a grim expression. The bewildered and unhappy man, small and delicate, wears an apron and taps his toe in frustration. The babies are bawling and a dish has fallen and broken. Even the cat with its fluffed tail held high seems alarmed at the woman's imminent departure. A sign at the bottom announces the "Hen Party" candidates: Mrs. Henry Peck for president and Mrs. William Nagg for Vice President. This cartoon portrays the fear of many anti-suffragists: if women voted the family would fall apart. Women would become aggressive, leave the house to go to meetings and bars. Men would be left to raise the children and clean house.

Eastman founds the Men's League for Woman Suffrage, whose members join women's parades and demonstrations. **Carrie Chapmann Catt**'s New York City's Woman Suffrage Party, organized last year, is growing and will increase to 500,000 within a decade. The National Association of Colored Women has endorsed female suffrage, and many local African-American groups campaign for enfranchisement. Supporters of suffrage now include immigrants, more working-class women, college students, and even the wealthy, as it is now considered a fashionable cause. Suffrage has replaced temperance as the largest mass movement of American women.[295]

LAW AND POLITICS

Women in the state of Washington have spent decades campaigning for the vote. This year the voters approve a state referendum providing full suffrage for females.

Oklahoma Democrat **Kate Barnard** is active in reform politics. Three years ago, at her urging, state legislators authorized a new elective position, a commissioner of charities and corrections. The thirty-two-year-old Barnard campaigned for the office and won, and she has been reelected this year. She wants to initiate reform and has developed a strategy to pass legislation. She appoints experts to draft a bill; then, before introducing it to legislators, she gets the support of constituents and publicly campaigns in her eloquent oratorical style. Barnard helps get many laws passed, including a compulsory education law, statutes prohibiting child labor, and legislation prohibiting unsafe working conditions in industry and forbidding blacklisting of union members.

Next year she will hire an attorney to investigate corruption in Indian affairs. The United States government recently gave the state authority to designate guardians of minor Indian children, but some appointees have robbed their young charges of lands with valuable timber, oil and gas deposits, and rich soils for agriculture. Barnard will recover nearly a million dollars for the young Native Americans, but state officials will be angry at her meddling. They will cut her staff, reduce her funding, and harass her office assistants. Barnard will not run again for public office, and she will be unsuccessful in raising private funds to continue her investigation.

— 1 9 1 1 —

WORK

Physician **Alice Hamilton** moved to Chicago in 1897 to teach pathology at the Women's Medical College at Northwestern University. When administrators abruptly closed the college in 1902, she became involved in industrial medicine. Living at Hull House and interacting with neighborhood residents made her aware of the poor health of many industrial workers. She researched industrial hazards, only to discover that Americans have ignored the issue. She found no safety laws for factories using hazardous substances such as lead, and no program for compensating poisoned workers. Hamilton was appointed to a new state commission on occupational diseases, and investigations and subsequent reports led to state laws compensating workers for diseases caused by poisonous gases, fumes, or dust. This year she is appointed special investigator for the United Sates Bureau of Labor, a position she will hold until 1920. Her thorough factory inspections, interviews with sick employees, and intensive laboratory work will allow her to correlate hazardous substances in industry with disease. Her findings will bring national attention and lead to regulatory legislation. As America's only expert, she will later be appointed assistant professor of industrial medicine at Harvard University. Her book *Industrial Poisons in the United States*, published in 1925, will be the first American text on the topic. She will remain one of the country's leading experts, and in 1949 she will revise her 1934 work, *Industrial Toxicology.*

EDUCATION AND SCHOLARSHIP

Educator **Jessie Field** publishes *The Corn Lady: The Story of a Country Teacher's Life.* Field, the daughter of Iowa pioneers, taught in rural schools and was later appointed the superintendent of schools in Page County, Iowa. She wanted to encourage an interest in farming in her students, and her text *Farm Arithmetic* had math problems of the sort farmers might need to solve. She often invited agricultural experts from local colleges to demonstrate new techniques in her classes. Most successful were her after-school activities. She organized corn clubs for boys, with corn, milk, and livestock judging contests, and home clubs for girls, with competition in crafts and cooking. Winners were awarded a pin whose design she created. It was a three-leaf clover, with a letter H on each leaf to represent head (technology), hands (agriculture), and heart (domestic science). These clubs are so successful that they will later became a national activity for rural youth sponsored by the United States Department of Agriculture as 4-H clubs (after adding another "H" for health).

Illustrator **Anna Botsford Comstock** also lectures on natural history at the University of Cornell. Her interest in natural history was heightened some years ago when she was appointed member of a state committee to promote agriculture. Hoping to curb the mass migration to cities and to encourage young people to become farmers, they established a program to teach natural history in the schools. Members hoped that an understanding of nature would inspire youth to live in rural areas. Comstock spoke on behalf of the group and prepared pamphlets for classroom. She has published books on insects, bees, butterflies, and trees, which she illustrates. This year Comstock publishes *The Handbook of Nature Study.* Designed for schoolteachers, it is an introduction to plant and animal life, with exercises for the students and ideas for class experiments. This will be her major work; it will be translated into six languages and used in the classroom for the next several decades.

Ellen Churchill Semple, whose college degree is from Vassar, has become a geographer. She studied in Leipzig in the 1890s with German geographer Friedrich Ratzel, who pioneered in anthropogeography. Eight years ago she published her first book, *American History and Its Geographic Conditions,* which relates American settlement to the physical landscape of the United States. Reviewers praised the work, and it established her reputation. Some American geographers define human geography as a study of the connection between people and their environment, and Semple's work helps give American geography (traditionally linked with geology) authority as a separate university discipline. This year Semple publishes her second work, *Influences of the Geographic Environment, on the Basis of Ratzel's System of Anthropo-Geography,* in which she examines how human behavior can be influenced by where people live. English and Scottish geographers praise the work, and a reviewer in an American journal calls it "the most scholarly contribution to the literature of geography that has yet been produced in America."[296] Within the next several years the concept of environmentalism will become outmoded in American intellectual thought, and Semple's work will be severely criticized by geographers. Although she is well published and has an excellent teaching reputation, Semple will be unable to find a full-time university position until 1921, when she will be appointed professor of anthropogeography at Clark University.

RELIGION

A recent census of American religion showed that women are two-thirds of all members in Protestant churches. Many men view this as a crisis; their anxiety is part of a larger concern that American males are becoming "effeminate." This year several Protestant leaders initiate an interdenominational religious revival, the Men and Religion Forward Movement. Using the motto "More Men for Religion, More Religion for Men," they open a central headquarters in New York City. They organize revivals, meetings, rallies, and sports outings for American men and boys, publicizing these activities through announcements and advertisements in newspapers, especially in the sports pages, and on billboards and neon signs in many cities. The revival will last through the next year, and more than one million males (mostly white, native-born, and middle-class) will attend events in seventy-six big cities and more than a thousand towns. By the 1920s there will be changes within the Protestant church. Male membership, which was 39 percent in 1906, will grow to 42 percent by 1926. Churchwomen will also lose power. In 1923 the Presbyterian General Assembly will incorporate all women's boards into men's groups.[297]

ARTS

Amy Cheney Beach composed piano waltzes at age four and begged her parents for lessons at age six. Unlike most prodigies' parents, the Cheneys decided Amy would study in the United States rather than Europe. She debuted at age sixteen with the Boston Symphony Orchestra and later taught herself composition. She has written a Mass, the *Festival Jubilate*, the *Gaelic Symphony*, a piano concerto, many chamber pieces, and songs. She is well known, and many American orchestras have performed her symphony. Critics praise her compositions, but they view her as a woman who writes music and refuse to compare her work with that of male contemporaries. This year, at age forty-four, her husband has died and she decides to sail to Europe. This is her first trip abroad,

and she will remain there for four years, performing in many cities. She will get rave reviews, adding international fame to her celebrity in the United States.

California dancer **Florence Treadwell Boynton** designs a new house and studio in Berkeley which she calls "Temple of the Wind." Its cement floor can be heated, and the canvas walls can be rolled up. Here she teaches dance and lectures women on healthier lifestyles, encouraging them toward a lighter diet and looser clothing. She has also developed a new form of expressive dancing, inspired by Asian art, which her students perform at the University of California's Greek Theater. Boynton's dancing style with its unstructured routines is a forerunner of modern dance.

JOINING FORCES

As more women work for suffrage, others organize more anti-suffrage groups. This year there are groups in six states working against suffrage. Members are primarily white Protestant native-born women in the upper and middle classes. Many are active outside the household in charitable work, and they do consider themselves reformers, but they oppose suffrage for various reasons. Some believe that politics is "dirty" and will degrade women, and some believe that a nonpartisan female reformer could better get the attention of national leaders. Others maintain that women already have enough work to do in the household and in their clubs and churches, and getting into politics would take too much energy. Still others link suffrage to socialism and radical causes such as free love, divorce reform, or birth control. This year the National Association Opposed to Woman Suffrage (NAOWS) opens a central office in New York City. They campaign for new members through flyers, posters, speeches, and letters to the newspapers, whose editors — often anti-suffrage themselves — are usually pleased to print. By 1915 NAOWS will have branches in twenty-five states with a total of 200,000 members.[298]

A suffrage parade, New York City, May 1912. (National Archives.) Parades called attention to the campaign, and this is the city's third annual parade, organized to protest a suffrage bill's defeat in the state legislature. Nearly 17,000 women marched, including women in industry, academia, and other professions. Many wear white to represent purity, and some carry gold and purple banners. The parade lasted two and one half hours. A New York Times *editorial called the leaders "unnatural" and opposed the cause, as did the Catholic Church. The crowd taunted and jeered.*

Three years later the state legislature will defeat another women's suffrage bill, but in 1917 New York will become the sixteenth state where women have full suffrage.

LAW AND POLITICS

California voters pass a female suffrage referendum by a margin of 3,500.[299] Suffragists, who have been campaigning for nearly forty years, are jubilant. The state is the sixth where women have full suffrage.

— 1912 —

WORK

This year Congress creates a Children's Bureau, a division of the Department of Commerce and Labor, to address children's needs and protect their interests. President William Howard Taft appoints **Julia Lathrop** to head the bureau. Lathrop has been active in reform. As a member of the Illinois Board of Charities, she helped get the nation's first separate juvenile court built in Chicago. Previously, youthful offenders were treated as adults in the courts and were often jailed with the sick and insane. She also recently returned from a world tour where she investigated systems of public education. Her staff will address high infant mortality rates, child labor, medical care for children in tenements and rural areas, and the treatment of juvenile delinquency. They will investigate problems and lobby for reform legislation. They will publish pamphlets on baby care that they will distribute throughout the United States, and they will respond to thousands of letters from parents on medical care. They will also investigate child labor — 15 percent of all children between ages ten and fifteen are employed this year. The bureau staff will help get the first child labor law passed in 1916.[300] Lathrop will retire from the bureau in 1921, but she will continue to write and campaign for social reform.

Charlotta Spears Bass, who lives in Los Angeles, owns and edits the *California Eagle* with her husband. It is the state's major black newspaper, and under their editorship it will become nationally prominent. Charlotta and her husband protest injustices in their publication. When the movie *Birth of a Nation* comes to town, they denounce its racism and the Ku Klux Klan. They support women's rights and urge all qualified African Americans to vote. They wage war against lynching and protest discrimination in housing and employment. They will give young blacks jobs at the newspaper to give them experience. Charlotta later organizes a local council to encourage black business ownership, and she will initiate another group to fight against segregated neighborhoods. Charlotta will run the paper after her husband dies and she will remain an activist. Noting the absence of women in the U.S.

A young textile mill worker and her boss, c. 1910. (Archives of Labor and Urban Affairs, Wayne State University.) In 1910, nine million children between the ages of ten and fifteen labored in factories. They were cheap labor, used to run errands and help operate machines. Most children worked to help support their impoverished families. Mills were hazardous working places since dust and thread particles were easily inhaled. Bosses were harsh on their young employees, gave them few rest breaks, and made them work long hours for low wages. While some states regulated or prohibited child labor, businesses engaged in interstate commerce were exempt.

Senate and House of Representatives, she tells women to run for office; she is later nominated as the vice-presidential candidate for the Progressive Party. In 1960 she will publish her autobiography, *Forty Years: Memoirs from the Pages of a Newspaper.*

RELIGION

Writer and teacher **Henrietta Szold** has been active in Judaism since age eighteen, when she wrote a column for the *Jewish Messenger*. She later founded a society to translate and print classics in Jewish literature for American Jews. Szold is also concerned with the welfare of Jewish people abroad, and on a recent trip to Palestine she was shocked at the lack of available health care. This year she founds Hadassah, a Zionist organization for women. They will promote the formation of a Jewish state in Palestine, where Szold hopes Arab and Jewish people would work and live together. Hadassah's first project is to provide better health care for the Palestinians, and members raise funds to send doctors, nurses, and hospital equipment abroad. Hadassah's initial membership is twelve, but it will expand into the world's largest Zionist organization.

ARTS

When writer **Mary Antin** was young, she fled persecution in Russia and, with her Jewish family, sailed to the United States. Although her parents were impoverished, they allowed her to become educated rather than work. Her teachers noted and encouraged Antin's writing talent. At age eighteen she published her first book, a compilation of letters she wrote to her uncle about being an immigrant. She now lives in New York City with her husband and writes for magazines. A series she published in the *Atlantic Monthly* comes out this year as her autobiography, *The Promised Land.* Written to "My American friend," she praises her new country as a golden land where newcomers'

dreams can be realized. "I was born, I have lived, and I have been made over," she announces with pleasure. Her book is a classic statement of the melting pot idea, where immigrants easily assimilate into American culture and help build a better country. It is a best-seller; nearly 85,000 copies will be sold, and it will have thirty-four printings. Antin, with thousands of other Jewish immigrants, will later fight against the increasing nativism in America, and she will campaign against legislation restricting immigration.[301]

JOINING FORCES

Agnes Inglis, who grew up in a wealthy Detroit family, spent her first thirty years helping to nurse her sick sister. When freed of the family claim, she attended college and has worked in settlement houses in Detroit and Chicago. She is now in Michigan as a social worker for the YWCA. This year she receives an appointment as a state factory inspector; she investigates working conditions in industry. Her work with the poor and her observations of prejudice and injustice toward the working class have helped to her shape her political beliefs. She has read and attended lectures on socialism and anarchism, further convincing her to fight injustices. Inglis joined the Industrial Workers of the World (IWW) and contributes money and time to labor reform. In the 1920s she will begin a second career working with the papers of anarchist Joseph Labadie. Since he donated them to the University of Michigan they had remained unsorted and nearly unused; Inglis will arrange, organize, and catalog them. She will also expand the collection to include papers of other prominent American radicals. Working until her death in 1952, she will build the Labadie Collection into the nation's largest and best on anarchism.

Lawrence, Massachusetts, is a leading cloth production center. Mill wages are so low that whole families (mostly southern and eastern European immigrants) work. More than half of the industry's 35,000 laborers are women and children. This year state legislators pass a law regulating women's and children's hours; in response, the mill owners cut everyone's hours. The workers are furious at the pay decrease, and they strike. The Women's Trade Union League, the American Federation of Labor, and the IWW send representatives to Lawrence. The IWW, whose officials give the most assistance, sends organizer **Elizabeth Gurley Flynn**. This twenty-one-year-old has been involved in labor protests for four years and has even been jailed several times. She is a colorful and flamboyant speaker and an energetic organizer. Under her leadership IWW members coordinate meetings for the strikers, find housing for the workers' children, raise money for strike relief, and get good national publicity. After three months the strike is called off, but conditions later worsen. While many workers get their demands met, mill owners later speed up machinery, forcing employees to work twice as fast. Nearly 14,000 workers joined the IWW, but the next year attacks by a local group that brands the new members "atheistic anarchists," as well as harassment by the Catholic Church, reduce the IWW membership by half.[302]

Unitarian minister **Marie Jennie Howe** has moved with her husband from Cleveland to Greenwich Village. Howe, long active in women's rights, forms the Heterodoxy Club. The initial twenty-five members are college graduates, and are writers, teachers, scholars, artists, social workers, industrial investigators, and journalists. Many are political radicals, most reject Christianity, and some are lesbians. They rebel against the traditional roles for women and reject the idea that women are morally superior. They will campaign for their rights rather than their duties as women. They meet on Saturday nights and discuss politics, art trends, scientific discoveries, labor reform, and new writings by scholars. They call themselves "feminists," a term (originally used in France in the late 1800s) that will gain common usage in the next several years. Club members will later organize mass meetings in New York City to explain their program of social reform.

LAW AND POLITICS

Voters in Oregon, Arizona, and Kansas adopt constitutional amendments giving women full suffrage.

— 1913 —

DOMESTICITY

Home economist **Christine Frederick**, the household editor of the *Ladies' Home Journal*, publishes *The New Housekeeping: Efficiency Studies in Home Management*. Addressing middle-class housewives, she compares the home to a business and suggests ideas for effective management. She advises women to prepare schedules for chores, plan meals, make records of all household items, and label drawers for easier storage. This will save time, she tells her readers — time that they can use for good grooming, supervising their children, learning about their husbands' business, and doing community volunteer work. Frederick advises mothers against taking jobs; she insists it is "unnatural" for women to want a career, and that baking a cake can be as fulfilling as office work. "The science of homemaking and of motherhood, if followed out on an efficient plan, can be the most glorious career open to any woman," she promises. Her book sells well and becomes a bible for middle-class housewives.[303]

EDUCATION AND SCHOLARSHIP

Sociologist **Elsie Clews Parsons** lives in New York City with her husband and four children. She has a doctorate from Columbia University, has taught at Barnard and Columbia, and writes. She has recently become acquainted with Franz Boas and is interested in anthropology. This year Putnam publishes her latest book, *The Old-Fashioned Woman: Primitive Fantasies about the Sex*. Parsons describes the stages in women's lives, shows how they are similar in different cultures, and points out the universal limitations placed on women. She believes the way Americans view women is a holdover from earlier stages of culture, when events like childbirth were not understood and viewed with awe. She writes that Americans promote sex differences by the kind of toys they give their children and their expectations of the sexes concerning dress, manners, and vocations. She challenges Americans' easy acceptance of custom and argues that too many women conform to society's expectations, passively accepting an active social life and marriage because it is the route to respectability. Parsons will later spend many seasons doing fieldwork in the Southwest with American Indians, publish extensively, and be respected by anthropologists and ethnographers. She will be elected as president of several professional organizations and for more than twenty years be associate editor of the *Journal of American Folklore*.

ARTS

The Society of American Artists and the National Academy of Design control which artists can be exhibited, and they prefer the traditional styles. Many younger artists are experimenting with modern techniques such as impressionism and need a place to exhibit. They form a new group, the American Society of Painters and Sculptors. With the help of their president, Arthur Davis, a wealthy art patron, they sponsor the International Exhibition of Modern Art. It will include several hundred works by American and European artists and takes place in New York City's National Guard Armory. Of the forty or so women who exhibit is **Marguerite Thompson Zorach**. While a student in Paris

she studied at an avant-garde school run by fauvists. She liked their use of bold colors and distortion to represent emotion. Back in New York she has completed *Study*, which she enters in the Armory show. In reviews, the critics denounce modern art and attack Zorach's piece with sarcasm. A reviewer notes the yellow eyes and purple lips of her figure and comments that the woman "is feeling very, very bad. She is portraying her emotions after a long day's shopping."[304] Zorach continues to paint, but even her later and more representational pieces will be derided. Her art will later be reevaluated and acclaimed by art historians during the 1960s.

Meta Warrick Fuller is a well-known black sculptor. When she studied in Europe she met master sculptor Auguste Rodin, who praised her sense of form. Back in the Philadelphia she was unable to get commissions, sales, or exhibits in the white community, so she turned to the black community, where she found support. She received a federal commission to do a piece for the Jamestown Tercentennial Exposition. Her studio is now in Framingham, Massachusetts, and she has a greater interest in African-American themes. This year W. E. B. Du Bois asks her to create a sculpture to celebrate the Emancipation Proclamation's fiftieth anniversary. Fuller creates the *Spirit of Emancipation*. Its three people, eight feet high, stand tall and proud, unlike works of earlier artists, whose figures were bowed in gratitude. Fuller also gives the female negroid features, and she is among the earliest sculptors to do this. She will work for fifty more years and get many commissions. She will work through her eighties using themes of African-American culture and religion and will become active in the civil rights movement, donating many works for the cause.

JOINING FORCES

This year Illinois lawmakers pass legislation allowing women to vote in municipal and presidential elections. Chicago activist **Ida Wells-Barnett** is pleased and establishes the Alpha Suffrage club to help black women vote intelligently. She founds a newsletter, *The Alpha Suffrage Record*, to inform women about issues and candidates. She travels throughout the state, urging women to register and vote, and some Alpha members serve as clerks, registering Chicago voters. Her group will give black women a strong voice in local politics, and within three years there will be two hundred members. As president, Well-Barnett travels to Washington, D.C., to join the Illinois contingent in a suffrage parade sponsored by the National American Woman Suffrage Association. When the parade organizers tell her she must join the African-American contingent who march behind the state delegations, Wells-Barnett joins the crowd on the sidewalk; then, when she sees the Illinois delegation, she steps out to march with them.[305]

Agnes Walz, Oil City, Pennsylvania c. 1913. (Alan Coppens.) Note her bobbed or "shingled" hair, a new popular style. Her grandfather, a German immigrant, cofounded Pennzoil, a successful oil company in Pennsylvania. Most of his wealth, nearly nine million dollars, was lost in the depression of 1890.

Agnes loved animals and wanted to become a veterinarian. But her father discouraged her, insisting she settle for marriage and children. Even with parental encouragement, Agnes might have been unable to fulfill her dream. The rising enrollment and academic success of college women during the turn of the century caused a backlash. Male administrators in higher education set quotas on female enrollment, and even established new and separate coordinate colleges for females, which had inadequate funding.

— 1 9 1 4 —

DOMESTICITY

Most Americans still view motherhood as women's main occupation and believe that white middle-class mothers should not hold outside jobs. Currently only 5 percent of white married women (but 30 percent of black married women) are employed. This year Congress passes a resolution creating Mother's Day. The resolution calls the American mother the "greatest source of the country's strength and inspiration ... [who does] ... so much for the home, for moral spirits and religion."[306]

WORK

Elinore Pruitt Steward describes her life in Wyoming in *Letters of a Woman Homesteader*, published this year. Steward is among thousands of women who have

moved west. In 1909 the young widow moved with her daughter to Wyoming to become a housekeeper for Clyde Steward, a cattle rancher, whom she later married. She also staked her own claim and built a house. Life was hard, they were isolated, and winters were harsh. On Steward's ranch she farmed, raised chickens and turkeys, milked cows, branded cattle, and cared for the livestock when they were sick. She also grew oats, hayed, and planted gardens. She loved the life. In her book she glows with praise about homesteading, calling it the solution to poverty. "Any woman who can stand her own company," she enthuses, "can see the beauty of the sunset, loves growing things, and is willing to put in as much time at careful labor as she does the washtub will certainly succeed; she will have independence, plenty to eat all the time and a home of her own at the end."[307]

EDUCATION AND SCHOLARSHIP

Leta Stetter Hollingworth lives in New York City with her husband, who teaches at Barnard. She wanted to teach school but could not get hired because she was married. She decided to begin graduate work at Columbia University's Teachers College, where some women were permitted to enroll. She studied with the psychologist Edward Thorndike and decided to do research on gender differences. She wanted to challenge the notion that during their menstrual periods women are less efficient in motor skills and intelligence. This year she publishes an article from her dissertation research, *Functional Periodicity: An Experimental Study of the Mental and Motor Abilities of Women during Menstruation*. Hollingworth tested twenty-eight women and two men (of varying ages and occupations) in mental and physical skills. She asked the women to note their cycles, and she concluded that women's periods have no effect on their mental abilities or motor skills. Her work adds to the growing body of studies on gender differences that help disprove earlier ideas about women. In her conclusion, Hollingworth urges women to become experimental physiologists so that someday a psychology of women can be written that is based "on truth, not opinion; on precise, not on anecdotal evidence; on accurate data rather than remnants of magic."[308]

ARTS

Gertrude Vanderbilt Whitney, the daughter of railroad magnate Cornelius Van-

derbilt, has been sculpting since shortly after she married. She has already earned several commissions and won prizes. Whitney has a studio in Greenwich Village, where she has befriended many young artists and offered space where they could have exhibits. This year she enters a contest for a commission to create a memorial for the 1,500 Americans who died when the *Titanic* sank two years ago. She wins first place. Her sculpture depicts a male figure eighteen feet high with his arms outstretched, leaning slightly forward, and in the shape of a cross. She will complete her work in 1931, and it will be placed by the Potomac River in Washington, D.C. Whitney will sculpt many other pieces but will be remembered most as a museum founder. In 1929, realizing that her vast personal collection of contemporary American art should be available to the public, she will offer the Metropolitan Museum of Art her collection and funding for housing it in a new wing. Their rejection will inspire her, two years later, to establish the Whitney Museum of American Art.

JOINING FORCES

The war in Europe began in August, and American attitudes toward the war reflect quite a diversity of opinions. President Woodrow Wilson has declared America neutral, but many citizens fear the United States will eventually get involved. Pacifists **Lillian Wald, Crystal Eastman**, Oswald Garrison Villard, Paul Kellogg, and others found the American Union Against Militarism (AUAM). Wald is elected president and Eastman as executive secretary. They meet with President Wilson, urging him to stay neutral, and hire lobbyists to persuade congressmen to keep America out of the conflict. They found a press service to publish articles promoting peace, and they establish local committees in a number of cities. When the United States does enter the war, there will be severe hostility against pacifists, protesters, and conscientious objectors. To defend free speech, the AUAM will create a Civil Liberties Board, which will later become the American Civil Liberties Union.

Thirty-three-year-old **Julia Grace Wales**, an English professor at the University of Wisconsin in Madison, is a pacifist. She is appalled by the conflict and believes there must be some way to obtain peace. During the semester break in December, she sketches out a plan for mediation. She suggests that delegates from neutral countries could formulate ways to end the conflict; then they could discuss these plans with heads of the warring countries to try to mediate an armistice. Even if no armistice could be obtained, delegates could still work for eventual peace. At the war's end, she suggests, an international body should be established to keep world peace. Her plan is published in a sixteen-page pamphlet, *Continuous Mediation without Armistice*. The Wisconsin state legislature will endorse it and send it to President Wilson and Congress.

Quaker and reformer **Alice Paul** spent several years in England studying at the London School of Economics. Now back in the United States, she has completed doctoral work in sociology at the University of Pennsylvania and decides to work for suffrage. While in England she helped British women in campaigning for suffrage. She is frustrated with how long it is taking to obtain suffrage for American women, and two years ago she was appointed to chair the Congressional Committee of the National American Woman Suffrage Association (NAWSA). Their job was to work for an amendment to the U.S. Constitution and to raise money supporting their campaigns. Paul recruited a hardworking group of women and set up headquarters in Washington, D.C. They started an aggressive publicity campaign and raised $25,000. Last year committee members organized a suffrage parade held the day before President Wilson's inauguration. The 5,000 marchers attracted huge crowds and much publicity.

Paul has changed the committee's name to the Congressional Union. While the NAWSA leadership has endorsed her work, conflict has arisen. Paul's aggressive tactics have irritated, angered, and embarrassed the main group. She has tried to convince leadership that a constitutional amendment should be their priority, and her strategy (borrowed from the British) is to blame the party in power for lack of suffrage. This year the parent group votes to oust the Congressional Union. Paul's group will continue to work for a federal amendment by picketing the White House, demonstrating, and campaigning against all Democrats, especially President Wilson.[309]

LAW AND POLITICS

Montana and Nevada voters adapt constitutional amendments giving women full suffrage.

— 1915 —

DOMESTICITY

As the suffrage debate intensifies, antisuffragist congressmen continue to promote the role of the "true" American woman. Representative Clark of Florida, who opposes female enfranchisement, speaks angrily to Congress, "I do not wish to see the day come when the women of my race in my state shall trail their skirts in the muck and mire of partisan politics. I prefer to look at the American woman as she has always been, occupying her proud estate as queen of the American home."[310]

WORK

Advertisers and home economists are promoting an additional job for housewives — consumer. With the increase in manufactured goods, marketing is becoming

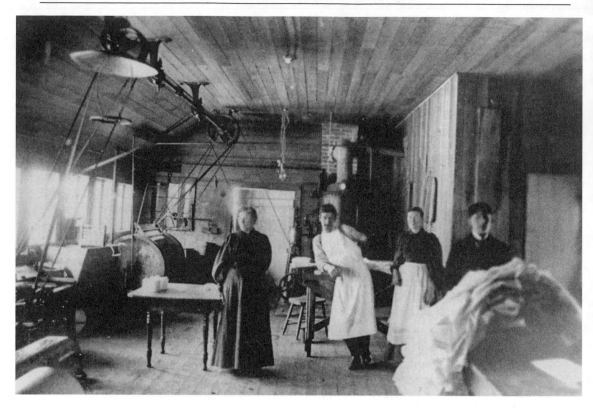

Workers at the Otsego, Michigan, Laundry, 1915. (Allegan County Historical Society.) The invention of the automatic washing machine led to the formation of commercial laundries, which employed many women. Some of these laundries thrived in urban areas in the early 1830s. They peaked in popularity during the 1920s, but since they were small, decentralized businesses they eventually needed to increase fees to remain profitable. At the same time, the booming home washing machine industry offered mass-produced appliances at low prices and financed national advertising campaigns. Home machines eventually replaced commercial laundry services.

important and in several years advertisers will spend half a billion dollars annually. Women do most of the family shopping, and this year they purchase nearly 90 percent of all consumer goods. Advertisers pitch their copy to middle-class housewives, urging them to buy the best to prove they love their families. Home economists also endorse this role and insist that women must be educated to become good consumers. An article in the *Ladies' Home Journal* announces that "the housewife is the buying agent for the home, and she must take time to spend wisely."[311]

Since the turn of the century, there are more job choices for female college graduates. The fields of social work, librarianship, and nursing have expanded, and more women are being hired as personnel managers for businesses and industries. Govern-

ment agencies also want female employees as researchers and clerks. And more women are interested in the sciences and in applying to law schools and medical colleges. This year, to help women make career decisions, staff members from several eastern women's colleges establish a Bureau of Vocational Information in New York City. They offer seminars, workshops, and lectures to college students about employment possibilities and will help graduates find jobs. The bureau will last until 1932.

Bertha Van Hoosen is a respected physician in Chicago. She has a thriving private practice, has taught clinical gynecology at the University of Illinois Medical School, and is chief of the gynecological staff at Cook County Hospital. Despite her prominence, because she is female she is barred from membership in the Chicago Gynecological and Obstetrical Society. Although she is a member of the American Medical Association, Van Hoosen is tired of being ignored at meetings. She believes that since there is prejudice against female doctors, they need a separate professional group. This year she founds the National Women's Medical Association (NWMA), the only national group for female physicians. Other doctors have formed similar organizations, but most failed from lack of interest and insufficient membership. Male physicians disapprove of the new group — as do some female physicians, who feel that separate groups are unnecessary — and they protest its formation. Membership in the NWMA will increase, but it will never have more than one-third of all American women physicians.[312]

EDUCATION AND SCHOLARSHIP

Most successful female physicians in the early twentieth century were educated at women's medical colleges. Now many of these schools have closed from lack of funds and an inability to compete with the larger programs, well-equipped laboratories, and better funding at large universities.

With the closure of these schools, more women have been attending coeducational medical schools. As some of the large medical schools at coeducation universities opened their doors to women, many women applied and female enrollments sometimes reached as high as 33 percent. This increase caused a backlash, as administrators feared that the women might eventually dominate the profession. Some university administrators closed their doors to female applicants, other established quotas, and still others, who had segregated schools, closed the women's facilities. As a result, the number of females in American medical schools has declined from 1,280 to 592 during the past thirteen years. Women have always been a minority of American doctors. The percentage of female doctors reached a high of 6 percent in 1910,

but it will continue to decrease annually, until the trend is reversed in 1970.[313]

There has been a steady increase in the number of women getting college degrees during the past fifteen years. In 1900 women earned 19 percent of all bachelor's degrees; this year they earn 28 percent.[314]

Ella Cara Deloria, a Dakota Sioux who grew up in South Dakota reservation, receives her B.A. in science from Columbia Teachers College this year. During her student days there she met anthropologist Franz Boas and did some translating for him. Boas will later hire her as an assistant, and she will work with him for nearly thirty years. As an anthropologist and linguist Deloria will accomplish a great deal. She will edit and translate many Sioux texts and compile a Dakota-English dictionary. Her fieldwork and extensive publications will provide one of the most comprehensive accounts of Dakota Sioux culture.

ARTS

Black actor **Anita Bush** grew up in New York City, where her father was a tailor for performers. Many actors befriended young Anita, and the stage was her second home. This year, at age thirty-two, she has noticed that most African Americans are guided into musical careers rather than into classical drama. She becomes interested in serious theater acting, and this year she forms a stock company for black actors. Known as the Layafette Players, they will perform in Harlem and travel to perform plays in many American cities. This pioneering black troupe will last for seventeen years, and many successful actors will get their start here.

Sculptor **Janet Scudder** completes a bronze piece for a proposed victory fountain in Washington, D.C., honoring the suffrage movement. Called *Femina Victrix*, it is a woman standing on a globe holding a wreath aloft. Scudder's model is dancer Irene Castle, whose slender shape will be the ideal body type for women during the next decade.

JOINING FORCES

Many American women are horrified by the war and want to work for peace. To reformer **Crystal Eastman** it makes sense that women should do this work, since women are mothers (or potential mothers) and therefore "have a more intimate sense of the value of human life." Eighty-six representatives from women's organizations attend the first meeting in Washington, D.C., and they elect Hull House director Jane Addams as president. After several days of debate they agree on a party platform: neutral nations should work to mediate the conflict; weapons manufacturing should be limited to avoid war profiteering; people in all countries should have a voice in foreign policy; women must have universal suffrage; and after the war an international body should be founded to keep peace. They establish headquarters in Chicago, and by the year's end there will be 25,000 members. When the United States enters the conflict, the group will split: some will actively support the war effort, some will continue to crusade for peace, and others devote time to domestic programs such as food conservation and collecting relief supplies.[315]

Suffragist **Aletta Jacobs**, who lives in the Netherlands, calls for an international congress of women to meet at The Hague to discuss peace. She invites members of the Women's Peace Party and groups from many other countries. Participants include forty-seven Americans and women from eleven other countries, some of whose nations are at war. They adopt Julia Wales's plan and will try to mediate an armistice. Several delegations are appointed as ambassadors. They will visit the heads of neutral and belligerent countries. The American delegates (including **Jane Addams**, **Alice Hamilton**, **Emily Balch**, and **Julia Wales**) visit Austria-Hungary, Belgium, France, Germany, Switzerland, Great Britain, the Scandinavian countries, and Russia. The women travel for five weeks and confer with prime ministers, presidents, a king, and the pope.

World reaction is unfavorable. Some spokesmen in belligerent countries insist that the group has been formed by one of their enemies. The press is hostile. A British newspaper denounces the group as "Pro-Hun Peacettes," Theodore Roosevelt calls the idea "silly and base," and a Washington, D.C., newspaper editor calls the women's work "utterly futile." President Wilson, who does agree to meet with a delegation, later remarks, "My heart is with them, but my mind has contempt for them. I want peace but I know how to get it and they do not."[316]

When the delegates return to The Hague, they report that a conference of neutral nations who attempt to mediate peace would be acceptable to some warring nations and that such a conference might bring peace. Some delegates at The Hague try to establish such a gathering of representatives of neutral nations, but because the women's congress lacks authority or power, and because of much infighting, they are unable to have effective discussion or reach an agreement. Before disbanding the congress creates a permanent peace committee, later called the Women's International League for Peace and Freedom, which will last into the late twentieth century. Their plan for a postwar international peacekeeping group will help lead to the establishment of the League of Nations.

— 1916 —

EDUCATION AND SCHOLARSHIP

Home economists have been successful in their campaign to introduce domestic science classes in high school and college curricula. This year 20 percent of all high schools now offer courses, and in colleges it is even more popular. Eleven years ago 213 college women took home economics, and this year course enrollment is more than 17,000.[317]

Psychologist **Jessie Taft**, whose Ph.D. is from the University of Chicago, publishes her dissertation, *The Woman's Movement from the Point of View of Social Consciousness*. Taft studied with philosopher and psychologist George Herbert Mead, who is interested in personality development. Taft took Mead's idea that social relations, rather than biology or environmental influences, shape our character, and applied it to women. In her study she maintains that women are formed by the social environment and are raised by their parents to develop traditional "female" traits. The "problem" women now have is finding a balance between the traditional "nurturing" world they are expected to live in and the outside, more rational world of higher education and work. She maintains that attitudes toward women need to change so they can be free from society's constraints. Taft disagrees with the still popular notion that women are morally superior and points out the damage done when virtues and characteristics are defined as masculine or feminine. Taft's study adds to the growing literature disproving traditional beliefs about men and women. Her work foreshadows later studies by scholars at the University of Chicago that will view blacks and Jews as "outsiders" trying to find a balance between two worlds.

ARTS

Los Angeles musician **Lauretta Green Butler** is a pianist who performs with black orchestras and plays for her local church. On a recent trip to Chicago she attended a performance of young African Americans and was impressed with their talents. This year she opens a school to train young black children in performance arts. The Butler Dance Studio accepts children from age two through teens, and they will learn discipline, dancing, singing, and mime. Next year she will found a Kiddie Minstrel Review, whose performances will become popular through the 1940s at social events, at nightclubs, and in the movies. She will train many future

child stars, including some who will join the casts of *The Little Rascals* and *Our Gang*.

Wealthy socialite **Alva Vanderbilt Belmont**, who lives in New York City, has turned to suffrage work. She has written articles on why women deserve the vote, raised thousands for the cause, and even rented a whole floor of a Fifth Avenue building as headquarters for the National American Woman Suffrage Association (NAWSA). Several years ago she sponsored British suffragist Christabel Pankhurst's lecture tour of the United States. This year she decides to write a musical. Collaborating with columnist, socialite, and songwriter **Elsa Maxwell**, Belmont composes an operetta, *Melinda and Her Sisters*. It concerns Melinda, youngest of eight daughters in a wealthy family, who rebels against fashion, social climbers, and reactionary politicians and becomes a suffragist. The drama is performed at the Waldorf-Astoria. Belmont convinced **Marie Dressler**, a famous comedian, to perform, and other actors are wealthy young socialites. The event gets much publicity and good reviews from critics. The tickets and sale of beautifully designed programs and bound librettos earn $8,000 for suffrage.

JOINING FORCES

Reformer and nurse **Margaret Sanger** has been crusading for American women's right to information about birth control. She has traveled in Europe, where in many cities information on birth control is openly given and there are even some clinics for women where nurses can advise them. In the United States the Comstock Law prohibits distribution of any contraception information, since this is considered obscene. Sanger has already faced arrest several times for printing and distributing birth control literature, and because of her friendships with anarchists and socialists, government officials are aware of her activities. This year she opens a clinic in Brooklyn, and nearly 500 Jewish and Italian immigrant women visit the clinic. It stays open for ten days, then officials close it down and arrest and imprison Sanger. Her court case and appeals will bring Sanger national fame and draw attention to the controversy. She will continue her crusade for several more decades.

Members of the American Union Against Militarism (AUAM) help the United States avoid a war with Mexico. In response to a skirmish in Mexico between American troops and Pancho Villa, a rebel leader, President Woodrow Wilson asks Congress to authorize sending American military forces to northern Mexico. When an American army officer who witnessed the skirmish reports that the Americans began the attack, the AUAM and other peace groups launch a massive publicity drive. Thousands of Americans send letters and telegrams to the White House requesting that no troops be sent, and the president changes his mind.

Carrie Chapman Catt has been working for suffrage for nearly thirty years. She helped establish an international suffrage group and is a former president of the NAWSA. Last year she was persuaded to again head the NAWSA, which has weakened and become fragmented. There is now more money for the campaign; Miriam Leslie, a wealthy publisher, left a million dollars in her will for Catt to use for suffrage work. This year Catt develops what she calls the "winning plan." She appoints a board of hardworking delegates who will work full-time and have pledged to convince their state legislators to support an amendment to the United States Constitution giving women full suffrage. Catt decides she needs President Wilson's personal support to reach this goal. She invites him to speak this year at the NAWSA convention in Atlantic City, and he indicates that they have his endorsement.

— 1917 —

WORK

In April the United States declares war on Germany and Austria-Hungary. As men join the services, women also want to support the war effort. At first prominent Americans are unsure of what women's role will be and tell them to "keep the home fires burning" and inspire patriotism in their men. A contributor to *World's Work* opines that women should not be "wearing trousers or an unbecoming uniform and try to do something that a man can do better." A Labor Department spokesman announces that women's labor is not needed in industry, so they should sew, knit socks, and conserve food. A British major speaks to a meeting of an American women's club and informs them, "Your part, ladies, is to *smile*."[318]

The government's attitude toward women's labor changes after the second draft that winter. They campaign for women in industry, and now more than 23,000 women are working in factories. They manufacture explosives and munitions and work in blast furnaces, foundries, brass smelting plants, oil refineries, steel mills, and chemical and fertilizer plants. They also manufacture automobiles, airplanes, and electrical tools. Some sew uniforms, and others work on railroads or as streetcar conductors, ice deliverers, and theater ushers. Most women who do war work are already in the labor market and are promoted to higher-paying jobs previously held by men. Another 4,000 females enter the labor force for the first time. Many men resist hiring women to work at jobs held by men, and some strike in protest.[319]

Thousands of black women migrate north hoping to get jobs in war industries, and many settle in Chicago, Detroit, and Cleveland. These women find it difficult to get hired, since they face a double prejudice. Most find little better than menial work as cleaners. Some with lighter skin are employed in segregated government offices or find work in stores as elevator operators or stock girls. Those who are hired in industry get the hardest and dirtiest jobs with the lowest pay. Black women are generally the last hired, and after the war they will be the first fired.

The Council of National Defense sets up a Committee on Women's Defense Work (the Women's Committee) and appoints **Anna Howard Shaw**, the former president of the National American Woman Suffrage Association (NAWSA) to lead it. Members are representatives of women's organizations. The group is an advisory body with no budget or actual authority. The secretary of war tells them their job is to coordinate "women's preparedness" for the war effort, but no one will explain just what this means. The committee does register women for volunteer work (although most are never called), and they appoint some volunteers to canvass neighborhoods asking women to sign food conservation pledges. They are also successful in selling war bonds. But because their mission is not spelled out, there is much duplication of effort, as other women's clubs are doing the same work. Nor do government leaders call upon the women's committee; when they want help they contact the Red Cross or the YWCA.

Many women enlist in the military. Nearly 13,000 join the Navy as Yeoman (F). They do clerical work, draft blueprints, help at enlistment offices, and serve as translators and radio technicians. The Marine Corps hires 300 "Marinettes" who do clerical and technical work. Others join the Women's Motor Corps, where they learn engine repair and drive trucks and ambulances.[320]

Women also enlist as medical personnel. The Army Nurse Corps sends more than 8,000 nurses abroad, and the Navy Nurse Corps sends more than 11,000. Red Cross leader **Jane Delano** establishes a Red Cross

American Red Cross nurses in uniform, c. 1912. (National Archives.) The United States joined the International Red Cross in 1882, thanks to the efforts of Clara Barton. Nearly 21,000 Red Cross nurses served during World War I. The Red Cross nurse was used as a symbol on war posters to inspire national pride at the sight of a (lovely, young) nurse. Note that all those in the photo are white. Hundreds of black trained nurses were eager to work, but their applications to the program were denied. Black leaders pressured the Red Cross, and a month before the war's end, some black nurses received jobs in American camps.

Nursing Corps as an auxiliary of the Army Nurse Corps; she also sets up a volunteer program for women to train as nurse's aides, for which Delano prepares training materials. Nearly 20,000 nurses and aides from the Red Cross will serve in American and European hospitals.[321]

Other nurses and female doctors want to join the war effort, but they are rejected. There are hundreds of qualified black nurses whose applications to the Army and Navy programs are turned down because of race. They then try to sign up for the Red Cross nurses program. **Adah Thoms,** president of the Colored Graduate Nursing Association, has a lengthy correspondence with Jane Delano regarding why black nurses have not been called to duty, but Delano's replies are evasive. Finally, a month before the war's end, twenty-four black nurses are appointed by the Red Cross to serve at camps in the United States.[322]

Female physicians also want to join the military, but they are denied appointments as commissioned surgeons because of gender. A group of female physicians sends the government a petition protesting the surgeon general's sex discrimination, but it has no effect. The National Woman's Medical Association encourages female physicians to work even without a commission, and fifty-five female doctors work in hospitals in Europe as contract surgeons, with no military status or benefits.[323]

Angry at the treatment of black nurses, some prominent African-American leaders meet in New York City to form the Circle for Negro War Relief. Their goal is to give support to black soldiers. They raise money to send food and supplies to soldiers overseas. In the United States they establish canteens and clubs for servicemen, offer programs and lectures, and provide supplies. They also make hospital visits and offer financial help to families who have lost sons or fathers. They initiate a nursing program (similar to the Red Cross) called the Blue Circle Nurses, and these women work in rural areas. Mem-

bers of the circle publicize their activities and encourage the formation of local groups. By next year there will be sixty branches throughout the country.[324]

Women's clubs contribute to the wartime effort. Members of the National Association of Colored Women raise money, sell Liberty Loans and bonds, volunteer in hospitals, and establish canteens for black servicemen. The General Federation of Women's Clubs initially opposed America's entry into the war, but now accept it with President Wilson's statement that it is the only way to get peace. They open an office in Washington, D.C., to coordinate activities and they raise millions to buy war bonds and support the Red Cross. They also join the crusade for moral purity, rallying against liquor and prostitution. The NAWSA supports the war at the urging of their president, Carrie Chapman Catt. They can raise thousands to establish a hospital in France, sell Liberty Bonds, and make supplies for the Red Cross. They include female workers in their suffrage parades, hoping to show the public how women are contributing to the war effort. The YWCA organizes groups of workers, technicians, and telephone operators and sends them to Europe. Other women establish patriotic societies. They form the American War Mothers this year, and later they will establish a Service Star League and an American Legion auxiliary.

President Wilson has created a Committee on Public Information in response to war opposition and public apathy. Its job is to inspire patriotism, promote war goals, and support the nation. Members and volunteers prepare brochures, design posters, write press releases, give speeches, and sponsor loyalty leagues. The Association of Collegiate Alumnae (ACA) meets this year in Washington, D.C., and decides to contribute to this campaign for patriotism. They write pamphlets and brochures on liberty and democracy, offer programs in schools, and establish a speakers bureau with a list of women who will give talks about the war needs in schools and churches and at movie theaters. ACA members also adopt French and Belgian orphans and teach in schools as substitutes.

More than 25,000 women will sail to Europe to help in war work.[325] About half of these are small groups or individuals who will volunteer in hospitals or wherever they are needed. Some have specific plans. Philanthropist **Anne Morgan**, daughter John Pierpoint Morgan, is active in France. She has already allowed the French government to use her large villa near Versailles for relief and reconstruction work. This year she creates and heads the American Committee for Devastated France. One project is to restore an area northeast of Paris that was ravaged by the war by planting crops and reconstructing farms. They will later build hospitals, orphanages, and kindergartens and raise millions for food and medical supplies.

Another woman in Europe is writer **Dorothy Canfield Fisher**, who has moved to France with her whole family for the war's duration. Her husband, John, drives ambulances, and Fisher, who is worried that many people may be blinded during the war, establishes a press to print books in Braille. She also founds an orphanage, does other relief work, and funds her activities by selling articles and short stories. Next year she will publish *Home Fires in France*, recounting her war work.

Poster of a young American woman working at a switchboard in Europe against a background of soldiers, horses, and guns, entitled, "Back our girls over there," 1918. (Library of Congress.) The poster was published by the YWCA, who recruited female workers and paid for their passage to Europe. They assigned hundreds to work the switchboards — a logical choice since most telephone operators were women. The image of a young, white, and attractive American female was commonly used on posters to arouse patriotism.

ARTS

Ethel Waters, whose mother was a twelve-year-old who had been raped, has been raised by her grandmother in Philadelphia. Ethel has musical talent, and at age thirteen, while working as a hotel maid, she would sing in front of the mirror. This year, while she was entertaining at a Halloween party, two agents from a vaudeville troupe like her singing and hire her to join their production. As "Sweet Mama Stringbean" she begins her professional career as a blues, jazz, and ballad singer. Several years later she will be a popular performer in Harlem. She will later have recording contracts with Black Swan Records and Columbia Records. Waters will have a successful career as singer and recording artist and later as a theater and film actor.

Artist **Georgia O'Keefe**, who has been painting and teaching for many years, decided to work in a new style. Living in Texas, she liked the skies and landscapes and began to paint southwestern scenes. Unbeknownst to her, a friend gave some of her studies to photographer Alfred Steiglitz, who exhibited them in New York. This year she moves to New York and becomes friends with Steiglitz, who introduces her to other artists in his circle. Here O'Keefe will begin to paint flowers, "organic" shapes, and abstracts. She will later become prominent for her brightly colored flowers and southwestern motifs.

Dancer **Martha Graham**, who grew up in California, joins the Denishawn Company in Los Angeles. Dancers Ruth St. Denis and Ted Shawn established the company to teach interpretive dance. They also stage pageants using simple costumes and minimal scenery, and they like to use Asian rhythms and Greek costumes. Graham is a promising student, and Shawn will write the ballet *Xochitl* for her. Graham will later create and head her own dancing studios, and she will become internationally famous for her dance. She will be considered a leader in modern dance and will gain much praise for unique choreography and for her own flexibility in performances.

Suffragist picketing the White House with a poster calling the president "Kaiser Wilson," c. 1918. (National Archive.) The National Woman's Party refused to support the war and continued to campaign for suffrage. Copying a British tactic, they blamed the party in power for the lack of nationwide female enfranchisement. NWP members denounced President Wilson as a hypocrite who urged Americans to fight for democracy while most American women were denied the vote. They picketed the White House with signs and posters that incurred outrage. National leaders wanted no dissent or controversy; they accused pacifists of treason, and denounced the NWP as pro–German. Many suffragists were arrested, thrown in prison, and beaten, and those who refused to eat were brutally force-fed.

JOINING FORCES

Alice Paul merges her Congressional Union with its western branch, the Woman's Party, into a new group, the National Woman's Party. They take no stance on the war and are concerned only with getting suffrage. Throughout the war, hundreds of members will picket the White House. They will hold signs calling the president "Kaiser

Wilson" and denoting the hypocrisy of fighting a war for democracy in a country where women are still denied the vote. Although the picketers are peaceful, many are arrested and imprisoned, where they are treated brutally.

There is much war hysteria in the nation. The phrase "one hundred percent

American" has been created, which demands loyalty, unity, and patriotism. There is intolerance against radicals, pacifists, and even immigrants, who are often regarded with suspicion. While the picketers for women's suffrage were tolerated before the war, they are now viewed as disloyal and even pro–German. The Sedition Act is passed this year and allows for the arrest of those suspected of being allied with the Germans.

Conditions have been very poor for black women workers, who make low salaries and have poor working conditions. Token efforts by members of the Women's Trade Union League to help black female wage earners are ineffective. The American Federation of Labor appoints a black social worker to establish a central office where problems can be addressed, but a lack of funding for the project makes the idea unsuccessful. A group of Washington, D.C., women led by **Mary Church Terrell** has organized the Women Wage-Earners Association (WWEA), a group that will help organize and protect black female workers. This year, in Norfolk, Virginia, some WWEA members are trying to help local workers organize. Some 600 waitresses, domestic servants, nurses, cigar makers, and tobacco stemmers decide to strike, demanding better working conditions. They are arrested by the police as "slackers." There is a new federal rule, "work or fight," which allows arrest of those who are not in the armed forces or working at home. The WWEA is investigated as a possible subversive organization, and this destroys the Virginia branch. Enforcement of the rule is biased, since local strikes by white males are not disrupted.

LAW AND POLITICS

Jeannette Rankin is from Montana, where she campaigned for female suffrage. She won a seat in the United States House of Representatives two years ago, and she is the first American woman to win a federal legislative office. She calls herself a Progressive Republican and works for female suffrage, protective legislation, prohibition, and peace. This year, in a special session of Congress in April, she is one of fifty-six representatives who vote not to enter the war.

There are several suffrage victories. New York passes an amendment to the state constitution to give women full suffrage. In Arkansas a new law gives women suffrage in primary elections, and in North Dakota, Nebraska, and Rhode Island women win suffrage in presidential elections.

Congress passes the Smith-Hughes Act, which offers federal grants for vocational education in schools. For boys there are a variety of industrial courses that can be offered; for girls, training is only in home economics, not in business or commercial courses. This helps sanction housekeeping as the primary job training for females.

— 1918 —

WORK

President Woodrow Wilson establishes a Women's Department of the National War Labor Board to address the pay inequity of women workers, who make one-half to two-thirds the wages of men in the same jobs. Although board members support equal pay for equal work, they are unable to make changes due to long-standing prejudice against female wage earners. They will formulate no consistent policies on wages, nor will they address the issue of women workers when male soldiers return home.

Another government agency established is the Women in Industry Service, part of the Labor Department. **Mary Van Kleeck**, a labor expert, is appointed head, and **Mary Anderson**, who is an official in the Women's Trade Union League, is hired as an assistant. Their job is to oversee working conditions for women in industry, but because the agency has little authority they accomplish little.

Next year Van Kleeck will retire, and Anderson will become head.

The British have established a corps of women to work on farms, and more than 40,000 have joined a land army. The United States also has a shortage of agricultural workers, and there is a movement to imitate the British. Last year, **Delia Marble**, a geology professor at Barnard who owns a dairy farm, hired several students to help out. It was so successful that she traveled with an associate throughout the United States, promoting the idea of a women's land army. The government establishes it this year. Young women — mostly college students — attend camps where they are trained in agricultural techniques, and then they are placed on farms throughout the United States. By the summer more than 15,000 women are working on farms in more than twenty-seven states. They hoe, plant crops, plow, drive harvesters, and work with livestock and poultry. Some farmers who were hesitant about hiring the women at first are now appreciative and welcome the new workers.[326]

Among women who are needed for government jobs are home economists. The president has established the U.S. Food Administration as an auxiliary group to the Department of Agriculture. There have been predictions of food shortages in Europe, and the Food Administration's job is to increase production and decrease consumption. Stanford president Ray Wilber, who heads the

Female students at the Asheville Normal and Collegiate Institute build a chicken coop, Asheville, North Carolina, c. 1918. (North Carolina Collection, Pack Memorial Public Library, Asheville, N.C.) Note the student's bobbed hair and short skirts, more practical for their labor.

The Woman's Board of Home Missions of the Presbyterian Church founded this school in 1892, one of several schools they founded in the mountains. This institute trained local girls as teachers and community workers. Students worked in the school's vegetable gardens, fruit orchards, poultry house, and dairy. Their labor kept tuition low and fed students and teachers. The girls took courses in the liberal arts, sewing, electricity and carpentry. The school flourished and by 1925 offered a Baccalaureate in Education. Unfortunately the church later withdrew financial support, and the institute closed in 1944.

A female mechanic working on a car, Seattle, Washington, c. 1918. (National Archives.) During the war women took jobs vacated by soldiers, in trades previously closed to them. This woman joined a Motor Corps program established by the National League for Women's Services. She learned automobile repair and maintenance. Other women manufactured steel plates and explosives, assembled electrical tools, worked in blast furnaces, oil refineries, and chemical and fertilizer plants, and helped repair railroads. Many women liked their new jobs, which challenged them and paid well. Some female leaders optimistically predicted that women would enter new vocations after the war, but this did not happen. As national leaders called upon women's loyalty to accept wartime jobs, so they urged women to patriotically resign when the troops returned. Those who refused were often fired. It is doubtful that this woman would have been able to work as a mechanic after the war.

Food Conservation Division, appoints two women to direct the home conservation section. They will help instruct housewives on reducing consumption and conserving food. A staff of eight will help prepare publications, organize cooking demonstrations, and initiate lecture series throughout the country. **Mary Swartz Rose** is the deputy director of the Bureau of Food Conservation for New York City. This year she publishes *Everyday Foods in Wartime*, showing housewives how to conserve. The Food Administration staff are successful. Food consumption drops 10 percent this year, and much of the surplus is sent to Europe.[327]

Women with graduate degrees have trouble finding war work. Most scientific projects are under the aegis of the military, which refuses to give commissions to women. Generally males use their networks to find scientists, and they hire friends, colleagues, and former students. Some female scientists are hired as "civilian assistants." Physicist **Louise McDowell**, from Wellesley, is hired by the National Bureau of Standards to work on radar, and physicist **Frances Wick** at Vassar is employed by the United States Signal Corps to work on gun sights and radios airplanes. The lack of women scientists hired during the war will affect their future employment. Most government positions in science in the postwar era will be offered to men who made contacts during the war.

Most female psychologists are unable to use their skills for war work. The army creates a Psychological Testing Program with several high-level positions. While there is a cadre of female psychologists who have spent years working in testing, only men are appointed — even some with no experience in testing. Major R. M. Yerks, the program's director, issues a press release stating that trained women might be hired as assistants, but he has no plans to hire staff female psychologists. Two female psychologists eventually get positions as assistants.

EDUCATION AND SCHOLARSHIP

Astronomy is considered an appropriate field for women, who are commonly hired at observatories to calculate and note positions of stars. Astronomer **Anne Jump Cannon**, a Wellesley graduate, has been employed to do stellar spectrography at the Harvard College Observatory. Building on work of her predecessors, she has refined their classification system, and this year she publishes another volume in a catalog of stars. When the project is completed, female astronomers will have cataloged 225,300 stars.[328] Cannon will be honored for her work in astronomy. She will become a member of several scientific societies and eventually be appointed curator of astronomical photographs at the Harvard College Observatory.

ARTS

Adella Prentiss Hughes is an arts patron in Cleveland, Ohio, who supports music. This year she convinces local businessmen to hire American violinist Nikolai Sokoloff as conductor of a new local orchestra. They agree and found the Cleveland Symphony Orchestra, which Hughes will manage for the next fourteen years. She will

help raise operating expenses, find a suitable auditorium, arrange tours, and develop educational programs. Several other women have also founded symphony orchestras. **Helen Taft** helped establish the Cincinnati Symphony, composer **Mary Howe** helped found the National Symphony Orchestra in Washington, D.C., and musician and philanthropist **Ima Hogg** helped organize the Houston Symphony.

Willa Cather publishes *My Ántonia*, which celebrates pioneer life and is based on her experiences growing up in Nebraska. Already a popular novelist, Cather is known for her graceful style and her description of the American West. Cather originally intended to become a scientist, but a teacher at the University of Nebraska noted her talent and encouraged her to write. Cather had taught high school and worked as a journalist before she began writing novels. She will write many more and eventually win a Pulitzer Prize. Cather is unhappy with the passing of the pioneer generation, and she will feel alienated by the fast pace and modern technology of the 1920s. Her later works will be set in Spanish New Mexico, antebellum Virginia, and French Quebec.

JOINING FORCES

Among women advocating the availability of birth control information is **Mary Coffin Ware Dennett**. She views contraception as a solution to the problem of world overpopulation and believes that women have the right to contraceptive advice. She also links birth control to sex education. Three years ago she wrote an essay on sex for her teenage sons in which she speaks of sex as joyful and positive, not something to be hidden. This year she publishes it in the *Medical Review of Reviews* as "The Sex Side of Life." It is so popular that thousands request reprints, including health departments and churches. By 1922 more than 25,000 copies will be circulated.[329] The postmaster general will later ban her essay as obscene; although

Dennett will be convicted, the ruling will later be reversed by a federal court.

LAW AND POLITICS

There are more state suffrage victories. Michigan, Oklahoma, and South Dakota lawmakers approve full suffrage by constitutional amendments. Texas passes a law enacting primary suffrage for women.

In January, Representative Jeannette Rankin introduces the Anthony Amendment, calling for a constitutional amendment for women suffrage. President Wilson addresses the House urging a yes vote. He says that women have worked hard for the war effort, and suffrage is "vital" to victory. The House votes for it and gets the two-thirds needed, but the Senate fails to pass it.

In November, the armistice has been signed and the war has ended.

— 1919 —

WORK

While many women liked their wartime jobs with higher pay and interesting challenges, most are dismissed from their positions after the war. Navy and Marine females are put on inactive duty and forbidden to reenlist. Most females who worked in war industry jobs are fired, or gradually phased out. Leaders call upon women to now go back to their homes, and "preserve democracy." The typical attitude is reflected in a comment from an official of the Central Federated Union of New York, who insists that "the same patriotism which induced women to enter industry during the war should induce them to vacate their positions after the war." In Detroit and Cleveland female streetcar conductors are fired, and in New York City twenty female judges are dismissed and told that their positions were valid only during the war emergency. Farm laborers are still

needed, and the Woman's Land Army has become a division of the United States Employment Services. But prejudice from farmers and problems of coordination force the division's closure. The federal government continues its discrimination against women by excluding them from many civil service jobs. A report shows that this year females are prohibited from testing for 60 percent of all civil service jobs.[330]

Typical of the postwar discrimination is the plight of female chemists. When the war started industrial chemists were needed, and many female chemists, previously unemployed, were hired. Their work was superb, and they liked the new jobs. William Brady, a chemist at the Illinois Steel Company, publishes an article in *The Journal of Industrial and Engineering Chemist* this year. He praises their work and their willingness to work long hours, noting that they have taken less sick time than their male colleagues. He predicts that female chemists are now part of the industry. "They have proved beyond a doubt that they can do ... careful, conscientious, reliable chemical work." Several months later, Brady's boss will fire all the female chemists.[331]

Leaders of the Circle for Negro War Relief have been successful. National membership is at 3,000, with fifty-three chapters in many cities.[332] They drop "War" from their name and develop a peacetime program. They will raise money for scholarships to educate more black nurses, and will convince some local health board officials to provide half of the annual salaries for black public health nurses. They will also raise funds to support kindergartens and day nurseries for African-American children and will fund local hospitals.

EDUCATION AND SCHOLARSHIP

Many American blacks are becoming more assertive and calling for racial pride. One is writer **Delilah Leontium Beasley**, an *Oakland Tribune* reporter. This year she publishes *The Negro Trail Blazers of California*, a book based on eight years of research. She wants to show black and white Americans the accomplishments of African Americans. Beasley, who grew up in Ohio, began writing at age twelve, and by fifteen she was writing a column for the *Cincinnati Enquirer*. She moved to California nine years ago. As a *Tribune* writer, she has crusaded to get the public to use the term "Negro" rather than "darkie" and to capitalize it. She is one of many strong voices urging equality for blacks.

ARTS

Sylvia Woodbridge Beach, who has lived in Paris and the United States, moved back to France several years ago. She befriended a popular bookseller whose shop was a literary center for young French writers. Beach wanted to open up a branch store in New York, but the cost was prohibitive. Assisted by her bookseller friend, this year she opens an English-language bookstore in Paris called Shakespeare and Company. The store, which also provides a lending library, will become a center for expatriate writers like Gertrude Stein, Ezra Pound, and Sherwood Anderson. Beach will also encourage writer Katherine Ann Porter and poet Hilda Doolittle. Beach will later help James Joyce prepare his *Ulysses* manuscript, and she will publish it under the bookstore's imprint. Her store will stay open until 1941, when war pressures force its closure.

Black teacher and writer **Jessie Redmon Fauset** moves to New York City to become the literary editor of *The Crisis: A Record of the Darker Races*. W. E. B. Du Bois founded the publication for the National Association for the Advancement of Colored People, and it is widely read. Fauset will remain editor through the 1920s. She will publish her own sketches and stories and encourage many young black artists to write, including Langston Hughes, who first publishes in *The Crisis*. The magazine's showcasing of so many young and talented black writers will help inspire the Harlem Renaissance.

Dorothea Lange, who grew up in New Jersey, had planned to become a teacher. Then, after taking a photography class with the well-known Arnold Genthe and several others at Columbia, she has decided to change careers. This year she moves to San Francisco and opens a portrait studio, finding clients among the wealthy. When the depression begins in the 1930s, she starts to take photos of the unemployed and of migrant workers, a new phase in her work. Lange will become well known for her superb work capturing the mood of the Great Depression. Her exhibits will be so effective that she will be hired as a photographer for the Farm Security Administration.

JOINING FORCES

There has been a decline of activity in some chapters of the General Federation of Women's Clubs as some establish more specialized clubs. This year women form the National Federation of Business and Professional Women. **Lena Madesin Phillips** is the group's first executive secretary. Their plan is to encourage teamwork and solidarity among working women and to lobby for legislation to improve women's wages. The early membership reflects employment trends: nearly half of the members are clerical workers. In three years women will establish more than three hundred local branches. They will prepare a list of skilled women for government appointments and publish their activities in the *Independent Woman*.

During the war, many workers were forced to pledge that they would not strike, but now that the war has ended, massive protests erupt among wage earners. This year nearly four million workers strike in 3,300 separate protests. Among the strikers are female telephone operators in the International Brotherhood of Electrical Workers. Their protest — one of the largest since 1909 — shuts down phone service in parts of

New England. This strike will be unsuccessful, but they will continue to protest during the 1920s.[333]

There has been a wave of fear about communists and socialists who might overthrow the American government, and officials are tracking down radicals. Congress has passed a bill authorizing deportation of people who might promote a revolution. This year they deport anarchist **Emma Goldman** to Russia. Goldman immigrated to American from Russia when she was sixteen and has been a popular leader, advocating radical change in society. She has agitated for free speech, birth control, and women's equality with men, including suffrage, and has denounced society's sexual double standard. She will travel through Europe for many years, and when she dies in 1940, officials allow her to be buried in Chicago.

LAW AND POLITICS

The Eighteenth Amendment, prohibiting the manufacture, sale, or transportation of liquor, is ratified this year, and Congress passes the Volstead Act to enforce it. During the war, as a patriotic act, thousands pledged to refrain from drinking. Public opinion in the South and West supports prohibition, and many states already enforce it. Groups like the Women's Christian Temperance Union, which has been crusading for temperance for nearly fifty years, are overjoyed.

Kentucky governor Edwin P. Morrow, surrounded by suffragists, signs the Nineteenth Amendment to the Constitution of the United States, January 1920. (Library of Congress.) Kentucky was the twenty-fourth state to ratify the amendment. Later that year Tennessee's approval became the needed thirty-sixth, and the amendment became law in August.

Prohibition will be difficult to enforce and will result in widespread lawlessness, corruption, and crime. The amendment will be repealed in 1933.

There are several state suffrage victories. In Indiana a law allowing presidential suffrage was challenged in court but is reenacted this year. Women win full suffrage in seven other states: Maine, Missouri, Iowa, Minnesota, Ohio, Wisconsin, and Tennessee.

In March, Congress passes the Nineteenth Amendment, enfranchising women. Members of suffrage groups now begin the campaign for ratification.

— 1920 —

DOMESTICITY

Although office work has become an acceptable vocation for women, there is still much discussion about it. Only the nature of the criticism has changed. In the 1890s and early 1900s, women were told they were too idealistic and morally superior for office work. Now the arguments have changed, and critics charge them with either becoming too masculine or with having the "feminine" characteristics of being silly and giggly and being hampered by their periods. Henry Norman writes an article for the *Forum*, "The Feminine Failure in Business." Women lose too much work time because of their periods to be effective employees, he argues, and they are not strong enough to have the mental concentration needed in office work. Another writer sends a piece to the *Literary Digest*, saying that women are unsuitable as receptionists, since they are too moody and temperamental and might be "sarcastic" or "flirt" with office visitors.[334]

The *Ladies' Home Journal* publishes an inspirational statement for its readers: "I believe in woman's rights; but ... in women's sacrifices also ... I believe in woman's suffrage; but ... many other things are vastly

Ida May Fayling and her children Lloyd, Jr., and Enid Celia, White Bear Lake, Minnesota, c. 1920. (Dione Miles.) This studio portrait represents an American ideal: a lovely young white, middle-class mother with her two children.

During the 1920s there was much pressure on middle-class white women to marry, have children, and stay at home. Most Americans maintained that female wage earners threatened the family's stability (ignoring the fact that 90 percent of female wage earners needed the income). National leaders, employers, and even some reformers insisted that women belong at home. Advertisers, speechwriters, sermons, and magazine and newspaper articles promoted this ideal. Most white married women whose husbands earned sufficient income chose marriage and motherhood as their vocation.

more important.... I believe in woman's brains; but I believe still more in her emotions."[335]

WORK

Congress has established the Women's Bureau of the Department of Labor from the wartime Women in Industry Service. **Mary Anderson**, former head of the service, now directs the bureau, and she will hold the position until 1944. Their mission is to find facts on women in labor, investigate situations and act as advocates, and develop standards for women wage earners. Anderson is a good administrator, and the bureau will get a reputation for thorough field investigations. However, Anderson is primarily allied with white middle-class groups. She supports protective legislation that will be challenged in courts during the 1920s, and her staff fails to address the rights of female African-American workers. With stronger female leadership during the 1960s, the bureau will help get a federal equal pay act passed in Congress and will persuade President John F. Kennedy to establish a commission on the status of women.

The war made little difference in the number of women employed in peacetime. Women are now 21 percent of the labor force (which is nearly forty-two million), but only 24 percent of all women hold jobs. Less than 5 percent of the women now working entered the labor force as a result of the war. While some wealthy, well-educated, or ambitious women have been able — and will continue to be able — to find good careers, until 1940 most women (86–90 percent) will be employed in less than a dozen occupations, with low wages and status.[336]

The war did affect trends in the kinds of employment for women. The United States now has new international markets in commerce, finance, communications, and advertising. This has opened more positions in white-collar jobs such as clerks, office workers, bookkeepers, secretaries, buyers, home decorators, and telephone and telegraph operators. Women are now 48 percent of all clerical workers, 92 percent of stenographers and typists, and 62 percent of social workers. They also comprise 94 percent of trained nurses, 79 percent of librarians, and 84 percent of teachers. The war did not bring changes in the number of women in manu-

facturing and industry. While the number of factory operatives has almost doubled since 1900, the percentage of women in this work has declined.[337]

Black female wage earners have made little progress. Although during the war some got jobs previously closed to them, after the war, like white women, most black women were fired. Their standing in the labor force has not improved, and this year 75 percent of them work in agricultural labor, domestic service, and laundry work.[338]

EDUCATION AND SCHOLARSHIP

This year women earn an even greater percentage of college and postgraduate degrees. They earn 34 percent of all bachelor's degrees; 30 percent of all master's degrees, and 15 percent of all doctorates. While the number of universities and colleges — and enrollment — will expand during the 1920s, women will lose ground in graduate degrees. The percentage of females with doctorates will drop to 10 percent by 1950 and will only rise again in 1970, with 13 percent.[339]

Margaret Mead, a young college student, transfers from DePauw to Barnard this year. She found DePauw provincial and inbred and wanted the excitement and the cosmopolitan atmosphere of New York City. At Barnard she will study with Franz Boas and Ruth Benedict, beginning work that will lead to her career as an anthropologist. Mead, like other young women coming of age after the war, is full of optimism about what she can do. These young women have a sense of personal autonomy that their mothers lacked. While Mead's mother was excited about reforming society, Mead is excited about her individual rights and intellectual growth. She will later recall, "We belonged to a generation of young women who felt extraordinarily free.... We laughed at the idea that a woman could be an old maid at the age of twenty five, and we rejoiced at the new medical care that made it possible to have a child at age forty."[340]

Labor activist **Mary Ritter Beard** publishes her second book, *A Short History of the American Labor Movement*, on the working class and social reform. After this she will turn to women's history, and she will pursue this work during the 1930s and 1940s. Even the book she will coauthor with her husband, Charles Beard, will include a great deal of information on women. Beard believes that earlier histories that emphasize the injustices done to women are not as useful as those stressing women's contributions, and in her works she writes of women's many activities. She will be a lone worker in women's history until the 1970s, when a new group of historians will begin to study women's past.

RELIGION

To help promote better race relations, a women's council from the Methodist Episcopal Church, South, makes a public statement supporting African Americans. They address what they believe are black women's needs: domestic service should be classified as a profession, and there should be more day nurseries and improved housing for blacks as well as prosecution for lynching. They fail to address suffrage. Next year the Southeastern Federation branch of the National Association of Colored Women responds. They offer specific suggestions of how white women can improve race relations and point out that white women should ensure that all women have suffrage.

ARTS

Nativism has increased in the United States, and immigration has decreased by 50 percent in the last decade. However, one woman who writes of her life as an immigrant has become quite successful. **Anzia Yezierska**, a Jewish immigrant from Poland and a prize-winning writer of short stories, publishes *Hungry Hearts*. Movie mogul Samuel Goldwyn buys her story for $10,000, and Yerzierska travels to Hollywood to help with the screenplay. She will later become discouraged by the compromises needed in adapting her story. Although she continues to publish, by the 1930s her books will be less popular. Her works will be rediscovered and appreciated again during the 1980s.[341]

JOINING FORCES

While female wage earners are 21 percent of the labor force, less than 8 percent are in unions. These who are organized are primarily in the clothing unions (50 percent of all female union members) and in printing and typographical unions (25 percent). Other organized women are meat packers, hotel employees, shoe and boot makers, and railroad clerks.[342]

Alice Paul believes women need more than suffrage for full equality, and she envisions an Equal Rights Amendment (ERA) to the Constitution. She will begin a campaign for this within the National Woman's Party. There will be a sharp division among women on the topic, as many believe it will destroy existing protective legislation for women. While there will be lengthy campaigns for the ERA, it will have failed to pass Congress by the late twentieth century.

LAW AND POLITICS

The Nineteenth Amendment is ratified, giving American women full suffrage.

At a victory party in February, the National American Woman Suffrage Association founds the League of Women Voters. They will be a nonpartisan group whose goal will be voter education. It will remain primarily a white middle-class organization, with most members married and at home full-time.

Appendix: Tables

TABLE 1-A
Population by Region and Gender, 1790–1860[1]
(in thousands)

Year	NE[2] females	NE males	NC[3] females	NC males	South[4] females	South males	West[5] females	West males	Total population[6]
1790	940	961	—	—	616	655	—	—	3,292
1800	1,248	1,303	23	—	830	874	—	—	5,309
1810	1,670	1,714	135	27	1,069	1,123	—	—	7,240
1820	2,169	2,187	406	151	2,163	2,255	—	—	9,638
1830	2,751	2,748	772	453	2,808	2,900	—	—	12,860
1840	3,364	3,397	1,594	838	3,423	3,528	—	—	17,064
1850	4,287	4,339	2,589	1,758	4,430	4,552	47	132	23,193
1860	5,329	5,226	4,354	2,814	5,478	5,655	197	422	31,433

TABLE 1-B
Population by Region and Gender, 1870–1920[1]
(in thousands)

Year	NE[2] females	NE males	NC[3] females	NC males	South[4] females	South males	West[5] females	West males	Total population[6]
1870	6,219	6,080	6,262	6,705	6,197	6,091	381	609	38,559
1880	7,347	7,161	8,348	9,016	8,244	8,272	698	1,070	50,189
1890	8,726	8,681	10,792	11,619	9,910	10,118	1,283	1,820	52,979
1900	10,522	10,525	13,589	12,744	12,119	12,405	1,794	2,298	76,213
1910	12,790	13,087	14,403	15,486	14,465	14,924	2,982	3,844	92,229
1920	14,783	14,879	16,562	17,494	16,352	16,773	4,149	4,754	106,022

[1]For 1800 through 1820, regional figures include whites only.
[2]NE: Northeast Region, includes CT, MA, ME, NH, NJ, NY, PA, RI, VT.
[3]NC: North Central Region, includes IA, IL, IN, KS, MI, MN, MO, NE, ND, OH, SD, WI.
[4]South Region includes AL, AR, DE, DC, FL, GA, KY, LA, NC, OK, SC, TX, VA, WV.
[5]West Region includes AZ, CA, CO, HI, ID, MT, NM, NV, OR, UT, WA, WY.
[6]Total population estimates from Series A 6–8 in *Historical Statistics*, 8.

Source: U.S. Bureau of the Census, *Historical Statistics of the United States, Colonial Times to 1970, Bicentennial Edition* (Washington, D.C., 1975), 8, 22.

TABLE 2
Black American Females, 1790–1860

Year	Total slave population	Total black females	Female slaves	Free black women[1]
1790	679,681	—	—	—
1800	893,602	—	—	—
1810	1,191,362	—	—	—
1820	1,538,022	870,800	750,010	120,790
1830	2,009,043	1,162,366	996,220	166,146
1840	2,487,355	1,440,760	1,240,938	199,822
1850	3,204,313	1,827,550	1,601,779	225,771
1860	3,953,760	2,225,086	1,971,135	253,951

[1]From 1820 through 1840, 14% of all black women were free; this declined to 12% in 1850 and 11% in 1860.

Source: U.S. Bureau of the Census, *Historical Statistics of the United States, Colonial Times to 1970, Bicentennial Edition* (Washington, D.C., 1975), 14, 17, 18.

TABLE 3
Birthrates, 1800–1920
(live births/1,000 population)

Year	Total population	White population	Black population
1800	—	55.0	—
1820	55.2	52.8	—
1840	51.8	48.3	—
1860	44.3	41.4	—
1880	39.8	35.2	—
1900	32.3	30.1	—
1920	27.7	26.9	35.0

Source: U.S. Bureau of the Census, *Historical Statistics of the United States, Colonial Times to 1970, Bicentennial Edition* (Washington, D.C., 1975), 49.

TABLE 4
Immigration from Great Britain, Ireland,
and Germany, 1820–1890

Year	Total number of immigrants	Percentage from Europe	European Immigrants[1]			
			Total from Europe	Percentage from Great Britain	Percentage from Ireland	Percentage from Germany
1820	8,385	92	7,691	29	43	12
1830	23,322	31	7,217	5	12	8
1840	84,066	95	80,126	3	47	35
1850	369,980	83	308,323	14	44	21
1860	153,640	92	141,209	19	32	35
1870	387,203	85	328,626	27	15	31

| Year | Total number of immigrants | Percentage from Europe | European Immigrants— | | | |
			Total from Europe	Percentage from Great Britain	Percentage from Ireland	Percentage from Germany
1880	457,257	76	348,691	16	16	19
1890	455,302	98	445,680	15	12	20

[1]Percentages are proportion of total immigration.
Source: U.S. Bureau of the Census, *Historical Statistics of the United States, Colonial Times to 1970, Bicentennial Edition* (Washington, D.C., 1975), 106.

TABLE 5
Immigration from Central, Southern, and Eastern Europe, 1890–1920

| Year | Total number of immigrants | Percentage from Europe | European Immigrants[1] | | | | |
			Total from Europe	Percentage from Austria and Hungary	Percentage from USSR and Baltic States	Percentage from Italy	Percentage Spain, Greece, and Portugal
1890	455,302	98	445,680	12	8	11	< 1
1900	448,572	95	424,700	26	20	22	2
1910	1,041,570	89	926,291	25	18	21	4
1920	430,001	57[2]	246,295	1	< 1	22	11

[1]Percentages are proportion of total immigration.
[2]Additional percentages from other countries: 21% from Canada and Newfoundland; 12% from Mexico; 10% other.
Source: U.S. Bureau of the Census, *Historical Statistics of the United States, Colonial Times to 1970, Bicentennial Edition* (Washington, D.C., 1975), 105, 106.

TABLE 6
Immigration of Females, 1820–1920[1]

Year	Total number of immigrants	Females as percentage of total	Year	Total number of immigrants	Females as percentage of total
1820	10,311	30	1875	227,498	38
1825	12,858	26	1880	457,257	37
1830	24,837	27	1885	395,346	43
1835	48,716	17	1890	455,302	38
1840	92,207	36	1895	279,948	47
1845	119,896	78	1900	448,572	32
1850	380,904	31	1905	1,026,499	29
1855	230,476	41	1910	1,041,570	29
1860	179,691	41	1915	326,700	43
1865	287,699	40	1920	430,001	42
1870	387,203	39			

[1]For 1820 through 1867 the figures include returning U.S. citizens.
Source: U.S. Bureau of the Census, *Historical Statistics of the United States, Colonial Times to 1970, Bicentennial Edition* (Washington, D.C., 1975), 112.

TABLE 7
High School Diplomas Earned by Females,
1870–1920

Year	Total diplomas awarded	Percentage earned by females
1870	16,000	56
1875	20,000	55
1880	24,000	54
1885	32,000	56
1890	44,000	57
1895	72,000	60
1900	95,000	60
1905	119,000	61
1910	156,000	60
1915	240,000	58
1920	311,000	60

Source: U.S. Bureau of the Census, *Historical Statistics of the United States, Colonial Times to 1970, Bicenten-nial Edition* (Washington, D.C., 1975), 379.

TABLE 8
Bachelor's Degrees[1] Earned by Females,
1870–1920

Year	Total degrees awarded	Percentage earned by females
1870	9,371	15
1875	11,932	17
1880	12,896	19
1885	14,734	18
1890	15,539	17
1895	24,106	18
1900	27,410	19
1905	31,519	21
1910	37,199	23
1915	43,912	28
1920	48,622	34

[1]Or first professional degree.
Source: U.S. Bureau of the Census, *Historical Statistics of the United States, Colonial Times to 1970, Bicenten-nial Edition* (Washington, D.C., 1975), 386.

TABLE 9
Graduate Degrees
Earned by Females,
1895–1920

Year	Total master's degrees[1] awarded	Percentage earned by females	Total doctorates[2] awarded	Percentage earned by females
1895	1,334	17	272	9
1900	1,583	19	382	6
1905	1,925	20	369	8
1910	2,113	26	443	10
1915	3,557	26	611	10
1920	4,279	30	625	15

[1]Or second professional degree.
[2]Or equivalent.

Source: U.S. Bureau of the Census, *Historical Statistics of the United States, Colonial Times to 1970, Bicentennial Edition* (Washington, D.C., 1975), 386.

TABLE 10
Paid Workers in Farm
and Nonfarm Occupations,
1820–1920
(in thousands of persons, age 10 or over)

Year	Total workers	Percentage in farm occupations	Percentage in nonfarm occupations
1820	2,881	72	28
1840	5,420	69	31
1860	10,533	59	41
1880	17,392	49	51
1900	29,073	38	62
1920	42,434	27	73

Source: U.S. Bureau of the Census, *Historical Statistics of the United States, Colonial Times to 1970, Bicentennial Edition* (Washington, D.C., 1975), 134.

TABLE 11
Female Employment, 1870–1920

Year	Total people employed[1]	Females as percentage of total people employed	Married females as percentage of total females employed	Employed females as percentage of total female population[2]
1870	12,506	15	NA	NA
1880	17,392	15	NA	NA
1890	22,736	17	14	19
1900	29,073	18	15	21
1910	38,167	21	25	25
1920	41,614	21	23	24

[1]Thousands of workers age 10 and over.
[2]Employed females age 15 and over.
Source: U.S. Bureau of the Census, *Historical Statistics of the United States, Colonial Times to 1970, Bicentennial Edition* (Washington, D.C., 1975), 129, 133.

TABLE 12
Females in Selected Occupations, 1870–1920

Year	Stenographers and Typists		Teachers[1]		Trained Nurses		Social, Welfare, and Religious Workers[2]	
	Total people employed	Females as percentage of total	Total people employed	Females as percentage of total	Total people employed	Females as percentage of total	Total people employed	Females as percentage of total
1870	154	5	84,548	66	1,154	96	68	0.1
1880	5,000	40	153,372	68	1,464	95	165	0.3
1890	33,400	64	244,467	71	4,206	92	1,143	1.0
1900	112,364	77	325,485	74	11,046	94	3,373	3.0
1910	316,693	83	478,027	80	76,508	93	8,889	56.0
1920	615,154	92	639,241	84	143,644	96	26,927	66.0

[1]Includes college teachers, but for women this is a very small proportion.
[2]Includes clergy from 1870 through 1900.

Source: Margery Davies, *Women's Place Is at the Typewriter: Office Work and Office Workers, 1870–1930* (Philadelphia, Temple University Press, 1982), data from tables 1 and 4.

TABLE 13
Females in Selected Occupations, 1900–1920
(in thousands of persons age 14 and over)

Year	White-Collar Workers				Manual and Service Workers			
	Total professional, technical, and kindred	Females as percentage of total	Total clerical and kindred	Females as percentage of total	Total operatives and kindred	Females as percentage of total	Total private household workers	Females as percentage of total
1900	1,234	35	877	24	3,720	34	1,579	57
1910	1,758	41	1,987	35	5,411	31	1,851	96
1920	2,283	44	3,385	48	6,587	27	1,411	96

Source: U.S. Bureau of the Census, *Historical Statistics of the United States, Colonial Times to 1970, Bicentennial Edition* (Washington, D.C., 1975), 129, 133.

Notes

INTRODUCTION

1. Many additional categories could be used for a portrayal of women's lives, for example, health, sexuality, or reproduction issues. However, these lie outside the scope of this work.

2. Gerda Lerner, *The Creation of Feminist Consciousness: From the Middle Ages to 1870* (New York: Oxford Univ. Press, 1993), 192.

3. Anne Firor Scott, *Natural Allies: Women's Associations in American History* (Urbana: Univ. of Illinois Press, Illini Book edition, 1993), 2.

TEXT

1. Rosemary R. Ruether and Rosemary S. Keller, eds., *Women and Religion in America*, vol. 2, *The Colonial and Revolutionary Periods* (San Francisco: Harper & Row, 1983), 226.

2. Gerda Lerner, ed., *The Female Experience: An American Documentary* (New York: Bobbs-Merrill, 1977; New York: Oxford Univ. Press, 1992), 209.

3. Joan M. Jensen, "Native Women and Agriculture: A Seneca Case Study," in Ellen Carol DuBois and Vicki L. Ruiz, eds., *Unequal Sisters: A Multicultural Reader in U.S. Women's History* (New York: Routledge, 1990), 54.

4. Quoted in Mary Beth Norton, *Liberty's Daughters: The Revolutionary Experience of American Women, 1750–1800* (New York: Harper-Collins Publishers, 1980), 246.

5. *Ibid.*, 137.

6. See table 2; Rosalyn Baxandall and Linda Gordon, eds., *America's Working Women: A Documentary History, 1600 to the Present*, rev. ed. (New York: W. W. Norton, 1995), 32–34.

7. Quoted in Frederick Rudolph, ed., *Essays on Education in the Early Republic* (Cambridge: Harvard Univ. Press, Belknap Press, 1965), 70.

8. Ruth Barnes Moynihan, Cynthia Russett, and Laurie Crumpacker, eds., *Second to None: A Documentary History of American Women*, vol. 1, *From the 16th Century to 1865* (Lincoln: Univ. of Nebraska Press, 1993), 187.

9. Linda K. Kerber, *Women of the Republic: Intellect and Ideology in Revolutionary America* (Chapel Hill: Univ. of North Carolina Press, 1980; reprint, New York: W. W. Norton, 1986), 153.

10. Moynihan et al., *Second to None*, vol. 1, 186.

11. For a full discussion this see Joan Scott, "The Woman Worker," in Georges Duby and Michelle Perrot, eds., *A History of Women in the West*, vol. 4, *Emerging Feminism from Revolution to World War I* (in Italian: Laterza & Figli Spa, Rome and Bari, 1991; reprint in English: Cambridge: Harvard Univ. Press paperback edition, 1995), 399–426.

12. Ruether and Keller, *Women and Religion*, vol. 2, 362.

13. Quoted in Susan Burrows Swan, *Plain and Fancy: American Women and Their Needlework, 1700–1850* (New York: Holt, Rinehart and Winston, Rutledge Books, 1977), 73.

14. Quoted in Miriam Brody, "Introduction," in *A Vindication of the Rights of Women*, by

Mary Wollstonecraft, ed. Brody. (London, 1792; reprint, London: Penguin Books, 1992), 13.

15. For a discussion of the Greene and Whitney relationship see Autumn Stanley, *Mothers and Daughters of Invention: Notes for a Revised History of Technology* (Metuchen, N.J.: Scarecrow Press, 1993; New Brunswick: Rutgers Univ. Press, 1995), 544–46.

16. Gary B. Mills, "Coincoin," in Darlene Clark Hine, Elsa Barkely, and Rosalyn Terborg-Penn, eds., *Black Women in America: An Historical Encyclopedia*, vol. 1 (Brooklyn: Carlson Publishing, 1993; Bloomington: Indiana Univ. Press, 1994), 258–59.

17. Quoted in Norton, *Liberty's Daughters*, 248.

18. Janet Whitney, *Abigail Adams* (Boston: Little, Brown and Co., 1947), 290.

19. Quoted in Joan Hoff, *Law, Gender, and Injustice: A Legal History of U.S. Women* (New York: New York Univ. Press, 1991), 100.

20. Michael S. Kimmel and Thomas E. Mosmiller, eds., *Against the Tide: Pro-Feminist Men in the United States, 1776–1990: A Documentary History* (Boston: Beacon Press, 1992), 71.

21. The percentage increase and number of free blacks are calculated from footnote 1 in the table of Population by Sex and Race, Series A-91-104, in U.S. Bureau of the Census, *Historical Statistics of the United States, Colonial Times to 1970, Bicentennial Edition* (Washington, D.C., 1975), 14.

22. Nancy F. Cott, ed., *Root of Bitterness: Documents of the Social History of American Women* (Boston: Northeastern Univ. Press, 1986), 105.

23. Moynihan et al., *Second to None*, vol. 1, 202.

24. U.S. Census, *Historical Statistics*, 35, 28.

25. Catherine Clinton, *The Other Civil War: American Women in the Nineteenth Century* (New York: Hill and Wang, 1984), 42.

26. Quoted in Nancy F. Cott, *The Bonds of Womanhood: "Woman's Sphere" in New England, 1780–1835* (New Haven: Yale Univ. Press, 1977), 44.

27. *Martin v. Commonwealth of Massachusetts*, I Mass. 347 (1805); quoted in Kerber, *Women of the Republic*, 133.

28. Moynihan et al., *Second to None*, vol. 1, 204.

29. Cott, *Root of Bitterness*, 113, 116.

30. Cott, *Bonds of Womanhood*, 132.

31. Barbara M. Wertheimer, *We Were There: The Story of Working Women in America* (New York: Random House, Pantheon Books, 1977), 55.

32. Quoted in Cott, *Bonds of Womanhood*, 148.

33. Quoted in *ibid.*, 86.

34. *Commonwealth v. Addicks*, 5 Benney (Pa.) 519 (1813); Hoff, *Law, Gender, and Injustice*, 132.

35. *Herbert v. Wren*, 7 Cranch 368, 3 L. Ed. 374 (1813).

36. Quoted in Cott, *Bonds of Womanhood*, 157.

37. Quoted in *ibid.*, 99.

38. Mimi Abramovitz, *Regulating the Lives of Women: Social Welfare Policy from Colonial Times to the Present* (Boston: South End Press, 1988), 122.

39. Quoted in G. J. Barker-Benfield and Catherine Clinton, eds., *Portraits of American Women: From Settlement to the Present* (New York: St. Martin's Press, 1991), 97.

40. U.S. Census, *Historical Statistics*, 30.

41. *Connor v. Shephard*, 15 Mass. 164 (1818); quoted in Hoff, *Law, Gender, and Injustice*, 107.

42. *Dartmouth College v. Woodward*, 17 U.S. 518 (1819); quoted in Hoff, *Law, Gender, and Injustice*, 104–5.

43. See table 4.

44. *Ibid.*

45. See table 2; quoted in Norton, *Liberty's Daughters*, 73.

46. Barbara N. Parker, "Sarah Goodridge," in Edward James, Janet Wilson James, and Paul Boyer, eds., *Notable American Women, 1607–1950: A Biographical Dictionary*, vol. 2 (Cambridge: Harvard Univ. Press, Belknap Press, 1971), 62.

47. Quoted in Cott, *Bonds of Womanhood*, 72.

48. See table 1-A.

49. Tanya Bolden, *The Book of African-American Women: 150 Crusaders, Creators, and Uplifters* (Holbrook, Mass.: Adams Media, 1996), 33.

50. Francis Trollope, *Domestic Manners of the Americans,* ed. Donald Smalley (New York: Alfred A. Knopf, Borzoi Book, 1949), 75.

51. See table 3 for decline in birthrates.

52. Quoted in Barbara M. Solomon, *In the Company of Educated Women: A History of Women and Higher Education in America* (New Haven: Yale Univ. Press, 1985), 36.

53. Glenda Riley, *Inventing the American Woman: An Inclusive History*, vol. 2 (Wheeling, Ill.: Harlan Davidson, 1995), 67.

54. Wertheimer, *We Were There*, 94.

55. See table 1-A; U.S. Census, *Historical Statistics*, 27, 30.

56. Baxandall and Gordon, *America's Working Women*, 63.

57. Quoted in Wertheimer, *We Were There*, 97.

58. Marilyn Richardson, *Maria W. Stewart, America's First Black Woman Political Writer* (Bloomington: Indiana Univ. Press, 1987), 38.

59. Linda Gordon, *Woman's Body, Woman's Right: Birth Control in America*, rev. ed. (New York: Penguin Books, 1990), 61, 48.

60. Ellen Skinner, ed., *Women and the National Experience: Primary Sources in American History* (New York: Addison-Wesley Educational Publishers, 1996), 34.

61. See tables 1-A and 4.

62. Mary Beth Norton et al., *A People and a Nation: A History of the United States*, vol. 1, *To 1877*, 4th ed. (Boston: Houghton Mifflin, 1994), 390.

63. Dorothy Sterling, ed., *We Are Your Sisters: Black Women in the Nineteenth Century* (New York: W. W. Norton, 1984), 181.

64. Shirley J. Yee, *Black Women Abolitionists: A Study in Activism, 1828–1860* (Knoxville: Univ. of Tennessee Press, 1992), 54.

65. Quoted in Alice Kessler-Harris, *Out to Work: A History of Wage-Earning Women in the United States* (New York: Oxford Univ. Press, 1983), 69.

66. Dawn Keeley and John Pettegrew, eds., *Public Women, Public Words: A Documentary History of American Feminism* (Madison: Madison House, 1997), 155.

67. Quoted in Kerber, *Women of the Republic*, 112.

68. Quoted in Swan, *Plain and Fancy*, 40.

69. Skinner, *National Experience*, 61.

70. Keeley and Pettegrew, *Public Women*, 157–58.

71. Yee, *Black Women Abolitionists*, 52.

72. Sterling, *We Are Your Sisters*, 128.

73. Skinner, *National Experience*, 61.

74. Moynihan et al., *Second to None*, vol. 1, 244.

75. Lerner, *Female Experience*, 334–35.

76. See table 4.

77. Kessler-Harris, *Wage-Earning Women*, 47.

78. Quoted in George Hochfield, ed., *Selected Writings of the American Transcendentalists* (New York: New American Library, Signet Classics, 1966), 296.

79. Mary P. Ryan, *The Empire of the Mother: American Writing about Domesticity, 1830–1860* (The Haworth Press, 1982; reprint, New York: Harrington Park Press, 1985), 33.

80. Lerner, *Female Experience*, 204.

81. Quoted in "Margaret Fuller: Woman in the Nineteenth Century," in Miriam Schneir, ed., *Feminism: The Essential Historical Writings* (New York: Random House, Vintage Books, 1972), 63.

82. Peter Quinn, "The Tragedy of Bridget Such-A-One," *American Heritage*, December 1997, 39.

83. Skinner, *National Experience*, 76.

84. Kimmel and Mossmiller, *Pro-Feminist Men*, 212.

85. Lillian Schlissel, *Women's Diaries of the Westward Journey* (New York: Schocken Books, 1982), 24.

86. Skinner, *National Experience*, 79.

87. Martha M. Solomon, ed., *A Voice of Their Own: The Woman Suffrage Press, 1840–1910* (Tuscaloosa: Univ. of Alabama Press, 1991), 31.

88. Moynihan et al., *Second to None*, vol. 1, 254.

89. Norton et al., *People and Nation*, vol. 1, 349.

90. Wertheimer, *We Were There*, 61.

91. See tables 4 and 6.

92. Schlissel, *Women's Diaries*, 64; U.S. Census, *Historical Statistics*, 25.

93. Norton et al., *People and Nation*, vol. 1, 406.

94. Lerner, *Female Experience*, 417.

95. Quoted in Aileen S. Kraditor, *Up from the Pedestal: Selected Writings in the History of American Feminism* (Chicago: Quadrangle Books, 1968), 189–90.

96. Sterling, *We Are Your Sisters*, 166.

97. Moynihan et al., *Second to None*, vol. 1, 276.

98. Quoted in Martha Solomon, *Woman Suffrage Press*, 188.

99. Ellen Carol DuBois, ed., *The Elizabeth Cady Stanton–Susan B. Anthony Reader*, rev. ed. (Boston: Northeastern Univ. Press, in arrangement with Schocken Books, 1992), 100.

100. Quoted in Ryan, *Empire of the Mother*, 112.

101. Baxandall and Gordon, *America's Working Women*, 77–78.

102. Cathy Davidson and Linda Martin-Wagner, eds., *The Oxford Companion to Women's Writing in the United States* (New York: Oxford Univ. Press, 1992), 103.

103. Quoted in *ibid.*, 784.

104. Quoted in Ryan, *Empire of the Mother*, 111.

105. U.S. Census, *Historical Statistics*, 106;

Baxandall and Gordon, *America's Working Women*, 73.

106. Quoted in Yee, *Black Women Abolitionists*, 46.

107. Wertheimer, *We Were There*, 102–3.

108. Kessler-Harris, *Wage-Earning Women*, 71.

109. Wertheimer, *We Were There*, 84.

110. Kessler-Harris, *Wage-Earning Women*, 335, n. 31.

111. See table 2; Wertheimer, *We Were There*, 108.

112. Sterling, *We Are Your Sisters*, 204.

113. Drew Gilpin Faust, *Mothers of Invention: Women of the Slaveholding South in the American Civil War* (Chapel Hill: Univ. of North Carolina Press, 1996; New York: Random House, Vintage Books, 1997), 22.

114. Katharine M. Jones, *Heroines of Dixie: Confederate Women Tell Their Story of the War* (New York: Bobbs Merrill, 1955), 32.

115. Hoff, *Law, Gender, and Injustice*, 144.

116. Scott, *Natural Allies*, 63.

117. Quoted in Helen E. Marshall, "Dix, Dorothea Lynde," in James et al., *Notable American Women*, vol. 1, 488–89.

118. Elizabeth D. Leonard, *Yankee Women: Gender Battles in the Civil War* (New York: W. W. Norton, 1994), 114.

119. Faust, *Mothers of Invention*, 82–83.

120. Mary Boykin Chesnut, *A Diary from Dixie*, ed. Ben Ames Williams (Boston: Houghton Mifflin, Sentry edition, 1961), 1.

121. Lori D. Ginzberg, *Women and the Work of Benevolence: Morality, Politics, and Class in the Nineteenth Century United States* (New Haven: Yale Univ. Press, 1990), 168.

122. Norton et al., *People and Nation*, vol. 1, 442; number of female nurses from Hoff, *Law, Gender, and Injustice*, 144.

123. Faust, *Mothers of Invention*, 96.

124. Mary P. Ryan, *Women in Public: Between Banners and Ballots, 1825–1880* (Baltimore: Johns Hopkins Univ. Press, 1990), 1.

125. See table 3.

126. Kessler-Harris, *Wage-Earning Women*, 76, 84.

127. Faust, *Mothers of Invention*, 17.

128. Quoted in Jones, *Confederate Women*, 259.

129. Catherine Clinton and Nina Silber, eds., *Divided Houses: Gender and the Civil War* (New York: Oxford Univ. Press, 1992), 245.

130. Lynn Sherr, *Failure Is Impossible: Susan B. Anthony in Her Own Words* (New York: Random House, Times Books, 1995), 35.

131. Quoted in Faust, *Mothers of Invention*, 47.

132. Quoted in *ibid.*, 91; salaries, p. 89.

133. *Ibid.*, 39.

134. Baxandall and Gordon, *America's Working Women*, 74–75.

135. Wertheimer, *We Were There*, 151.

136. Elizabeth Cady Stanton, *Eighty Years and More: Reminiscences, 1815–1897* (N.p.: T. Fisher Unwin, 1898; reprinted with an introduction by Ellen Carol DuBois and afterword by Anne D. Gordon, Boston: Northeastern Univ. Press, 1993), 238, 240.

137. James West Davidson et al., *Nation of Nations: A Narrative History of the American Republic* (New York: McGraw Hill, 1990), 581.

138. Faust, *Mothers of Invention*, 78.

139. Wertheimer, *We Were There*, 153–54.

140. Ellen Carol DuBois, *Feminism and Suffrage: The Emergence of an Independent Women's Movement in America, 1848–1869* (Ithaca: Cornell Univ. Press, 1978), 60.

141. Scott, *Natural Allies*, 68; Jeannie Attie, "Warwork and the Crisis of Domesticity in the North," in Clinton and Silber, *Divided Houses*, 257.

142. Wertheimer, *We Were There*, 158.

143. Sterling, *We Are Your Sisters*, 385.

144. Quoted in Thurman Wilkins, "Ream, Vinnie," in James et al., *Notable American Women*, vol. 3, 123.

145. Rosalyn Terborg-Penn, "Discrimination against Afro-American Women in the Women's Movement, 1830–1920," in Sharon Harley and Rosalyn Terborg-Penn, eds., *The Afro-American Woman: Struggles and Images* (Port Washington, N.Y.: Kennikat Press, 1978), 20.

146. Lerner, *Female Experience*, 409.

147. Anne L. Macdonald, *Feminine Ingenuity: Women and Invention in America* (New York: Ballantine Books, 1992), 42.

148. Quoted in Norton Juster, *A Woman's Place: Yesterday's Women in Rural America* (Golden, Colo.: Fulcrum Publishing, 1996), 60, 8.

149. Quoted in *ibid.*, 267–68.

150. Lerner, *Female Experience*, 237.

151. DuBois, *Feminism and Suffrage*, 103.

152. William C. McLoughlin, "Van Cott, Margaret Ann Newton," in James et al., *Notable American Women*, vol. 3, 507.

153. Macdonald, *Women and Invention*, 45.

154. Beverly Beeton, *Women Vote in the West: The Woman Suffrage Movement, 1869–1896* (New York: Garland Publishing, 1986), 1.

155. Hoff, *Law, Gender, and Injustice*, 176.

156. DuBois, *Feminism and Suffrage*, 128; see table 4.

157. Kessler-Harris, *Wage-Earning Women*, 54.

158. See table 7.

159. See table 8.

160. Quoted in Hoff, *Law, Gender, and Injustice*, 163.

161. Martha Solomon, *Woman Suffrage Press*, 87.

162. U.S. Census, *Historical Statistics*, 35, 37.

163. Ruth Barnes Moynihan et al., eds., *Second to None: A Documentary History of American Women*, vol. 2, *From 1865 to the Present* (Lincoln: Univ. of Nebraska Press, 1993), 43.

164. Marion Meade, *Free Woman: The Life and Times of Victoria Woodhull* (New York: Alfred A. Knopf, 1976), 126.

165. Barbara Solomon, *Educated Women*, 56.

166. Mary Beth Norton et al., *A People and a Nation: A History of the United States*, vol. 2, *Since 1865*, 4th ed. (Boston: Houghton Mifflin, 1994), 492.

167. *Bradwell v. Illinois*, 83 U.S. 130 (1873); Hoff, *Law, Gender, and Injustice*, 165–66.

168. Quoted in Hoff, *Law, Gender, and Injustice*, 157.

169. See table 3.

170. Scott, *Natural Allies*, 95.

171. *Ibid.*, 96; Doris Weatherford, *American Women's History* (New York: Prentice Hall, 1994), 378.

172. Keeley and Pettegrew, *Public Women, Public Words*, 282.

173. Juster, *Woman's Place*, 259.

174. Margery W. Davies, *Woman's Place Is at the Typewriter: Office Work and Office Workers, 1870–1930* (Philadelphia: Temple Univ. Press, 1982), 35, 54, 37.

175. Quoted in Barbara Solomon, *Educated Women*, 48.

176. Scott, *Natural Allies*, 104.

177. Quoted in Hoff, *Law, Gender, and Injustice*, 164.

178. *Minor v. Happersett*, 88 U.S. 162 (1875); Hoff, *Law, Gender, and Injustice*, 173.

179. Lerner, *Female Experience*, 179.

180. Quoted in Hoff, *Law, Gender, and Injustice*, 180.

181. Quoted in Dorothy Schneider and Carl Schneider, *American Women in the Progressive Era, 1900–1920* (New York: Doubleday, Anchor Books, 1934), 166.

182. Quoted in Charlotte Streifer Rubinstein, *American Women Artists: From Early Indian Times to the Present* (Boston: G. K. Hall; New York: Avon Books, 1982), 114.

183. Sterling, *We Are Your Sisters*, 372.

184. Quoted in Rubinstein, *American Women Artists*, 56.

185. Norton et al., *People and Nation*, vol. 2, 535; see table 12.

186. See table 1-B; Linda Peavy and Ursula Smith, *Pioneer Women: The Lives of Women on the Frontier* (New York: Smithmark Publishers, Saraband Books, 1996), 106.

187. See table 12.

188. See table 8; Barbara Solomon, *Educated Women*, 63; *ibid.*, 26.

189. Frances Paul Prucha, ed., *Americanizing the American Indians: Writings by the "Friends of the Indians," 1800–1900* (Cambridge: Harvard Univ. Press, 1993), 20.

190. Quoted in Juster, *Woman's Place*, 72.

191. Beverly Guy-Sheftall, "Spelman College," in Hine et al., *Black Women in America*, vol. 2, 1091.

192. Sterling, *We Are Your Sisters*, 357; Elizabeth Clark-Lewis, "Domestic Workers in the North," in Hine et al., *Black Women in America*, vol. 1, 341.

193. Quoted in Rubinstein, *American Women Artists*, 92.

194. James Playsted Wood, *Magazines in the United States: Their Social and Economic Influence* (New York: The Ronald Press, 1949), 106; John Tebbel and Mary Ellen Zuckerman, *The Magazine in America, 1741–1990* (New York: Oxford Univ. Press, 1991), 60.

195. Julian T. Baird, Jr., "Wilcox, Ella Wheeler," in James et al., *Notable American Women*, 608.

196. Ray Ginger, *Age of Excess: The United States from 1877 to 1914* (New York: Macmillan, 1965), 79.

197. Cott, *Root of Bitterness*, 311–13, 318.

198. *Civil Rights Cases*, 109 U.S. 3 1883.

199. Moynihan et al., *Second to None*, vol. 2, 33.

200. Tebbel and Zuckerman, *Magazine in America*, 57, 102–3.

201. Christine Ammer, *Unsung: A History of Women in American Music* (Westport, Conn.: Greenwood Press, 1980), 96.

202. Karin Pendle, ed., *Women and Music: A*

History (Bloomington: Indiana Univ. Press, 1991), 149.

203. Wertheimer, *We Were There*, 182, 189.

204. Kraditor, *Up from the Pedestal*, 196.

205. *Rosencranz v. Territory of Washington*, 267, 5 P. 335 (1884); *Harland v. Territory*, 3 Wash. Terr. 131, 13 P. 453 (1887); Hoff, *Law, Gender, and Injustice*, 225.

206. Quoted in Scott, *Natural Allies*, 74.

207. Tebbel et and Zuckerman, *Magazine in America*, 96.

208. For increase of female office workers see table 12; quoted in Davies, *Office Workers*, 81–82.

209. Sara M. Evans, *Born for Liberty: A History of Women in America* (New York: Macmillan, Free Press, 1989), 150

210. See table 11; Nancy Woloch, *Women and the American Experience* (New York: McGraw-Hill, 1994), 222, 225

211. See table 12.

212. Woloch, *Women and the American Experience*, 227–28.

213. Barbara Solomon, *Educated Women*, 44; see table 8.

214. Linda M. Perkins, "The Impact of the 'Cult of True Womanhood' on the Education of Black Women," *Journal of Social Issues* 39, no. 3 (1983): 33.

215. Woloch, *Women and the American Experience*, 337.

216. *New York Times* article quoted in "Quest for Dignity: Black Women in the Professions, 1865–1900," in Bettina Aptheker, *Woman's Legacy: Essays on Race, Sex, and Class in American History* (Amherst: Univ. of Massachusetts Press, 1982), 91; Darlene Clark Hine, "Physicians, Nineteenth Century," in Hine et al., *Black Women in America*, vol. 2, 923.

217. Reuther and Keller, *Women and Religion*, vol. 1, 208, 205.

218. Macdonald, *Women and Invention*, 179; quoted in Rubinstein, *American Women Artists*, 152.

219. Patricia A. Schechter, "Temperance Work in the Nineteenth Century," in Hine et al., *Black Women in America* vol. 2, 1155.

220. Schneider and Schneider, *Progressive Era*, 72.

221. An earlier University of Chicago closed in the late 1800s from financial troubles; Rosalind Rosenberg, *Beyond Separate Spheres: Intellectual Roots of Modern Feminism* (New Haven: Yale Univ. Press, 1982), 43; Barbara Solomon, *Educated Women*, 58.

222. Barbara Solomon, *Educated Women*, 58.

223. Janet Scudder, "Modeling My Life," in Jill Ker Conway, ed., *Written by Herself: Autobiographies of American Women: An Anthology* (New York: Random House, Vintage Books, 1992), 356.

224. Alice Kessler-Harris, "Where Are the Organized Women Workers?" *Feminist Studies* 3 (Fall 1975): 96; see table 11; Wertheimer, *We Were There*, 195.

225. Quoted in David W. H. Pellow, "Annie J. Cooper," in Jessie Carney Smith, ed., *Epic Lives: One Hundred Black Women Who Made a Difference* (Detroit: Gale Research, Visible Ink Press, 1993), 127; Mary Helen Washington writes that Cooper may have abandoned her feminist theme in her writings because of discouragement and "professional uncertainty." From the 1890s through the 1940s, black female scholars and activists were generally ignored or discounted by the African-American men who dominated American black intellectual thought and discourse. See Mary Helen Washington, Introduction to *A Voice from the South* (Xenia, Ohio: Aldine, 1892; New York: Negro Universities Press, 1969; reprinted with an introduction by Mary Helen Washington, New York: Oxford Univ. Press, 1988), xxviii, xxxix–xl.

226. Gail Bederman, *Manliness and Civilization: A Cultural History of Gender and Race in the United States, 1880–1917* (Chicago: Univ. of Chicago Press, 1995), 70.

227. Norton et al., *People and Nation*, vol. 2, 614; James Davidson et al., *Nation of Nations*, 779.

228. Macdonald, *Women and Invention*, 202.

229. Margaret W. Rossiter, *Women Scientists in America: Struggles and Strategies to 1940* (Baltimore: Johns Hopkins Univ. Press, 1982), 46.

230. Quoted in Bert J. Lowenberg and Ruth Bogin, eds., *Black Women in Nineteenth Century Life: Their Words, Their Thoughts, Their Feelings* (University Park: Pennsylvania State Univ. Press, 1976), 275–76.

231. Barbara Solomon, *Educated Women*, 54.

232. Moynihan et al., *Second to None*, vol. 2, 83.

233. Statistics in Ronald Takaki, *A Different Mirror: A History of Multicultural America* (Boston: Little, Brown and Co., 1993), 238.

234. U.S. Census, *Historical Statistics*, 105–6; quoted in Aileen S. Kraditor, *The Ideas of the Woman Suffrage Movement* (New York: Columbia

Univ. Press, 1965; reprint, New York: W.W. Norton, 1981, 131.

235. *Ibid.*, 133.

236. *In re Lockwood*, 154 U.S. 116 (1894).

237. See table 7.

238. See table 8.

239. Statistics from a 1956 study by Walter Crosby Eells, "Earned Doctorates for Women in the Nineteenth Century," cited in Rossiter, *Women Scientists*, 32.

240. *Ibid.*, 33–34; U.S. Census, *Historical Statistics*, 386; table 9.

241. Maureen Fitzgerald, "The Religious Is Personal Is Political: Foreword to the 1993 Edition of *The Woman's Bible*," in *The Woman's Bible*, by Elizabeth Cady Stanton (New York: New York European Publishing Co., 1895, 1898; reprint, Boston: Northeastern Univ. Press, 1993), xxix.

242. Gerda Lerner, ed., *Black Women in White America: A Documentary History* (New York: Random House, Vintage Books, 1973), 442.

243. Eleanor Flexner, *Century of Struggle: The Woman's Rights Movement in the United States*, rev. ed. (Cambridge: Harvard Univ. Press, Belknap Press, 1975), 230.

244. "Farmer, Fannie Merrit," in Robert McHenry, ed., *Famous American Women: A Biographical Dictionary from Colonial Times to the Present* (Springfield, Mass.: G. and C. Merriam Co., 1980, as *Liberty's Women*; reprint, New York: Dover Publications in arrangement with G. and C. Merriam, 1983), 125.

245. Paula Giddings, *When and Where I Enter: The Impact of Black Women on Race and Sex in America* (New York: William Morrow, 1984; New York: Bantam Doubleday Dell Publishing Group in arrangement with William Morrow, 1988), 95.

246. Quoted in Baxandall and Gordon, *America's Working Women*, 163.

247. Lynne D. Gordon, *Gender and Higher Education in the Progressive Era, 1900–1920* (New Haven: Yale Univ. Press, 1990), 52.

248. Barbara Ehrenreich and Deirdre English, *For Her Own Good: 150 Years of the Experts' Advice to Women* (Garden City, N.Y.: Doubleday, Anchor Books, 1978; reprint, New York: Doubleday, Anchor Books, 1989), 195.

249. Norton et al., *People and Nation*, vol. 2, 670.

250. Figure (cited as more than 4,000 by 1900) from Vicki L. Ruiz, "Chicanas and Mexican American Women," in Wilma Mankiller et al., *The Reader's Companion to U.S. Women's History* (New York: Houghton Mifflin, 1998), 84.

251. Carl N. Degler, Introduction to Charlotte Perkins Gilman, *Women and Economics: A Study of the Economic Relation between Men and Women as a Factor in Social Evolution* (Boston: Small, Maynard & Co., 1898, 1899; reprint of 1899 edition, edited and with an introduction and notes by Carl N. Degler, New York: Harper & Row, Torchbook edition, 1966), xiii.

252. Percentage is from a study quoted in Barbara Solomon, *Educated Women*, 87.

253. Elsa Barkley Brown, "Womanist Consciousness: Maggie Lena Walker and the Independent Order of St. Luke," in DuBois and Ruiz, *Unequal Sisters*, 211.

254. Enrollment in public day schools from U.S. Census, *Historical Statistics*, 369; figures on number of teachers and percentages estimated from table 12.

255. Maxine L. Margolis, *Mothers and Such: Views of American Women and Why They Changed* (Berkeley: Univ. of California Press, 1985), 200; see table 8; Margolis, *Mothers and Such*, 49.

256. See tables 10 and 11.

257. Norton et al., *People and Nation*, vol. 2, 537; see table 11; Schneider and Schneider, *Progressive Era*, 50.

258. Kessler-Harris, "Organized Women Workers," 93; see table 12.

259. Takaki, *Different Mirror*, 288; Carolyn D. McCreesh, "International Ladies' Garment Workers' Union," in Mankiller et al., *Reader's Companion*, 308; Wertheimer, *We Were There*, 316.

260. Paul Avrich, *An American Anarchist: The Life of Voltairine deCleyre* (Princeton: Princeton Univ. Press, 1978), 144, 4.

261. Lynn Y. Weiner, *From Working Girl to Working Mother: The Female Labor Force in the United States, 1820–1980* (Chapel Hill: Univ. of North Carolina Press, 1985), 41.

262. See table 5.

263. Albert Erlebacher, "Kander, Lizzie Black," in James et al., *Notable American Women*, vol. 2, 306.

264. Merrit Cross, "White, Alma Bridwell," in *ibid.*, vol. 3, 582.

265. U.S. Census, *Historical Statistics*, 107–8; Amy Ling, "Chinese American Writing," in Cathy Davidson and Wagner-Martin, *Oxford Companion*, 184–85.

266. Rosenberg, *Intellectual Roots*, 44.

267. Lynne D. Gordon, *Gender and Higher Education*, 112.

268. Bederman, *Manliness and Civilization*, 202.

269. Tebbel and Zuckerman, *Magazine in America*, 99, 98.

270. Quoted in Ruether and Keller, *Women and Religion*, vol. 1, 204.

271. Statistic from museum's web page: http://www.boston.com/gardner/museumhist.htm.

272. Esther Stineman, *Mary Austin: Song of a Maverick* (New Haven: Yale Univ. Press, 1989), 90.

273. Elinor Richey, "Morgan, Julia," in Barbara Sicherman and Carol H. Green, eds., *Notable American Women: The Modern Period: A Biographical Dictionary* (Cambridge: Harvard Univ. Press, Belknap Press, 1980), 500–501; Elizabeth G. Grossman and Lisa B. Reitzes, "Caught in the Crossfire: Women and Architectural Education, 1880–1910," in Ellen Perry Berkeley and Matilda McQuaid, eds., *Architecture: A Place for Women* (Washington, D.C.: Smithsonian Institution Press, 1989), 30–31.

274. Kessler-Harris, *Wage-Earning Women*, 152; Wertheimer, *We Were There*, 207.

275. Evans, *Born for Liberty*, 150; Skinner, *National Experience*, 117–18.

276. Margolis, *Mothers and Such*, 136.

277. Lynne D. Gordon, *Gender and Higher Education*, 68.

278. Statistic on sales of sheet music from Carolyn Lindeman, introductory notes to *Pickles and Peppers and Other Rags by Women*, audiocassette, Northeastern Records NR 225-C, 1987.

279. Cynthia Grant Tucker, *Prophetic Sisterhood: Liberal Women Ministers of the Frontier, 1880–1930* (Bloomington: Indiana Univ. Press, 1994), 3, 155. The school was named after a prominent nineteenth-century Unitarian.

280. Thomas Vennum, Jr., "Densmore, Frances Theresa," in Sicherman and Green, *Notable American Women*, 185.

281. Ellen Carol DuBois, "Working Women, Class Relations, and Suffrage Militance," in DuBois and Ruiz, *Unequal Sisters*, 189.

282. Nancy F. Cott, *The Grounding of Modern Feminism* (New Haven: Yale Univ. Press, 1987), 25.

283. Lerner, *Black Women in White America*, 380.

284. Robert W. Lovett, "Knox, Rose Markward," in James et al., *Notable American Women*, vol. 2, 284.

285. Arnold T. Schwab, "MacDowell, Marian Griswold Nevins," in Sicherman and Green, *Notable American Women*, 448.

286. *Muller v. Oregon*, 208 U.S. 412 (1908); quote from decision in Henry Steele Commager, ed., *Documents of American History*, vol. 2 (New York: Meredith Publishing Company, Appleton-Century-Crofts, 7th edition, 1963), 44; Hoff, *Law, Gender, and Injustice*, 197; 1914 statistic from Kessler-Harris, *Wage-Earning Women*, 188.

287. Micheal Flug, "Harsh, Vivian Gordon," in Hine et al., *Black Women in America*, vol. 1, 543.

288. Quoted in Margolis, *Mothers and Such*, 49.

289. Thomas J. Schlereth, *Victorian America: Transformations in Everyday Life* (New York: HarperCollins, 1991), 188–90; Wertheimer, *We Were There*, 237.

290. Mari Jo Buhle, *Women and American Socialism, 1870–1920* (Urbana: Univ. of Illinois Press, Illini Books, 1983), 191; Wertheimer, *We Were There*, 297, 308.

291. Membership statistic from the NAACP webpage: http:// www.naacp.org/.

292. See tables 11 and 12.

293. Schlereth, *Victorian America*, 256; Dee Garrison, "The Tender Technicians: The Feminization of Public Librarianship, 1876–1905," in Mary Hartman and Lois W. Banner, eds., *Clio's Consciousness Raised: New Perspectives on the History of Women* (New York: Harper & Row, Harper Colophon, 1974), 158–59.

294. Rosalyn Terborg-Penn, *African American Women in the Struggle for the Vote, 1850–1920* (Bloomington: Indiana Univ. Press, 1998), 165; Elizabeth Clark-Lewis, "Domestic Workers in the North," in Hine et al., *Black Women in America*, vol. 1, 341.

295. Flexner, *Century of Struggle*, 257; Buhle, *Women and American Socialism*, 225.

296. Quoted in John K. Wright, "'Miss Semple's Influences of Geographic Environment': Notes toward a Biobibliography," *Geographical Review* 52 (1962): 351.

297. Gail Bederman, "'The Women Have Had Charge of the Church Work Long Enough': The Men and Religion Forward Movement of 1911–1912 and the Masculinization of Middle-Class Protestantism," in Susan Juster and Lisa MacFarlane, eds., *A Mighty Baptism: Race, Gender, and the Creation of American Protestantism* (Ithaca: Cornell Univ. Press, 1996), 115, 108, 107, 134, 138.

298. Manuela Thurner, "'Better Citizens without the Ballot': American Anti-suffrage Women and Their Rationale during the Progressive Era," in Marjorie Spruill Wheeler, ed., *One Woman, One Vote: Rediscovering the Woman*

Suffrage Movement (Troutdale, Ore.: New Sage Press, 1995), 206.

299. Joan M. Jensen and Gloria Ricci Lothrop, *California Women: A History* (San Francisco: Boyd & Fraser, 1987), 65.

300. Norton et al., *People and a Nation*, 540.

301. C. Beth Burch, "Fiction," in "Jewish American Writing," in Davidson et al., *Oxford Companion*, 440; Ruth Yu Hsiao, "Antin, Mary," ibid., 57.

302. Ardis Cameron, *Radicals of the Worst Sort: Laboring Women in Lawrence, Massachusetts, 1860–1912* (Urbana: Univ. of Illinois Press, Illini edition, 1995), 98; Wertheimer, *We Were There*, 368.

303. Quoted in Margolis, *Mothers and Such*, 144.

304. Quoted in Rubinstein, *American Women Artists*, 174.

305. Wanda Hendricks, "Ida B. Wells-Barnett and the Alpha Suffrage Club of Chicago," in Wheeler, *One Woman, One Vote*, 268.

306. Statistic calculated from table 6 in Weiner, *Working Girl to Working Mother*, 89; quote from Margolis, *Mothers and Such*, 47.

307. See table 1; Elinore Pruitt Stewart, *Letters of a Woman Homesteader* (The Atlantic Monthly Company, 1914; Boston: Houghton Mifflin paperback, 1988), 215.

308. Quoted in Rosenberg, *Intellectual Roots*, 103.

309. Statistics from Evans, *Born for Liberty*, 166.

310. Quoted in Kraditor, *Woman Suffrage Movement*, 26.

311. Statistics from Schlereth, *Victorian America*, 157, 141; quote from Margolis, *Mothers and Such*, 136.

312. Mary Roth Walsh, *"Doctors Wanted: No Women Need Apply": Sexual Barriers in the Medical Profession, 1835–1975* (New Haven: Yale Univ. Press, 1977), 217.

313. Statistics on medical students: Thomas Neville Bonner, *To the Ends of the Earth: Women's Search for Education in Medicine* (Cambridge: Harvard Univ. Press, 1992), 156, 162; statistics on female doctors in Walsh, *Doctors Wanted*, table 5 on p. 186.

314. See table 8.

315. William L. O'Neill, *Everyone Was Brave: The Rise and Fall of Feminism in America* (Chicago: Quadrangle Books, 1969), 175–76, 178.

316. Schneider and Schneider, *Progressive Era*, 199, 298, 201, quote from Wilson, 203; comments from Roosevelt and the newspaper in O'Neill, *Everyone Was Brave*, 179.

317. Ehrenreich and English, *For Her Own Good*, 164.

318. Quote from Riley, *Inventing*, 217; Schneider and Schneider, *Progressive Era*, 214.

319. Riley, *Inventing*, 219.

320. Schneider and Schneider, *Progressive Era*, 228.

321. Riley, *Inventing*, 218; Jeannette P. Nichols, "Delano, Jane Arminda," in James et al., *Notable American Women*, vol. 1, 459.

322. Darlene Clark Hine, "Nursing, World War I," in Hine et al., *Black Women in America*, vol. 2, 892.

323. Walsh, *Doctors Wanted*, 218.

324. Dorothy Salem, "World War I," in Hine et al., *Black Women in America*, vol. 2, 1287.

325. Schneider and Schneider, *Progressive Era*, 232.

326. Penny Martelet, "The Woman's Land Army, World War I," in Mabel Deutrich and Virginia Purdy, eds., *Clio Was a Women: Studies in the History of American Women* (Washington, D.C.: Howard Univ. Press, 1980), 136, 142.

327. Rossiter, *Women Scientists*, 120.

328. G. Kass-Simon and Patricia Farnes, eds., *Women of Science: Righting the Record* (Bloomington: Indiana Univ. Press, 1993), 99.

329. Christopher Lasch, "Dennett, Mary Coffin Ware," in James et al., *Notable American Women*, vol. 1, 465.

330. William H. Chafe, *The Paradox of Change: American Women in the Twentieth Century* (New York: Oxford Univ. Press, 1991), 66.

331. Rossiter, *Women Scientists*, 118.

332. Hine, "Nursing, World War I," in Hine et al., *Black Women in America*, vol. 2, 893.

333. Norton et al., *People and a Nation*, 709, 545.

334. Quoted in Davies, *Office Workers*, 89, 85.

335. Quoted in Schneider and Schneider, *Progressive Era*, 18.

336. See table 11; Chafe, *Paradox of Change*, 66; Kessler-Harris, *Wage-Earning Women*, 249.

337. See table 12; Barbara Solomon, *Educated Women*, table 5, p. 127; see table 13.

338. Kessler-Harris, *Wage-Earning Women*, 238.

339. See table 8; U.S. Census, *Historical Statistics*, 386.

340. Quoted in Margaret Mead, *Blackberry Winter: My Earlier Years* (New York: Simon and Schuster, Touchstone, 1972), 108.

341. See table 5; Jules Chametkzy, "Yezier-ska, Anna," in Sicherman and Green, *Notable American Women*, 753.

342. Kessler-Harris, *Wage-Earning Women*, 152.

Bibliography

Abramovitz, Mimi. *Regulating the Lives of Women: Social Welfare Policy from Colonial Times to the Present.* Boston: South End Press, 1988.

Ammer, Christine. *Unsung: A History of Women in American Music.* Westport, Conn.: Greenwood Press, 1980.

Anderson, Karen. *A History of Racial Ethnic Women in Modern America.* New York: Oxford Univ. Press, 1996.

Andrews, William L., ed. *Sisters of the Spirit: Three Black Women's Autobiographies of the Nineteenth Century.* Bloomington: Indiana Univ. Press, 1986.

Apple, Rima D., ed. *Women, Health, and Medicine in America: A Historical Handbook.* New Brunswick: Rutgers Univ. Press, 1990.

Aptheker, Bettina. *Woman's Legacy: Essays on Race, Sex, and Class in American History.* Amherst: Univ. of Massachusetts Press, 1982.

Armitage, Susan, and Elizabeth Jameson, eds. *The Women's West.* Norman: Univ. of Oklahoma Press, 1987.

Bacon, Margaret Hope. *Mothers of Feminism: The Story of Quaker Women in America.* San Francisco: Harper & Row, 1986.

Bank, Mirra. *Anonymous Was a Woman.* New York: St. Martin's Press, 1979.

Barker-Benfield, G. J., and Catherine Clinton, eds. *Portraits of American Women: From Settlement to the Present.* New York: St. Martin's Press, 1991.

Battle, Kemp. *Hearts of Fire: Great Women of American Lore and Legend.* New York: Harmony Books, 1997.

Baxandall, Rosalyn, and Linda Gordon, eds. *America's Working Women: A Documentary History, 1600 to the Present.* Rev. ed. New York: W. W. Norton, 1995.

Baym, Nina. *American Women Writers and the Work of History, 1790–1860.* New Brunswick: Rutgers Univ. Press, 1995.

Bederman, Gail. *Manliness and Civilization: A Cultural History of Gender and Race in the United States, 1880–1917.* Chicago: Univ. of Chicago Press, 1995.

Beeton, Beverly. *Women Vote in the West: The Woman Suffrage Movement, 1869–1896.* New York: Garland Publishing, 1986.

Bekin, Carol Ruth, and Mary Beth Norton. *Women of America: A History.* Boston: Houghton Mifflin, 1979.

Berkhofer, Robert F., Jr. *Salvation and the Savage.* New York: Atheneum, 1976.

Bernhard, Virginia, Betty Brandon, Elizabeth Fox-Genovese, and Theda Perdue, eds. *Southern Women: Histories and Identities.* Columbia: Univ. of Missouri Press, 1992.

Bolden, Tanya. *The Book of African-American Women: 150 Crusaders, Creators, and Uplifters.* Holbrook, Mass.: Adams Media, 1996.

Bonner, Thomas Neville. *To the Ends of the Earth: Women's Search for Education in Medicine.* Cambridge: Harvard Univ. Press, 1992.

Boydston, Jeanne. *Home and Work: Housework, Wages, and the Ideology of Labor in the Early Republic.* New York: Oxford Univ. Press, 1990.

Brown, Richard D. *Knowledge Is Power: The Diffusion of Information in Early America,*

1700–1865. New York: Oxford Univ. Press, 1989.

Buhle, Mari Jo. *Women and American Socialism, 1870–1920*. Urbana: Univ. of Illinois Press, Illini Books, *1983*.

Campbell, Karlyn Kohrs, ed. *Man Cannot Speak for Her*. 2 vols. New York: Praeger, 1989.

Chafe, William H. *The Paradox of Change: American Women in the Twentieth Century*. New York: Oxford Univ. Press, 1991.

Clifford, Geraldine J. *Lone Voyagers: Academic Women in Coeducational Institutions, 1870–1937*. New York: Feminist Press at the City University of New York, 1989.

Clinton, Catherine. *The Other Civil War: American Women in the Nineteenth Century*. New York: Hill and Wang, 1984.

_____, and Nina Silber, eds. *Divided Houses: Gender and the Civil War*. New York: Oxford Univ. Press, 1992.

Cogan, Frances B. *All-American Girl: The Ideal of the Real Womanhood in Mid-Ninteenth-Century America*. Athens: Univ. of Georgia Press, 1989.

Conrad, Susan P. *Perish the Thought: Intellectual Women in Romantic America, 1830–1860*. Secaucus, N.J.: Citadel Press, 1978.

Conway, Jill K. *The Female Experience in Eighteenth- and Nineteenth-Century America: A Guide to the History of American Women*. Princeton: Princeton Univ. Press, 1985.

_____, ed. *Written by Herself: Autobiographies of American Women: An Anthology*. New York: Random House, Vintage Books, 1992.

Cooper, James L., and Sheila M. Cooper, eds. *The Roots of American Feminist Thought*. Boston: Allyn and Bacon, 1973.

Cott, Nancy F. *The Bonds of Womanhood: "Woman's Sphere" in New England, 1780–1835*. New Haven: Yale Univ. Press, 1977.

_____. *The Grounding of Modern Feminism*. New Haven: Yale Univ. Press, 1987.

_____, ed. *Root of Bitterness: Documents of the Social History of American Women*. Boston: Northeastern Univ. Press, 1986.

Davidson, Cathy N., and Linda Wagner-Martin, eds. *The Oxford Companion to Women's Writing in the United States*. New York: Oxford Univ. Press, 1995.

Davidson, James West, et al. *Nation of Nations: A Narrative History of the American Republic*. New York: McGraw Hill, 1990.

Davies, Margery W. *Woman's Place Is at the Typewriter: Office Work and Office Workers, 1870–1930*. Philadelphia: Temple Univ. Press, 1982.

DePauw, Linda Grant, and Conover Hunt. *Remember the Ladies: Women in America, 1750–1815*. New York: Viking Press, Studio Book, 1976.

Devens, Carol. *Countering Colonization: Native American Women and Great Lakes Missions, 1630–1900*. Berkeley: Univ. of California Press, 1992.

Dewhurst, C. Kurt, Betty MacDowell, and Marsha MacDowell. *Artists in Aprons: Folk Art by American Women*. New York: E. P. Dutton in association with the Museum of American Folk Art, 1979.

Douglas, Ann. *The Feminization of American Culture*. New York: Alfred A. Knopf, 1977.

DuBois, Ellen Carol. *Feminism and Suffrage: The Emergence of an Independent Women's Movement in America, 1848–1869*. Ithaca: Cornell Univ. Press, 1978.

_____, and Vicki L. Ruiz, eds. *Unequal Sisters: A Multicultural Reader in U.S. Women's History*. New York: Routledge, 1990.

Duby, Georges, and Michelle Perrot, eds. *A History of Women in the West*. Vol. 4, *Emerging Feminism from Revolution to World War I*. In Italian: Rome and Bari: Laterza & Figli Spa, 1991. Reprinted translation: Cambridge: Harvard Univ. Press, 1995.

Ebert, John, and Katherine Ebert. *American Folk Painters*. New York: Charles Scribner's Sons, 1975.

Edwards, Rebecca. *Angels in the Machinery: Gender in American Party Politics from the Civil War to the Progressive Era*. New York: Oxford Univ. Press, 1997.

Ehrenreich, Barbara, and Deirdre English. *For Her Own Good: 150 Years of the Experts' Advice to Women*. Garden City, N.Y.: Doubleday, Anchor Books, 1978. Reprint, New York: Doubleday, Anchor Books, 1989.

Epstein, Barbara Leslie. *The Politics of Domesticity: Women, Evangelism, and Temperance in Nineteenth-Century America*. Middletown, Conn.: Wesleyan Univ. Press, 1991.

Evans, Sara M. *Born for Liberty: A History of Women in America*. New York: Macmillan, Free Press, 1989.

Faust, Drew Gilpin. *Mothers of Invention: Women of the Slaveholding South in the American Civil War*. Chapel Hill: Univ. of North Carolina Press, 1996; New York: Random House, Vintage Books, 1997.

Flexner, Eleanor. *Century of Struggle: The Woman's Rights Movement in the United States*. Rev. ed. Cambridge: Harvard Univ. Press, Belknap Press, 1975.

Foster, Frances Smith. *Written by Herself: Literary Productions by African-American Women, 1746–1892*. Bloomington: Indiana Univ. Press, 1993.

Fox-Genovese, Elizabeth. *Within the Plantation Household: Black and White Women of the Old South*. Chapel Hill: Univ. of North Carolina Press, 1988.

Frankel, Noralee, and Nancy S. Dye, eds. *Gender, Class, Race, and Reform in the Progressive Era*. Lexington: Univ. Press of Kentucky, 1991.

Giddings, Paula. *When and Where I Enter: The Impact of Black Women on Race and Sex in America*. New York: William Morrow, 1984; New York: Bantam Doubleday Dell Publishing Group in arrangement with William Morrow, 1988.

Ginzberg, Lori D. *Women and the Work of Benevolence: Morality, Politics, and Class in the Nineteenth Century United States*. New Haven: Yale Univ. Press, 1990.

Gordon, Ann D., ed. *African American Women and the Vote, 1837–1965*. Amherst: Univ. of Massachusetts Press, 1997.

Gordon, Linda. *Woman's Body, Woman's Right: Birth Control in America*. Rev. ed. New York: Penguin Books, 1990.

Gordon, Lynne D. *Gender and Higher Education in the Progressive Era, 1900–1920*. New Haven: Yale Univ. Press, 1990.

Harley, Sharon, and Rosalyn Terborg-Penn, eds. *The Afro-American Women: Struggles and Images*. Port Washington, N.Y.: Kennikat Press, 1978.

Harris, Ann Sutherland, and Linda Nochlin. *Women Artists, 1550–1950*. New York: Alfred A. Knopf and the Los Angeles County Musem of Art, 1977.

Hine, Darlene Clark. *Black Women in United States History*. Brooklyn: Carlson Publishing, 1990.

_____, Elsa Barkley Brown, and Rosalyn Terborg-Penn, eds. *Black Women in America: An Historical Encyclopedia*. 2 vols. Brooklyn: Carlson Publishing, 1993; Bloomington: Indiana Univ. Press, 1994.

Hoff, Joan. *Law, Gender, and Injustice: A Legal History of U.S. Women*. New York: New York Univ. Press, 1991.

Hoffman, Ronald, and Peter J.Albert, eds. *Women in the Age of the American Revolution*. Charlottesville: Univ. Press of Virginia, 1989.

James, Edward, Janet Wilson James, and Paul Boyer, eds. *Notable American Women, 1607–1950: A Biographical Dictionary*. 3 vols. Cambridge: Harvard Univ. Press, Belknap Press, 1971.

Jensen, Joan M., and Gloria Ricci Lothrop. *California Women: A History*. San Francisco: Boyd & Fraser, 1987.

Jezic, Diane Peacock. *Women Composers: The Lost Tradition Found*. New York: Feminist Press at the City Univ. of New York, 1988.

Johnson, Paul. *The Birth of the Modern: World Society, 1815–1830*. New York: HarperCollins Publishers, 1991.

Jones, Katharine M. *Heroines of Dixie: Confederate Women Tell Their Story of the War*. New York: Bobbs-Merrill, 1955.

Juster, Norton. *A Woman's Place: Yesterday's Women in Rural America*. Golden, Colo.: Fulcrum Publishing, 1996.

Juster, Susan, and Lisa MacFarlane, eds. *A Mightly Baptism: Race, Gender, and the Creation of American Protestantism*. Ithaca: Cornell Univ. Press, 1996.

Kaminer, Wendy. *A Fearful Freedom: Women's Flight from Equality*. Reading, Mass.: Addison-Wesley Publishing, 1990.

Kass-Simon, G., and Patricia Farnes, eds. *Women of Science: Righting the Record*. Bloomington: Indiana Univ. Press, 1993.

Keeley, Dawn, and John Pettegrew, ed. *Public Women, Public Words: A Documentary History of American Feminism*. Madison: Madison House, 1997.

Keller, Rosemary Skinner, and Rosemary Radford Ruether, eds. *In Our Own Voices: Four Centuries of American Women's Religious Writing*. New York: HarperSanFrancisco, 1995.

Kerber, Linda K. *Women of the Republic: Intellect and Ideology in Revolutionary America*. Chapel Hill: Univ. of North Carolina Press, 1980. Reprint, New York: W. W. Norton, 1986.

Kessler-Harris, Alice. *Out to Work: A History of Wage-Earning Women in the United States*. New York: Oxford Univ. Press, 1983.

_____. *Women Have Always Worked: A Historical Overview*. New York: The Feminist Press, 1981.

Kimmel, Michael S. *Manhood in America: A Cultural History*. New York: The Free Press, 1996.

_____, and Thomas E. Mosmiller, eds. *Against the Tide: Pro-Feminist Men in the United States, 1776–1990: A Documentery History*. Boston: Beacon Press, 1992.

Kraditor, Aileen S. *The Ideas of the Woman*

Suffrage Movement, 1890–1920. New York: Columbia Univ. Press, 1965. Reprint, New York: W. W. Norton, 1981.

_____, ed. *Up from the Pedestal: Selected Writings in the History of American Feminism.* Chicago: Quadrangle Books, 1968.

Leonard, Elizabeth D. *Yankee Women: Gender Battles in the Civil War.* New York: W. W. Norton, 1994.

Lerner, Gerda. *The Creation of Feminist Consciousness: From the Middle Ages to 1870.* New York: Oxford Univ. Press, 1993.

_____, ed. *Black Women in White America: A Documentary History.* New York: Random House, Pantheon Books, 1972; New York: Random House, Vintage Books, 1973.

_____, ed. *The Female Experience: An American Documentary.* New York: Bobbs-Merrill, 1977. New York: Oxford Univ. Press, 1992.

Lindley, Susan Hill. *"Your Have Stept Out of Your Place": A History of Women and Religion in America.* Louisville: Westminster John Knox Press, 1996.

Lowenberg, Bert J., and Ruth Bogin, eds. *Black Women in Nineteenth Century American Life: Their Words, Their Thoughts, Their Feelings.* University Park: Pennsylvania State Univ. Press, 1976.

Lunardini, Christine. *What Every American Should Know about Women's History: Two Hundred Events That Shaped Our Destiny.* Holbrook, Mass.: Bob Adams, 1994.

Macdonald, Anne L. *Feminine Ingenuity: Women and Invention in America.* New York: Ballantine Books, 1992.

Maniero, Lina, ed. *American Women Writers: A Critical Reference Guide for Colonial Times to the Present.* 4 vols. New York: Frederick Unger Publishing, 1979.

Mankiller, Wilma, et al. *The Reader's Companion to U.S. Women's History.* New York: Houghton Mifflin, 1998.

Margolis, Maxine L. *Mothers and Such: Views of American Women and Why They Changed.* Berkeley: Univ. of California Press, 1985.

Matthews, Glenna. *"Just a Housewife": The Rise and Fall of Domesticity in America.* New York: Oxford Univ. Press, 1987. Reprint, 1989.

_____. *The Rise of Public Woman: Woman's Power and Woman's Place in the United States, 1630–1970.* New York: Oxford Univ. Press, 1992.

Moynihan, Ruth Barnes, Cynthia Russett, and Laurie Crumpacker, eds. *Second to None: A Documentary History of American Women.* 2 vols. Lincoln: Univ. of Nebraska Press, 1993.

Myers, Sandra L. *Westering Women and the Frontier Experience, 1800–1915.* Albuquerque: Univ. of New Mexico Press, 1986.

Nies, Judith. *Seven Women: Portraits from the American Radical Tradition.* New York: Viking Penguin, 1977.

Norton, Mary Beth. *Liberty's Daughters: The Revolutionary Experience of American Women, 1750–1800.* New York: HarperCollins Publishers, 1980.

_____, ed. *Major Problems in American Women's History: Documents and Essays.* Lexington, Mass.: D. C. Heath, 1989.

Norton, Mary Beth, et al. *A People and a Nation: A History of the United States.* 2 vols. 4th ed. Boston: Houghton Mifflin, 1994.

Ogden, Annegret S. *The Great American Housewife: From Helpmate to Wage Earner, 1776–1986.* Westport: Greenwood Press, 1986.

O'Neill, William L. *Everyone Was Brave: The Rise and Fall of Feminism in America.* Chicago: Quadrangle Books, 1969.

Parker, Gail, ed. *The Ovenbirds: American Women on Womanhood, 1820–1920.* Garden City, N.Y.: Doubleday, Anchor Books, 1972.

Peavy, Linda, and Ursula Smith. *Pioneer Women: The Lives of Women on the Frontier.* New York: Smithmark Publishers, Saraband Books, 1996.

Pendle, Karin, ed. *Women and Music: A History.* Bloomington: Indiana Univ. Press, 1991.

Prucha, Frances Paul, ed. *Americanizing the American Indians: Writings by the "Friends of the Indians," 1800–1900.* Cambridge: Harvard Univ. Press, 1973.

Riley, Glenda. *Inventing the American Woman: An Inclusive History.* 2 vols. Wheeling, Ill.: Harlan Davidson, 1995.

Rogers, Kathrine M., ed. *The Meridian Anthology of Early American Women Writers: From Anne Bradstreet to Louisa May Alcott, 1650–1865.* New York: Penguin Books USA, Meridian Book, 1991.

Rosenberg, Rosalind. *Beyond Separate Spheres: Intellectual Roots of Modern Feminism.* New Haven: Yale Univ. Press, 1982.

_____. *Divided Lives: American Women in the Twentieth Century.* New York: Hill and Wang, Noonday Press, 1992.

Rossi, Alice S., ed. *The Feminist Papers: From Adams to deBeauvoir.* New York: Columbia Univ. Press, 1973. Reprint, Boston: Northeastern Univ. Press, 1988.

Rossiter, Margaret W. *Women Scientists in America: Struggles and Strategies to 1940.* Baltimore: Johns Hopkins Univ. Press, 1982.

Rothman, Sheila M. *Woman's Proper Place: A History of Changing Ideals and Practices, 1870 to the Present.* New York: Basic Books, 1978.

Rubinstein, Charlotte Streifer. *American Women Artists: From Early Indian Times to the Present.* Boston: G. K. Hall; New York: Avon Books, 1982.

Rudolph, Frederick, ed. *Essays on Education in the Early Republic.* Cambridge: Harvard Univ. Press, Belknap Press, 1965.

Ruether, Rosemary R., and Rosemary S. Keller, eds. *Women and Religion in America.* Vol. 1, *The Nineteenth Century.* San Francisco: Harper & Row, 1981.

_____, eds. *Women and Religion in America.* Vol. 2, *The Colonial and Revolutionary Periods.* San Francisco: Harper & Row, 1983.

Ryan, Mary P. *The Empire of the Mother: American Writing about Domesticity, 1830–1860.* New York: The Haworth Press, 1982. Reprint, New York: Harrington Park Press, 1985.

_____. *Women in Public: Between Banners and Ballots, 1825–1880.* Baltimore: Johns Hopkins Univ. Press, 1990.

Schlereth, Thomas J. *Victorian America: Transformations in Everyday Life, 1876–1915.* New York: HarperCollins, 1991.

Schlissel, Lillian. *Women's Diaries of the Westward Journey.* New York: Schocken Books, 1982.

Schneider, Dorothy, and Carl Schneider. *American Women in the Progressive Era, 1900–1920.* New York: Doubleday, Anchor Books, 1994.

Schneir, Miriam, ed. *Feminism: The Essential Historical Writings.* New York: Random House, Vintage Books, 1972.

Scott, Ann Firor. *Making the Invisible Woman Visible.* Urbana: Univ. of Illinois Press, 1984.

_____. *Natural Allies: Women's Associations in American History.* Urbana: Univ. of Illinois Press, Illini Book edition, 1993.

Sellers, Charles. *The Market Revolution: Jacksonian America, 1815–1846.* New York: Oxford Univ. Press, 1991.

Sherr, Lynn. *Failure Is Impossible: Susan B. Anthony in Her Own Words.* New York: Random House, Times Books, 1995.

Shoemaker, Nancy, ed. *Negotiators of Change: Historical Perspectives on Native American Women.* New York: Routledge, 1995.

Sicherman, Barbara, and Carol H. Green, eds. *Notable American Women: The Modern Period: A Biographical Dictionary.* Cambridge: Harvard Univ. Press, Belknap Press, 1980.

Skinner, Ellen, ed. *Women and the National Experience: Primary Sources in American History.* New York: Addison-Wesley Educational Publishers, 1996.

Smith-Rosenberg, Carroll. *Disorderly Conduct: Visions of Gender in Victorian America.* New York: Afred A. Knopf, 1985. New York: Oxford Univ. Press, 1986.

Solomon, Barbara M. *In the Company of Educated Women: A History of Women and Higher Education in America.* New Haven: Yale Univ. Press, 1985.

Solomon, Martha M., ed. *A Voice of Their Own: The Woman Suffrage Press, 1840–1910.* Tuscaloosa: Univ. of Alabama Press, 1991.

Stanley, Autumn. *Mothers and Daughters of Invention: Notes for a Revised History of Technology.* Metuchen, N.J.: Scarecrow Press, 1993; New Brunswick: Rutgers Univ. Press, 1995.

Stanton, Elizabeth Cady. *Eighty Years and More: Reminiscences, 1815–1897.* N.p.: T. Fisher Unwin, 1898. Reprinted with an introduction by Carol Ellen DuBois and afterword by Ann D. Gordon, Boston: Northeastern Univ. Press, 1993.

Sterling, Dorothy, ed. *We Are Your Sisters: Black Women in the Nineteenth Century.* New York: W. W. Norton, 1984.

Strasser, Susan. *Never Done: A History of American Housework.* New York: Pantheon Books, 1982.

Strickland, Rennard. *Fire and the Spirits: Cherokee Law from Clan to Court.* Norman: Univ. of Oklahoma Press, 1975.

Swan, Susan Burrows. *Plain and Fancy: American Women and Their Needlework, 1700–1850.* New York: Holt, Rinehart and Winston, Routledge Books, 1977.

Takaki, Ronald. *A Different Mirror: A History of Multicultural America.* Boston: Little, Brown, 1993.

Tebbel, John, and Mary Ellen Zuckerman. *The Magazine in America, 1741–1990.* New York: Oxford Univ. Press, 1991.

Terborg-Penn, Rosalyn. *African American Women in the Struggle for the Vote, 1850–1920.* Bloomington: Indiana Univ. Press, 1998.

Trollope, Francis. *Domestic Manners of the Americans.* Ed. by Donald Smalley. New York: Alfred A. Knopf, Borzoi Books, 1949.

Ulrich, Laurel Thatcher. *A Midwife's Tale: The Life of Martha Ballard, Based on Her Diary, 1785–1812.* New York: Alfred A. Knopf, 1990. New York: Vintage Books, 1991.

Walsh, Mary Roth. *"Doctors Wanted: No Women*

Need Apply": Sexual Barriers in the Medical Profession, 1835–1975. New Haven: Yale Univ. Press, 1977.

Weatherford, Doris. Foreign and Female: Immigrant Women in America, 1840–1930. New York: Facts on File, 1995.

Weiner, Lynn Y. From Working Girl to Working Mother: The Female Labor Force in the United States, 1820–1980. Chapel Hill: Univ. of North Carolina Press, 1985.

Wertheimer, Barbara M. We Were There: The Story of Working Women in America. New York: Random House, Pantheon Books, 1977.

Wheeler, Marjorie Spruill, ed. One Woman, One Vote: Rediscovering the Woman Suffrage Movement. Troutdale, Ore.: New Sage Press, 1995.

Woloch, Nancy. Women and the American Experience. New York: McGraw-Hill, 1994.

Wood, James Playsted. Magazines in the United States: Their Social and Economic Influence. New York: The Ronald Press, 1949.

Yee, Shirley J. Black Women Abolitionists: A Study in Activism, 1828–1860. Knoxville: Univ. of Tennessee Press, 1992.

Index

Page numbers in italics indicate photographs